Political Parties in the Arab World

Continuity and Change

Edited by Franceso Cavatorta and Lise Storm

EDINBURGH
University Press

For my two spirited little ladies and all the freedom fighters.
Heads up, backs straight.
L.S.

Edinburgh University Press is one of the leading university presses in the UK. We publish academic books and journals in our selected subject areas across the humanities and social sciences, combining cutting-edge scholarship with high editorial and production values to produce academic works of lasting importance. For more information visit our website: edinburghuniversitypress.com

© editorial matter and organisation Franceso Cavatorta and Lise Storm, 2018
© the chapters their several authors, 2018

Edinburgh University Press Ltd
The Tun – Holyrood Road
12 (2f) Jackson's Entry
Edinburgh EH8 8PJ

Typeset in 12/14 Arno and Myriad by
IDSUK (Dataconnection) Ltd, and
printed and bound in the United States of America

A CIP record for this book is available from the British Library

ISBN 978 1 4744 2406 6 (hardback)
ISBN 978 1 4744 2407 3 (paperback)
ISBN 978 1 4744 2408 0 (webready PDF)
ISBN 978 1 4744 2409 7 (epub)

Contents

Figures and Tables

Figures

Tables

Acknowledgements

Political Parties in the Arab World: Continuity and Change has been long in the making. The idea for the book grew out of numerous conversations at academic conferences and workshops with party politics specialists and scholars working on the Middle East and North Africa. As scholars bridging both fields, we were repeatedly met with questions about the role and importance of parties within the political systems of the Arab world and whether one can, indeed, even speak of parties being present there. These conversations egged us on, kept us on our toes, made us think. This book is the result of the thought process.

A special thanks goes to those academics and practitioners who first queried the role of parties in the Arab world, and who genuinely wanted to know more. Who were crying out for more rigorous scholarship on the topic, and who therefore encouraged us to press ahead with the volume: Thomas Carothers, André Gerrits, Peter Burnell, Jeff Haynes, Jorge Valledares, Lars Svåsand, Robert Elgie, Anthony Smith, Dina Melhem, Fernando Casal-Bértoa, Susan Dodsworth, Nic Cheesemean, Marina Ottaway, Annika Savill, Frederik Uggla, Eva Wegner, Miquel Pellicer, Vincent Durac, Paola Rivetti, Alex Baturo, Janine Clark, Rory McCarthy, and Patrick Bernhagen. Thanks also to the anonymous reviewers and their helpful suggestions, which assisted us in producing better work, and to Nicola Ramsey who believed in the project from the outset. Finally, we would also like to thank the people who initially inspired us to go down the path of party politics and acted as mentors along the way: Michael Laver, Ken Benoit and the late Gunnar Sjöblom and Peter Mair.

Preface

With very few exceptions, political parties have been ignored in studies of the Middle East and North Africa and no major systematic work analysing their role has appeared in recent times. This reality is related to the fact that parties in the Arab world tend to be weakly organised, ideologically fuzzy and play a different role in politics if compared with parties in other regions of the world. However, as this edited volume demonstrates, parties in the Arab world do exist, and some of these have even become institutionalised. That said, often parties are not vehicles for citizen representation and champions of democracy, but that does not mean they play an insignificant role in politics, nor does it imply that Arab parties should therefore be ignored. A comprehensive command of the region's political parties is crucial to understanding the dynamics of electoral authoritarian regimes and authoritarian resilience across the Arab world as well as processes of regime change, and they are also crucial in understanding the political dynamics within individual countries. Arab parties are key actors in the political arena and they simply play a *different* role to parties in the west. Compared with parties in other non-democratic and newly democratic regimes, however, they share many similarities in terms of their role and functions.

A number of excellent studies of individual parties in the Arab world as well as single-country case studies of parties in the region do exist and more and more are being published in recent years as the Arab Uprisings have generated a renewed interest in the internal political dynamics of the region. That said, the body of scholarship that sets out to discuss the role and functions of parties across the Arab world in a systematic manner, exploring continuity and change across cases and themes is rare indeed. Consequently, this is where our book fits in. It is an edited volume structured along themes, allowing at the same time for in-depth case studies. The key features of the book are four-fold: it sets out an innovative research agenda on an under-researched topic; it provides a comparative perspective on political parties across the region; it analyses the ways in which political parties in the Arab world matter and develop; and finally, it offers a more systematic understanding of the functioning of Arab regimes by incorporating the role political parties play in them.

The book is structured along three interrelated themes and some chapters therefore naturally overlap, thereby serving as bridges between the different parts. Chapter 1 by Storm and Cavatorta deals with the current debates on political parties, both in the Arab world and more generally. Among the issues discussed are whether parties are still important, whether the Arab world is exceptional, and how parties have performed in elections in the region around the time of the Arab Uprisings, the analysis centring on the question of whether Arabs do not do parties.

Following on from this initial analysis of party politics, which serves as a foundation and benchmark for the analysis in the various chapters included in the volume, is a section on **party families**, which covers the left (Chapter 2 by Resta), the secular – at times labelled liberal/leftist – parties (Chapter 3 by Wolf), moderate Islamist parties (Chapter 4 by El Kyak) and Salafi parties (Chapter 5 by Pall). In short, the chapters in this cluster look at families of parties across the region to analyse and explain how they have changed over time and what their difficulties and challenges are in deepening their roots in society. More specifically, the contribution by Resta is dedicated to the study of left-wing parties (with particular focus on the Egyptian and Tunisian cases), dealing with the significant transformations they have gone through. The chapter attempts to explain how they went from being dominant opposition parties in the first few decades following independence only to have become marginalised today. If anything, the relative weakness of the left in a region where popular demands would seem to be in line with left-wing political engagement is a paradox worth exploring.

Following on from Resta, Wolf discusses the region's so-called secular parties and what it means to be one. Most of the scholarly work on the Arab political systems points to the divide between Islamist and secular parties, but we have very little notion of what secular parties stand for, how they relate to other actors in the system, and in what way they define secularity and *laïcité*.

On the topic of Islamist parties, which have been very much *en vogue* in recent years, El Kyak examines in detail how mainstream Islamist parties have become relatively institutionalised and how, despite significant set-backs as in the case of the Egyptian Muslim Brotherhood, they continue to work within the institutions in place, be they fairly open and democratic or still closed off and authoritarian. This has implications for the political systems they operate in, but also for their organisational structures.

Pall dedicates his analysis to what some scholars have termed a new phenomenon within broader Islamist politics, namely the launch and rise of Salafi parties. Salafis traditionally shunned engagement in institutional politics through the creation of political parties, but the uprisings seem to have modified this traditional attitude and a number of countries have seen the participation of Salafis through parties. The case of Egypt is of course the most significant and best known, but Salafi parties are also active in Yemen, Kuwait and Tunisia. This new phenomenon deserves attention because Salafi parties not only compete with liberal, secular and socialist ones, but also with parties that find their roots in the Muslim Brotherhood, extending therefore the arena of party competition.

The second cluster of chapters focuses on **international constraints**. Daher's contribution (Chapter 6) looks at Lebanon's *Hezbollah* and the extent to which – as well as how – the party has been shaped by international factors, while Jamal (Chapter 7) examines how international constraints and Israeli occupation in particular have impacted on party politics in Palestine. The two chapters both highlight the nature of the external constraints some parties and party systems operate under and how this modifies national interactions, including the very problematic nature of parties having an integrated armed militia.

The remaining two contributions to this section deal specifically with cases where externally driven processes of regime change provided the opportunity for political parties to play a much greater role than they had in the past (Chapter 8 by Edwards on Iraq and Chapter 9 by Kamel on Libya). In both cases, however, parties failed to consolidate new party systems, resisting by implication the traditional role expected of them in building a pluralist political system. Rather than confirming their irrelevance, these two cases indicate that institutional failures might be the outcome of political party dynamics not conducive to compromise, particularly, as in Iraq and Libya, when ascriptive identities come to dominate the political game. Other contributions touch tangentially instead on the relative success that political parties have had. In Tunisia, for example, they have been able to shape the new political institutions through bargaining and negotiations, leading the country to consolidate its electoral democracy in a reasonably short period of time, defying in the process the assumption that parties in the region are irrelevant.

The third and final group of chapters analyses issues relating to **societal constituents**, taking their lead from Kamel, who highlights the role of tribalism as one of the main factors in shaping party politics in Libya. Alles (Chapter 10) discusses the impact of tribalism on parties in Yemen, in terms of both their role and functions, while Kraetzschmar (Chapter 11) centres his analysis on Kuwaiti politics and the relationship between the country's proto-parties and the tribes. Taken together, the contributions by Kamel, Alles and Kraetzschmar showcase just how much variety there is between parties operating within supposedly similar countries within the region. In Yemen and Libya, for instance, political parties are legal, while in Kuwait they are yet to be legalised and gain official status. In Yemen parties are institutionalised, in Kuwait the proto-parties are somewhat institutionalised (albeit in decline), while in Libya parties are very much not institutionalised. In all three countries parties are highly personalistic – as they are also in Iraq (Edwards in Chapter 8) and Mauritania (Ojeda-García in Chapter 12) – and, more importantly, they are viewed by the citizenry as less powerful than the tribes, a reality which has resulted in parties not being acknowledged as relevant actors in the cases of Libya and Kuwait, while in Yemen they are seen as essential.

Ojeda-García on Mauritania's parties places these observations in a wider perspective. The case of Mauritania – a country often classified as 'African' rather than Middle Eastern or Arab – has clear commonalities with these cases, the parties being highly personalistic, weakly institutionalised (as in the case of Libya, where institutionalisation is even lower), and strongly focused on providing clientelistic and directive linkage. Similar to the situation in Iraq, Libya and Yemen, political parties are legal in Mauritania, and their weakness does not stem from being excluded from the formal channels of power, but rather from the constraints imposed by the role of the military in politics and the extreme importance within party politics of personalism and citizen control as directed by the regime.

The two final contributions to Part 3 are by Debuysere (Chapter 13) and Yaghi (Chapter 14) on women and youth respectively. Debuysere analyses the role of women in political parties across the region with particular emphasis on the case of Tunisia, highlighting the different drivers of women's participation in parties and institutional politics. Yaghi examines instead the reasons why young activists failed to build competitive and strong political parties in the aftermath of the overthrow of the incumbent authoritarian regimes in Tunisia and Egypt. In fact, having been among the protagonists of the uprisings and their main initiators, young activists did not evolve into central figures of the subsequent political systems in the two countries. Older politicians and established political parties remained the central actors in both Tunisia and Egypt, sidelining young activists. This marginalisation and, to an extent, choice of disengagement are accounted for in Yaghi's study.

Finally, the concluding chapter by Cavatorta and Storm (Chapter 15) broadens the focus to parties elsewhere in the world and is consequently dedicated to a discussion of the extent to which the lessons learnt from the Arab world are applicable transnationally, covering issues such as the lack of the left as an alternative, charismatic leadership, the rise of populism, and the wider dissatisfaction with party politics.

In summary, there are two broad objectives this edited volume intends to achieve. First, the different chapters provide a novel analysis of parties in the Arab world to allow scholars to better understand regional debates and issues that are not necessarily linked to democratisation processes. Second, the edited volume aims at placing Arab political parties in the much wider literature on the functions, roles and challenges of parties more broadly. For instance, how women and young people integrate parties (or their relative absence of engagement in them) can speak to similar phenomena taking place outside the region. Studies of Arab political parties with armed militias can be similarly useful to highlight how similar dynamics exist elsewhere. Thus, there is a wider comparative element that this volume offers.

Chapter 1

Do Arabs not do parties? An introduction and exploration

Lise Storm and Francesco Cavatorta

With very few exceptions, political parties have been ignored in studies of the Middle East and North Africa and no major systematic work analysing their role has appeared in recent times. This is for two broad reasons. First of all, political parties are inherently associated with democracy or democratising institutions. Given the absence of democracy and genuine democratisation processes in the region (with the notable current exception of Tunisia), scholars argued that it was not necessary to study actors deemed irrelevant to the understanding of Arab politics. Second, party politics and political parties in the Arab world rarely have deep societal roots, they are generally weakly organised, and are more often than not personalistic in nature. This reality – often incorrectly interpreted as the absence of institutionalisation – coupled with the parties' limited direct influence on political decisions justifies their neglect to many scholars viewing them through a western lens.

Nevertheless, the contention of this project is that political parties do matter and are worth investigating. With the Arab Uprisings, an increasing number of scholars, but also the general public, have taken a keen interest in the local politics of the Arab world. Most extant analyses, however, focus on prospects for democracy, authoritarian entrenchment, and issues related to security, including migration, and EU foreign policy. Consequently, very few studies take into consideration the role of parties, and those that do only deal with parties in a rather superficial manner (Carothers 2006; Lawson and Ibrahim 2010; Ottaway and Hamzawy 2009; Penner Angrist 2006; Perthes 2004; Pratt 2007; Sadiki 2009, 2014). This reality is undoubtedly linked to the fact that political parties do not figure as prominently in Arab politics as elsewhere. Yet, their current 'irrelevance' might not last forever and a better understanding of their role – or potential role – can be very useful. After all, the Arab Uprisings themselves came as a surprise and their protagonists were also 'unusual suspects' (Aarts and Cavatorta 2013) such as youth movements and trade unions, suggesting that looking beyond what one might think of as 'relevant' and powerful actors is not a futile exercise.

This volume argues that parties in the Arab world are pivotal and that they play a key role in political life. Not because the region is democratising and that we therefore need to study political parties in that context. Rather, the book builds on the general assertion that *political parties are important in their own right because of the functions they have regardless of the type and nature of the regimes within which they operate*. The Arab world is no different. Parties are important here too, even if the setting is authoritarian and the parameters under which they operate are different to those in the established democracies. This volume, accordingly, sets out to discuss the role and functions of parties across the Arab world, exploring continuity and change across cases and themes with a view to ensure longevity, and focusing in particular on the issue of linkage (clientelistic, directive, electoral and participatory). Hence, the discussion covers parties and tribes, women, religion, the Arab left, and charismatic leadership to mention just a few key topics. Little has been written on Arab political parties in such a broad comparative perspective, and several of the themes are hitherto understudied, yet crucial if we are to understand the intricate dynamics of Arab politics past and present, anchoring the discussion of the region's parties much further back than the Arab Uprisings, and providing a solid foundation for analyses stretching further into the future than these famed uprisings. It is also important to move away from studies focusing exclusively on the 'structure of the conflict' between authoritarian ruling elites and opposition parties (Lust-Okar 2005). The book is, in other words, a historically moored, deep comparative political analysis structured around themes that have relevance to the region today and in the years to come, and which extend across boundaries. It is not a historical account of the development of the party systems in each Arab country, as a number of excellent works exist on this (Tachau 1994; Penner Angrist 2006; Lawson and Ibrahim 2010; Randjbar-Daemi et al. 2017). The book is also not about the role of parties in the impending Arab democratisation process, because in general – as already stated – the Arab world is not democratising.

Why are parties so important?

Parties matter and this is the case in democracies as well as in authoritarian regimes. Parties matter in any regime. They serve as vehicles for citizen representation in democracies, they are vessels of elite co-optation in many authoritarian regimes, in totalitarian regimes the party is one of the arms of the ruler, and in those regimes where parties are entirely prohibited they tend to still exist, serving the cause of the clandestine opposition. In short, parties are powerful, and they play a prominent role in politics, regardless of whether as legal entities or clandestinely. Equally important, and something we tend to forget, parties are not just key players within the realms of democracy. Parties are important in their own right. Understanding the role of functions of parties in any country is vital if we are to accurately grasp the workings of the regime in place and, potentially, make predictions about its future development. According to Pettitt (2014: 3), political parties 'are simply the most important political organisation in the modern world'.

Political parties in democratic regimes

In the west, scholars have long argued that 'modern democracy is unthinkable save in terms of parties' (Schattschneider 1942: 1). As a matter of fact, the reality that there is no single fully-fledged democracy today that does not have political parties (in plural) speaks volumes about their role. Parties are essential if democracy is to survive, because parties act as vehicles through which voters and representatives are mobilised behind a cause. Parties, in short, aggregate and articulate the interests of the citizenry and formulate political programmes, thereby strengthening their voice. Of course, one could argue that other organisations could fulfil these functions, but research shows that political parties are superior to other ways of solving collective-action problems; they are better at aggregating interests, coordinating decision-making in parliament, and at ensuring vertical accountability, that is, when power necessarily is delegated from the citizenry to a select group of representatives (Aldrich 1995; Przeworski et al. 1999; Schedler 2002, 2007). Moreover, parties create 'linkage' between governments and voters, affording the citizenry not only the opportunity to *participate* (and mobilise and socialise), but also the ability to hold their *elected* representatives accountable, particularly at election time when citizens select their representatives (Pedersen 1989).

Parties also provide what is often termed 'clientelistic' and 'directive' linkage in democratic regimes, although some more than others. Clientelistic linkage, where a vote for a party is expected to result in certain investments in the local area, and directive linkage, where those in power use the party as a means to control the citizenry, can work for or against democracy. Because these two types of linkage are less prominent than electoral and participatory linkages in democratic regimes today, they are often afforded a marginal role in discussions of modern parties, particularly in the western world. However, as this book highlights, parties in the Arab world are largely geared towards providing clientelistic and directive linkage, while electoral and participatory linkage has been given much less of a priority. With recent developments in the Arab world coupled with the decline of membership-based politics in the west (van Biezen and Poguntke 2014), there is reason to believe that the scholarship on party politics will be undergoing serious review in the coming years. There is a real necessity to broaden – if not revise – our understanding of the role and functions of political parties globally. Most notably, there is the above-mentioned void in our knowledge of parties that emphasise clientelistic and directive linkage as discussed in this book, but there is also a pressing demand for scholarship exploring where the 'traditional' or more 'ideal type' parties prioritising electoral and participatory linkage will be heading at a time when party apathy and anti-establishment sentiment is growing, and has been for quite some years. Could it be, for instance, that the two types of parties are coming closer together as horizontal engagement is becoming an increasingly popular form of mobilisation, not only in the Arab world as highlighted in this volume, but also in the west (van Biezen 2014; Mair 2006)?

What do we know about parties in non-democratic and newly democratic regimes?

Although relatively little is written about Arab parties, there is reason to believe that parties in the region are similar to those in other non-democratic regimes and in new democracies. A frequent critique of such parties is that they are ideologically and organisationally weak, functioning as personal vehicles of political entrepreneurs (and their families) and consequently dominated by a cadre that is not actually interested in building a party if understood along the lines of citizen representation and interest aggregation. These parties are top-heavy and suffer from weak internal democracy too, and they are therefore unlikely to build strong party organisations because there is no incentive for the party leadership to do so. On the contrary, increased internal democracy is often seen as a challenge. While less organisationally weak, similar critiques – particularly with regard to the issue of internal democracy – have been levied against the parties that sprang from independence movements in the Middle East and elsewhere and, at present, the Islamist parties, which have come to prominence in recent years, especially in the wake of the Arab Uprisings (Carothers 2006; Storm 2013; Svåsand 2014; Martínez 2017).

Some scholars argue that the reality that parties in non-democratic and newly democratic regimes differ from those in the west is hardly surprising given the different context (Sartori 1976; Kitchelt 1995; van Biezen 2003, 2005; Webb and White 2007; Reilly and Nordlund 2008):

> Elites and masses in new democracies have not had the same opportunity as their counterparts in Europe to gradually adapt to changing political institutions and social and economic processes. Instead, political transitions have been compressed in time and occurred simultaneously with economic transformations, technological changes and a strong impact of international events, actors and processes. (Svåsand 2014: 16)

Furthermore, in many of these countries where political parties are a relatively new phenomenon, the notion of what constitutes a party is very much contested, and often it differs from that in the west (Catusse and Karam 2010). Organisations labelling themselves as political parties do not necessarily have an interest in party building, actors do not always identify with their parties' ideas, and the parties do not necessarily unite political actors that share similar interests and, consequently, mobilise support for such. As a consequence of this reality, some scholars have come to query whether parties can be said to exist in such countries, and where they do, if they play a central role in politics.

Is the Arab world exceptional after all?

Given the fact that the Arab world is the least democratic region in the world, it is hardly astonishing that Arab parties, in particular, are a hotly contested topic, as the issue of the role and functions of parties is closely linked to the debate on prospects for democracy. Mirroring the discussion of the compatibility of democracy and Catholicism prior to the so-called Third Wave, a debate has raged within the academic community in recent decades over whether the Arab world or, indeed, the Muslim world can be said to be exceptional (Stepan and Robertson 2003; Hinnebusch 2017). Some scholars have argued that Islam and democracy are incompatible, thus explaining why the region is the most hostile in the world to the advance of democracy. Their argument, in short: the Arab world is exceptional. Others contend that Islam and democracy are compatible, but as fostering democracy takes time, those hoping to see democracy take hold in the region must be armed with patience. Hence, the Arab world is not exceptional. Then there are those on the fence. Those who argue that democracy is essentially a western concept, and therefore the Arab world is neither exceptional nor unexceptional, but rather misunderstood. According to this group of scholars, we need to broaden our understanding of democracy and look at Arab definitions of democracy, such as Islamic democracy, if we are to adequately assess the prospects of democracy in the region (Bellin 2012; Brumberg 2014; Cavatorta 2010; Pace and Cavatorta 2012; Hess 2013, 2016; Hinnebusch 2015; Valbjørn 2012; Valbjørn and Bank 2010).

Here we argue that while we think democracy is *possible* in the region despite the fact that very few countries have yet made the transition, many may not *want* to undergo such a process. Thus, democratisation is not the key issue at hand. Rather, parties are. What they look like, how they operate, and the ways in which they contribute to change and/or the perpetuation of the status quo; that is what matters.

Do Arabs not do parties?

Given the central role political parties play in both democratic and non-democratic regimes, it is somewhat ironic that scholars working on Arab parties are often met with questions about the need for parties in the region. As if parties are not relevant, as if they do not play a crucial role in how politics is conducted. As if the Arab world is exceptional as just discussed above. From where we are sitting, the Arab world is either exceptional, being the only region where political parties are not needed to provide linkage – either because unlike elsewhere, (a) other organisations provide this linkage or (b) linkage is simply not necessary – or the

Arab world is not exceptional, but rather under-studied and therefore badly understood, at least on the party front. In short, do Arabs not do parties? We think they do, we just do not know very much about them.

It is true that the many parties in the Arab world are less developed than parties in most other parts of the world, and that the region's parties tend to play a different role in politics than they do in democratic regimes as shall be discussed in more detail below and, of course, throughout the book. However, this reality by no means implies that political parties do not exist, or that they do not play a central role in political life.

Some twenty-five years ago, Tachau (1994: xv) argued that 'mass political awareness and demands for greater and more effective political participation are evident throughout the region', a reality that rings no less true today, particularly in the wake of the Arab Uprisings. When Tachau edited his seminal volume on *Political Parties of the Middle East and North Africa*, one of the main challenges facing the contributors was how to define parties, ensuring that their definition was not too narrow, yet not so broad as to water down the concept entirely. The problem was that most definitions of political parties were developed with the western world in mind, and a key element of these was, accordingly, the fielding of candidates in competitive parliamentary elections (see, for example, Sartori 1976). Yet, in many Arab states there was no such contestation, either because parliaments did not exist, or because direct popular elections were not the method for selecting the representatives in parliament. Some definitions also maintained that political parties demonstrate a modicum of longevity, that is, 'continuity in organisation' meaning that to qualify as a party an organisation would not be dependent upon the life span of current leaders, a characteristic that many Arab parties did not share at the time (LaPalombara and Weiner 1966).

The rise of competitive authoritarianism

Things have changed considerably in the Arab world since the time Tachau and his colleagues were writing. Most notably, parliaments are now found throughout the region, and most members of parliament are elected in direct popular elections. The days of totalitarianism and closed authoritarian regimes are long gone for most parts of the region (Stepan and Robertson 2003; Sadiki 2009; Brownlee 2011; Lust 2014). That is not to say, however, that the Arab world has undergone a wave of transitions to democracy and that parties are now afforded a role in political life identical to that of their counterparts in democratic regimes. Rather, the region is currently in the age of 'competitive authoritarianism', a state where non-democratic regimes utilise democratic methods to maintain their grip on power. In the words of Levitsky and Way, who coined the term:

> in competitive authoritarian regimes, formal democratic institutions are widely viewed as the principal means of obtaining and exercising political authority. Incumbents violate these rules so often and to such an extent, however, that the regime fails to meet conventional minimum standards for democracy. (Levitsky and Way 2002: 52)

Put differently, the violations of the rules create an uneven playing field between the government and the opposition:

> Although elections are regularly held and are generally free of massive fraud, incumbents routinely abuse state resources, deny the opposition adequate media coverage, harass opposition candidates and their supporters, and in some cases manipulate electoral results. Journalists, opposition politicians, and other government critics may be spied on, threatened, harassed, or arrested. Members of the opposition may be jailed, exiled, or – less frequently – even assaulted or murdered. (Levitsky and Way 2002: 53)

As competitive authoritarianism has taken hold in the Arab world, with most of the region's regimes now falling into this category, some of the difficulties Tachau and his colleagues experienced when settling on a definition of political parties that also applied to the Middle East and North Africa have ceased to be important. The Arab world is presently awash with political groups 'identified by an official label that presents at elections, and is capable of placing through elections (free or non-free) candidates for public office' as per Sartori's (1976: 63) classical definition. The parties in the 'new' Arab world evidently do not play the same role in politics as parties did during the previous regimes given the (somewhat) recent reliance on competitive elections, nor do they perform the exact same functions as parties in the west, although some are of course shared (Gandhi 2008). Hence, the time has arguably come to take stock with a view to, on the one hand, improve our understanding of the region's political parties as well as, on the other, enrich our knowledge of parties in general. In short, *in this changed political environment, what role do Arab political parties currently play, what characterises these parties, what difficulties do they face, and what lessons can the rest of the world learn from the region?*

The Arab Uprisings and changes to the party landscape in the Arab world

The eruption of the Arab Uprisings in December 2010 and the subsequent wave of unrest that swept the Middle East and North Africa from 2011 onwards resulted in considerable changes within the party landscape in the region. This reality has been largely overlooked by scholars in their preoccupation with assessing democratic advances and prospects for democracy in the Arab world following the upheaval. Prior to the Arab Uprisings, one- and two-party systems dominated the region, bearing evidence of strictly limited contestation and electoral choice in those countries that did formally allow political parties to operate. This situation has now changed. In the post-Arab Uprisings environment, political pluralism has improved considerably, and most Arab states now operate with party systems that can either be characterised as cases of moderate pluralism (three to five political parties) or extreme pluralism (six to eight-plus parties). Egypt and Tunisia, which were previously one-party systems, can now most accurately be described as cases of moderate pluralism as can Libya, which did not allow for political parties during the reign of Gaddafi and consequently held its first competitive legislative elections in 2012. Algeria remained in the 'moderate pluralism' category, and Iraq and Morocco continued to belong in the category of 'extreme pluralism', although Iraq is clearly atomised with numerous parties contesting national elections on the slates of obscure alliances (Storm 2017). It should be noted that Lebanon, Palestine and Yemen have not held legislative elections since the Arab Uprisings. Syria held elections in 2012 and 2016, but these were neither free nor fair and have therefore not been counted. Yemen was a one-party system prior to the Arab Uprisings, Palestine and Syria had two-party systems in place, and Lebanon was a case of extreme pluralism.

The reality that a considerable degree of party system change has taken place in the Arab world with the advent of the Arab Uprisings is not only highly interesting given the overall lack of democratic progress in most cases, but also very important for scholars of party politics when one takes a closer look at the developments. Of course, change was always going to happen if measured in terms of electoral volatility as countries across the region moved to legalise previously repressed opposition forces and prohibit the vehicles of the old regime, while new parties mushroomed alongside. What is noteworthy, however, and also somewhat surprising is the realisation that the Arab Uprisings resulted in the emergence of very few sizeable and durable new parties. Most new parties were, in fact, loose political alliances based on local interests and militia or tribal allegiances, often fronted by a charismatic leader, such as *al-Aridha* in Tunisia. These parties never even came close to resembling genuine political parties, and the great majority were unsurprisingly gone in a flash. The Freedom and Justice Party (FJP) in Egypt could have been the exception to the rule, but the party was shut down by the military regime in the wake of the *coup d'état* of 2013 due to the party's close links to the Muslim Brotherhood.

Moreover, very few of the parties that were established in the wake of the uprisings were so-called externally created parties, that is, genuinely new entities, and of these not a single one managed to survive for more than one legislative election (Storm 2017).[1] For those preoccupied with democratisation in the region, this is arguably a disappointing fact, but for those concerned with Arab parties it is a very different matter. The reality that the traditionally dominant parties remained the central actors within the party systems supports previous findings on Arab parties and party systems (Storm 2013), namely that these have become institutionalised as Table 1.1 shows. They are not necessarily forces for democracy, nor do they necessarily play the same role and have the same functions as parties in the west as discussed in more detail below, but they are key actors, and durable too.

Table 1.1 reveals several important issues not only about the state of parties in the Arab world, but also about their status in politics. For instance, with reference to longevity, the average age of the top two parties in at least one of the two most recent legislative elections was above thirty years in a significant number of instances (Algeria, Egypt, Lebanon, Morocco, Palestine and Sudan), in some countries covering cases from both the pre- and post-Arab Uprisings era. What the data presented in Table 1.1 does not disclose, but which full election data makes readily apparent, is the reality that while in a number of countries the average of the top two parties has declined following the unrest, this by no means implies that the old parties have ceased to exist. Rather, in the majority of cases it is simply a consequence of electoral volatility, which is high in the region due to the parties' weak roots in society.

Poor rootedness is a cause for concern from the perspective of those hoping for democracy to take hold in the Arab world, and for the region's parties to play a more central role within the upper echelons of power and, of course, as vehicles of citizen representation and mobilisation. Much more worrying, however, is the reality that the top two parties tend

Table 1.1 Parties and elections in the Arab world[a]

	Election year	Average age of top two parties (years)	Combined seat share of top two parties (%)	Parties	Seat share (independent candidates) (%)	Notes/*
Algeria	2012	36.5	59.7	FLN, RND	3.9	
	2007	31.5	50.6	FLN, RND	8.5	
Bahrain	2014	12	7.5	al-Wefaq, al-Asalah	92.5	
	2010	8.5	52.5	al-Asalah, al-Menbar Islamic Society	42.5	Boycott by al-Wefaq.
Egypt	2015	2.5	20.8*	Free Egyptians Party; Nation's Future Party	56.9*	* Of the 568 directly elected seats.
	2011–12	0	65.9	FJP, al-Nur	4.2*	* Independents not affiliated with any party.
	2010	32*	82.9	NDP, al-Wafd	13.6*	* Independents incl. those affiliated with the NDP and the Muslim Brotherhood.
Jordan	2016	19.5	15.4	al-Wasat, IAF	76.9	
	2013	6	3.3	al-Wasat, Stronger Jordan	82.0	* Three parties won two seats: Stronger Jordan, the Homeland, and the NUP. Stronger Jordan won a larger vote share than its two competitors. IAF boycott.
Lebanon	2009	7.5	35.2	Future Movement, FPM	0.8	
	2005	31.5	40.6	Future Movement, PSP	1.6	
Libya	2014	–*	–*		100.0	* Independents only.
	2012	0	70*	NFA, JCP	60.0	* Of the 80 seats reserved for parties. Another 120 were set aside for independents.

Table 1.1 Parties and elections in the Arab world[a] (cont.)

	Election year	Average age of top two parties (years)	Combined seat share of top two parties (%)	Parties	Seat share (independent candidates) (%)	Notes/*
Mauritania	2013	5	62.3	UFP, Tewassoul	–	
	2006	2	58.9	RDF, al-Mithaq	–	
Morocco	2016	13*	57.5	PJD, PAM	–	* Conservatively dating the PJD according to its formal establishment in 1998 (and not its previous forms tracing back to 1967).
	2011	43.5*	42.3	PJD, PI	–	* See above.
Palestine	2006	33	90.2	Hamas, Fatah	3.0	
	1996	37	64.0*	Fatah	36.0	* *Fatah* was the only party to formally win any seats. Affiliated independents and other independents won the remainder. Hamas and the PFLP boycotted the elections.
Sudan	2015	41	81.7	National Congress Party, DUP-Original	4.2	
	2010	20.5	93.8	National Congress Party, SPLM*	0.7	* SPLM is now part of the political framework in South Sudan following the partition.
Tunisia	2014	2.5*	71.4	Nidaa Tounes, Ennahda	1.4	* Conservatively dating the *Ennahda* according to its formal establishment in 2011 (and not its previous forms tracing back to 1981).
	2011	0*	53	Ennahda, PP	3.7	* See above.
Yemen	2003	17	91.3	GPC, al-Islah	4.7	
	1997	11	80.3	GPC, al-Islah	18.1	

[a] The table excludes war-torn Syria, Iraq due to inadequate election data at the party level, and those Arab Gulf States that do not formally allow for political parties and/or where election data is inadequate.

to command a very sizeable share of the seats in the legislature. In non-democratic regimes, this is generally a sign of limited room being afforded the opposition in practice, even if opposition parties are legalised and invited to contest elections. This is a theme touched upon in most of the chapters in this book, often with references to authoritarian legacies and the authoritarian context. In tightly controlled Algeria, the combined seat share of the top two parties, which were both regime parties, was above 50 per cent in the two most recent legislative elections. This was also the case in Egypt prior to the Arab Uprisings (in excess of 80 per cent), in Palestine during the conflict between *Hamas* and *Fatah* in 1996, which saw the latter party boycott the elections, and then again in 2006 when the two parties jointly commanded more than 90 per cent of the seats in the legislature. In post-partition Sudan, the seat share of the top two parties was above 80 per cent in the most recent elections of 2015, a situation similar to that in Yemen in both 1997 and 2003. Worryingly, despite having gone to great lengths to avoid a return to a dominant/hegemonic party system, the two parties performing the best in the Tunisian legislative elections in the post-Arab Uprisings era have won in excess of 50 per cent of the seats between them, both in 2011 (53 per cent) and 2014 (71.4 per cent), with the trend going in the wrong direction.

Finally, adding further to the words of caution is the reality that independent candidates continue to play a disproportionately central role in legislative politics in the Arab world, underlining yet again – and as discussed further below – the lack of party rootedness and legitimacy in the eyes of the electorate as well as, of course, the limited role of ideology, although the latter does play a part when it comes to Salafi parties for instance. This is a particularly worrying observation in countries where parties are not formally legalised, such as for instance in Bahrain, where independent candidates commanded in excess of 40 per cent of the seats in the legislature in 2010 and more than 90 per cent in 2014, and in those cases where parties are struggling to assert themselves as central actors within the political system, such as is the case in Jordan and Libya. In Jordan, 82 per cent of the seats went to independents in the 2013 elections, and in 2016 their share was 76.9 per cent. In Libya, 60 per cent of all contested seats were reserved for independents in the first post-Arab Uprisings elections in 2012, and some two years later, in 2014, all seats were set aside for independents, robbing budding parties of the opportunity to assert themselves at the polls. Egypt under the current military regime has also increased its reliance on so-called independent candidates, and these now command a seat share close to 60 per cent.

What we can learn from the parties of the Arab world

If the Arab world can teach us one thing about parties, it is that the *local* context matters. It is impossible to understand the role and function of political parties in under-studied regions if we examine them from a regional perspective or from a western ideal. Of course, international and regional factors matter, but local contextual knowledge is paramount. There is tremendous variety among Arab parties, within and across countries and within so-called party families, whether the left, secular parties, Islamist parties or resistance parties. The wealth of different parties found in the region cannot be explained solely by culturalist explanations as championed most notably by Bill and Springborg (1994), nor can they be reduced to structural factors, such as the issue of rentierism (Luciani and Beblawi 1987; Ross 2001), weak rule of law, poverty, and anti-political legacies (Carothers 2006). The research behind the contributions to this book clearly highlights that both types of factors are important, and often at the same time. Rentierism has evidently played a great role in shaping party politics – and the role of parties in politics – not only in the Arab Gulf States, but also in the case of Libya and to some extent Tunisia, while tribalism has been (and continues to be) a key determining factor in countries such as Yemen, Libya and Kuwait, and similarities can be found in the Tunisian case in the form of allegiance to a *za'im*, which often takes priority over political ideology. Weak rule of law has had a negative impact on party development across the Arab world, as have anti-political legacies as discussed by most contributors to this volume. The research demonstrates that what characterises those parties that have managed to survive – that is, institutionalise – has less to do with political ideology and strong party programmes, and more to do with the ability of parties to provide clientelistic and directive linkage, which are both linked to tribalism, charismatic leadership and authoritarian legacies. However, not only do people *vote* for parties based on the above factors, these factors also shape why people *join* political parties as well as largely determining the *role* and *functions* of parties in the Arab world.

In most of the Arab world, the chief function of political parties is to provide clientelistic linkage (Lust-Okar 2009; LeDuc et al. 2014; Lust 2016). That is, party membership or a vote for a party is expected to result in benefits to the party member, the voter, and the geographical area represented by the party. This reality is to a certain extent caused by a situation where legislative elections are effectively contested like local elections, that is, where the emphasis is on the constituency and the candidates themselves rather than politics at the national level. But the two also reinforce and perpetuate each other, and this is one of the main challenges facing political parties in the region today. How to build strong political parties with national appeal that can serve a more central role in political life when they have never done so – with a few exceptions – in the past, and in an environment where the dominant actors within the political elite are not affording them much space to do so and the electorate is disillusioned with the political establishment? Save to a degree for the parties that emerged from the various independence movements, political parties in the Arab world are faced with the task of having to develop not in tandem with the emergence of mass politics as in the west, but in a day and age where party de-alignment and anti-party sentiment is growing. Of course, these problems are not exclusive to the Arab world, but the context is rather. The complex interplay of tribalism, rentierism and competitive authoritarianism coupled with international constraints exists nowhere else at such a level and intensity.

A further issue is, of course, that the parties may very well not wish to reconsider their role. As Kraetzschmar points out in his chapter in this volume, while from the perspective of party and party system development a debate on the future of political parties is paramount, it appears that there is little interest in doing so. The parties themselves and the politicians at the forefront appear content with their present role as long as it does not diminish in importance, hence they bolster (competitive) authoritarianism because they benefit from it. The parties are clients of the upper echelons of the regime (whether a king, president, royal family, the military, etc.), and in some cases – such as in Kuwait, Libya and Yemen – also of the tribes, while the electorate are clients of the parties (see, in this volume, Chapters 5–7, 9–11, 14). The parties that have done the best at institutionalising themselves consequently serve two functions: they provide clientelistic and directive linkage. On the one hand, they provide services to their constituents and members (clientelistic linkage), as Blaydes (2011) also finds, while on the other they are instruments of the regime – used as a means to co-opt and appease the opposition and other potentially challenging forces within society, including the tribes (directive linkage). In Morocco this is epitomised in the *makhzen*. In some cases, particularly in the Arab Gulf States and in those countries with pronounced societal cleavages, such as in Lebanon, Mauritania and Yemen, evidence of both clientelistic and directive linkage is highly visible. In others, for example in Morocco, a degree of contextual knowledge is necessary to detect this. However, across the region it rings true that parties have become marginalised and co-opted at the institutional level, while utilised as alternative mobilising forces at the societal level via selective accommodation (Lust 2016; this volume, chs 2, 3, 5). This dynamic is at the core of the functioning of the electoral authoritarian regimes in the Arab world.

Arab parties as vehicles for citizen participation and representation

There is no arguing against the reality that a typical Arab voter will be facing the following sequence of questions when deciding where to put their tick at election time. First, the voter will establish whether he or she will vote for a pro-regime or anti-regime (legal opposition) candidate, a decision which for many voters is linked to tribalism, ethnicity or religious affiliation. Then, the question is which *local* candidate is most likely to deliver something of benefit to the voter based on the strength of the candidate's *personal* connections to the regime and within the party, which is an issue very much related to directive and clientelistic linkage. If more than one candidate meets the requirements, then the typical voter will take into consideration which of the candidates he or she feels closest to ideologically. Ideology and party programmes are, in other words, not particularly important at the polls, and consequently not that much of a priority to the parties. This rings true both in the Arab republics and the monarchies alike.

Consequently, the parties that have traditionally emphasised participatory and electoral linkage, while downplaying – or failing to provide – clientelistic and directive linkage have fared less well. This point is well illustrated by the performance of the Arab leftist parties, which largely centred their attention on mass mobilisation and socialisation in the first few decades following independence. Having failed to provide stable, participatory regimes alongside affordable housing, employment, education, and so on, the parties of the left have lost appeal and have thus largely been abandoned by the electorate despite the fact that survey data clearly indicates that the population is generally left-leaning (Achcar 2013; Abdel Muti 2013; Jamal 2013; Masoud 2014; Yom 2015; this volume, chs 2, 7). That said, participatory and electoral linkage are not without importance in the Arab world today. Both in the run-up to the Arab Uprisings and in their aftermath, Islamist parties in particular have demonstrated the merits of a focus on mobilising the masses (Schwedler and Clark 2006; Hamdok et al. 2010; al-Anani 2012). The ability to mobilise the electorate, coupled with the fact that many Islamist parties were viewed as the only hope for the future if compared with the alternatives, which had either failed (the left, the old regime parties) or were without much substance (the new populist parties). As a consequence of their success at the polls, Islamist parties were vilified as radicals – usually unjustly – particularly in the case of Egypt's Freedom and Justice Party and Tunisia's *Ennahda*, neither of which had the intention of turning time back to the days of the Prophet. This is not to say that Egypt's President Morsi was not attempting to concentrate power in his own hands, because he was indeed. However, his motives were personal and his actions not initiated by the FJP.

Following on from these Islamist victories, which saw the FJP rise to power in Egypt, the *Ennahda* win in Tunisia, and the *Parti de la Justice et du Développement* (PJD) emerge victorious in Morocco in the first legislative elections to be held after the outbreak of the Arab Uprisings, came a populist backlash. In Egypt the popularly elected president, the Islamist Mohamed Morsi, was ousted in a popularly supported military coup, which eventually saw the orchestrator (General Abdel Fattah el-Sisi) legitimise his power and the effective military regime via the polls in presidential elections in 2014. In Tunisia, populist, anti-Islamist forces (in the shape of *Nidaa Tounes*) with ties to the old Ben Ali regime won the legislative elections of 2014 as well as the presidential elections that same year, while in Morocco the party of the King's close friend, the *Parti Authenticité et Modernité* (PAM), came second just behind the Islamist PJD. Quite a few countries had, it appeared, come full circle, with the electorate flocking to the parties perceived as able to provide clientelistic linkage and ensure stability, even if as a consequence of directive linkage via non-democratic forces higher up in the system.

Note

1. Tunisia's *Ennahda* and the *Congrès pour la République* were not newcomers, but rather newly legalised previously clandestine entities, while Morocco's PAM pre-dates the Arab Uprisings even if it had not contested the elections as a party prior to the events. Tunisia's *Nidaa Tounes* had close relations to Ben Ali's now defunct regime party, the *Rassemblement Constitutionnel Démocratique*. The only genuine newcomer was Egypt's *Hizb al-Nur*.

Bibliography

Aarts, Paul, and Francesco Cavatorta (2013), *Civil Society in Syria and Iran: Activism in Authoritarian Contexts*, Boulder, CO: Lynne Rienner.

Abdel Muti, Ayman (2013), 'The Egyptian Revolution and the Role of the Left: Success and Failure Factors', in Ellen Jarrar (ed.), *The Left and the Arab Revolutions*, Cairo: Rosa Luxemburg Foundation, pp. 13–33.

Achcar, Gilbert (2013), *The People Want: A Radical Exploration of the Arab Uprising*, Oakland, CA: University of California Press.

Aldrich, John (1995), *Why Parties? The Origin and Transformation of Party Politics in America*, Chicago: University of Chicago Press.

al-Anani, Khalil (2012), 'Islamist Parties Post-Arab Spring', *Mediterranean Politics* 17: 3, 466–72.

Bellin, Eva (2012), 'Reconsidering the Robustness of Authoritarianism in the Middle East: Lessons from the Arab Spring', *Comparative Politics* 44: 2, 127–49.

Bill, James, and Robert Springborg (1994) *Politics in the Middle East*, New York: HarperCollins.

Blaydes, Lisa (2011), *Elections and Distributive Politics in Mubarak's Egypt*, Cambridge: Cambridge University Press.

Brownlee, Jason (2011), 'Executive Elections in the Arab World: When and How Do They Matter?', *Comparative Political Studies* 44: 7, 807–28.

Brumberg, Daniel (2014), 'Theories of Transition', in Marc Lynch (ed.), *The Arab Uprisings Explained: New Contentious Politics in the Middle East*, New York: Columbia University Press, pp. 29–54.

Carothers, Thomas (2006), *Confronting the Weakest Link: Aiding Political Parties in New Democracies*, Washington DC: Carnegie Endowment for International Peace.

Catusse, Myriam, and Karam Karam (2010), 'Back to Parties? Partisan Logics and Transformations of Politics in the Arab World', in Myriam Catusse and Karam Karam (eds), *Returning to Political Parties? Political Party Development in the Arab World*, Paris: Presses de l'Ifpo.

Cavatorta, Francesco (2010), 'The Convergence of Governance: Upgrading Authoritarianism in the Arab World and Downgrading Democracy Elsewhere?', *Middle East Critique* 19: 3, 217–32.

Gandhi, Jennifer (2008), *Political Institutions under Dictatorship*, Cambridge: Cambridge University Press.

Hamdok, Abdalla, Marina Vaccari, Rosa Balfour, Ferruccio Pastore, Battistina Cugusi, Roberto Aliboni and Daniela Pioppi (2010), *Islamist Mass Movements, External Actors and Political Change in the Arab World*, Stockholm and Rome: International Institute for Democracy and Electoral Assistance, Centro Studi di Politica Internazionale and Istitute Affari Internazionali.

Hess, Steve (2013), 'From the Arab Spring to the Chinese Winter: The Institutional Sources of Authoritarian Vulnerability and Resilience in Egypt, Tunisia, and China', *International Political Science Review* 34: 3, 254–72.

Hess, Steve (2016), 'Sources of Authoritarian Resilience in Regional Protest Waves: The Post-Communist Colour Revolutions and 2011 Arab Uprisings', *Government and Opposition* 51: 1, 1–29.

Hinnebusch, Raymond (2015), 'Introduction: Understanding the Consequences of the Arab Uprisings – Starting Points and Divergent Trajectories', *Democratization* 22: 2, 205–17.

Hinnebusch, Raymond (2017), 'Political Parties in MENA: Their Functions and Development', *British Journal of Middle Eastern Studies* 44: 2, 159–75.

Jamal, Manal A. (2013), 'Beyond Fatah Corruption and Mass Discontent: Hamas, the Palestinian Left and the 2006 Legislative Elections', *British Journal of Middle Eastern Studies* 40: 3, 273–94.

Kitchelt, Herbert (1995), 'Formation of Party Cleavages in Post-Communist Democracies: Theoretical Propositions', *Party Politics* 1: 4, 447–72.

LaPalombara, Joseph, and Myron Weiner (1966), *Political Parties and Political Development*, Princeton, NJ: Princeton University Press.

Lawson, Kay, and Saad Eddin Ibrahim (2010), *Political Parties and Democracy: The Arab World*, New York: Praeger.

LeDuc, Lawrence, Richard Niemi and Pippa Norris (2014) *Comparing Democracies 4: Elections and Voting in a Changing World*, London: Sage.

Levitsky, Steven, and Lucan Way (2002), 'The Rise of Competitive Authoritarianism', *Journal of Democracy* 13: 2, 51–66.

Luciani, Giacomo, and Hazem Beblawi (1987), *The Rentier State*, London: Croom Helm.

Lust, Ellen (2014), 'Elections', in Marc Lynch (ed.), *The Arab Uprisings Explained: New Contentious Politics in the Middle East*, New York: Columbia University Press, pp;. 218–45.

Lust, Ellen (2016), *The Middle East*, London: Sage.

Lust-Okar, Ellen (2005), *Structuring Conflict in the Arab World: Incumbents, Opponents, and Institutions*, Cambridge: Cambridge University Press.

Lust-Okar, Ellen (2009), 'Legislative Elections in Authoritarian Regimes: Competitive Clientelism and Regime Stability', *Journal of Democracy* 20: 3, 122–35.

Mair, Peter (2006), *Ruling the Void*, London: Verso.

Martínez, José Ciro (2017), 'Jordan's Self-Fulfilling Prophecy: The Production of Feeble Political Parties and the Perceived Perils of Democracy', *British Journal of Middle Eastern Studies* 44: 3, 356–72.

Masoud, Tarek (2014), *Counting Islam: Religion, Class and Elections in Egypt*, Cambridge: Cambridge University Press.

Ottaway, Marina, and Amr Hamzawy (2009), *Getting to Pluralism: Political Actors in the Arab World*, Washington DC: Carnegie Endowment for International Peace.

Pace, Michelle, and Francesco Cavatorta (2012), 'The Arab Uprisings in Theoretical Perspective: An Introduction', *Mediterranean Politics* 17: 2, 125–38.

Pedersen, Mogens (1989), 'En kortfattet oversight over det danske partisystems udvikling', *Politica* 21: 3, 265–78.

Penner Angrist, Michele (2006), *Party Building in the Modern Middle East*, Seattle: University of Washington Press.

Perthes, Volker (ed.) (2004), *Arab Elites: Negotiating the Politics of Change*, Boulder, CO: Lynne Rienner.

Pettitt, Robin (2014), *Contemporary Party Politics*, London: Palgrave Macmillan.

Pratt, Nicola (2007), *Democracy and Authoritarianism in the Arab World*, Boulder, CO: Lynne Rienner.

Przeworski, Adam, Susan Stokes and Bernard Manin (1999), *Democracy, Accountability, and Representation*, Cambridge: Cambridge University Press.

Randjbar-Daemi, Siavush, Eskandar Sadeghi-Boroujerdi and Lauren Banko (2017), 'Introduction to Political Parties in the Middle East: Historical Trajectories and Future Prospects', *British Journal of Middle Eastern Studies* 44: 2, 155–8.

Reilly, Benjamin, and Per Nordlund (2008), *Political Parties in Conflict-Prone Societies*, New York: United Nations University Press.

Ross, Michael (2001), 'Does Oil Hinder Democracy?', *World Politics* 53: 3, 325–61.

Sadiki, Larbi (2009), *Rethinking Arab Democratization: Elections without Democracy*, Cambridge: Cambridge University Press.

Sadiki, Larbi (2014), *Routledge Handbook of the Arab Spring*, London: Routledge.

Sartori, Giovanni (1976), *Parties and Party Systems: A Framework for Analysis*, Cambridge: Cambridge University Press.

Schattschneider, Elmer Eric (1942), *Party Government*, New York: Holt, Rinehart and Winston.

Schedler, Andreas (2002), 'The Menu of Manipulation', *Journal of Democracy* 13: 2, 36–50.

Schedler, Andreas (2007), *Electoral Authoritarianism: The Dynamics of Unfree Competition*, Boulder, CO: Lynne Rienner.

Schwedler, Jillian, and Janine Clark (2006), 'Islamist–Leftist Cooperation in the Arab World', *ISIM Review* 18, 10–11.

Stepan, Alfred, and Graeme Robertson (2003), 'An "Arab" More than a "Muslim" Democracy Gap', *Journal of Democracy* 14: 3, 30–44.

Storm, Lise (2013), *Party Politics and the Prospects for Democracy in North Africa*, Boulder, CO: Lynne Rienner.

Storm, Lise (2017), 'Parties and Party System Change', in Inmaculada Szmolka (ed.), *Political Change in the Middle East and North Africa: After the Arab Spring*, Edinburgh: Edinburgh University Press.

Svåsand, Lars (2014), *International Party Assistance – What Do We Know about the Effects?*, Stockholm: EBA.

Tachau, Frank (ed.) (1994), *Political Parties of the Middle East and North Africa*, Westport, CT: Greenwood Press.

Valbjørn, Morten (2012), 'Upgrading Post-Democratization Studies: Examining a Re-politicized Arab World in a Transition to Somewhere', *Middle East Critique* 21: 1, 25–35.

Valbjørn, Morten, and André Bank (2010), 'Examining the "Post" in Post-Democratization: The Future of Middle Eastern Political Rule through Lenses of the Past', *Middle East Critique* 19: 3, 183–200.

van Biezen, Ingrid (2003), *Political Parties in New Democracies*, Basingstoke: Palgrave Macmillan.

van Biezen, Ingrid (2005), 'On the Theory and Practice of Party Formation and Adaptation in New Democracies', *European Journal of Political Research* 44: 1, 147–74.

van Biezen, Ingrid (2014), 'The End of Party Democracy as We Know It? A Tribute to Peter Mair', *Irish Political Studies* 29: 2, 177–93.

van Biezen, Ingrid, and Thomas Poguntke (2014), 'The Decline of Membership-Based Politics', *Party Politics* 20: 2, 205–16.

Webb, Paul, and Stephen White (2007), *Party Politics in New Democracies*, Oxford: Oxford University Press.

Yom, Sean (2015), 'The New Landscape of Jordanian Politics: Social Opposition, Fiscal Crisis, and the Arab Spring', *British Journal of Middle Eastern Studies* 42: 3, 284–300.

Part 1

Party families

Chapter 2

Leftist parties in the Arab region before and after the Arab Uprisings: 'unrequited love'?

Valeria Resta

The relative weakness of the left in the Middle East, a region where popular demands would seem to be in line with left-wing political engagement, is a disorienting, yet disregarded, issue. Dominant opposition forces in the 1970s, leftist parties have consistently lost appeal across the Arab world while political Islam has imposed itself as a major political force. More intriguingly, the Arab Uprisings seemingly unveiled the existence of a rather progressive society in line with the values and policies of the left. Yet, in post-uprising democratic elections in Tunisia, Egypt and Morocco, leftist parties have been largely marginalised to the advantage of their main competitors: Islamist parties. While the literature is largely concerned with investigating the reasons underpinning the political affirmation of Islamists, this chapter delves into the causes of the left's decline and poor electoral performances.

Drawing on Hinnebusch (1981), the causes of the rollback of leftist parties might be attributed either to the social environment or to the structures of the state, or both. After a look at the development of leftist parties in the region, the hypothesis that their decline has more to do with the structures and mechanisms of the undemocratic rule than with a change in the political demands of societies will be tested against two very different cases: Egypt and Lebanon. The two countries differ in the degree of homogeneity of society, with Egypt exemplifying the evolution of a considerable number of countries in the area and with Lebanon having a unique institutional set-up. Yet, in both cases, leftist parties were perceived as a major threat to regime stability and beginning in the 1970s they were repressed, co-opted and reduced to empty shells. While generally speaking sham pluralist reforms robbed all representative institutions of any meaning, regimes in power targeted very successfully the left's constituency. The Arab Uprisings, by shaking the structures of many Arab states, offered the opportunity to restore genuine patterns of partisan mobilisation that, it was believed, would benefit the left. Yet, the return of the left to a protagonist's role in Arab politics has not occurred.

Definition and historical development of the Arab left

When appraising leftist parties in the Arab World, it is necessary to examine the complexities of determining what Leftism implies in the region. In Tamimi's words, 'the use of this term, left, has become so subdivided to cover a wide range of views which describes the different streams gathered under the umbrella of the left' (Tamimi 2013: 35). Despite such variety, a blueprint of the Arab left nonetheless emerges. This is the result of the communist ideology imported in the early 1920s and influenced by both regional contingencies and processes of state-building in which Arab leftist parties operated. In light of these developments, the programmes and strategies of leftist parties have gone through three different periods.

During the first phase (from the 1920s to the late 1950s/early 1960s), the parties of the Arab left had nationalist tendencies. The Marxists' struggle for the emancipation of the working classes from capital found an echo in the national struggle for the emancipation from colonial rule (Bustani 2014). Leftist parties provided both ideological justification and material support to the fight for national independence, encountering the enthusiastic support of the population and becoming at once the first ideological and mass parties of the region (Salem 1994). This was for instance the case of the *Istiqlal* in Morocco, the *Neo-Destour* in Tunisia and the Free Officers Movement in Egypt, which subsumed leftist tenets in claims for national independence. Later, acknowledging that 'the correspondence between patriotic sentiments and the national boundaries of newly independent states was, at best, sporadic' (Gelvin 2004: 194) and witnessing the inception of the Palestinian–Israeli conflict, leftist politics served the cause of pan-Arabism. Examples of this are the Nasserist ideology, the Popular Front for the Liberation of Palestine (PFLP) in Palestine and Jordan and, more marginally, the *Ba'athist* parties active in the region in those years.

In a second stage, from the mid-1960s to the early 1980s, leftist parties became increasingly critical of the authoritarian traits postcolonial nationalist regimes displayed and of the introduction of free-market oriented economic policies (Rogan 2012; Murphy 1999). New leftist parties saw the light of day, although they were often the result of splits from the ranks of the ruling party. This was the case of the Democratic Social Movement in Tunisia (MDS), the Yemeni Socialist Party or the National Progressive Union Party (NPUP) in Egypt. Nationalist enthusiasm gave way to democratic concerns with considerable attention paid to social justice and redistribution because of the progressively invasive World Bank and IMF-led economic liberalisation (Perkins 2004; Gelvin 2004). At that time, the left dominated the oppositional landscape, despite the fact that political pluralism was severely restricted across the region. In most countries these new leftist parties, operating either overtly or underground, were well entrenched within trade unions, professional associations or students' unions and were able to mobilise people against the regime in strikes and local protests (Hendriks 1983). Precisely because these parties proved to be strong opposition actors, they suffered from harsh repression. Such was the fate of the newly born NPUP in Egypt, and of many Communist parties.

Third, and lastly, the years from the mid-1980s to the 2011 uprisings witnessed the decline of the left as a partisan entity. Co-opted through sham processes of political liberalisation and deprived of any channel of mobilisation to compete in manipulated elections for ineffective parliaments, legal leftist parties, more or less consciously, turned into lifeless engines of undemocratic rule while illegal leftist parties became almost totally irrelevant or disappeared (Lust-Okar 2005; Maghraoui 2002; Geddes 2006). Highly bureaucratised and unable to provide responses to social claims, leftist parties displayed two of the three symptoms that Tarrow (1998) attributes to the decline of collective action, namely withdrawal and fractionalisation.[1] The latter implies the creation of new organisations and is absolutely striking when looking at civil society since the early 2000s. The new millennium brought with it the creation of new – small – leftist parties and organisations, and, more importantly, a shift of balance within the Arab left between political parties and civic associations in favour of the latter as far as genuine opposition to the regime was concerned. In light of the inefficacy of partisan engagement, the new generation of leftist activists chose the path of engagement with the civil society. This trend led to the emergence of movements such as the April 6 Youth Movement and *Kifaya* in Egypt, the Palestinian Youth Association for Leadership and Rights Activation or the Tunisian League for Human Rights (LTDH). Despite their leftist leanings, these new activists do not describe themselves as leftist, finding it problematic to have partisan or ideological affiliations (Langohr 2004; Cavatorta 2012). New leftist parties also arose. However, these do not genuinely represent the working classes, thus acknowledging the rupture with their natural constituencies that occurred during the 1980s and 1990s, and focus instead on the wider themes of democratisation, social justice and human rights. The creation of the *Congrès pour la République* (CPR) in Tunisia, the emergence of the *Karama* in Egypt and the Democratic Left Party in Lebanon are instances of this evolution.

This new left, fragmented and shallow in its ideological connotations, worked for the creation of electoral coalitions within the broader leftist camp and issue-based coalitions with other opposition forces, such as the Socialist Alliance in Egypt and *Nidaa Tounes* in Tunisia. All these ventures played a role in 'restoring the leftist voice which had completely disappeared in the nineties' (Abdel Muti 2013: 18) and in weakening Arab regimes, eventually leading to their contestation or fall. Yet, the uprisings of 2010 and 2011 did not restore the old patterns of leftist mobilisation and partisanship (Yom 2015). This became evident in the elections that followed the revolts, when no leftist party could stand in the way of the impressive victories the Islamists obtained.

Explaining the decline of leftist parties in the Arab region

The historical evolution of leftist parties across the Arab world describes a parabolic trajectory that ends in their current substantial marginalisation. How did this happen since, from the 1940s until the early 1980s, the spirit of Leftism was there, and strongly influenced Arab nationalism (Achcar 2013; Rogan 2012)? According to Hinnebusch (2005: 335), political parties in the Middle East, as their counterparts in western consolidated democracies, can be considered as barometers of 'the nature and development of politics [...] in the region'. In particular, parties are deemed to: (1) 'reflect the inherited societal tradition', and with it the power of sub-national and trans-national identities; (2) 'reflect societal change', in terms of '*composition, ideologies,* and *organizational capacit[ies]*'; and to (3) reflect and affect 'the process of *state formation*' (Hinnebusch 2005: 335; original emphasis). Out of this theoretical framework, the very reasons for the decline of leftist parties in the Arab world are to be found within the society, intended as its inner characteristics and its perception of political changes, and within national polities. It might then be the case that either Leftism did not chime any longer with mass aspirations or that the evolution of Arab regimes has been detrimental to leftist parties. Or both.

Indeed, each of the explanations attributed to the decline of leftist parties falls within one of these two referent environments, namely the social and the institutional. As for the former, some have argued that the importance of transnational identities the left embodied, namely Communism, Socialism and Nasserism, lost their attractiveness because of the failure of the USSR and of the Nasserist socio-economic and political experiments (Hilal 2014; Graham 2004; Murphy and Ehteshami 1996). Others see in the organisational rigidity of leftist parties a problematic Soviet importation that undermined the capacity of the Arab left to accommodate social dynamism (Yacoub 2014). By contrast, others point to the reliance of leftist parties on the charisma of their leaders, thus reflecting the regional praxis of the personalisation of politics (Shteiwi 2014). Along similar lines, the decline of leftist parties has been attributed to their poor institutionalisation (Storm 2013; Hilal 2014). This goes hand in hand with the claim that leftist parties were too elitist and too concerned with intellectual work to develop any meaningful link with their societies (Guessoumi 2014). Although all these accounts enhance our comprehension of the phenomenon under investigation, a reappraisal is needed.

On the one hand, arguing that Leftism has lost appeal because of its past failures might be misleading. First, as Masoud (2014: 57) brilliantly puts it, 'such arguments assume that the Egyptian peasant or the Yemeni tribesman (or the American political science professor) decide whom to vote for by weighting the historical records of alternative worldviews'. After all, Latin American countries proved throughout the 2000s that leftist politics had not been buried under the ruins of the USSR. Second, these readings completely disregard the fact that many people in the Arab world self-place on the left side of the political spectrum (Tessler 2011; Masoud 2014) and that their personal orientations support leftist agendas, a point to which we return later. On the other hand, conceiving the decline of leftist parties as a result of their organisational deficiencies that translate into their detachment from the public might be myopic. Considering the mobilisation capacities these parties have enjoyed up to the late 1970s, such accounts confound the causes with the effects of other intervening variables. And this leads to the introduction of institutional explanations.

Most countries of the region are, indeed, non-democratic regimes, with the majority being cases of competitive authoritarianism (Levitsky and Way 2002; Schedler 2006; Lust-Okar 2006). That is, they display some traits of political liberalisation, namely inclusion and competition, aimed at the survival of the incumbent authoritarian ruler. According to an increasing numbers of authors, the unevenness in opportunity structures underpinning the resilience of these regimes has been particularly detrimental to legalised opposition parties, wherein leftist parties belong (Hilal 2014; Wickham 2002; Masoud 2014; this volume, ch. 15). It is so because while competitive authoritarian regimes allow those parties to contest elections, they deny them any meaningful access to the channels of mobilisation and secure overwhelming victories for the ruling parties at the polls through what one can label 'creative elections', that is, ad hoc electoral laws, frauds, violence or other illegal means (Schedler 2002, 2006; Posusney 2002; Lust-Okar 2005; Shehata 2010; Kraetzschmar and Cavatorta 2010). In light of these poor electoral performances, legalised opposition parties become dependent on the benevolence of the regime for their survival and therefore mitigate their oppositional stances. In such way, these parties, while contributing to the maintenance of these regimes (Lust-Okar 2005; Storm 2017), gradually detach themselves from their electorate, thus entrenching this vicious circle of regime dependence, political feebleness and electoral irrelevance.

In line with institutional accounts, this contribution argues that the aforementioned non-democratic dynamics have been particularly detrimental for the fate of both banned and legalised opposition parties of the left and this is also at the root of their inability to compete with their major contenders – Islamist parties – in the years proceeding and following the Arab Uprisings. Compared with the Islamist parties, legalised leftist parties suffer from a double handicap. First, the regime undermined and entirely occupied all their traditional and structured channels of politicisation and mobilisation – trade unions, professional syndicates and student unions – through co-optation and patronage practices (Posusney 1997; Allal 2009; Baroudi 1998). Such crucial aspect holds also for banned leftist parties that could not find space to pursue underground activities. Second, by playing by the rules of the games with their party labels, legalised leftist parties rightly began to be perceived as part of the authoritarian set-up. Simply put, the Arab left does not enjoy the same degree of party institutionalisation and the same level of attractiveness as their Islamist counterparts because of the unevenness in the opportunity structures undemocratic regimes created. Indeed, this has been the case of both competitive authoritarian Egypt and of the consociational confessional democracy of Lebanon to which the next section is dedicated.

Feeding, domesticating or killing the left: the political dynamics in Egypt and Lebanon before 2010

When talking about the Arab left, the risk of falling into problematic overgeneralisations or into excessive simplification is high. In light of this, the selection of Egypt and Lebanon as objects of an in-depth investigation relies on the criterion of the most dissimilar design strategy. According to this technique, selected cases differ on all relevant aspects other than the *explanandum* and the causal factor of theoretical interest. This ensures a broad representativeness of the sample under investigation, thus providing a sound basis for generalisation (Seawright and Gerring 2008). Egypt is in North Africa, while Lebanon is in the Levant. They differ in their process of state formation: the first is the result of a national revolution, whereas the second is a case of state-building by decree (Gelvin 2004). Moreover, while Egypt has a homogenous society – the presence of Copts not affecting this formulation – above which ruled a regime exemplifying the common traits of Arab authoritarianism (Schlumberger 2007; Heydemann 2007; Ghalioun 2004), Lebanon is a unique example of a consociational confessional democracy (Harris 2014; Ismael and Ismael 2011) set up in such a way as to appease the tensions stemming from a particularly heterogeneous society. Finally, Lebanon has been lacerated by a civil war that heavily shaped its party system and displays the effects of the intermestic venues (i.e. the influence of international factors in domestic politics) of Arab politics in a more accentuated way (Calculli 2015; Korany 2010).

The Egyptian left confronts the Pharaoh

As already mentioned, Egypt exemplifies the political evolution of a large number of regimes in the area – such as Tunisia, Algeria, Turkey or Iran – whose processes of state- and nation-building resulted from revolution or conquest. 'In each of these cases, the national myth recounting the deeds of a heroic leader or founding generation created a firmer foundation for nation-building than that enjoyed by the states created in the Levant and Mesopotamia' (Gelvin 2004: 184). These regimes, instantiated by the Egyptian case, have been described as authoritarian-populist in their early decades, post-populist since the mid-1970s, and upgraded authoritarian from the 1990s to the Arab Uprisings (Hinnebusch 2005; Heydemann 2007).

The only remarkable leftist parties in Egypt until the 2011 uprisings were the Communist Party, banned since 1953, and the National Progressive Union Party (NPUP), also known as *Tagammu*, founded in 1976 under Sadat's impulse to introduce a semblance of political liber- alisation and part of the left wing of the Nasserist coalition (Hinnebusch 1981). Because of the circumstances surrounding its creation, the NPUP was initially regarded with ambiguity. Soon after though, the party's involvement in the 1977 bread riots signalled a clear rupture with the regime and its position as a genuine opposition party was reinforced. Thus, its following went far beyond an already politicised constituency and the party obtained the support of the wider working class, sectors of the middle class, and progressive intellectuals and professionals. In particular, the NPUP seemed to have strongholds among the working class in the major districts of al Cairo and Alexandria. As Hendriks reports:

> Of approximately one hundred eighty registered party members in one Cairo *qism* (district), thirty-one per cent were workers, forty-one per cent were muwazzafin [clerks, rev], and the remaining twenty-eight per cent were students. The official figures underesti- mate actual workers' support. In this district, one worker, who was a member of the local leadership group (*lejnat el qism*), collected membership fees from thirty-one colleagues, many of whom did not want to register officially. Given the risk of being known as a Tajammu'awi for people who feel more vulnerable vis-a-vis [sic] the authorities than do educated muwazzaf, it is probable that this under-enumeration occurs elsewhere as well. (Hendriks 1983: 267)

In a relatively short period of time, the party succeeded in developing a complex organisational structure and in penetrating trade unions – despite government interference – the professional association of journalists, and the bar, making inroads in the countryside as well (Hendriks 1983). This made the NPUP '(with the possible exception of the *Ikhwan*) [. . .] the only political force in Egypt which possesses cadres and basic units on a serious scale' (Hinnebusch 1981: 338). However, this increasing appeal drew Sadat's attention. In his mind, the party had simply moved too far beyond the permissible. In September 1978 a wave of repressive measures were implemented against NPUP members and the party was virtually banned, while a tame leftist alternative to the NPUP, the Socialist Labour Party (SLP), was created. Finally, in 1980 the 'Law of Shame' stated that anyone trying to corrupt the youth by denying religious values or criticising state policy could be punished in Court. This law is indicative of Sadat's strategy to support Islamism to counterbalance Nasserist elements in general, and the NPUP in particular, for its secular ideology, portrayed as a 'denial of divine laws', and for its oppositional stance, depicted as 'disloyalty to the nation' (Law 95/1980).

Despite such circumstances, the party's activities continued underground until the advent of Mubarak who eased, at least at first glance, the pressure on the party. However, the NPUP continued facing significant obstacles concerning both the channels of mobilisation available to it and access to parliament because the new president succeeded in devising his survival through the electoral machine and his control over society. As Masoud explains, the electoral dynamics of the authoritarian regime under Mubarak were particularly detrimental to the NPUP. From 1984 to 1987, Egypt used a proportional system with a closed list. Even though priority was given to parties rather than candidates, the NPUP was badly defeated, gaining no seats in both elections due to its inability to compete with the ruling party in terms of political as well as economic resources. The situation worsened for the NPUP when, from 1990, Egypt returned to a majoritarian system that, for opposition parties, was 'something close to a death knell' (Masoud 2014: 68). The influence of political parties declined due to the influx of local notables and businessmen who had more economic resources to meet the demands of voters. In addition, as in the past, there was a resurgence of networks of patronage and kinship – networks also detrimental to the NPUP's hope of expanding beyond its cradle-districts (Masoud 2014). Finally, the regime continued to occupy the major channels of leftist political mobilisation (Posusney 1997). Serving as channels of mobilisation under Nasser, trade unions became, under Sadat and Mubarak, channels of demobilisation to control the working class. This strategy of demobilisation reached its apex in 1995 with the trade union law, which prevented workers employed on temporary contracts from voting in union elections, thereby easing the re-election of incumbent union leaders (Kienle 2001; Posusney 1997; Shehata 2010). What happened from the mid-1980s onward tells a tale of partisan demobilisation within the left and the subsequent activation of new forms of political engagement in civil society, which was totally disconnected from the party. Such partisan disengagement within the NPUP did not recover in time for the first free and fair parliamentary elections of 2011 and 2012. Thus, the party only gained four seats, far behind the Freedom and Justice Party (FJP) and other conservative parties.

Such an outcome might be attributed to the fact that even though it is true that all opposition parties were repressed before the fall of the Mubarak regime, the effects of the competitive authoritarian Egyptian regime have not been the same on all opposition parties. The right represented by the New Wafd party, for instance, had the support of a wealthy and liberal-conservative constituency that did not threaten the regime. Therefore, it enjoyed a certain amount of economic resources and autonomy that made it less vulnerable than the NPUP to the regime's infiltration of trade unions and other important channels of mass mobilisation. With regard to the Muslim Brotherhood (MB or *Ikhwan*), Bianchi (1989) speaks of a 'policy of selective accommodation'. While the radical groups were repressed, non-violent Islamic groups and associations were tolerated. It is so because, as Wickham (2002) puts it, Mubarak wanted to avoid any public accusation of interference with religion, but also because he thought they were innocuous. Hence, the MB arrived at the 2011 elections with a double advantage over the left. First, it could count on a vast network of mobilised supporters developed since the 1970s. Second, given the formal ban it suffered from – even though Islamist candidates had run as independents since the 1980s – it could present its party brand to voters as completely detached from the previous regime.

The Lebanese left between the social boundaries of consociational democracy and foreign interferences

The political system of Lebanon is the emanation of the National Pact that 'institutionalized consociational democracy as a constitutional reality' (Hanf 2015: 73) by precisely assigning the spoils available to each community in order to foster a peaceful coexistence among different confessions within the independent and sovereign state. Following a so-called procedural definition of democracy, such a system can hardly be considered fully democratic for the obstacles that it poses to the mechanisms of representation and selection of the political elite (Dahl 1971). Therefore, it has been defined as a 'unique case'. On the one hand, contrary to the Arab authoritarian regimes, Lebanon lacked a dictator mobilising masses around a developmental project of national unity, and the presence of several political parties prevented the country from turning into a one-party or hegemonic party system. On the other hand, contrary to representative democracy, the preservation of its parliamentary regime and 'democratic' system relies on the weakness and ineffectiveness of political parties that depart from confessional representation (Suleiman 1967). Hence, genuine ideological and cross-sectarian political parties are deemed to represent a threat to the Lebanese political system. In this respect, leftist parties are regarded as particularly threatening, for 'the Lebanese left is defined as parties opposing the sectarian quota' (Yacoub 2014: 84). It follows that much has been done to weaken their presence and influence.

In line with the regional trend, the origins of the Lebanese left go back to the mandate period in the 1920s with the emergence of the Communist Party (LCP).[2] Then, the Syrian Social Nationalist Party (SSNP) and the Progressive Socialist Party (PSP) emerged in 1932 and in 1949 respectively. These parties can be considered only marginally leftist, as Haugbølle argues (2013).[3] All the aforementioned parties enjoyed their highest point during the period between 1970 and 1975, which is remembered as the 'period of political assertion of leftist parties' (al-Khazen 2003: 609). Those years witnessed the politicisation of trade unions along with an increase in leftist membership among university students and professionals. It is reported that in 1973, 70 per cent of university students supported leftist parties. Of them, 7.8 per cent, 18.6 per cent and 12.9 per cent stood for the PSP, the SSNP and the LCP respectively (Hanf 1973: 18). Moreover, new political and social forces arose, such as the Organization of Communist Action (OCAL) or the Islamic *Harakat al-Mahrumin*, to limit the outflow of Shi'i individuals towards secularist parties. The rise of this new form of political activism wherein 'ideology [i]s an unsettling force in Lebanese politics' is deemed to be 'first and foremost' the result of the Palestinian presence in the country following the events of Black September 1970 (Haugbølle 2010: 39). Regardless of sect, all leftist parties could not avoid supporting the Palestinian cause for it presented a revolutionary initiative against the western oppressor they themselves were committed to (Hazran 2010). This consideration had not escaped Jumblatt.[4] He quickly established an alliance with the PLO and, because of this, was able to gather for the first time in Lebanese history all the leftist parties in the Front for Nationalist and Progressive Parties and Forces. This enjoyed an impressive following and became in 1972 the National Movement.

Beside the importance of the Palestinian question, the resurgence of ideology found fertile ground due to regional and internal developments. Regionally, the 1967 defeat and the death of Nasser in 1970 'liberated' the different leftist forces that were all grouped under Nasserism. At the same time, inspired by worldwide protests (al-Khazen 2003), non-Nasserist leftists found the opportunity to propose their political agenda. Internally, Lebanese society underwent a massive transformation during the 1960s as a result of Chehab's presidency. On the one hand, thanks to favourable international conditions, his economic policies created a new intellectual middle class (one that would eventually suffer the most from the unfulfilled expectations that the spread of unemployment and inflation in the early 1970s provoked). On the other hand, he fostered a political landscape that favoured the reception of the discourse of leftist parties. Under his mandate, a new political course, emancipated from confessional affiliation, saw the light of day and this allowed the proliferation of modern and ideological parties that were mostly of the left (Hanf 2015). Yet, 'Chehab's revolution of the state was half cooked' (Haugbølle 2010: 42) and paved the way for a clash between pre-modern, that is, Gemayel's Lebanese Forces, versus modern politics, namely Jumblatt's National Movement (Hanf 2015: 131–40).

The civil war weakened and fragmented the Lebanese left. Since the disintegration of the National Movement, the left has undergone a series of splits regarding the appraisal and the meaning of the civil war (Haugbølle 2013). Moreover, all parties involved in the conflict were regarded with distrust in Lebanese society once the conflict ended (Hanf 2015) and there was little these parties could do to change this perception. The process of militarisation that leftist movements underwent during the war irreparably altered their structures, depriving them of the openness and flexibility required to 'approach' the population (Yacoub 2014). In addition to the deficiencies in parties' structures the civil war produced, leftist parties suffered also from the political compromise the peace-making process brought about. In the aftermath of the war, the *Pax Syriana* (1990–2005) silenced all political forces not aligned with Damascus's policies and foreign relations. Despite their participation in the national dialogue, the LCP and the OCAL were excluded from parliamentary representation, governmental responsibility and defensive tasks – the latter being entrusted entirely to *Hezbollah*. The PSP, by contrast, was granted parliamentary representation but, adapting to the new situation, gradually lost its leftist traits. Faced with the aphasia of the partisan left, leftist activism revolved around civil society associations and students' movements. A new party did arise to gather members of the old partisan left and young activists from associational life – Democratic Left (2004) – and it eventually entered in the Parliament. However, this success did not lead to any reversal of fortunes for the left because 'fundamental disagreements over the 2006 war between Hezbollah and Israel and the Syrian conflict since 2011 [...] compounded internal splits and further marginalization of the established leftist parties' (Haugbølle 2013: 431). In addition, like pre-war Lebanon, post-2005 Lebanon relies on what Haugbølle refers to as 'social boundaries', that is, 'institutions that organize (un)equal access to resources' (Haugbølle 2013: 427). This entails an

> ever-expanding but holistic complex ensemble, one that operates at the structural, institutional, and individual levels, and aims at entrenching and reproducing sectarianism modes of subjectifica-tion and mobilisation, while sabotaging challenges to the material underpinnings and ideological hegemony of the sectarian system. (Salloukh et al. 2015: 174)

Personal status legislation, limits on civic activism, media demonisation and the electoral system – based on gerrymandering and malappor-tionment (Salamey 2014; Harris 2014) – are all pivots of the sectarian structure that makes ideological, and especially left-leaning, parties in Lebanon 'parties in search of partisans' (al-Khazen 2003) even in the aftermath of the Arab Uprisings.

Political dynamics after the Arab Uprisings and the implications for the left

While it is not the scope of this chapter to investigate whether the Arab Uprisings were actually revolutions against neo-liberal authoritarian regimes led by leftist-inspired forces, as some authors contend (Zemni et al. 2013), it is nonetheless true that across the region they spoke a leftist jargon, demanding bread, jobs and dignity (Achcar 2013; Chomiak and Entelis 2011). In addition, generally speaking, it seems that through the years the Arab left has been superficially successful in promoting its vision of a political system and society. By combining the survey data from all the waves of Arab Barometer polls, it is possible to capture personal orientations regarding some of the values that correspond to the tenets of the Arab left, namely the need for pluralism, secularism, women's rights and economic redistribution (Figure 2.1).[5]

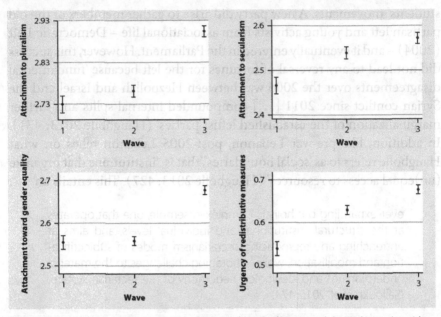

Note: Scores above 2.5 (red line) denote substantial agreement with the reported items; scores below 2.5 denote substantial disagreement; scores in decimal values from 0 to 1 denote percentage of respondents indicating economic issues (i.e. fighting poverty and unemployment) as the major challenges of their country.

Figure 2.1 Individuals' attachment to leftist values (2006–14). (Source: Arab Barometer, waves I, II and III, <http://www.arabbarometer.org/content/ab-waves>, last accessed November 2016)

On average, with the passing of time an increasing number of people believe that a parliamentary system, wherein all parties can compete in elections, would be appropriate for their country. Even though this is not a uniquely leftist claim, leftist parties have nonetheless championed the introduction of a genuine parliamentary system and political pluralism for a long time. During the same period, more and more people, worried about the economic situation of their country, consider poverty and unemployment as being the major challenges to deal with – hence, in the absence of a survey question in the polls specifically aimed at grasping individual support for economic redistribution, it would not be misleading to think of those respondents as supporters for redistributive measures. They also increasingly believe that religion should be disentangled from social and political life, and that women should have the same opportunities and rights as men. However, the rise of progressive values historically prompted by the left corresponds to the resurgence of Islamist parties in terms of both mass support and, when allowed, parliamentary representation within competitive authoritarian regimes. Moreover, the countries that experienced their first free and democratic elections as a consequence of the Arab Uprisings – Tunisia and Egypt – have recorded Islamist electoral victories.

The combination of the resurgence of political Islam, often expressed in gains at elections, with the concomitant emergence of a secular, progressive Arab society, suggests that there is a gap between individuals' political orientations and voters' choices in the region. This gap is possibly the result of uneven structures for political opportunities created by non-democratic regimes, which have been particularly unfavourable to the left. Lust-Okar (2005) has shown how competitive authoritarian regimes shape different structures of competition, thus indicating that opposition parties and movements are not treated equally under such rules. The cases of Lebanon and Egypt, despite their differences, have demonstrated how leftist parties have suffered the most significant losses. In both cases these parties were marginalised or co-opted and excluded from their mobilisation channels. In fact, the consequences of such treatment are evident even once the Arab Uprisings brought about the breakdown of authoritarian regimes and the transition to democracy in Tunisia.

At the time of their first free and democratic elections, Tunisia and Egypt displayed, in a more or less pronounced manner, two different, yet intertwined, aspects of the aforementioned electoral gap that can be attributable to undemocratic patterns of unbalanced control of the political opposition. These are (1) the inconsistency of the electoral offer; and (2) individuals' misperception of such offer. The first can be understood as a lack of coherence between the political aspirations of society and the party system at election time. Since 2011, Tunisia is an example of this, inasmuch as the left side of the political spectrum is fragmented into a multitude of small political parties despite the attempts to unify it. This situation is clearly the result of the Ben Ali regime's co-optation of the older parties of the left (such as the MDS) that produced two effects. On the one hand, it has triggered the creation of a multitude of political parties reacting to the political aphasia of the established parties, resulting in a schizophrenic representation of the left. On the other hand, it has generated mistrust towards established political parties that, while harming the left, renders religious institutions more effective than political parties when it comes to their ability to meet individuals' needs.

This latter aspect introduces the second element of the aforementioned electoral gap, namely the inability of individuals to appraise correctly different political alternatives and choose the one that is closest to their own needs and values, which is the result of the ousting of the left from its natural channels of mobilisation in tandem with the regime's accommodation of Islamist charitable associations. As Masoud explains about the 2011 Egyptian elections:

> though the majority of poor Egyptian voters prefer significant re-distribution and a large welfare state, they are unable to connect these preferences with parties that most espouse them [i.e. the left parties], voting instead for Islamist politicians who, by virtue of their embeddedness in dense networks of religious organizations, are able to speak to voters in ways that leftists are not. (Masoud 2014: 181)

In light of the pervasiveness of competitive authoritarianism in the region, these findings are hardly unique to the cases of Tunisia and Egypt and are indicative of the complexities of recovering from undemocratic legacies even when authoritarian regimes collapse. By looking at the World Values Survey longitudinal data, a regional trend of progressive lack of confidence in national parliaments (Figure 2.2) and political parties (Figure 2.3) emerges through the period 1999–2014. As expected, Figure 2.4 illustrates that there is a significant correlation between the two phenomena. From a statistical point of view, correlation is not causation. Yet, the discussion above suggests that the modest appeal of political parties in the region is the result of the building of undemocratic rule, which started with the weakening of national parliaments and entailed, *inter alia*, the marginalisation of bottom-up initiatives of political representation. Deprived of any meaningful channel of politicisation and political representation, individuals turned to religious institutions, which proliferated during the same period in which leftist parties began to be repressed. Such organisations answered the everyday problems of citizens and satisfied their needs for social and political belonging. In short, religious institutions became a perfect substitute for political parties insofar as there is a correlation between perceiving the latter as useless and perceiving the former as capable and trustworthy. Such effect is even more evident when considering medium- to high-income respondents who, according to some empirical contributions (Masoud 2014; Campante and Chor 2012; Pellicer and Wegner 2014; Resta 2016), are more likely to engage in social and political activism and to cast their genuine ballots in elections (Figure 2.5).

It was hoped the Arab Uprisings would pave the way for a more balanced and competitive political landscape, giving leftist parties the possibility to reorganise and retrieve their lost ascendancy among Arab citizens. Yet, confronted with the continuous grip of authoritarianism and regional instability, there is little reason to believe this could happen in the near future. However, there is also little reason to be totally pessimistic. From the perspective of party politics, it is just too early to draw any conclusions

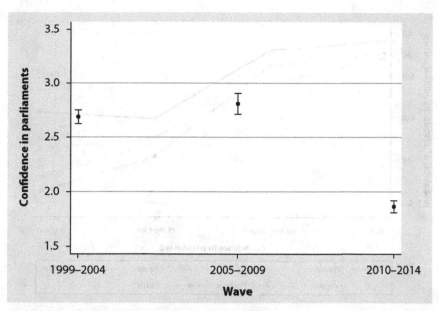

Note: Scores below 3 indicate substantial mistrust towards national parliaments.

Figure 2.2 Confidence in national parliaments (1999–2014). (Source: World Values Survey longitudinal data, 1999–2014, <http://www.worldvaluessurvey.org/WVSContents.jsp>, last accessed November 2016)

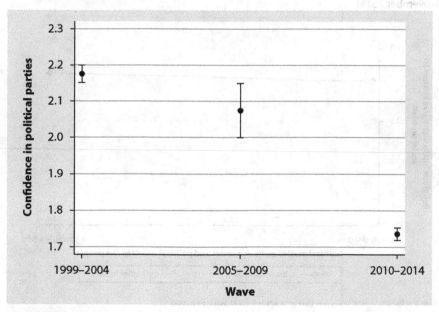

Note: Scores below 3 indicate substantial mistrust toward political parties.

Figure 2.3 Confidence in political parties (1999–2014). (Source: World Values Survey longitudinal data, 1999–2014, <http://www.worldvaluessurvey.org/WVSContents.jsp>, last accessed November 2016)

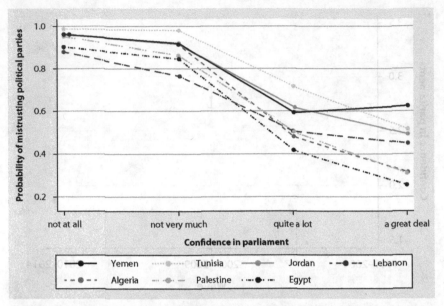

Note: Results from logistic regression wherein the variable 'confidence in parliament' has been interacted with the country variable to grasp the variance for each level of confidence in parliament and within each country.

Figure 2.4 Marginal effects of considering political parties as irrelevant depending on confidence in national parliaments. (Source: World Values Survey longitudinal data, 1999–2014, <http://www.worldvaluessurvey.org/WVSContents.jsp>, last accessed November 2016)

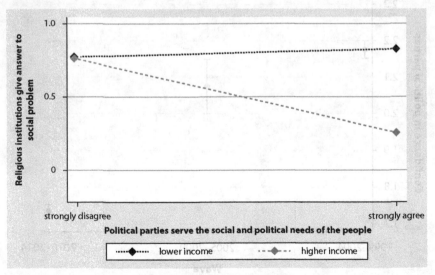

Note: Results from logistic regression. Data accounts only for Algeria (1999–2004).

Figure 2.5 Predicted probabilities of seeing in religious institutions a substitute for parties depending on their perceived irrelevance. (Source: World Values Survey longitudinal data, 1999–2014, <http://www.worldvaluessurvey.org/WVSContents.jsp>, last accessed November 2016)

regarding how the uprisings affected the leftist parties of the region. Given the poor premises, establishing, or re-establishing in this case, roots in society and undertaking the way to party institutionalisation will take far more than the span of time we have observed thus far (Mainwaring and Scully 1995; Randall and Svåsand 2002). In the long run, the Arab left may profit from two factors to re-emerge and institutionalise. First, the Arab Uprisings, while shaking pre-existent structures of political participation, have demonstrated the existence of a young and progressive generation in search of a political voice (Cavatorta 2012; Achcar 2013). Second, the case of Tunisia, which represents the best outcome of the revolts, may provide the left with the best practices necessary to adapt and survive with renewed strength under new political circumstances.

Conclusion

The decline of leftist parties across the Arab world seems to be more the effect of the functioning of competitive authoritarian regimes and their legacy than of the left's inner deficiencies. There is no doubt that the left, as in other countries of the world, is extremely fragmented and trapped in self-referential debates resulting from both its intellectual elite and years of political isolation, co-optation or war (Hammad 2002; Yacoub 2014). It is also true that the Islamist appeal is particularly strong because it calls for the restoration of morality and because of its relative novelty (Wickham 2002). Yet, these are in large part two sides of the same coin resulting from marginalisation and co-optation of political parties at the institutional level and selective accommodation of the alternative mobilising forces at the social one. These two mechanisms guaranteed the survival of non-democratic regimes in the area but damaged leftist parties more than other opposition forces. The fact that Arab society displays leftist leanings and that leftist parties proved powerful when fewer obstacles hindered their mobilisation potential, as the cases of Egypt and Lebanon demonstrated, are counterfactual evidence that the decline of the Arab left does not derive from a change in the demand of political representation. Rather, it reflects the process of formation and consolidation of non-democratic Arab polities. However, even with the advent of the uprisings, the Arab left is still 'stuck' in the long-lasting effects of the yoke of undemocratic regimes. A new momentum, or at least renewed relevance, for parties of the left might come from further destabilisation of the regimes in power when a more progressive society enjoying new forms of mobilisation can operate. In addition, the failure of Islamists in power may help the left recover credibility. In any case, it will be a long process.

Appendix

Table 2.1 Construction of indices, coding and inter-items correlation for Figure 2.1. (Source: World Values Survey longitudinal data, 1999–2014, <http://www.world valuessurvey.org/WVSContents.jsp>, last accessed November 2016)

Index	Questions (AB)	Coding	Inter-items correlation
Pluralism	Would a parliamentary system in which nationalist, left-wing, right-wing, and Islamist parties compete in parliamentary elections be appropriate for your country?	1 = very bad 2 = bad 3 = good 4 = very good	
Secularism	The government and parliament should enact laws in accordance with the Islamic law	1 = strongly disagree 2 = disagree 3 = agree 4 = strongly agree	0.703 (Cronbach's α)
	Your country is better off if religious people hold public positions in the state	1 = strongly agree 2 = agree 3 = disagree 4 = strongly disagree	
	Religious leaders (imams, preachers, priests) should have influence over government decisions	1 = strongly agree 2 = agree 3 = disagree 4 = strongly disagree	
	Religious practices are private and should be separated from social and political life	1 = strongly disagree; 2 = disagree; 3 = agree; 4 = strongly agree	
Gender equality	A married woman can work outside the home	1 = strongly agree 2 = agree 3 = disagree 4 = strongly disagree	0.76827* (Eigenvalue)
	In general, men are better at political leadership than women	1 = strongly disagree 2 = disagree 3 = agree 4 = strongly agree	
	University education for males is more important than university education for females	1 = strongly disagree 2 = disagree 3 = agree 4 = strongly agree	
Support for redistributive measures	What is the most important challenge your country is facing today?	1 = the economic situation (poverty, unemployment and price increases) 0 = others	

*This low value derives from the fact that two dimensions regarding attitudes toward gender equality have been put together (see Kostenko et al. 2016; Resta 2016).

Table 2.2 Arab barometer sample description (supporting Figure 2.1). (Source: World Values Survey longitudinal data, 1999–2014, <http://www.worldvaluessurvey.org/WVSContents.jsp>, last accessed November 2016)

Country	Wave			Total
	2006–2009	*2010–2011*	*2012–2014*	
Algeria	1,300	1,216	1,220	3,736
Egypt	0	1,219	1,196	2,415
Iraq	0	1,234	1,215	2,449
Jordan	1,143	1,188	1,795	4,126
Lebanon	1,195	1,387	1,200	3,782
Morocco	1,277	0	1,116	2,393
Palestine	1,270	1,200	1,200	3,670
Sudan	0	1,538	1,200	2,738
Tunisia	0	1,196	1,199	2,395
Yemen	717	1,200	1,200	3,117
Total	**6,902**	**11,378**	**12,541**	**30,821**

Table 2.3 World Value Survey sample description (supporting Figures 2.2–2.5). (Source: World Values Survey longitudinal data, 1999–2014, <http://www.worldvaluessurvey.org/WVSContents.jsp>, last accessed November 2016)

Country	Wave			Total
	1999–2004	*2005–2009*	*2010–2014*	
Algeria	1,282	0	1,200	2,482
Palestine	0	0	1,000	1,000
Jordan	1,223	1,200	1,200	3,623
Lebanon	0	0	1,200	1,200
Tunisia	0	0	1,205	1,205
Egypt	3,000	3,051	1,523	7,574
Yemen	0	0	1,000	1,000
Total	**5,505**	**4,251**	**8,328**	**18,084**

Table 2.4 Construction of variables (supporting Figures 2.2–2.5). (Source: World Values Survey longitudinal data, 1999–2014, <http://www.worldvaluessurvey.org/WVSContents.jsp>, last accessed November 2016)

Variable	Questions (WVS)	Coding
Trust in parliament	Confidence: in parliament	1 = not at all 2 = very much 3 = quite a lot 4 = a great deal
Trust in political parties	Confidence: in political parties	1 = not at all 2 = very much 3 = quite a lot 4 = a great deal
Effectiveness of political parties	Political parties serve the social and political needs of people	0 = no 1 = yes
Religion as political substitute	Churches give answers to social problems	0 = no 1 = yes

Notes

1. Another one is the institutionalisation of the collective action (Tarrow 1998: 147–50).
2. Indeed, the Lebanese Communist Party was formalised in 1943 out of the decision to create two national parties from the Communist Party of Syria and Lebanon.
3. The first belongs to the Lebanese left only inasmuch as it questions the sectarian status quo but turns out to be 'in no recognizable manner socialistic [for] it rejects state capitalism, social security schemes, and labour unions' (Suleiman 1967: 143). The PSP, by contrast, belongs to the left for its programme but not for its functioning. On the one hand, it pursues a leftist agenda and calls for the abolition of the sectarian system. On the other, it works like any other notable party, its leader Kamal Jumblatt being not only the president but also the *za'aim* of a party entrenched in the Druze community (al-Khazen 1998). Probably owing to this combination, the party has been incredibly incisive in Lebanese political life. It was the only party that succeeded in entering both parliament and government and it was the party of the man who worked for the resurgence and the unification of the leftist opposition in Lebanon (Hazran 2010).
4. Kamal Jumblatt was a prominent political figure in Lebanon. Elected to parliament in 1943, he became minister of the economy (1946/7). Yet, soon after, he founded the Progressive Socialist Party and led the anti-government forces in the Lebanese civil war.
5. Arab Barometer is a project aimed at detecting personal orientations in the Arab world through face-to-face surveys in a wide range of Arab countries. For item identification, please refer to the appendix at the end of this chapter.

Bibliography

Abdel Muti, Ayman (2013), 'The Egyptian Revolution and the Role of the Left: Success and Failure Factors', in Ellen Jarrar (ed.), *The Left and the Arab Revolutions*, Cairo: Rosa Luxemburg Foundation, pp. 13–33.

Achcar, Gilbert (2013), *The People Want: A Radical Exploration of the Arab Uprising*, Oakland, CA: University of California Press.

Allal, Amin (2009), 'Ici, si ça ne bouge pas ça n'avance pas! Les mobilisations protestataires de l'année 2008 dans la région minière de Gafsa. Réformes néo libérales, clientèlismes et contestation', in Myriam Catusse, Blandine Destremau and Éric Verdier (eds), *L'État face aux débordements du social au Maghreb: Formation, travail et protection sociale*, Paris: Karthala, pp. 173–86.

Baroudi, Sami E. (1998), 'Economic Conflict in Postwar Lebanon: State–Labor Relations between 1992 and 1997', *Middle East Journal* 52: 4, 531–50.

Bianchi, Robert (1989), *Unruly Corporativism: Associational Life in Twentieth-Century Egypt*, New York: Oxford University Press.

Bustani, Hisham (2014), 'Dissonances of the Arab Left', *Radical Philosophy* 184 (March/April), 35–42.

Calculli, Marina (2015), 'Sub-regions and Security in the Middle East: "Hierarchical interdependence" in Gulf–Levant Relations', in Elizabeth Iskander Monier (ed.), *Regional Insecurity after the Arab Uprisings: Narratives of Security and Threat*, Basingstoke: Palgrave Macmillan, pp. 58–81.

Campante, Filipe R., and Davin Chor (2012), 'Why Was the Arab World Poised for Revolution? Schooling, Economic Opportunities, and the Arab Spring', *Journal of Economic Perspectives* 26: 2, 167–87.

Cavatorta, Francesco (2012), 'Arab Spring: The Awakening of Civil Society. A General Overview', in European Institute of the Mediterranean (IEMed) (ed.), *IEMed Mediterranean Yearbook*, Barcelona: IEMed, pp. 75–85.

Chomiak, Laryssa, and John P. Entelis (2011), 'The Making of North Africa's Intifadas', *Middle East Report* 259, 8–15.

Dahl, Robert (1971), *Polyarchy: Participation and Opposition*, New Haven, CT and London: Yale University Press.

Geddes, Barbara (2006), 'Why Parties and Elections in Authoritarian Regimes?', revised version of a paper prepared for presentation at the annual meeting of the American Political Science Association, Washington DC, 2005, <https://www.scribd.com/document/133702645/Barbara-Geddes-Why-Parties-and-Elections-in-Authoritarian-Regimes-2006> (last accessed 1 September 2017).

Gelvin, James (2004), *The Modern Middle East: A History*, New York: Oxford University Press.

Ghalioun, Burhan (2004), 'The Persistence of Arab Authoritarianism', *Journal of Democracy* 15: 4, 126–32.

Graham, Fuller (2004), *The Future of Political Islam*, London: Palgrave.

Guessoumi, Mouldi (2014), 'The Map of the Tunisian Left', in Khalil Kalfat (ed.), *Mapping of the Arab Left*, Cairo: Rosa Luxemburg Stiftung North African Office, pp. 16–43.

Hammad, Hanan (2002), 'Arwa Salih's *The Premature*: Gendering the History of the Egyptian Left', *Arab Studies Journal* 24: 1, 118–42.

Hanf, Theodor (1973), 'Le Comportement politique des étudiants libanais, *Travaux et Jours* 46: 5–52.

Hanf, Theodor (2015), *Coexistence in Wartime Lebanon: Decline of a State and Rise of a Nation*, 2nd edn, London: I. B. Tauris.

Harris, William (2014), 'Republic of Lebanon', in Mark Gasiorowski (ed.), *The Government and Politics of the Middle East and North Africa*, 7th edn, Boulder, CO: Westview Press, pp. 79–110.

Haugbølle, Sune (2010), *War and Memory in Lebanon*, New York: Cambridge University Press.

Haugbølle, Sune (2013), 'Social Boundaries and Secularism in the Lebanese Left', *Mediterranean Politics* 18: 3, 427–43.

Hazran, Yusri (2010), 'The Lebanese Crisis: The Limits of Consociational Democracy', *Muslim World* 100: 1, 157–76.

Hendriks, Bertus (1983), 'The Legal Left in Egypt', *Arab Studies Quarterly* 5: 3, 260–75.

Heydemann, Steven (2007), 'Upgrading Authoritarianism in the Arab World', Analysis Paper 13, Washington DC: The Saban Center for Middle East Policy at the Brookings Institution.

Hilal, Jamil (2014), 'Introduction: On the Self-Definition of the Left in the Arab State', in Jamil Hilal and Katja Herman (eds), *Mapping of the Arab Left: Contemporary Leftist Politics in the Arab East*, Cairo: Rosa Luxemburg Stiftung Regional Office Palestine, pp. 8–33.

Hinnebusch, Raymond (1981), 'The National Progressive Unionist Party: The Nationalist-Left Opposition in Post-Populist Egypt', *Arab Law Quarterly* 3: 4, 325–51.

Hinnebusch, Raymond (2005), 'Political Parties and Trade Unions', in Youssef Choueiri (ed.), *A Companion to the History of the Middle East*, Oxford: Blackwell Publishing, pp. 334–54.

Ismael, Tareq, and Jacqueline Ismael (2011), *Government and Politics of the Contemporary Middle East: Continuity and Change*, New York: Routledge.

al-Khazen, Farid (1998), 'Kamal Jumblatt, the Uncrowned Druze Prince of the Left', *Middle Eastern Studies* 24: 2, 178–205.

al-Khazen, Farid (2003), 'Political Parties in Postwar Lebanon: Parties in Search of Partisans', *Middle East Journal* 57: 4, 605–25.

Kienle, Eberhard (2001), *A Grand Delusion: Democracy and Economic Reform in Egypt*, London: I. B. Tauris.

Korany, Bahgat (ed.) (2010), *The Changing Middle East: A New Look at Regional Dynamics*, Cairo: The American University in Cairo Press.

Kostenko, Veronica V., Pavel A. Kuzmuchev and Eduard D. Ponarin (2016), 'Attitudes towards Gender Equality and Perception of Democracy in the Arab World', *Democratization* 23: 5, 862–91.

Kraetzschmar, Hendrik, and Francesco Cavatorta (2010), 'Bullets over Ballots: Islamist Groups, the State and Electoral Violence in Egypt and Morocco', *Democratization* 17: 2, 326–49.

Langohr, Vickie (2004), 'Too Much Civil Society, Too Little Politics: Egypt and Liberalizing Arab Regimes', *Comparative Politics* 36: 2, 181–204.

Levitsky, Steven, and Lucan Way (2002), 'The Rise of Competitive Authoritarianism', *Journal of Democracy* 13: 2, 51–66.

Lust-Okar, Ellen (2005), *Structuring Conflict in the Arab World: Incumbents, Opponents, and Institutions,* Cambridge: Cambridge University Press.

Lust-Okar, Ellen (2006), 'Elections under Authoritarianism: Preliminary Lessons from Jordan', *Democratization* 13: 3, 456–71.

Maghraoui, Abdeslam (2002), 'Depoliticization in Morocco', *Journal of Democracy* 13: 4, 24–32.

Mainwaring, Scott, and Timothy Scully (1995), *Building Democratic Institutions: Party Systems in Latin America,* Stanford: Stanford University Press.

Masoud, Tarek (2014), *Counting Islam: Religion, Class and Elections in Egypt,* Cambridge: Cambridge University Press.

Murphy, Emma (1999), *Economic and Political Change in Tunisia: From Bourguiba to Ben Ali,* London: Palgrave Macmillan.

Murphy, Emma, and Anoushiravan Ehteshami (1996), 'Transformation of the Corporatist State in the Middle East', *Third World Quarterly* 17: 4, 753–72.

Pellicer, Miquel, and Eva Wegner (2014), 'Socio-economic Voter Profile and Motives for Islamist Support in Morocco', *Party Politics* 20: 1, 116–33.

Perkins, Kenneth (2004), *A History of Modern Tunisia,* Cambridge: Cambridge University Press.

Posusney, Marsha Pripstein (1997), *Labor and the State in Egypt: Workers, Unions and Economic Restructuring,* New York: Columbia University Press.

Posusney, Marsha Pripstein (2002), 'Multi-party Elections in the Arab World: Institutional Engineering and Oppositional Strategies', *Studies in Comparative International Development* 36: 4, 34–62.

Randall, Vicky, and Lars Svåsand (2002), 'Party Institutionalization in New Democracies', *Party Politics* 8: 1, 5–29.

Resta, Valeria (2016), 'Is It a Question of Religion? Is It a Real Cleavage? An Analysis of Voting Behaviour in 2011 Elections in Tunisia and Egypt', paper presented at the IPSA 24th World Congress of Political Science, Poznan, 23– July.

Rogan, Eugene (2012), *The Arabs: A History,* London: Penguin Books.

Salamey, Imad (2014), *The Government and Politics of Lebanon,* Abingdon: Routledge.

Salem, Paul (1994), *Bitter Legacy: Ideology and Politics in the Arab World,* Syracuse: Syracuse University Press.

Salloukh, Bassel, Rabie Barakat, Jinan al-Habbal, Lara Khattab and Shoghig Mikaelian (2015), *The Politics of Sectarianism in Postwar Lebanon,* London: Pluto Press.

Schedler, Andreas (2002), 'The Menu of Manipulation', *Journal of Democracy* 13: 2, 36–50.

Schedler, Andreas (2006), *Electoral Authoritarianism: The Dynamics of Unfree Competition,* Boulder, CO: Lynne Rienner.

Schlumberger, Oliver (2007), *Debating Arab Authoritarianism: Dynamics and Durability in Nondemocratic Regimes,* Stanford: Stanford University Press.

Seawright, Jason, and John Gerring (2008), 'Case Selection Techniques in a Menu of Qualitative and Quantitative Options', *Political Research Quarterly* 61: 2, 294–308.

Shehata, Dina (2010), *Islamist and Secularists in Egypt: Opposition, Conflict and Cooperation,* New York: Routledge.

Shteiwi, Musa (2014), 'The Jordanian Left: Today's Realities and Future Prospects', on Jamil Hilal and Katja Herman (eds), *Mapping of the Arab Left: Contemporary Leftist Politics in the Arab East*, Cairo: Rosa Luxemburg Stiftung Regional Office Palestine, pp. 56–82.

Storm, Lise (2013), *Party Politics and the Prospects for Democracy in North Africa*, Boulder, CO: Lynne Rienner.

Storm, Lise (2017), 'Parties and Party System Change', in Inmaculada Szmolka (ed.), *Political Change in the Middle East and North Africa: After the Arab Spring*, Edinburgh: Edinburgh University Press, pp. 63–88.

Suleiman, Michael W. (1967), *Political Parties in Lebanon: The Challenge of a Fragmented Political Culture*, Ithaca, NY: Cornell University Press.

Tamimi, Sonia (2013), 'The Predicaments of Tunisian Left', in Ellen Jarrar (ed.), *The Left and the Arab Revolutions*, Cairo: Rosa Luxemburg Foundation, pp. 35–52.

Tarrow, Sidney (1998), *Power in Movement: Social Movements, Collective Action and Contentious Politics*, Cambridge: Cambridge University Press.

Tessler, Mark (2011), *Public Opinion in the Middle East: Survey Research and the Political Orientations of Ordinary Citizens*, Bloomington: Indiana University Press.

Wickham, Carrie Rosefsky (2002), *Mobilizing Islam: Religion, Activism, and Political Change in Egypt*, New York: Columbia University Press.

Yacoub, Hussein (2014), 'The Lebanese Left: The Possibility of the Impossible', in Jamil Hilal and Katja Herman (eds), *Mapping of the Arab Left: Contemporary Leftist Politics in the Arab East*, Cairo: Rosa Luxemburg Stiftung Regional Office Palestine, pp. 82–101.

Yom, Sean (2015), 'The New Landscape of Jordanian Politics: Social Opposition, Fiscal Crisis, and the Arab Spring', *British Journal of Middle Eastern Studies* 42: 3, 284–300.

Zemni, Sami, Brecht De Smet and Koenraad Bogaert (2013), 'Luxemburg on Tahrir Square: Reading the Arab Revolutions with Rosa Luxemburg's *The Mass Strike*', *Antipode* 45: 4, 888–907.

Chapter 3

What are 'secular' parties in the Arab world? Insights from Tunisia's *Nidaa Tounes* and Morocco's PAM

Anne Wolf

The immediate aftermath of the 2010/11 popular uprisings in the Middle East and North Africa saw the rise and electoral victories of Islamist parties. Their surge has led an increasing number of scholars to analyse political developments in the region through the binary lens of 'Islamists versus secularists' – the latter typically referring to the countries' more established powerbrokers which have dominated the political landscape since independence (Zeghal 2013; Lust et al. 2012; Maâti 2011). Within this framework of analysis, Islamist parties are frequently accused of promoting a counter-modernisation platform, whilst secular actors are characterised as liberal and supportive of western values. For example, the *Guardian* reported the victory of Tunisia's 'secular' *Nidaa Tounes* (Call for Tunisia) in the October 2014 parliamentary elections by stating that '[a] liberal party [. . .] has taken the most seats' (*The Guardian* 2014). In an editorial the Deputy Director of Brookings Doha Center, Ibrahim Fraihat (2013), contrasted Tunisia's 'secularist liberals' with its nascent Salafi movement. Morocco expert Hanspeter Mattes (2016: 2) of the German Institute of Global and Area Studies called the Kingdom's 'secular' Authenticity and Modernity Party (PAM) a 'liberal, centrist' movement.

Whilst many scholars of the Arab world nowadays use casually the labels secular and secularism to describe the non-Islamist political spectrum, these notions first emerged in a specific western context, namely at a time modern nation-states were created, laying the foundation of the later establishment of democracy. In the west secularism served to resolve conflicts amongst rival religious dominations and occurred alongside industrial progress. Thereby it became closely associated with modernisation and liberalisation, concepts that were juxtaposed to religion and tradition. However, as Talal Asad (2003: 25) notes, the secular 'is not the opposite' of the religious and sometimes even overlaps with it. For example, many secular states in the west nowadays continue to devise religious policies. The aim of this chapter is to develop a more nuanced understanding of 'the secular' in the Arab world through an in-depth analysis of the internal dynamics, set-up, and ideological and strategic visions of *Nidaa Tounes* and the PAM, two important parties in the region commonly branded as secular, but whose inner workings and platforms remain poorly understood.

The cases of *Nidaa Tounes* and the PAM are particularly relevant because unlike in war-torn Libya and Syria, or in Egypt, where the Muslim Brotherhood-led government was overthrown in a military coup in the summer of 2013, Islamists in Tunisia and Morocco have managed to establish themselves as integral and powerful forces alongside the countries' more established power holders. In Tunisia, the Islamist *Ennahda* party emerged as the strongest force following the October 2011 Constituent Assembly elections. A month later, Morocco's Islamist Justice and Development Party (PJD) came first in competitive general elections following a tentative political opening, a process launched in 2011 under the aegis of the palace. In Tunisia, the legislative elections in October 2014 initially shifted the balance of power towards *Nidaa Tounes*, until many of its deputies resigned as a consequence of a major internal party crisis that erupted just a few months later. The party's divisions benefited *Ennahda*, whose deputies became the largest parliamentary bloc in the legislature and key coalition partners in government. In Morocco's October 2016 general elections the PAM closely trailed the PJD. Naturally, the Islamists' sway has had a direct impact on the platforms, membership bases and strategic priorities of non-Islamist forces.

This chapter first highlights the central features of the Tunisian and Moroccan political landscapes and how they must be understood in the context of the countries' particular political traditions and institutions, resorting to Michael Willis's (2002a, 2002b) typology of political parties in the Maghreb, which takes their historic, geographical and ethnic specificities into account. The following section shows that the ascent of Islamist forces provided the context for the creation of *Nidaa Tounes* and the PAM, a trend explaining their heterogeneous membership. Indeed, in many ways, both *Nidaa Tounes* and the PAM were established primarily to defend the countries' long-time powerbrokers from their Islamist adversaries. They are therefore distinct from traditional parties organised around a particular set of ideological values (Bohrer et al. 2000). The chapter then illustrates that the core issue uniting the diverse members of both parties is their opposition to Islamists, a stance which has come dramatically to the fore following the electoral victory of *Ennahda* and the PJD in 2011. Yet far from being secular, the last section shows that *Nidaa Tounes* and PAM activists see themselves as the guardians of their countries' 'true' Islamic heritage, promote their own brand of Islam, and increasingly resort to religious speech to further their political aims.

Beyond the 'secularists against Islamists' paradigm

Unlike in the western world, the key divide between parties in Tunisia and Morocco – and in much of the rest of the Arab world – is their stance towards the main power holders in the state, not their ideological leanings as the 'secularists against Islamists' paradigm suggests (Willis 2002a: 2). Regime interference in the political system is pervasive and parties are typically led by a single figure known as the *za'im* (the leader) with close ties to the central power (Willis 2002b: 12). Indeed, for almost twenty-five years in Tunisia power resided with former president Ben Ali and a close circle of cronies within his extended family, the political and business elites. Politically, they were organised in the Democratic Constitutional Rally (RCD) party, a heterogeneous party defending the interests of the president and his allies. The RCD emerged under Ben Ali as a rebranding of the Socialist Destourian Party (PDS), which under its previous name, the *Neo-Destour*, led the fight for independence. Both the PDS and the RCD were de facto *partis uniques*, as the legal opposition lacked any real sway in parliament. Even after Ben Ali's ousting in January 2011, much of the formal and informal networks of cronyism continued to exist, with his previous allies determined to protect their political and economic privileges. Founded in June 2012, *Nidaa Tounes* became the main vehicle to defend such interests, as the RCD was banned in 2011.

Unlike Tunisia and most other countries in the region, Morocco retained a multi-party system upon independence. However, real power remains concentrated in the hands of the monarchy and the *makhzen* – influential members of the deep state, including the military, the security and business sectors. In an attempt to divide the political scene and weaken its most fervent opponents, the monarchy traditionally supported the creation of a number of pro-palace parties to compete with genuine opposition movements. The PAM, founded in 2008 by Fouad Ali El Himma, an adviser to King Mohammed VI, emerged as the most influential of these forces.

The most fervent opponents to these pro-regime parties over the last few decades have been Islamist activists, who have gained relevance since the late 1960s. During this period in Tunisia, religious dissidents created the Islamic Group, which was renamed the Islamic Tendency Movement (MTI) in 1979 and *Ennahda* in 1989. In 1981, MTI activists applied for the authorisation to form a political party, but their request was rejected and subsequent decades saw a stand-off between them and state authorities, who fiercely cracked down on powerful religious opponents (Wolf 2017). As a consequence, many of *Ennahda's* members were either imprisoned or exiled starting from the late 1980s and only re-emerged on the political scene after the Ben Ali regime was overthrown in 2011 (Cavatorta and Merone 2013; Wolf 2013). Morocco's PJD also has its roots in the 1960s, when its founder Abdelkrim El Khatib announced the creation of the Popular Democratic and Constitutional Movement (MPDC), which, together with the Movement of Unity and Reform (MUR)[1] would become the PJD in 1998. Whilst the PJD was granted a party licence, another Islamist movement, the *Al Adl Wal Ihsane* (Justice and Spirituality) – arguably the most fervent political opposition – has remained underground ever since its creation in 1973 by Sheikh Abdessalam Yassine (Sakthivel 2014).

Compared with these Islamist movements, other opposition forces remained weak and fragmented. This is in part because they lack a clear ideology and are perceived as elitist. Indeed, whilst *Ennahda* and the PJD have benefited from close ties with their grass roots, non-Islamist contenders are often seen as detached from the concerns of ordinary citizens and their support base is typically limited to major urban zones. In addition, in Tunisia they have historically remained divided over strategic priorities and competing leadership aspirations – a tendency highly visible amongst members of the Progressive Democratic Party (PDP), *Ettakatol*, the Congress for the Republic (CPR) and the Tunisian Workers' Communist Party (PCOT).[2] There were efforts to unite in a pro-democracy coalition, most importantly in the framework of the so-called October 18 Movement launched in 2005, but they never gained momentum (Haugbølle and Cavatorta

2011). In addition, such a coalition could not achieve much without the inclusion of Islamists.

In Morocco cooperation centred on the Socialist Union of Popular Forces (USFP) and the *Istiqlal* (Independence) party.[3] Yet, similar to the October 18 Movement in Tunisia, both parties lacked unity at key moments. Mutual animosity and personal rivalries prevented party leaders from pushing for political reforms even at times when the opportunity arose. For instance, in the 1990s King Hassan II was in need of both parties' collaboration to enhance his reformist image and he even decided to include them in the so-called *alternance* government (1998–2002). Yet despite this important window of opportunity, the USFP and *Istiqlal* failed to press for real political change (Wegner and Pellicer 2011: 304). The parties' popularity suffered a serious blow because of such inefficiency, and allegations of corruption further undermined their support base (Boussaid 2009: 414; Boukhars 2011; Storm 2013).

The failure of non-Islamist parties to challenge the real wielders of power reinforced the leverage of *Ennahda* and the PJD. Both the monarchy in Morocco and Ben Ali in Tunisia attempted to counter Islamists through a threefold strategy: (1) denouncing them as 'extremists' by linking them to violent groups; (2) reinforcing their own religious underpinnings; as well as (3) committing to 'modernity' and western values. As part of the latter strategy, authorities in both countries have had a hand in the creation of a number of prominent western-style women's rights associations, which have received much praise from their western partners. For the authorities, promoting the inclusion of famous women's activists into the RCD/*Nidaa Tounes* and the PAM was instrumental in boosting their supposed modern credentials, a throwback to the state feminism of the previous authoritarian regime. Often, these female activists were promoted to important posts, a tendency that is key to understanding why these parties enjoy a secular image amongst western observers.

The secular image that parties such as the RCD/*Nidaa Tounes* and the PAM enjoy in the west, however, stands in contrast with what a number of Moroccans and Tunisians believe when they state that 'there are no "true" secular parties in the Arab world', when comparing them with their counterparts in Europe.[4] This seems quite evident given that, just as in most other countries in the region, Islam is the official religion of both Tunisia and Morocco, meaning that the religious dimension is a central component of the state. Historically, moreover, key powerbrokers never adhered to the principles of secularism or its French counterpart, *laïcité*.

Indeed, in an attempt to enhance their Islamic credentials, Ben Ali and RCD officials were frequently portrayed in the media in religious dress and praying. The former president also created a Ministry of Religious Affairs, built the Zine el-Abidine Ben Ali mosque in the suburb of Carthage, and boasted of providing the deprived with free food and presents during the holy month of Ramadan. The religious dimension of the state is even more pronounced in Morocco. There the monarchy's very legitimacy derives from the King's claim to be a descendant of the Prophet Mohammed. King Mohammed VI also holds the title of the 'Commander of the Faithful' and is frequently seen on television leading prayers. *Al Adl Wal Ihsane* and some critical voices within the PJD are the only ones challenging his religious leadership. Far from secularists versus Islamists, the religious contention between *Nidaa Tounes*/PAM and their Islamist adversaries is about the appropriation and the 'correct' interpretation of Islam. Naturally, therefore, both *Nidaa Tounes* and PAM activists have been alarmed by the Islamists' quickly rising profile.

The birth of the PAM and *Nidaa Tounes*

Whilst four years apart, the creation of the PAM and that of *Nidaa Tounes* are a direct consequence of the surge of Islamist forces, alongside religious radicals in Morocco and Tunisia. In 2003, the stability in Morocco was severely tested when a series of suicide bombers blew themselves up in Casablanca. In total forty-five people were killed in the attacks, including twelve suicide bombers. Authorities accused *Salafia Jihadia*, an offspring of the Moroccan Islamic Combatant Group, of masterminding the bombings. Leaders of the PJD and *Al Adl Wal Ihsane* fiercely condemned the attacks. Yet these leaders' growing popularity, alongside that of violent activists, deeply unsettled the authorities. They feared that their Islamic leadership – upon which the monarchy's overall authority depends – was under threat. The rising profile of religious opponents was accentuated at that time by growing popular disillusionment with the more established parties. In March 2006, a leaked opinion poll, secretly conducted by the International Republican Institute, lay bare the extent to which old parties lacked popular support. Of those surveyed, only 15 per cent stated that they would cast a vote for the USFP in the next parliamentary elections, compared with 13 per cent who supported *Istiqlal*. Almost half of the respondents were still unsure as to which party they would support in the ballots. When accounting for their political leanings, the poll showed that the PJD might score up to 46 per cent of the vote.[5] Naturally, this alarmed the Moroccan authorities. As one of the PAM's founding members explained:

> During the process that led to the creation of the PAM, we observed two things: the mounting prominence of conservative forces, sometimes even with violent manifestations, such as was the case during the terrorist attacks in Casablanca [...]. Moreover, there was very little popular interest in politics, which was quite worrying.[6]

Clearly, the lack of popular support for the old political parties and their perceived inability to counterbalance the Islamists was the main driving force behind the creation of the PAM. Storm (2013: 50) highlights that its founder 'el-Himma made little secret of' the fact that 'the PAM was to weaken the PJD'.

This echoes the reasons for the establishment of *Nidaa Tounes*. In Tunisia, the post-uprising period saw the emergence of *Ennahda* as the strongest political force. After its electoral victory in October 2011, it formed the so-called Troika government together with the CPR and *Ettakatol*, two left-of-centre parties. However, its two coalition partners were weak compared with the Islamists. Furthermore, the parliamentary opposition had limited political sway in a country with a long history of being dominated by a single force. As a consequence, many non-Islamist actors quickly came to fear 'unchecked Islamism' (Wolf 2014a). Tensions reached fever pitch with the assassination of two opposition politicians, Chokri Belaïd and Mohammed Brahmi, by religious radicals in February and July 2013 respectively. *Ennahda* leaders fiercely denounced the killings. Yet many of the party's opponents were keen on blaming *Ennahda* for the assassinations, accusing its leaders of having turned a blind eye to the rise of religiously motivated violence after the uprisings. Opposition to *Ennahda* was bolstered at the time by the overthrow of the Muslim Brotherhood in Egypt, which provided anti-Islamist forces in Tunisia with renewed confidence. In the summer of 2013, they created the National Salvation Front, which was led by *Nidaa Tounes* and sought to overthrow the Troika government. A *Nidaa Tounes* member summed up the main rationale behind the establishment of the party and its prominent role within the National Salvation Front: 'secular forces needed to unite and force *Ennahda* out of power'.[7] The *Nidaa Tounes'* member calling the National Salvation Front 'secular' despite its considerable heterogeneity highlights that the terms secular and secularism are essentially used by Tunisians to express opposition to the Islamists.

While the surge of Islamist forces alongside violent Salafis provided the context for the birth of *Nidaa Tounes* and the PAM, the creation of a new political party of course demands careful planning and significant political experience. Just like many parties in the region, *Nidaa Tounes* and the PAM were created by a single political figure with close ties to the countries' central powerbrokers; a *za'im*. The extent of a *za'im's* name recognition, charisma, political experience and personality cult is indeed far more important than his ideological leanings or that of his party. In Morocco, El Himma (a former classmate, close friend and adviser of King Mohammed VI) became the leading figure. El Himma drew upon vast political experience and many consider him to be one of Morocco's most powerful officials. In 2000 he became the Deputy Interior Minister in what is speculated to be a sort of shadow interior minister post (Eibl 2012: 46). Following the Casablanca terrorist attacks of 2003, he also led the country's secret services. Yet despite his high-level career, in 2007 El Himma suddenly decided to run as an independent in the elections, a move many suspected was part of a palace intrigue (Eibl 2012: 45). Upon acquiring a seat, El Himma became tasked with leading the foreign affairs committee in parliament. He also led the Modernity and Authenticity bloc, which grouped thirty-six deputies. In parallel, El Himma created, together with a number of political associates, the association Movement for All Democrats (MTD). Its members set up organisational branches throughout the Kingdom, often with the help of local notables, many of whom joined the MTD's chapters in remote areas (Boussaid 2009: 415). With its wide regional network, the MTD provided the backbone of PAM's later support base. In 2008 it merged into the PAM, together with a number of smaller association and political parties, such as *Al Ahd*, the National Democratic Party (PND) and the Alliance of Liberties (ADL).

In Tunisia as well, a strongman, Beji Caïd Essebsi, who enjoyed for a long time close relations with the political establishment, created *Nidaa Tounes*. In the 1960s he was Minister of the Interior and Minister of Defence, at a time when the regime of Tunisia's first president, Habib Bourguiba, harshly cracked down on leftists. After Ben Ali took over power in 1987, Essebsi integrated the RCD party. He became Ambassador to West Germany and President of the Chamber of Deputies. Yet he was marginalised within the RCD from the mid-1990s onwards, at a time when the party became increasingly dominated by cronies of the president and his family. Essebsi's almost two-decade absence from the political scene facilitated his political comeback after Ben Ali's ousting.[8] He became interim prime minister, a position in which he organised the legislative elections. Founding members of *Nidaa Tounes* claim that, from early 2012 onwards, when the dominance of *Ennahda* became strikingly apparent in parliament, various political forces longed for the establishment of a party that would unite the fragmented opposition. An experienced politician who, despite his long absence from politics never cut his close ties with powerful members of the ruling elite, Essebsi emerged as their natural candidate.[9] In April 2012 he first created the *Nidaa Tounes* initiative, which, two months later, became a political party. So ultimately, *Nidaa Tounes* and the PAM were created by strongmen to counter Islamists, but this occurred more out of a desire to defend their strategic interests than for ideological reasons. As such, both *Nidaa Tounes* and the PAM initially adopted a distinctly negative identity centred on their desire to keep Islamism in check. In short, they did not follow any explicitly secular agenda.

Divided they stand

The promise of countering Islamist forces and religious radicals helped Essebsi and El Himma to garner a wide membership base behind their parties. It consisted of key state powerbrokers – former RCD members and the *makhzen* respectively – as well as entrepreneurs, leftists and women's rights activists. Within this heterogeneous set-up, the RCD and *makhzen* are, by far, the parties' most powerful blocs. In Morocco, El Himma himself, Secretary General of the PAM until 2011, is of course representative of this constituency, yet other leading figures also made their careers within the *makhzen* before joining the party. They include Mohammed Cheikh Biadillah, a former Minister of Health, and Abdelouahad Khouja, a previous financial inspector at the Ministry of Foreign Affairs (Eibl 2012: 50). In Tunisia, Essebsi, *Nidaa Tounes'* founder and Secretary General until being elected president in 2014, is representative of RCD former members now in *Nidaa Tounes*. In fact, even as President of the Republic, Essebsi continues to pull many strings within the party. Indeed, via his son Hafedh, who took the important position of vice president of *Nidaa Tounes* and is responsible for its organisation in the provinces, the president monitors and influences internal party affairs. Other key figures of the former Ben Ali regime also acquired leading posts within *Nidaa Tounes*. Most famously perhaps, the RCD's last Secretary General, Mohamed Ghariani, joined *Nidaa Tounes* in 2013, although he later distanced himself from the party.[10]

Another important constituency within both parties consists of businessmen, many of whom have long entertained close ties to the Moroccan monarchy and the Ben Ali regime. *Nidaa Tounes'* Faouzi Elloumi, a member of the party's executive committee and CEO of Elloumi Group, one of the most successful companies in the country, is a former RCD deputy and mayor. Ridha Charfeddine, CEO of a pharmaceutical laboratory and president of Club Omnisports, was elected *Nidaa Tounes* deputy in October 2014 for the district of Sousse. Within the PAM, Ali Belhaj, a member of the party's political bureau who leads an important family business in Casablanca, is typical of this constituency of influential entrepreneurs. In interviews with the author, many businessmen stated that, far from ideological reasons, they joined these parties to protect their economic interests. As one successful entrepreneur in Tunis explained:

> Here in Tunisia we have a saying: if you stay too far away from the fire you will freeze, if you get too close to it you will get burned. For me, joining politics was a way to ensure that my business will survive. However, we businessmen need to be careful that we don't get burned, [...] we can't get too much involved in power battles.[11]

Whilst entrepreneurs alongside the RCD/*makhzen* constituency provide *Nidaa Tounes* and the PAM respectively with the necessary financial and political leverage to become major players, leftists and women's rights activists help to bestow them with a liberal, pro-western image. They are also the ones who care about the parties' ideological underpinnings. Many members of the parties' leftist wing have a long history of human rights activism and some were in the past engaged in anti-regime militancy. Severely repressed in the past, they were co-opted by the current power holders. In Morocco, the PAM's current Secretary General, Ilyas El Omari, who was sentenced to five years in prison under former King Hassan II, represents this category (TelQuel 2016b). It also includes Jamal Chichaoui, a member of the political bureau who was jailed and tortured for being part of a group that sought to overthrow the late king.[12] In the case of *Nidaa Tounes*, leftist figureheads include former General Secretary and Minister of Foreign Affairs, Taieb Baccouche, who used to be a leader of the country's powerful labour organisation, the General Tunisian Labour Union (UGTT). Mohsen Marzouk – a founding member of *Nidaa Tounes* who later left the party – was arrested and tortured under Bourguiba for his activism within the leftist General Tunisian Student Union (UGET) (Carpenter 2008). In later years he worked for the Arab Institute for Human Rights and the Arab Democracy Foundation. Some figures like him have now changed their strategy and believe that rather than fighting the remnants of the former regime, they might be able to foster political change from within *Nidaa Tounes*, even if that means working alongside former RCD officials.

Yet even more so than leftists, the presence of prominent women activists underpins the supposed 'liberal' image of PAM and *Nidaa Tounes*. Most famous perhaps is Bochra Belhaj Hmida, a former member of *Nidaa Tounes'* executive committee. A prominent lawyer, in 1989 she co-founded the Tunisian Association of Democratic Women (ATFD) and later became its president (1994–8). Under the Ben Ali regime, the ATFD was an important tool to propagate western-style women's rights and the former president was keen on linking its achievements to his rule. Another prominent woman in the party is Selma Elloumi Rekik, the sister of Faouzi Elloumi, a famous businesswoman and Minister of Tourism. In an interview with the author, she explained that her main motivation for joining *Nidaa Tounes* was to support a modern social project.[13] Many of PAM's female activists provided very similar justifications for joining the party, although they remained vague about the specificities of this 'modern' project. Generally it entailed an active role for women in state and society, a status they viewed as threatened by the Islamists, and a somewhat flexible interpretation of Islam – with limits, however. Indeed, one self-described so-called modern woman deplored in front of the author that not all Moroccan Muslims fast during the holy month of Ramadan.[14]

Although the set-up of *Nidaa Tounes* and that of the PAM clearly bear important similarities, each party also has specificities related to the particular geographic and demographic landscapes of their respective countries. In Morocco, the PAM has been keen to portray itself as a pro-*Amazigh* voice to attract supporters of this important ethnic group in the country. In January 2016, Aziz Benazouz, head of the party's parliamentary group, created an outcry when asking a question in *tamazigh* in parliament (TelQuel 2016a). Moreover, demographically, the PAM has succeeded in integrating sectors of the youth. Many young people view joining the party as one of the only ways of ascending the political ladder, denouncing that prominent family clans dominate the USFP and the *Istiqlal*. A young leader of the PAM's political bureau explained:

> When I was 27 years old I became interested in politics. My father told me that we are not a powerful family and that in Morocco you need a big family name to impose yourself on the political scene. He explained that I will have to fight by myself and that I don't have a family that can protect me [...] However, when the PAM was created a few years later, I saw an opportunity to establish myself.[15]

Many of PAM's young people hail from rural areas, where the party also managed to attract local notables and business owners (Sater 2007). As a result, rural areas have become its main electoral stronghold.[16] By contrast, *Nidaa Tounes'* support base is more urban. The party is particularly strong in the capital Tunis and the cities of the Sahel, the area encompassing the country's coastline to the east. Under Bourguiba and Ben Ali, both of whom hailed from the Sahel, most of the investment was directed there and to Tunis, a process that reinforced the marginalisation of rural areas. Important former cronies of Ben Ali still dominate economic affairs in the coastal cities and the capital and attempt to defend their interests through *Nidaa Tounes*. Its party leaders have sought to enhance their sway within the regions by reviving former RCD cells. They have also encouraged activists from the UGTT, which has local chapters throughout the country, to join the party. However, most of the UGTT members who are politically active have preferred to support the competing leftist Popular Front coalition, whose activists fiercely opposed the political comeback of former RCD officials.

It is therefore no surprise that *Nidaa Tounes* failed to promote young people. Those activists who are relatively young and have acquired important posts within the party, such as Firas Guefrech, a presidential adviser, have a track record of RCD activism. Recently, *Nidaa Tounes'* RCD members sought to revive their image by calling themselves *Destourians*, a term alluding to Tunisia's independence movement.[17] Yet only some of *Nidaa Tounes'* oldest members, including its founder Essebsi, can actually claim a *Neo-Destour* legacy. Despite being a minority, these figures have an important role in bestowing the party with a sense of historical legitimacy and continuity.[18] Clinging to the achievements of Tunisia's independence movement, however, only reflects that *Nidaa Tounes'* vision and political strategy, loosely defined around a modern, anti-Islamist project, remain shallow.

A minimalist ideology

Naturally, the heterogeneous membership of the PAM and *Nidaa Tounes* makes it difficult for their leaders to formulate a clear and coherent party programme. Indeed, it is even questionable whether devising a detailed platform is even a priority for some leaders, especially from the RCD/*makhzen* and businessmen constituencies, who seem to be more concerned with bolstering their own power than representing ordinary citizens. When asked about the ideological foundations of their parties, many PAM and *Nidaa Tounes* activists chuckle. Bemused, a member of the PAM's political bureau asked: 'you actually think that there are still political parties based on ideology?'[19] Others suddenly became quite nervous at the prospect of having to recall the party's ideological tenets, visibly trying to remember the basic lines of the last manifesto they had glanced at. This highlights that people were drawn to the party for a variety of reasons, such as respect for its *za'im*, not necessarily because of its programme. After a little thought, most provided a vague answer that included the wish to create a modern country and promote economic development – goals obviously not exclusive to either the PAM or the *Nidaa Tounes*, although they were typically cast in opposition to the Islamists. The difficulty of explaining the basic building blocks of the party's official programme was much starker among *Nidaa Tounes* activists, probably because it is younger compared with the PAM and emerged during a period of rapid political change.[20]

Over the past years, the *Nidaa Tounes* leaders have sought to develop what can be called a minimalist ideology, which also guides much of the PAM strategy and constitutes an attempt to unify the party's diverse constituencies. As we have seen, the basic tenets of the *Nidaa Tounes* platform are anti-Islamism, a commitment to modernity, and a related endeavour to promote prosperity and security. According to its official website, the party seeks to defend the gains of the modern Tunisian state since independence, particularly the personal status code (*moudawana*),[21] a (for the region) pioneering set of women's rights which some religiously conservative sectors of society have challenged publicly. *Nidaa Tounes* also called for 'social justice and development' through a non-exclusionary project.[22] Its senior members have pushed for an economic reconciliation law that allows former state employees to return money embezzled from public funds in exchange for amnesty and immunity from any further prosecution (Samti 2015). Clearly, this legislation benefits *Nidaa Tounes*' RCD constituency and entre-preneurs, and some of the party's leftists and women's rights activists have distanced themselves from it. Moreover, after the 2014 elections, senior members of *Nidaa Tounes* also advanced a more liberal economic programme, which caused frictions with its left-leaning activists, who advocated a more state-centred approach.

Yet leftists were willing to compromise on the economic front as long as *Nidaa Tounes*' main objective remained countering *Ennahda*. It is important to highlight that, whilst leftist opposition to the Islamists has deep historical and ideological roots, the RCD constituency and entre-preneurs rallied against *Ennahda* for more pragmatic reasons, specifically to protect their economic and political privileges from a major political rival. Thus, very early on, anti-Islamism became the very *raison d'être* and unifying force behind *Nidaa Tounes*' distinct currents. When major protests erupted after Tunisia's second political assassination in the summer of 2013, *Nidaa Tounes* leaders resorted to fierce anti-Islamist rhetoric to enhance the party's profile and bolster its support base. In subsequent months, senior *Ennahda* members tried very hard to convey that they would henceforth keep a lower profile and not challenge Ben Ali's former entourage, a stance which led many of its former RCD members and businessmen to gradually propose more conciliatory politics towards the Islamists. This illustrates the extent to which their relation towards *Ennahda* is defined more by strategic calculations rather than ideological cleavages. Shortly before the October 2014 elections, Essebsi even went as far as to announce that he did not rule out forming a coalition with *Ennahda*. To the dismay of many leftists and women's activists, his words were translated into action once it became apparent that *Nidaa Tounes* needed the Islamists to form a stable parliamentary majority. Suddenly *Nidaa Tounes*' unifying objective, that is, countering *Ennahda*, disappeared.

The creation of a coalition government that included *Ennahda* occurred shortly after Essebsi was elected president, a post that required him to cede all party responsibilities. Even though he kept yielding influence within *Nidaa Tounes* through his son, the formal departure of the party's unifying figure and *za'im* – along with the frustration of many of its members with the newly formed coalition with the Islamists – meant that frictions between rival party clans quickly burst out into the open. On 15 November alone, thirty-one *Nidaa Tounes* deputies resigned in protest over the party's coalition with *Ennahda* as well as the increasing sway of Essebsi's son within the party, especially as his influence came without any tangible political experience. As a result, *Ennahda* became once again the biggest parliamentary bloc (Marzouk 2015).

The PAM's initial dependence on El Himma carried similar risks of internal implosion. Major tensions erupted within the party during the 2011 pro-democracy protests when some within the party accused the *makhzen* of failing to live up to its promise of bringing about a gradual democratic opening. Tensions heightened when some demonstrators started calling upon El Himma to *dégage* (get lost) (TelQuel 2011), a slogan used during Tunisia's 2010/11 uprising against Ben Ali. As many Moroccans considered palace authorities to be untouchable, they decided to instead attack El Himma, their most prominent political representative.

However, in contrast to *Nidaa Tounes*' dependence upon Essebsi, El Himma was under the aegis of the monarchy, which continued to pull many strings within the party, particularly through its *makhzen* constituency and businessmen. The palace's influence helped keep the party together despite major internal frictions in 2011 and El Himma's subsequent departure, allegedly a deliberate act to downplay the monarchy's sway within the party.[23] Moreover, as we have seen, the PAM's ideological foundations are somewhat more nuanced compared with *Nidaa Tounes*' and this also helped the party remain somewhat united. The PAM's leaders promote a social democratic ideology and claim to realise this through close ties to the grass roots, including in remote areas. Its party platform advocates 'regional decentralisation' in the 'fight against poverty, vulnerability, marginalisation and exclusion' and calls for 'participation as a way to create wealth'.[24] Party leaders have also proposed a detailed programme to promote regionalisation, including through the election of regional councils (Eibl 2012). If the party's stated socio-economic priorities seem at least partially contradictory given the leverage of the *makhzen* and businessmen in its internal affairs, in recent years the PAM has indeed managed to renew itself through close ties with its rank-and-file and by continuously promoting new figures.

Moreover, the PAM's seemingly contradictory claim to both authenticity and modernity also helped to make the party less vulnerable compared with *Nidaa Tounes*. Whilst clearly emphasising the goal to 'consolidate the achievements of the modernists',[25] PAM leaders have made it a priority to reassure more traditional constituencies that modernity and authenticity can be combined, that is, that the modern does not stand in opposition to or fight against religion or tradition. This stands in contrast to western perceptions of the modern and modernity, typically situating them alongside secularisation processes that push back the hold of tradition and religion in politics and society. The choice of the PAM party symbol, a tractor, is a case in point. It is a reference to a 1959 photograph of King Mohammed V on a tractor at a time when innovative technology was introduced into agricultural production. Pictured wearing traditional Moroccan dress, the late king seemed to suggest that technological advancement can be coupled with respecting tradition. Boussaid (2009: 415) argues that the high value PAM leaders place on keeping traditions alive is a way 'to ensure that the existing political parties are not outflanked by the PJD'. Indeed, compared with their counterparts in *Nidaa Tounes*, PAM leaders have also been less apparently anti-Islamist. For example, whereas *Nidaa Tounes* members frequently equate *Ennahda* followers with the more conservative Salafis or even accuse them of complicity in terrorism, PAM activists have refrained from similar charges against the PJD, at least in public.[26] Despite this, opposition to the Islamists is also a powerful unifying force behind the PAM's different constituencies and ensures that leftists and women activists remain drawn to the party, even though they do not always have much in common with the *makhzen* and its entrepreneurs. One female PAM member explained:

> I will defend the [PAM's] project as long as I live. Because I am against living in a country led by an obscurantist, totalitarian political party [the PJD], which excludes others and does not follow national objectives, but the international goals of the Muslim Brotherhood. I am for democracy, but [. . .] I don't want their democracy. Frankly, I prefer to be in a stable and secure country, which is open and tolerant, to having a democracy led by them. They are the true danger we are facing nowadays.[27]

Such fierce anti-Islamist rhetoric directed towards the PJD is, however, rarely uttered in public, as PAM members fear being labelled by their adversaries as atheists or 'enemies of religion' – a common way to denounce non-Islamist parties in the region. Rather, PAM leaders have resorted to a discourse presenting their party as the guardian of the country's true Islamic heritage. In fact, the PAM proposes a nationalist religion in contrast to the PJD's supposed transnational Islamic affiliations, a strategy that has also become increasingly prominent amongst *Nidaa Tounes* activists.

Nidaa Tounes and PAM's brand of Islam

During the October 2014 election campaign in Tunisia, many observers noticed that *Nidaa Tounes* focused more on religious themes than *Ennahda*, whose programme privileged issues related to economic development. In September 2014, just a month before the elections, the *Nidaa Tounes* Forum of Dialogue, Civilizations, Religions and Cultures – a sort of academy created in an attempt to strengthen the party's identity – held an event devoted to 'religious discourse and political and partisan propaganda in Tunisia: between neutrality and bias' (Konrad Adenauer Stiftung 2014). A similar workshop, focusing on 'religion and cultures of coexistence in the world: realities and dangers', had already taken place a year earlier (Konrad Adenauer Stiftung 2014). In part an opportunity to warn of the 'self-proclaimed spokespersons of Islam' – an allusion to *Ennahda* and the Salafis – the event also placed considerable importance on reinforcing *Nidaa Tounes*' own religious legitimacy. Amongst other statements, during the workshop Essebsi clarified that *Nidaa Tounes* follows 'an approach that promotes a balance between authenticity and openness', echoing the PAM's rhetoric. Essebsi warned of confusing Islamism and Islam, which, he affirmed, 'is a religion of openness, a religion that accepts the cohabitation with other religions' (Babnet 2013).

One of the main tools used to reinforce *Nidaa Tounes*' religious credentials are its ties to the Zaytouna establishment, Tunisia's historic Islamic centre of learning and teaching. Before independence the Zaytouna's status was similar to that of Egypt's al-Azhar University, but it was dismantled under Bourguiba, who reduced it to a simple faculty of sharia and theology. Nevertheless, the Zaytouna still represents much of Tunisia's historic Islamic tradition. After Ben Ali took power, he sought to strengthen the RCD's links to the institution to prop up its religious credentials and counter the rising prominence of political Islam, a strategy *Nidaa Tounes* now pursues. In 2013 Essebsi recalled 'the historical role of the Zaytouna mosque and the Tunisian *ulama* in fostering moderate Islamic thought, which had an enormous influence throughout the Maghreb and Arab world' (Babnet 2013). *Nidaa Tounes* leaders have also presided over important religious ceremonies at the Zaytouna mosque (Businessnews 2015). Clearly, they seek to portray *Nidaa Tounes* as a party that defends Tunisia's traditional Islamic legacy in contrast to *Ennahda*, whose vision, they assert, is linked to the more transnational goals of the Muslim Brotherhood. *Ennahda* leaders' deliberate distancing from the Zaytouna establishment, which they accuse of having colluded with the former Ben Ali regime, has somewhat facilitated *Nidaa Tounes'* claim to its heritage.

The Moroccan context is different given the King's leadership in religious affairs and his status as the Commander of the Faithful. Yet PAM officials have also sought to prop up their Islamic credentials in a way similar to their counterparts in *Nidaa Tounes*. One PAM member explained that the party 'defends what we call "Moroccan Islam", in all its diversity, openness, and moderation. It is an Islam which does not contradict modernity.'[28] To underpin religious elements within the party and its claim to 'authenticity', some PAM activists have created links to the influential pro-regime Sufi orders, particularly the *Tijaniyya* and *Boutchichiya*. Sufi adepts have joined the party, including some in leadership posts, although their religious affiliations have often been kept a secret so as not to alienate the leftists within the party and encourage charges of their orders being co-opted. The Sufi nexus has influenced the PAM in several important ways. First of all it created an important electoral constituency given that many Sufi leaders have called on their followers to support the party.[29] It also triggered a debate about Islam within the party as many adepts advocate a more pronounced religious policy. As one of them, also a member of the PAM's political bureau, explained: 'I wished my party did more to promote the true religious face of Morocco [. . .]. We are currently discussing how we could do that. Now we must take action and launch initiatives.'[30] However, when consulting leftists about the role of Sufis within the party, many downplayed their influence, while others did not even know their main representatives. When providing them with examples, some leftists affirmed it was impossible that they were indeed Sufi adepts, hence denying them a constituency within the party. This illustrates the contested relationship that exists within the PAM between its more secular and religious factions, and that the balance between the two, alongside that between authenticity and modernity, remains constantly in flux.

Conclusion

The PAM and *Nidaa Tounes'* ties to religious institutions are just one important instance illustrating the organic relationship they have both with the secular and the religious. The parties' religious underpinnings can also be observed in some of their political counterparts in other parts of the region, such as in Egypt. There the surge of the Muslim Brotherhood has caused state authorities and the military to reinforce their ties to al-Azhar (Bano 2015). Moreover, Algeria's National Liberation Front (FLN) – the country's main political force that emerged out of its anti-colonial struggle – has intensified its Islamic rhetoric in recent years, even though Islamists there have retained a lower profile compared with those in neighbouring states. Moreover, like the Moroccan officials, Algerian authorities have promoted Sufi leaders to key posts in party and government in an attempt to convey their claim over the country's traditional Islamic heritage and keep the Islamists in check (Werenfels 2014). Whilst secular parties in the region in part utilise religion to keep Islamist competitors in check, this chapter has highlighted that they have themselves a religious constituency. In both Morocco and Tunisia increased liberties following the 2010/11 uprisings forced secular parties to become more accountable to the people and to reflect their religious sensibilities. As much research has over the past years focused upon the rise of Muslim Brotherhood-type and Salafi movements, more nuanced analyses of the non-Islamist camp are needed to better understand complex political transformations in the region.

Notes

1. The MPDC emerged in 1967 through a split from the royalist Popular Movement party (MP). The MUR was founded in 1996 by Ahmed Raissouni and Abdelilah Benkirane through the fusion of the associations The League of the Islamic Future and Reform and Renewal.
2. Centred on its leader Moncef Marzouki, the CPR combines human rights discourses with socialist and pan-Arab ideas. Ettakatol (FDTL) describes itself as a popular social-democratic force, even though most of its leaders hail from upper-class backgrounds. The PDP centres around the human rights militancy of its two founders, Nejib Chebbi and Maya Jribi.
3. The USFP emerged in 1975 out of a split from the National Union of Popular Forces (UNFP). The latter is itself a breakaway from Istiqlal, the main political force during Morocco's nationalist independence movement.
4. Author interview with Nidaa Tounes leader, Tunis, April 2014.
5. US Embassy in Rabat 2006, 'IRI Poll Shows Voters Have Little Faith in Political Parties, Predicts Strong Showing by PJD in 2007', 22 February, accessed via WikiLeaks.
6. Author interview with PAM founding member, Rabat, February 2016.
7. Author interview with Nidaa Tounes member, Tunis, August 2013.

8. Essebsi has attempted to frame his absence from the political scene in terms of his opposition to Ben Ali's regime. See, for details, *Nidaa Tounes'* official website, available at <http://nidaa-tounes.org/site/الرئيس/الفريق/السيد-الباجي-قائد-السبسي/the president)> (last accessed 21 March 2016).

9. Author interview with *Nidaa Tounes* founding member, Tunis, July 2013.

10. In January 2016 Mohamed Ghariani joined *Al Moubadara*, a competing pro-regime force led by Kamel Morjane, a former Minister of Defence and distant relative of Ben Ali (Businessnews 2016).

11. Author interview with Tunisian businessman, Tunis, September 2013.

12. Author interview with Jamal Chichaoui, Rabat, February 2016.

13. Author interview with Selma Elloumi Rekik, Tunis, September 2013.

14. Author interviews with female PAM members, Rabat, January and February 2016.

15. Author interview with Ghizlane Drousse, Rabat, February 2016.

16. Many PAM members concede that they are also doing well in rural areas because of limited electoral oversight there, which makes it easy to influence voters through informal networks and money. Author interviews, Rabat, January and February 2016.

17. *Nidaa Tounes'* official website states that the party seeks to regroup the fifth generation of the nationalist independence movement. See <http://nidaa-tounes.org/site/التاريخية/الحزب/الخلفية-الخلفية التاريخية/historical background)> (last accessed 21 March 2016).

18. Essebsi was a member of the *Neo-Destour* and the PDS before joining the RCD. Mohamed Ennaceur, *Nidaa Tounes'* interim chairperson, was also an important personality in the independence movement. However, his role within *Nidaa Tounes* is mainly symbolic.

19. Author interview with Habib Belkouche, Rabat, February 2016.

20. Indeed, in the summer of 2013 – just a year after its creation – a senior *Nidaa Tounes* official advised that for queries related to its platform, the author should contact a German foundation which closely cooperates with the party and, according to the official, wrote much of its programme. Author interviews with *Nidaa Tounes* leaders, Tunis, July and August 2013.

21. For details, see *Nidaa Tounes'* official website, available at <http://nidaa-tounes.org/site/حركتنا/الحزب/حركتنا/our movement)> (last accessed 21 March 2016).

22. For details, see *Nidaa Tounes'* official website, available at <http://nidaa-tounes.org/site/حركتنا/الحزب/حركتنا/our movement)> (last accessed 21 March 2016).

23. PAM senior members have been keen on stressing that El Himma was just 'a leader amongst others' and did not play 'any particular role within the party', accusing the media and opposition forces of exaggerating his influence. Author interviews with PAM senior members, Rabat, February and March 2016.

24. For details, see PAM's official website, available at <http://www.pam.ma/20/2015-10-12-12-18-39 (الأصالة والمعاصرة)/الأهداف الأساسية لحزب/the basic objectives of PAM)> (last accessed 20 March 2016).

25. For details, see PAM's official website, available at <http://www.pam.ma/20/2015-10-12-12-18-39 (الأصالة والمعاصرة)/الأهداف الأساسية لحزب/the basic objectives of PAM)> (last accessed 20 March 2016).

26. Author interviews with PAM and *Nidaa Tounes* members, Tunis, August 2014 and Rabat, February 2016.

27. Author interview with female PAM leader, Rabat, February 2016.
28. Author interview with PAM activist, Rabat, February 2016.
29. Author interview with Sufi leader, Fez, January 2016.
30. Author interview with member of PAM's political bureau, Rabat, February 2016.

Bibliography

Asad, Talal (2003), *Formations of the Secular: Christianity, Islam, Modernity*, Stanford: Stanford University Press.

Babnet (2013), 'Tunisie: Nidaa Tounes prône un Islam modéré fondé sur une approche réformatrice éclairée (Caïd Essebsi)', *Babnet Tunisie*, 8 October, <http://www.babnet.net/cadredetail-72536.asp> (last accessed 23 March 2016).

Bano, Masooda (2015), 'Protector of the "al-Wasatiyya" Islam: Cairo's al-Azhar University', in Masooda Bano and Keiko Sakurai (eds), *Shaping Global Islamic Discourses: The Role of Al-Azhar, Al-Madinah and Al-Mustafa*, Edinburgh: Edinburgh University Press, pp. 73–90.

Barrada, Hamadi (2009), 'Mohamed Cheikh Biadillah: "Nous sommes tous équidistants de Mohammed VI !"', *Jeune Afrique*, 15 April, <http://www.jeuneafrique.com/204036/politique/mohamed-cheikh-biadillah-nous-sommes-tous-quidistants-de-mohammed-vi/> (last accessed 20 March 2016).

Bohrer II, Robert, Alexander Pacek and Bemjamin Radcliff (2000), 'Electoral Participation, Ideology, and Party Politics in Post-Communist Europe', *The Journal of Politics* 62: 4, 1161–72.

Boukhars, Anouar (2011), *Politics in Morocco: Executive Monarchy and Enlightened Authoritarianism*, Abingdon: Routledge.

Boussaid, Fareed (2009), 'The Rise of the PAM in Morocco: Trampling the Political Scene or Stumbling into It?', *Mediterranean Politics* 14: 3, 413–19.

Businessnews (2015), 'À la Grande Mosquée de la Zitouna, Béji Caïd Essebsi préside la cérémonie de la Nuit du Destin', *Businessnews*, 13 July, <http://www.businessnews.com.tn/a-la-grande-mosquee-de-la-zitouna-beji-caid-essebsi-preside-la-ceremonie-de-la-nuit-du-destin,520,57451,3,> (last accessed 23 March 2016).

Businessnews (2016), 'Mohamed Ghariani rejoint Al Moubadara', *Businessnews*, 17 January, <http://www.businessnews.com.tn/mohamed-ghariani-rejoint-al-moubadara,520,61771,3> (last accessed 17 March 2016).

Carpenter, Scott (2008), 'Dissident Watch: Mohsen Marzouk', *Middle East Quarterly* 15: 3, <http://www.meforum.org/1973/dissident-watch-mohsen-marzouk> (last accessed 20 March 2016).

Cavatorta, Francesco, and Fabio Merone (2013), 'Moderation through Exclusion? The Journey of the Tunisian Ennahda from Fundamentalist to Conservative Party', *Democratization* 20: 5, 857–75.

Eibl, Ferdinand (2012), 'The Party of Authenticity and Podernity (PAM): Trajectory of a Political Deus ex Machina', *Journal of North African Studies* 17: 1, 45–66.

Fraihat, Ibrahim (2013), 'Tunisia's Lessons for the Middle East', <https://www.brookings.edu/articles/tunisias-lessons-for-the-middle-east/> (last accessed 25 June 2017).

The Guardian (2014), 'Tunisia Election Results: Nida Tunis Wins Most Seats, Sidelining Islamists', The Guardian, 30 October.

Haugbølle, Rikke, and Francesco Cavatorta (2011), 'Will the Real Tunisian Opposition Please Stand Up? Opposition Coordination Failures under Authoritarian Constraints', British Journal of Middle Eastern Studies 38: 3, 323–41.

Howe, Marvine (2005), Morocco: The Islamist Awakening and other Challenges, Oxford: Oxford University Press.

Konrad Adenauer Stiftung (2014), 'Le Discours religieux et la propagande politique et partisane en Tunisie: Entre neutralité et partialité', Konrad Adenauer Stiftung, 17 September, <http://www.kas.de/tunesien/fr/publications/38806/> (last accessed 23 March 2016).

Lust, Ellen, Gamal Soltan and Jacob Wichmann (2012), 'After the Arab Spring: Islamism, Secularism, and Democracy', Current History 111: 749, 362–4.

Maâti, Monjib (2011), 'The "Democratization" Process in Morocco: Progress, Obstacles, and the Impact of the Islamist–Secularist Divide', Working Paper 5, Washington DC: Saban Center for Middle East Policy.

Marzouk, Zeineb (2015), 'Thirty-one Deputies Resign as Nidaa Tounes Loses Majority', Tunisia Live, 9 November, <http://www.tunisia-live.net/2015/11/09/thirty-one-deputies-resign-as-nidaa-tounes-loses-majority/> (last accessed 19 March 2016).

Masbah, Mohammed (2014), 'Islamist and Secular Forces in Morocco. Not a Zero-Sum Game', SWP Comments C51, November.

Mattes, Hanspeter (2016), 'Islamistischer Wahlsieg in Marokko löst Krise bei der Regierungsbildung aus' [Islamist Electoral Victory Causes Crisis of Government Formation], GIGA Focus Nahost 05/2016, Hamburg: GIGA.

Sakthivel, Vish (2014), 'Al-Adl wal-Ihsan. Inside Morocco's Islamist Challenge', Policy Focus 135, August, Washington DC: Washington Institute for Near East Policy.

Samti, Farah (2015), 'In Tunisia, a New Reconciliation Law Stokes Protest and Conflict Instead', Foreign Policy, 15 September, <http://foreignpolicy.com/2015/09/15/in-tunisia-a-new-reconciliation-law-stokes-protest-and-conflict-instead/> (last accessed 19 March 2016).

Sater, James (2007), Civil Society and Political Change in Morocco, London: Routledge.

Storm, Lise (2013) Party Politics and the Prospects for Democracy in North Africa, Boulder, CO: Lynne Rienner.

TelQuel (2011), 'Analyse. Tous contre El Himma', TelQuel, 23 July, <http://telquel.ma/2012/02/29/analyse-tous-contre-el-himma_1494> (last accessed 10 March 2016).

TelQuel (2016a), 'Une question en amazigh crée polémique au parlement', TelQuel, 6 January, <http://telquel.ma/2016/01/06/question-en-amazigh-cree-polemique-au-parlement_1476676> (last accessed 10 March 2016).

TelQuel (2016b), 'Portrait-Enquête: Le mystérieux Ilyas El Omari', TelQuel, 25 January, <http://telquel.ma/2016/01/25/portrait-enquete-mysterieux-iliass-el-omari_1479378> (last accessed 10 March 2016).

Wegner, Eva, and Miquel Pellicer (2011), 'Left–Islamist Opposition Cooperation in Morocco', British Journal of Middle Eastern Studies 38: 3, 303–22.

Werenfels, Isabelle (2014), 'Beyond Authoritarian Upgrading: The Re-emergence of Sufi Orders in Maghrebi Politics', Journal of North African Studies 19: 3, 275–95.

Willis, Michael (2002a), 'Political Parties in the Maghrib: Ideology and Identification: A Suggested Typology', *Journal of North African Studies* 7: 3, 1–28.

Willis, Michael (2002b), 'Political Parties in the Maghrib: The Illusion of Significance?', *Journal of North African Studies* 7: 2, 1–22.

Wolf, Anne (2013), 'An Islamist "Renaissance"? Religion and Politics in Post-Revolutionary Tunisia', *Journal of North African Studies* 18: 4, 560–73.

Wolf, Anne (2014a), 'Can Secular Parties Lead the New Tunisia?', Washington DC: Carnegie Endowment for International Peace.

Wolf, Anne (2014b), 'Power Shift in Tunisia. Electoral Success of Secular Parties Might Deepen Polarization', *SWP Comments* C54, December.

Wolf, Anne (2017) *Political Islam in Tunisia: The History of Ennahda*, London: Hurst.

Zeghal, Malika (2013), 'Competing Ways of Life: Islamism, Secularism, and Public Order in the Tunisian Transition', *Constellations* 20: 2, 254–74.

Chapter 4

The institutionalisation of Islamist political parties after the uprisings

Anass El Kyak

Since Islamist political parties attained considerable electoral achievements in a number of Arab countries after the 2011 uprisings, political Islam has been again at the centre of scholarly and policy-making attention. In particular, observers focused on the factors that propelled these movements to power, as the uprisings had not seen Islamists play a central role in the protests. As Resta mentions in her chapter in this volume, issues more attuned to leftist values and thinking were the drivers of the uprisings. Various explanations contribute to highlight the specificities of Islamist political parties, but beyond the ontological and teleological debate about their ambivalent nature, a pragmatic analysis of the way they behave in society and within established institutions is needed at this juncture. Among the various Islamists movements, only non-violent ones will be analysed in this chapter; that is, those pursuing peaceful social and political activism to reach a considerable level of institutionalisation through democratic means.

Since the uprisings, scholars have argued about the actual impact they had on the countries' political systems (Lynch 2014). Some studies have stated that the forced transition under the pressure of popular demonstrations has led to instability and confusion. There is no doubt that, given the initial enthusiasm for the political transformations under way, the situation in Syria, Libya, Egypt and Yemen validates their conclusions. Thus, there are studies suggesting that we are witnessing an Arab winter (de la Puerta 2016), although the cases of Morocco, Tunisia, United Arab Emirates and Jordan seem to indicate that a degree of democratic progress has been achieved. Irrespective of the assessment one may put forth regarding the Arab Uprisings (Hinnebusch 2015), the rise of religious actors and movements remains a common finding in post-Arab Uprisings research. From the popularity of moderate movements looking to attain governmental responsibilities and work within the institutions of the state to the multiplication of radical revolutionary groups, Islamism has been and still is a powerful player in the political life of the Arab world.

The ascent of political Islam in the Arab world is not a new post-Arab Uprisings trend. It is, in fact, the result of a long postcolonial process of gestation and a direct consequence of the 1970s Islamic revival or awakening that pervaded all Arab countries (Krämer 2008). Islamist movements were formed in reaction to the perceived westernisation of those countries' elites and have had conflicting relationships with the authoritarian unaccountable regimes in place (Rashwan 2007). In many Arab countries, the genesis of the confrontation had taken place on the ideological front between nationalist ruling forces and Islamist intellectuals and activists since the series of military coups in the 1950s. This antagonism fuelled by a virulent reciprocal de-legitimation was transformed into an open political struggle, which increased during the period of free market reforms of the 1980s. Structural adjustment programmes were adopted then in non-oil-producing MENA countries and led to significant social problems, giving rise in particular to the economic difficulties of a well-educated youth in a weak socio-economic position at the margins of the political process (Woltering 2002). This situation created a fertile terrain for Islamist movements, which, thanks to their charitable service provision (Clark 2004) and their mobilisation capabilities, seemed to show up the regimes' failures. In short, they demonstrated that religion-based activism could be more effective and fairer than national belonging and citizenship. It follows that the same factors of social inequality, the inadequacies of the education system, general economic shortcomings and political stagnation pushed many ordinary citizens to mobilise in favour of change. Over recent decades, these deficiencies became the main incubator for the emergence of the Islamic doctrine as an alternative political project that fed new forms of political activism.

Since their early days, Islamist movements have enjoyed considerable legitimacy by dint of their concrete actions and have gained a solid internal identity thanks to their reformist goals. These two elements – legitimacy and identity – constitute the first pillar ensuring the expansion of early Islamist movements across Egypt (Muslim Brotherhood), Jordan (Muslim Brotherhood), Morocco (*Al Islah Wal Tajdid*) and Tunisia

(Islamic Tendency Movement). They were indeed initially formed thanks to a value-based commitment among their members and supported by deeply held beliefs in their mission. In addition, these movements preaching change have over time acquired the necessary skills and developed strategies by which they continue to ensure a stable framework for their social and political objectives. From their very establishment as social movements and until the inclusion of their political wings in state political institutions and throughout their interactions in a complex political environment, they have managed to both survive and thrive.

Across regimes and institutions and through an alternation between conflictual and negotiated relationships with other political actors, Islamist political parties have undergone a process of institutionalisation. Thus, to portray the emergence and the development of this process, we will go beyond examining the already answered questions such as 'whether democracy and Islam are compatible, whether inclusion or exclusion is a better strategy for deflating Islamic challenges, or whether Islamists treat democracy as a strategic or tactical option, [. . .]' (el-Said and Rauch 2015: 52).

Despite the existence of an important literature that covers the topic of Islamist ideology and movements from an explanatory angle, the issue of Islamist political parties as a distinct object of research continues to be slightly under-researched when it comes to their interactions with states and regimes and the role they play in the MENA countries' democratisation processes during the post-Arab Uprising period. The literature focuses, in fact, on contingent research questions such as how they managed to get to power or how they performed once in government (Guazzone 2013; Pioppi 2013).

Thus, this chapter's different approach relies on the introduction of the concept of institutionalisation, which will serve as an analytical tool to understand the contextual evolution of Islamist political parties and to measure the scope of their positioning within the political systems of the countries this study looks at. First, we will focus on defining the concept of institutionalisation and discuss the relevance of its use in reviewing the evolution of the organisational aspects, practical strategies and political behaviour of the Moroccan Party of Justice and Development (PJD) and the Tunisian *Ennahda* party. We will follow this examination with an analysis focused on how each party devised and implemented its strategies during the uprisings and on the opportunities and threats the conditions of the events posed on the two parties' institutionalisation processes.

Building on crucial aspects of their evolution before the uprisings, we will turn our attention on each political party's institutionalisation process through a qualitative examination of some of the main institutionalisation indicators such as adaptability, complexity, autonomy and coherence (Huntington 1968). More specifically, a focus on the PJD's institutionalisation process within the Moroccan political landscape will be provided and an assessment will be conducted regarding the participation and the institutional behaviour of the party during major recent political events, namely the government coalition bargaining in Morocco after the last two legislative elections. We will end the chapter with a discussion of the future perspectives and the challenges facing the institutionalisation of Islamist political parties across the Arab world.

Applicability of the concept of institutionalisation to the PJD and *Ennahda* cases

Going beyond the theoretical disagreement among scholars of institutionalism, especially between adepts of rational choice and sociological theorists who address the issues of institutionalisation from a teleological angle and emphasise principal–agent frameworks and normative behavioural views, we adopt a wider understanding of this process given the fact that there is no consensual definition of institutionalisation and no rigorous delimitation of its attributes with regard to political parties. Nevertheless, a recurrent definition of this concept appears in the literature dealing with the subject; it is that of Huntington (1968: 12), who defines institutionalisation as a 'process by which organizations and procedures acquire value and stability'. Through this process, organisations learn to adapt to the external dynamic environment (i.e. functional adaptability) by developing differentiated internal structures (i.e. organisational complexity) that imply stability. Furthermore, by becoming institutionalised, organisations tend to seek independence and protection from external influence and control (i.e. decisional autonomy) and to ensure internal discipline and unity within their ranks (i.e. internal coherence) by implementing institutional procedures (Eberlein 2011). By projecting the parameters of Huntington's definition onto political parties as particular organisations committed to influence and gain ground within a political system designed in a certain manner, we distinguish a priori two dimensions of the institutionalisation process. There is one concerning the political parties themselves as organisations and another related to the party system as a political construction. Our focus in this chapter will be directed uniquely towards the first dimension, namely individual parties' process of institutionalisation.

From the very inception of its core reformist idea to its complete institutionalisation, three major phases are identified in the development of a party: 'first, the period of developing a message and establishing identification; second, a period of organisation and electoral growth; and third, the period of stabilisation when the emphasis is on establishing the party's credibility as well as dependability' (Harmel and Svåsand 1993: 71). This is why dealing with parties as common organisations can lead to confusion especially in the understanding of their institutionalisation process. In fact, political parties are specific structures providing assemblies and meetings to men and women 'who profess the same political doctrine' (Constant 1837). Based on ideas that feed a specific representation of the world as it should be, political parties derive their desire for change and their struggle for reforms from the allegiance of individuals and groups holding common beliefs manifested within particular currents of the society. Also, they crystallise and maintain networks capable of upholding the interests of specific factions or groups within the state, the economy and the social structures. Thus, the prospective vision, specific objectives, intended reforms, goals, necessary means or projected results are contained in manifestos and policies designed to be operationalised and implemented using the instruments of the state and its institutions after winning the necessary popular support through periodic election processes. In addition, political parties' surrounding environment plays a significant role in this process of institutionalisation insofar as it provides the necessary and sufficient conditions for its applicability. By external environment we mean the system of government, the institutional design, and the distribution of power within the state, which allows (or not) political parties to pursue their objectives.

In the Arab world, authoritarian regimes have centralised power for decades. The 'predominance of personal power over institutional norms' (Nathan 2003: 6) constrained the spontaneous formation and participation of political parties in public life. Control and regulation of the political arena through different means – ranging from coercion to co-optation – to maintain all of the state's strategic levers at the full disposal of the ruling elite was the guiding political principle. This reality was clearly observable in the MENA countries before attempts at reform some regimes conducted in reaction to the 2011 uprisings. The activism of social and political movements seeking political change had not led to the institutional integration of political parties representing them. This was the case in both Morocco and Tunisia where, before the emergence of Islamist political parties, leftist ones were prevented from participating in state affairs because of the popular support they enjoyed. Thus, the *Union Socialiste des Forces Populaires* (USFP) in Morocco and the *Mouvement des Démocrates Socialistes* (MDS) in Tunisia, as representative examples, struggled against the regimes in place in the 1970s and 1980s. Whether it was under the absolute monarchical rule of Morocco or under the authoritarian republican system of Tunisia, the fear of change pushed these two regimes to employ a number of methods and strategies to thwart the ascent of political parties opposing the system as it stood. From the atomisation of the political scene to coercion and to electoral frauds, gerrymandering, and cutting off sources of support, opposition parties were subjected to multiple types of interference that sought to weaken their reformist message in society, as Resta also makes clear in her chapter in this volume on the Arab left. Even though they were at times formally allowed to exist and participate in elections, these political parties were unable to cross the red lines regimes drew that rigorously regulated all aspects of institutional political life before the uprisings. In short, party systems existed, but they were under the strict tutelage of the ruling elite and had very little to no room to manoeuvre.

From the early 1980s, Islamist political movements have in turn suffered from the regimes' authoritarian practices. Their particularity lies in the fact that they were important forums of reform ideas and that they approached public life with the support of a powerful religious framework informing their discourse of change. The alternatives they proposed and the goals they had found their place in the political awareness of the 'post-Islamic awakening' generations. Initially confronting the ills of secularisation and westernisation of predominantly Muslim societies, the Islamist political struggle was not limited to attacking the regimes in place. In fact it went beyond that, to confront also some of the main opponents of the regimes, especially those who aspired to a more modern conception of the state such as leftists and, more broadly, secular movements advocating the application of the principles, rights and liberties contained in universal treaties and conventions. A strong and sometimes violent antagonism emerged between these two opposing socio-political tendencies. This was the case in Morocco, where the 1970s clandestine

Moroccan Islamist movement *Al-Shabiba-Al-Islamiyya* (Islamic Youth) or the 1980s *Al-Jama'a-Al-Islamiyya* (Islamic Group) movement were in constant and open conflict with socialist and communist movements, particularly on university campuses, to take over the *Union Nationale des Étudiants du Maroc* (UNEM), the largest students' union in the country. This struggle between Islamists and secular leftists constituted an opportunity for authoritarian regimes to fuel and instrumentalise their confrontation to ensure that any attempt to establish a common front between them would fail, especially on issues of governance and power sharing (Schlumberger 2007). It is only from 2005 onwards in Tunisia, for instance, with the creation of the *Collectif du 18 octobre pour les droits et les libertés*, that political actors affiliated to these competing factions reached common ground for dialogue, contributing to the establishment of a shared convergent rhetoric based on freedom of expression, freedom from persecution, fight against torture, and broad democratic principles (Limam 2016). This Islamo-leftist tendency (Bruckner 2010), despite its tactical and temporary nature, federated previously divergent voices against authoritarian rule. The factions in this alliance/coalition, previously inconceivable, finally succumbed to pragmatism, a condition *sine qua non* in the political game of regime change.

It is this same pragmatism that governed the actions of a number of Islamist political movements across the region. By the late 1980s they had understood that their initial goals, such as the imposition of religious law or the reinstauration of the Caliphate, were not realistic objectives and had no place in a world of increased interdependence where the doctrine and practice of universal values had also taken hold. Indeed, their initial radical views and objectives offered a valid alibi to the regimes in place to 'rightly' repress their actions and target their structures because they were accused of promoting a retrograde and medieval doctrine with strong totalitarian undertones – often labelled Islamo-fascism (Schwartz 2006). This reality urged Islamist political parties to operate their first ideological shift and they committed to work on major revisions of their policy platform. In doing so they integrated the elementary and procedural acceptance of democracy in their literature and practices. They thereby conceded their original vision of the world and the state as a compromise that was the cornerstone of their institutionalisation process.

By operating such a change, a new episode in the conflictual relationship with the regimes occurred. In officially disavowing violence and extremism and recognising the legitimacy of the modern state and positive law,

Islamist political movements chose the path of normalisation. They began then to promote peaceful militancy and public activism within the existing institutions and through legislative means, demanding participation. Nevertheless, their doctrinal turn had not resolved the persistent constraining measures the regimes had imposed. This was the case of the Tunisian Movement of Islamic Tendency (later *Ennahda*), whose leaders and activists, after the wind of change and inclusion Ben Ali promised when he took power in 1987, were severely repressed right after the 1989 elections and completely banned from the Tunisian official political scene in 1992. In Morocco, the fate of the Islamist movement was different. It was in fact oriented towards finding a compromise with the regime in place. Even before their break with clandestine activism in 1992 and 'despite their potential for anti-regime activity, however, King Hassan II allowed the growth of Islamic opposition in the early 1980s attempting to counter his secular [and leftist] opponents [...fostering thus] a divided political environment' (Lust-Okar 2005: 59).

The PJD

If the *Ennahda* party carefully rooted the basic inputs of its process of institutionalisation by counting on popular legitimacy and by seeking international acceptance, the PJD, in addition to the same strategies, wanted to obtain an early presence in regional and national decision-making bodies. To this end, the party leaders knowingly considered that the process to attain a solid institutionalisation necessarily passed through the establishment of a relationship of trust with the monarchy. In fact, 'the recognition of the monarchy's political and religious legitimacy is a prerequisite for any party to gain and maintain legal status' (Pellicer and Wegner 2015: 35). Therefore, their failure to obtain legal recognition from the regime to form a new Islamist Party *Hizb At-Tajdid Al-Watani* (National Renewal Party) pushed the members of the more moderate Islamist *Harakat Al-Islah Wat-Tajdid* (Unity and Reform Movement) to enter the official political framework by joining the ranks of the *Mouvement Populaire Démocratique Constitutionnel* (MPDC), an empty shell party created in 1967 from a split of the centre-right party *Mouvement Populaire* (MP), both co-opted parties close to the monarchy. Since 1997, Dr Abdelkrim al-Khatib, an important figure in the national liberation struggle with links to the palace, founder of the MPDC and co-founder of the MP, was the main architect of the smooth integration of Islamists into the Moroccan political game until 2004 when he withdrew from politics. By providing them full access to the MPDC as an organisational platform for their political activities after several meetings with the powerful Driss Bassri, the Moroccan Minister of the Interior at the time, and the executives of *Harakat Al-Islah Wat-Tajdid*, al-Khatib's party was ready to accept the arrival of massive numbers of Islamists of the *Chabiba Al-Islamiyya* and *Jama'a Al-Islamiyya*, which modified the identity of the party for good (Mohsen-Finan and Zeghal 2006). Indeed, one year after this arrival, and after having avoided its dilution by declining the proposal to symbolically take part in the 1997 USFP-led government of *alternance*, the MPDC became officially *Le Parti de la Justice et du Développement* (PJD) in 1998, inheriting 9 out of 325 seats in the House of Representatives. Thus, Moroccan Islamists officially turned from opposition to His Majesty to the opposition of His Majesty (Catusse 2013).

With the arrival of King Mohammed VI to the throne in 1999, elections have become more transparent and increasingly respectful of international standards. A new political era began, one in which the Islamist electorate was able to find genuine political representation in the PJD, leading to a new push for the emergence of an institutionalised relationship between the PJD and essentially urban populations. With 42 seats in the lower House in 2002, 46 in 2007, 107 in 2011 and 125 in 2016, the PJD, acquiring increasing strength from the hundreds of associations affiliated with its mother movement *Harakat At-Tawhid Wal-Islah*, and equipped with the necessary legality that distinguishes it from other Islamist formations, has embarked on a march to power, upsetting in the process the political calculations of both the regime and traditional political actors. However, despite the popular credibility and support it has gained throughout its twenty years of official existence, the PJD, fully aware of the nature of the regime, the nature of the electoral system and the complex interconnections of the ruling elite's interests, has never short-circuited the will of the *makhzen*. Even after the May 2003 terrorist attacks in Casablanca, when all Islamist movements were under siege without distinction between moderates and extremists, the PJD remained committed to the principles of democracy and acted within the institutions, carefully managing the crisis and escaping serious attempts at its dissolution (Catusse 2013). The party declared insistently its unwavering allegiance to the monarchy and its recognition of its spiritual aspect – namely the role of Commander of the Faithful – in addition to its firm condemnation of violence. In the face of all these difficulties, which acted against the achievement of its complete institutionalisation, the PJD's signs of goodwill towards the regime and its persistence in mobilising voices of change produced strong electoral results in the 2007 legislative elections when the party obtained the second largest number of seats in the House of Representatives. It is important to note that in the period before the uprising the party held firm in parliament, refusing to accommodate the governments of the time and holding them instead accountable for their shortcomings. In addition, its achievements in local government, mainly in major urban districts, contributed to maintaining its popularity and credibility. However, from 2008 onwards, the PJD had to contend with the advent of the *Parti de l'Authenticité et de la Modernité* (PAM) on the political scene, as Wolf details in her chapter in this volume. This supposed catch-all party has been the leading force in local politics after the 2009 communal elections. If many of its senior officials have declared that they were determined to fight Islamists (Macé and Chevance 2016), many of them do not enjoy the necessary legitimacy to make their party become a major political force in Morocco and one with which the voices of change can identify. Therefore, in accordance with its symbol of the tractor, the PAM has found its political support in rural areas where vote buying and other dubious electoralist practices prevail.

The political context the arrival of the PAM foreshadowed a desire to establish a virtual bipolarity of the Moroccan political field likely to limit the attraction of the PJD. It can be observed that the rise of the PAM was in fact reminiscent of that of the 1963 *Front pour la Défense des Institutions Constitutionnelles* (FDIC), an ad hoc party created by Ahmed Reda Guédira, a close friend and adviser to King Hassan II, to counter the hegemony of the nationalist *Istiqlal* party. However, the 2011 uprising constituted an opportunity for Abdelilah Benkirane (leader of the PJD since 2008) and his lieutenants to openly discredit the political project of the PAM by initiating a virulent political campaign against its main figures and their links with corruption networks.

The *Ennahda*

While all these developments in Moroccan Islamist politics occurred on the official political scene at a reasonably slow pace from 1992 to 2010, Tunisian Islamism, banned during the same period from the official political arena, existed only in exile and outside formal institutions. Indeed, after the brief participation in Ben Ali's High Council of the National Pact, the Islamic Tendency Movement, which changed its name to the *Ennahda* movement in 1989, was quick to reopen the confrontation with the regime after being banned in the aftermath of the 1989 parliamentary elections. At the time, Rachid Ghannouchi, the main figure of the movement, left Tunisia for London from where he began coordinating a strategy of confrontation against the regime's wave of prosecution (Netterstrøm 2015). It was only in June 1996, when the *Ennahda* held its first congress in Belgium, that delegates voted overwhelmingly to abandon this strategy of confrontation in favour of a more moderate policy of opposition. From there, a new phase of moderation (Cavatorta and Merone 2013) was launched with dialogue and compromise as major watchwords. If the PJD's mechanism of institutionalisation confirms the applicability of the moderation through inclusion hypothesis, the case of the *Ennahda*, because of the different nature of the Tunisian political and socio-cultural model, requires the consideration of other explanatory variables to grasp its return in force during the Tunisian post-revolutionary era and, overall, its path towards institutionalisation.

Opportunities and threats in the context of the Arab Uprisings

In this section, we focus on the context of the uprisings in both Tunisia and Morocco and we identify the main opportunities and threats that have emerged from the events that brought unprecedented uncertainty to the politics of the MENA region. Specifically, we examine the way in which Islamist movements in Tunisia and Morocco dealt with the waves of protests to highlight the strategies and tactics they adopted during and after these events as well as the impact on their respective institutionalisation processes.

A few months before Mohammed Bouazizi set himself on fire on 17 December 2010, no one predicted Ben Ali's ousting on 14 January 2011 or the announcement King Mohammed VI made on 9 March 2011 concerning a process of constitutional reform aimed at reducing his powers. With slogans such as 'Ben Ali, get lost' in Tunisia, 'the people want the fall of the regime' in Egypt, or 'the people want the fall of despotism and corruption' in Morocco, the socio-economic injustice and political stagnation that citizens had railed against in private became the drivers of large demonstrations and civil resistance in Tunisia, Egypt, Bahrain, Morocco and Jordan and fuelled insurgencies and civil wars across Syria, Libya, Yemen and Iraq.

The uprising in Tunisia was the direct result of the persistence of dictatorship, corruption and inequality. Those factors, coupled with the regime's repressive practices, had existed for some time, but were insufficient conditions for a widespread wave of protests similar to that of December 2010. At the turn of the millennium, Tunisia was best known for its promising economic prospects with the international media covering mainly stories about the 5 per cent annual GDP growth and the ability of this North African industrialising, touristic and export-oriented country to attract private investments. Yet, the hidden reality of prebendalism,[1] high unemployment, absence of wealth redistribution, social injustice and inflation emerged after the 2011 uprisings. In 2008, for example, blatant favouritism and clientelism in the allocation of jobs in the state-owned Gafsa Phosphate Company engendered a large protest movement that was heavily repressed. Six months of rioting and street fighting spread throughout the whole southwestern region and constituted a serious premise of what would become, eighteen months later, what is commonly referred to in Tunisia as the Jasmine Revolution.

After decades of political stagnation, the departure of Ben Ali was a turning point and an opportunity that the *Ennahda* seized strategically to re-enter Tunisian politics. Despite the strength of its grass-roots networks in the country, the party chose to prevent its sympathisers from openly participating in the demonstrations under its banner, 'partly to avoid giving the regime an excuse to paint the demonstrations as the work of an opposition group seeking to take power' (Ghannouchi 2016: 62). Absent from the front line as a mobilising and organising force, the *Ennahda* adopted a 'wait and see' posture in public, but it did not neglect the background hard work of its restructuration to ensure the political return of its leaders from exile to prepare for the post-Ben Ali era. The Islamist party, because of its ban, did not participate in the interim national unity government formed on 17 January 2011 by Mohamed Ghannouchi. Many figures of Ben Ali's *Rassemblement Constitutionnel Démocratique* (RCD) were renewed as ministers in this new cabinet, giving the impression that nothing had changed. Therefore, street protests continued demanding the resignation of the old regime's allies in the government and the disbandment of the RCD. With the public declaration of the Tunisian Armed Forces chief of staff Rachid Ammar on 24 January 2011 in which he undertook to defend the uprisings, the return of the iconic *Ennahda* leader, Rachid Ghannouchi, was ensured. The resignation of Prime Minister Mohamed Guannouchi nearly one month later after several failed measures to legitimise his cabinet indicated that the structure of the old regime was decomposing rapidly and change began to take shape. In the wake of these events, the *Ennahda* was legalised on 1 March 2011. This shift put the Islamist party on a new trajectory of institutionalisation, forcing it to deal with secular political forces. This tactical move would crystallise in the Constituent Assembly of 23 October 2011 after the party came in first place in the legislative elections. However, large components of Tunisian society rejected – and many still do – the idea that religion could be intermeshed with politics lest this undermine the achievements of the Tunisian secular model.

While Islamist movements in Tunisia were dealing with the imposing secular structure and ethos of the state to negotiate a more central place for the values of Islam in the post-revolutionary state, Moroccan Islamists did not have to go through a similar process insofar as the monarchy, a political and religious institution, remains the principal defender and the permanent upholder of religion's role in the society.

In spite of this fundamental systemic difference, the PJD, like *Ennahda*, did not allow its members to participate officially in the youth-led 20th February Movement. Stating that any involvement in street protests could lead to instability, this tactical move was a signal to the monarchy; a sign of goodwill to prove that the party was not waiting for the opportunity to weaken the most powerful institution in the country. Islamist figures in the PJD, led by Benkirane, who later became prime minister, called for calm and peaceful dialogue, and offered themselves as partners to overcome this critical period in the history of the country.

As of February 2011, the slogan 'bread, dignity and respect of the people' was the one that the demonstrators of the 20th February 'melting-pot' Movement – composed of leftists, liberals and Islamists – shared. None of the groups that openly took part in protests was sufficiently institutionalised to lead the spontaneous movement to a more important role and none of the demonstrators was a figure likely to incarnate the whole movement and to be the spokesperson for change. This may have been the reason why the regime succeeded in containing the demonstrations quickly by adopting a carrot and stick approach. It is certain that the scale of events in Morocco was not similar to that of Tunisia and other Arab countries because the central institution was not directly targeted. The major and unexpected event was the early announcement by the King of constitutional reforms likely to ensure a more democratic distribution of the executive prerogatives between the monarchy and accountable elected government officials, a concrete separation of powers and an effective recognition of pluralism, civil rights and liberties. Thus, the turbulence quieted rapidly, giving way to a more reflective and inclusive process of consultations bringing together the monarchy – through its key advisers – and the traditional parties represented in parliament. Even other factions hitherto excluded[2] were invited to set forth their proposals for constitutional reforms to the ad hoc Advisory Committee on the Revision of the Constitution responsible for issuing to the people, by 1 July 2011, a concerted new constitution for referendum. This reform dynamics isolated the 20th February Movement's demands, given the fact that, unlike in other Arab countries, the breaking point of demanding the departure of the supreme executive power had never been reached. Therefore, it is in the context of so-called Moroccan exceptionalism that the transition process was implemented with a reconfiguration of authoritarianism and a containment of hostilities and violence (Dalmasso 2012).

The PJD, the main opposition party until the uprising, played an important role in the absorption of popular claims. The party in fact appropriated the major slogan of the demonstrations – the end of corruption – to make it its own battle cry during the electoral campaign following the adoption of the new constitution. Through a very accessible discourse appealing to broad segments of society, the PJD adopted a populist rhetoric, which led it to denounce the corruption and the control on the part of the elites – crucially not the monarchy – of institutional and political life. Even personalities close to the palace, including the powerful Fouad Ali El Himma and the influential Mounir Majidi, private secretary to the King, were not spared by PJD senior officials' electoral offensive. Even though the PJD did not adopt the major political claim of the 20th February Movement's left-wing trends, namely the transformation of the country into a parliamentary monarchical system (that is, a genuine constitutional monarchy), it made inequality and corruption – the two preoccupations of the lower classes – central to its discourse. The widespread social desire for change coupled with the PJD's reformist discourse, in which the abuses of the elite were severely denounced, explain the party's popularity, unprecedented for a Moroccan political party since that of the leftist movements of the 1970s and 1980s. Therefore, the 'power' the Moroccan Islamist party gained during the context of social upheaval made it an indispensable parameter in the regime's appeasement equation.

Despite the democratic promises of the monarchy, one must not forget that Morocco has a very conservative system of governance, which contains tendencies of change and digests them slowly by operating targeted readjustments in accordance with the peculiarities of the country. It is thus the *makhzen*, this traditional ubiquitous apparatus of monarchical rule, with which the PJD has to contend to accomplish its institutionalisation.

The stabilisation of the political and institutional behaviour of the PJD

Having set forth the institutional behaviour of both the PJD and the *Ennahda* in light of the first two phases, namely identity-building and political growth, we turn to the stabilisation phase by dissecting the practicality of its aspects considering only the case of the PJD and its context of institutionalisation. In this regard, Huntington's criteria of functional adaptability, organisational complexity, decisional autonomy and internal coherence will be employed to determine the institutional practices of the Moroccan Islamist party and its ability to influence the course of events in accordance with its ideals, its social project and its contextual tactical objectives.

Indeed, this stabilisation period is crucially important in the party's institutionalisation process inasmuch as the solidity of its two markers – credibility and dependability – is challenged whenever substantial issues or major events emerge in the country demanding significant mobilisation of the party's capacities. This reality is particularly clear in democratising countries like Morocco and Tunisia where the western-like party system has yet to be proven, and where relatively independent and stable political parties face considerable challenges. Their journey towards complete institutionalisation and their accession to government can be a difficult mission especially during transition periods where new political and social configurations are being designed. This was the case of the Moroccan PJD after winning the parliamentary elections in 2011 and

2016.[3] Its leader, Benkirane, was responsible for forming the government coalition; and it was also the case of the Tunisian *Ennahda* after winning the 2011 Constituent Assembly elections. In both cases, ideological cleavages weighed on coalition-building.

For the purposes of assessing the impact the transitional events in Morocco have had on the PJD's stabilisation phase, we rely on a comprehensive model to be applied to the institutionalisation of an Islamist party in the Arab world during the post-uprising context. In this model, we distinguish two dimensions of institutionalisation: internal and external. Each dimension oscillates between structural and attitudinal aspects (Randall and Svåsand 1999: 9). The internal dimension includes, on the one hand, the structural aspects of organisational complexity and internal coherence. On the other hand, we have the attitudinal value infusion. In addition, the external dimension is based on the variables of functional adaptability and decisional autonomy as structural aspects, and on reification capacity as the attitudinal aspect.

The internal dimension

The 2011 legislative elections in Morocco, which saw the PJD become the largest party[4] and allowed it for the first time in its history to accede to government, constituted a shift in the collective thinking of its leaders and sympathisers who saw in this event a deserved victory and an opportunity to continue the fulfilment of the party's reformist project. The rapid and uncontroversial appointment of Benkirane as prime minister and the relative ease with which negotiations with other political parties were conducted led to a relatively quick formation of the 2012 government coalition.[5] Mistrust towards an authoritarian regime that had managed party politics since its independence and during the critical times described above seemed suddenly to turn into a more concerted and stable relationship with the palace. Indeed, the Islamists of the PJD have made their place during the transition period through their close involvement in the drafting of the new constitution of 2011, which provides more prerogatives for the executive branch. Furthermore, the 2012 Islamist-led government clearly contributed to the appeasement of the Moroccan political scene after a period, albeit brief, of uncertainty and instability. PJD leaders, henceforth 'his Majesty's Islamists', have invested in the rhetoric according to which they played the crucial role of 'stabilising agents' during the 2011 social unrest to consolidate their party's institutionalisation in a system where power is distributed depending on the proximity to and alliance with the palace and managed through patron–client relationships (Liddell 2010).

The PJD's institutionalisation process rests on its organisational structure, reflecting a complex interconnected system of commissions, committees, councils, units and assemblies built on and kept together by a clear ideological vision and value-based objectives. The widely promoted ethical considerations that mark the party's actions and seduce those who identify themselves with its project are based on the capacity of the PJD and its leaders to emphasise its role as the political vehicle of Islamic consciousness and values within the society. Thus, by gradually assuming political responsibilities, either in parliament or in local politics, PJD members act as torchbearers of Islamic ethics within public institutions, reinforcing thereby the value infusion that links its members. Consequently, their reputation for discipline and integrity as well as their piety makes them the right people in the eyes of many voters to fight corruption, spread justice and find solutions to Morocco's socio-economic problems. Moreover, internal solidarity and cohesion among the members are maintained through the belief that the PJD is continuously targeted by what Benkirane calls 'demons and crocodiles', namely, unknown influential adversaries whose interests would be compromised if the PJD's project of reform were to be fully and successfully carried out.

The sum of these internal attributes – organisational complexity, value infusion and internal coherence – have allowed the party to gain ground progressively as a monolithic construction with a social project which differs from all other political tendencies. What distinguishes the PJD lies in the nature of the politically heterodox ideas it defends, and, unlike the other competing parties, in the organisational and normative design by which it extends its influence. Thus, for example, thanks to the party's democratic centralism, according to which the members' opinions are free but the party's decision is compulsory, no apparent discord was observed among PJD leaders even during the most challenging periods. Also, its care to avoid harmful political competition between its members through a very centralised mechanism of candidate selection helped the party prevent internal conflicts. In fact, the PJD's candidate selection and recommendation committees, backed by written procedures, hold the exclusive power to put the 'right' people in the 'right' place at the 'right' time to achieve the party's objectives. From the initial proposal to the attribution of the position – whether for those who will be assuming organisational and political responsibilities within the party or for those who are going to be nominated to be on the ballot papers – all candidates are put through a binding process of examination within which aspects of organisational complexity meet the PJD members' commitment to the values of their party.

Through its internal institutionalisation, the PJD is equipped with the necessary attributes enabling it to pursue its penetration into the structures of power in Morocco. There is no doubt that accession to government has been one of the PJD's pillar objectives in its grand strategy of political institutionalisation. However, in the context of Morocco, the pursuit of this objective tested the party's functional adaptability, decisional autonomy and reification capacity.

Before assessing the external dimension of its institutionalisation, we should take into account the antidote role that Islamists of the PJD had come to play on the Moroccan political scene. They were able, first, to contain the leftists during the 1980s and 1990s. Then they succeeded in incarnating and channelling the political representation of the return of Islam in Morocco; and most recently they have found the political recipe that allowed them to contribute, by their accession to government, to the appeasement of the 2011 political situation.

The external dimension

The institutionalisation of the PJD, particularly in its external dimension, is a zero-sum game. Through their strategy of concessions, Islamists seek to be a fully co-opted party in a scene where winning elections is never enough to rule. Moreover, in a context where 'the electoral system, which Giovanni Sartori calls the most specific manipulative instrument of politics, may be of even greater importance than the constitution' (Hamid 2014: 135), and where the regime apparatus is omnipresent, flexibility for political parties, especially those with a reform-oriented social project, is indispensable to reach a 'least cost' institutionalisation. However, the dilemma for the PJD resides in the fact that its popularity could be inversely proportional to the scope of the concessions it makes to be integrated in a political process that provokes increasing aversion and dissatisfaction among ordinary citizens.

In fact, from the existence of the PJD in 1998 until now, turnout at legislative elections has been diminishing. The rate of registered votes cast was 58.3 per cent in 1997, 51.6 per cent in 2002, 37 per cent in 2007, 45.5 per cent in 2011 and 42.3 per cent in 2016. The rate of effective voters who have expressed valid ballots was 50 per cent, 42.7 per cent, less than 25 per cent, 35.3 per cent and 37 per cent during the same timeline (Nohlen et al. 1999; Inter-Parliamentary Union n.d.; National Democratic Institute 2007, 2011; Moroccan Ministry of the Interior 2016). Furthermore, one can point to the imbalances of the electoral system,[6] which undermine the real representativeness of political parties requiring tactical calculations in the nomination of candidates. To this should be added the nature of the Moroccan monarchy, which is based on the unanimous acceptance by the country's major actors of its constitutional prerogatives and effective role of arbiter and guarantor of the integrity and continuity of the state.

Despite these challenges, the PJD has demonstrated great adaptive abilities. Low voter turnout has benefited the party insofar as it has maintained its capacity to mobilise voters during the electoral campaigns. PJD sympathisers' strong presence in universities, civil society, trade unions, local authorities, the civil service, parliament and, since 2012, government, reflects the party's bottom-up strategy which provides it with the ability to survive what they call *Tahakoum*, that is, the meddling in parties' affairs and the control of the political scene on the part of the monarchy. The PJD's external functional adaptability responds primarily to the contextual requirements of the party–state relationship. Thus, during their first mandate in government, PJD leaders maintained a justified vigilance in the management of the balance of power inside the government. As they were aware of the constitutional and customary limits of the prerogatives of the prime minister, they have carefully managed the relations with ministers who fall under the sovereign powers of the King, particularly in strategic sectors such as the interior, national defence, foreign affairs and religious affairs. Furthermore, with the PJD leading the government, its detractors, whether within the political opposition or within the *makhzen*, did not cease feeding the media and the electorate views holding, rightly or wrongly, Benkirane and his party responsible for unpopular neo-liberal policies like the reform of pensions and compensation funds, or for the failure of major public policies such as employment and education. In these circumstances, the challenge for the PJD resided in countering the vectors of negative influence on its electorate without venturing beyond the limits imposed by the duty of reserve of Benkirane and his party's ministers, and by taking into account the delicate relations with the palace. The point here is that the party needs to keep a fine balance between deflecting criticism where it might rightfully belong – the palace – and appearing competent in running public affairs. To this end, the party has multiplied meetings, media interactions and public forums to explain the scope of these reforms and policies, and to subtly remind public opinion that the prime minister remains under the orders of an executive monarch.

The October 2016 electoral results saw the PJD increase its support and the results backfired on its opponents who had sought to undermine the popularity of the Islamists. Since the 2016 legislative elections, a new political struggle has begun, this time on the front of the negotiations with the loyalist parties to include them in the government coalition. After five months of what was known in the media as 'government blockage', the King, in a sudden but unsurprising decision, replaced Benkirane as designated prime minister. Indeed, the PJD leader, after having reluctantly accepted the exclusion of the *Istiqlal* party from his coalition after the declarations of its leader Hamid Chabat who provoked a negative reaction from the palace,[7] refused the entry of the USFP into government.[8] The party strongly supported Benkirane during this period of tense political bargaining, especially when the three most loyalist parties to the palace, namely, the *Rassemblement National des Indépendants* (RNI), the *Union Constitutionnelle* (UC) and the *Mouvement Populaire* (MP) formed a bloc which included the USFP in order to force Benkirane's hand in accepting their conditions. The blockage required that someone be held responsible and, therefore, the King appointed the PJD's deputy on 17 March 2017. Thus, the choice of Saadeddine el-Othmani – a former Minister of Foreign Affairs and Secretary General of the PJD – as a flexible, even malleable figure, constituted a shift that will test both the functional adaptability and internal coherence of the whole party, especially with the dissatisfaction members of the party voiced after el-Othmani accepted the appointment without resistance, hiding behind the sovereign's will and the nation's interest. The constraints of operating in a system where royal prerogatives and power are considerable weigh even on tightly run parties like the PJD.

Similarly, the issue of the party's complete decisional autonomy as a necessary condition for its institutionalisation provokes disagreement among observers. Its interdependence vis-à-vis its environment and the level of its differentiation regarding other groups in society remain determining factors of the party's autonomy (Kalua 2011; Randall 2006). As a structural criterion, a party's decisional autonomy is often understood through two external dimensions. First, with respect to the governing system and the regime apparatus and its extent in defining or influencing the party's positions, strategies and policies according to a permission/restriction logic. Second, the autonomy towards sponsoring movements or organisations and the level of their interference and interactions with the party, particularly when the latter is originally formed as their 'political arm' (Randall 2006).

The PJD's decision-making system oscillates between its General Secretariat and its National Council. Most binding decisions fall within the competencies of these two central bodies, which operate by majority rule. Compared with other major political parties with strong political representation in Morocco, the PJD is characterised by a relative autonomy in its political decisions. However, despite displaying a degree of resistance to the regime's traditional interference in political parties' internal affairs, the PJD is not completely different from other political movements when it comes to operating in a system of political micromanagement where the rules of the game require acceptance of the palace's political adjustments. Thus, the PJD's political decisions have increasingly been adopted under the vague pretext of 'national interest' since the party has been in government. Indeed, governing problematises the PJD's principle of decisional autonomy, not because the monarchy manipulates directly the course of events within the party, but because leading the government implies proximity to the palace and therefore imposes self-restraint in terms of the timing and depth of specific decisions.

In addition, it cannot be omitted that the PJD maintains strong links with its mother movement, the *Harakat At-Tawhid Wal-Islah*, and its subsidiary bodies. The movement is a crucial and solid platform for the party both electorally and in terms of broader links in civil society, although the two entities are legally distinct and organisationally detached. The party remains connected to the movement thanks to the double membership of many of its leaders and militants (Willis 1999). Nevertheless, the close relationship between these two entities and the lack of autonomy of the party vis-à-vis its movement of origin do not prevent the institutionalisation of the party. In this respect, one can underline the parallels between the PJD and the Labour Party in

Great Britain as far as the lack of a full independence from a social group (i.e. the Labour Party and the British trade union movement) does not necessarily undermine the complete institutionalisation of the party (Janda 1970).

As an external attitudinal parameter in the institutionalisation equation, the reification capacity of the PJD, that is, the extent to which it has become part of popular consciousness via its 'organisational strength and its access to effective means of communication' (Randall and Svåsand 1999: 21), remains one of the party's most durable traits, rooting it in society and explaining thereby its political and electoral rise. Although it manifests itself very clearly during electoral campaigns, the popularity of the PJD transcends them. With the strong presence of its members during public debates, their continuous background work in conjunction with civil society and their reactivity regarding the important issues, the party shapes to a large extent its environment and demonstrates that it is not an entity expected to weaken or disappear. Thus, due to the values it claims to represent and the political positions it takes, the PJD has forged its reputation as a vector of long-term reforms and marked thereby the public imaginary, especially after 2011.

If many Moroccans have been interested in politics and public affairs thanks to the populist discourse of the party's leaders, many others, especially the youth, have drawn their political consciousness from the post-uprising context during which the PJD was strongly present. In fact, the projection of the party's ideas and political vision to a wider public is ensured in a large part by its capacity to exploit social media, aware that the digital era, in addition to providing more opportunities for political communication, requires the control of some virtual niches of influence that many other parties neglect. Thus, conscious that official broadcasting and traditional media no longer constitute an effective link to approach wider public opinion, the so-called electronic battalions of the PJD are very active on the Internet and dedicated to the promotion, advocacy and support of their party. This provides the PJD with a clear advantage in the political competition and a 'digital reification' highly beneficial in the institutionalisation process.

Above all, time, as the 'vital requirement for reification' (Randall 2006: 27), remains a decisive factor that puts to the test the criteria of institutionalisation. This is actually a dimension useful to predict whether the PJD will hold as a political construct on its own or if its recognition as an established political force is due only to the charismatic leadership of Benkirane and his close lieutenants. This speaks to the role of the *za'im* that Wolf discusses in her chapter in this volume about 'secular' political parties in the Arab world.

The institutionalisation of the PJD raises the fears of the elite, which will lose out if the party's proposed socio-economic and political project is applied in full. The ruling elite, and in particular the faction that 'bet' on an internal fracture of the PJD likely to erode its process of institutionalisation, is clearly unnerved. The elite's strategy to weaken the PJD was primarily to induce a virtual bipolarity by strengthening the PAM's electoral capabilities, as Wolf discusses in her chapter. This strategy did not pay off, as the astonishing legislative results in 2016 indicate. Henceforth, the PJD's antagonists rely on a grouping of loyalist parties (RNI, MP, UC), to which is added a discredited USFP, in order to weaken and dilute its influence inside the government and limit political achievements that might increase further the PJD's popularity.

Conclusion

Post-uprising political Islam in the Arab world experienced very different trajectories after 2011. Islamist leaders, who have always been in the opposition, struggled at the beginning of their mandates to adapt to conducting state affairs. Some have stood the test of power (the Moroccan PJD), others have strategically withdrawn from the front line of power (the Tunisian *Ennahda*), others still have boycotted the race to power despite their potential electoral attraction (the Jordanian Islamic Action Front), and others finally have failed (the Egyptian Muslim Brothers).

In this chapter, we adopted a comprehensive approach likely to contribute to fostering the knowledge about the political behaviour of two major Islamist parties, which have attracted considerable attention since their full participation in state institutions. If the Moroccan PJD and the Tunisian *Ennahda* as modern political parties have in common the willingness to take part in their countries' political and institutional life that prompted them to constantly rethink and adjust their doctrinal orientation without fully breaking with their ideological background, the conditions of their respective institutionalisation had imposed on them different paths.

When we look at the MENA's Islamist political parties from the angle of their institutionalisation processes, we understand that the post-uprising ascent of political Islam in the Arab world is neither sudden nor accidental. Like any other autonomous political party, Islamist ones behave and act similarly when it comes to seeking organisational strength, social legitimacy, popular rooting, electoral gains and political achievements.

In young democracies, individual political parties may be institutionalised, but their operation in a party system may not be (Casal Bértoa 2017). As we noted previously, this distinction comes from the fact that the conclusions drawn from the analysis of a single party's institutionalisation process should not be interchangeable with an eventual assessment of the institutionalisation of the party system as a whole. Certainly, political parties remain central variables in both cases, but the analytical framework that led to analyse the latter differs from the former.

If there is a consensus among authors that the movement of the third wave of democratisation (Huntington 1991) did not reach the coasts of the MENA region, there is no particular agreement on whether the Arab Uprisings constitute a prelude to a new wave of democracy or simply a populist and limited manifestation of an aborted need for change. However, there is no doubt that the latent collective urge for substantial democracy mixed with the Islamist parties' willingness to lead a drive for reforms through procedural democracy remain the obvious trends emerging from the tumultuous reality of the Arab world.

Notes

1. Term used by Joseph (1987) to describe the sense of entitlement that many people in Nigeria feel they have to the revenues of the Nigerian state. Elected officials, government workers, and members of the ethnic and religious groups to which they belong feel they have a right to a share of government revenues. We use this term to point mainly to the practice of corruption used by Ben Ali's family.
2. The will to legitimate this constitutional reform urged the regime to convene its most ardent political opponents to the consultation process; however, many of them boycotted the hearings. Senior activists of the 20th February Movement, Moroccan Association of Human Rights (AMDH), Unified Socialist Party (PSU) and Democratic Way (VD or *Annahj Addimocrati*) are the main factions which have argued that, in the absence of a constituent assembly, they will not take part in a process that will result in a 'granted constitution'.
3. In accordance with Article 47 of the Moroccan Constitution of 2011, the King had designated the PJD's leader, Benkirane, prime minister in both 2011 and 2016 after his party arrived first in the legislative elections. For a discussion of the

obstacles facing Benkirane in forming a government following the 2016 elections, please see below.

4. The PJD obtained 107 seats in the lower house. These results are, indeed, unprecedented in the post-protectorate political history of Morocco. The Islamist party won 1,080,914 votes, representing 27.08 per cent of the total vote, which allowed it to win sixty-one seats more than in the 2007 parliamentary elections.

5. The negotiations to form the first Benkirane government lasted only thirty-five days from the date of his appointment until the date of the official appointment of his government by the King on 3 January 2012. As mentioned, the negotiations following the 2016 elections were fraught.

6. In its 2007 final report on the Moroccan Legislative Elections, the National Democratic Institute gave the following example of such imbalances in the system: the number of votes needed to win at least one seat in the Chamber of Representatives varies widely from 2,476 and 4,563 in the Aousserd and Assa-zag districts to 27,893 and 26,068 in Chefchaouen and Alhaouz respectively.

7. At a meeting of the General Union of Workers of Morocco (UGTM), the Secretary General of the *Istiqlal* party, Hamid Chabat, said that Mauritania was part of Morocco, a declaration viewed by its neighbour to the south as an attack on its sovereignty. In reaction to this the Ministry of Foreign Affairs described these statements as 'dangerous and irresponsible', thus undermining the conduct of negotiations and the *Istiqlal*'s access to a future government.

8. Benkirane, backed by his party, insisted on the refusal to let the USFP into the government coalition especially after the controversial election of one of its main leaders, Habib El Malki, as speaker of the lower house despite the mediocre score of his party in the 2016 legislative elections, when the USFP won only 20 seats out of 395.

Bibliography

Badie, Bertrand, Dirk Berg-Schlosser and Leonardo Morlino (2011), *International Encyclopaedia of Political Science*, London: Sage.

Boudarham, Mohammed (2012), 'La Vérité sur l'assassinat de Omar Benjelloun', *TelQuel* 531, <http://telquel.ma/2012/07/19/Enquete-la-verite-sur-l-assassinat-de-Omar-Benjelloun_531_3631> (last accessed 1 September 2017).

Bruckner, Pascal (2010), *The Tyranny of Guilt: An Essay on Western Masochism*, Princeton, NJ: Princeton University Press.

Casal Bértoa, Fernando (2017), 'Political Parties or Party Systems? Assessing the "Myth" of Institutionalisation and Democracy', *West European Politics* 40: 2, 402–29.

Catusse, Myriam (2013), 'Beyond "Opposition to His Majesty": Mobilizations, Protests, and Political Conflicts in Morocco', *Pouvoirs* 145, 31–46.

Cavatorta, Francesco, and Fabio Merone (2013), 'Moderation through Exclusion? The Journey of the Tunisian Ennahda from Fundamentalist to Conservative Party', *Democratization* 20: 5, 857–75.

Clark, Janine (2004), *Islam, Charity, and Activism: Middle-Class Networks and Social Welfare in Egypt, Jordan, and Yemen*, Bloomington: Indiana University Press.

Constant, Benjamin (1837), *Cours de Politique Constitutionnelle*, <https://archive.org/details/coursdepolitiqu00consgoog> (last accessed 1 September 2017).

Dalmasso, Emanuela (2012), 'Surfing the Democratic Tsunami in Morocco: Apolitical Society and the Reconfiguration of a Sustainable Authoritarian Regime', *Mediterranean Politics* 17: 2, 217–32.

de la Puerta, Javier (2016), 'Politics in the Middle East: The Arab Winter', *The Economist*, <http://dare-think.com/2016/02/politics-in-the-middle-east-the-arab-winter/> (last accessed 1 September 2017).

Eberlein, Burkard (2011), 'Institutionalization', in Badie Bertrand, Dirk Berg-Schlosser and Leonardo Morlino (eds), *International Encyclopedia of Political Science*, Thousand Oaks, CA: Sage.

Ghannouchi, Rachid (2016), 'From Political Islam to Muslim Democracy: The Ennahda Party and the Future of Tunisia', *Foreign Affairs* 95: 5, 58–67.

Guazzone, Laura (2013), 'Ennahda Islamists and the Test of Government in Tunisia', *International Spectator* 48: 4, 30–50.

Hamid, Shadi (2014), 'Political Party Development before and after the Arab Spring', in Mehran Kamrava (ed.), *Beyond the Arab Spring: The Evolving Ruling Bargain in the Middle East*, Oxford: Oxford University Press, pp. 131–50.

Harmel, Robert, and Lars Svåsand (1993), 'Party Leadership and Party Institutionalisation: Three Phases of Development', *West European Politics* 16: 2, 67–88.

Hinnebusch, Raymond (2015), 'From Arab Spring to Arab Winter: Explaining the Limits of Post-Uprising Democratisation', *Democratization* 22: 2, 205–374.

Huntington, Samuel (1968), *Political Order in Changing Societies*, New Haven, CT: Yale University Press.

Huntington, Samuel (1991), *The Third Wave: Democratization in the Late Twentieth Century*, Norman: University of Oklahoma Press.

Inter-Parliamentary Union (n.d.), 'Morocco: Majliss-annouwab (House of Representatives)', <http://www.ipu.org/parline-e/reports/2221_E.htm> (last accessed 4 September 2017).

Janda, Kenneth (1970), *A Conceptual Framework for the Comparative Analysis of Political Parties*, Beverly Hills: Sage.

Joseph, Richard (1987), *Democracy and Prebendal Politics in Nigeria: The Rise and Fall of the Second Republic*, Cambridge: Cambridge University Press.

Kalua, Phaniso (2011), 'The Extent of Political Party Institutionalization in Malawi: The Case of United Democratic Front (UDF) and Malawi Congress Party (MCP)', *Forum for Development Studies* 38: 1, 43–63.

Krämer, Gudrun (2008), *A History of Palestine*, Princeton, NJ: Princeton University Press.

Liddell, James (2010), 'Notables, Clientelism and the Politics of Change in Morocco', *Journal of North African Studies* 15: 3, 315–31.

Limam, Wajdi (2016), 'Les Leçons du Mouvement tunisien du 18 octobre, de l'unité contre la dictature à la lutte pour la sauvegarde de la démocratie', *Huffington Post*, 5 October, <http://www.huffingtonpost.fr/wajdi-limam/democratie-tunisie-18-octobre_b_9571270.html> (last accessed 1 September 2017).

Lust-Okar, Ellen (2004), 'Divided They Rule: The Management and Manipulation of Political Opposition', *Comparative Politics* 36: 2, 159–79.

Lust-Okar, Ellen (2005), *Structuring Conflict in the Arab World: Incumbents, Opponents, and Institutions*, Cambridge: Cambridge University Press.

Lynch, Marc (2014), *The Arab Uprisings Explained, New Contentious Politics in the Middle East*, New York: Columbia University Press.

Macé, Celian, and Margot Chevance (2016), 'Maroc: Les islamistes au centre du jeu', *Libération*, 6 October, <http://www.liberation.fr/planete/2016/10/06/maroc-les-islamistes-au-centre-du-jeu_1520196> (last accessed 1 September 2017).

Mohsen-Finan, Kadja, and Malika Zeghal (2006), 'Opposition islamiste et pouvoir monarchique au Maroc. Le cas du Parti de la Justice et du Développement', *Revue française de science politique* 56: 1, 79–119.

Moroccan Ministry of the Interior (2016), 'Elections législatives du 7 octobre 2016', <http://www.maroc.ma/fr/actualites/elections-legislatives-2016> (last accessed 25 June 2017).

Nathan, Andrew (2003), 'Authoritarian Resilience', *Journal of Democracy* 14: 1, 6–17.

National Democratic Institute (2007), *Final Report on the Moroccan Legislative Elections of 2007*, Washington DC: National Democratic Institute, <https://www.ndi.org/sites/default/files/2316_ma_report_electionsfinal_en_051508_1.pdf> (last accessed 1 September 2017).

National Democratic Institute (2011), *Final Report on the Moroccan Legislative Elections of 2011*, Washington DC: National Democratic Institute, <https://www.ndi.org/sites/default/files/Morocco-Final-Election-Report-061812-ENG.pdf> (last accessed 25 June 2017).

Netterstrøm, Kasper (2015), 'The Islamists' Compromise in Tunisia', *Journal of Democracy* 26: 4, 110–24.

Nohlen, Dieter, Bernard Thibaut and Michael Krennerich (1999), *Elections in Africa: A Data Handbook*, Oxford: Oxford University Press.

Pellicer, Miquel, and Eva Wegner (2015), 'The Justice and Development Party in Moroccan Local Politics', *Middle East Journal* 69: 1, 32–50.

Pioppi, Daniela (2013), 'Playing with Fire. The Muslim Brotherhood and the Egyptian Leviathan', *International Spectator* 48: 4, 51–68.

Randall, Vicky (2006), 'Party Institutionalization and Its Implications for Democracy', paper presented at the IPSA Conference in Fukuoka, 9–13 July, <http://archives.cap.anu.edu.au/cdi_anu_edu_au/cdinews/featured_articles/featured-articles_dowloads/2006_08_CDI.News_AUG_SEP_FA_2_Randall.pdf> (last accessed 1 September 2017).

Randall, Vicky, and Lars Svåsand (1999), *Party Institutionalization and the New Democracies*, paper for the ECPR Joint Session of Workshops, Mannheim, 23–31 March.

Randall, Vicky, and Lars Svåsand (2002), 'Party Institutionalization in New Democracies', *Party Politics* 8: 1, 5–29.

Rashwan, Dina (2007), *The Spectrum of Islamist Movements Vol. 1*, Berlin: Verlag Hans Schiler/al-Ahram Centre for Political and Strategic Studies.

el-Said, Hamed, and James Rauch (2015), 'Education, Political Participation, and Islamist Parties: The Case of Jordan's Islamic Action Front', *Middle East Journal* 69: 1, 51–73.

Schlumberger, Oliver (2007), *Debating Arab Authoritarianism: Dynamics and Durability in Nondemocratic Regimes*, Stanford: Stanford University Press.

Schwartz, Stephen (2006), 'What Is "Islamofascism?"', *The Weekly Standard*, 16 August, <http://www.weeklystandard.com/what-is-islamofascism/article/13723> (last accessed 1 September 2017).

Willis Michael (1999), 'Between *Alternance* and the *Makhzen*: At Tawhid wa Al Islah's Entry into Moroccan Politics', *Journal of North African Studies* 4: 3, 45–80.

Woltering, Robert (2002), 'The Roots of Islamist Popularity', *Third World Quarterly* 23: 6, 1133–43.

Chapter 5

Do Salafi parties represent a contradiction in terms? The development and fragmentation of Kuwait's Salafi Islamic Group

Zoltan Pall

Salafism is best known as a proselytisation (*da'wa*) movement that intends to change the religious identity of other Muslims. Salafis intend to imitate the religious practices and morality of the first three generations of believers (*al-salaf al-salih*, righteous ancestors), and to do so they adopt a literal understanding of the scripture.

The ultimate aim of Salafism is make other Muslims leave other inter-pretations that are seen as distorted from the pure form of religion and accept that their version of Islam is the orthodox one. To achieve this aim, Salafis mostly focus on the correctness of minute details of religious practice and belief, and seem to be much less interested in political issues (Wiktorowicz 2006; Haykel 2009; Gauvain 2013). Yet, Salafis have been participating in parliamentary politics and established political parties in the early 1980s in Kuwait (Pall 2017), and after the 2011 Arab Uprisings Salafi parties have appeared on the scene in Egypt (Hoigilt and Nome 2014), Tunisia (Merone and Cavatorta 2013) and Yemen (Kuschnitzki 2014). Salafi parties also exist in Bahrain and Pakistan.

A number of recent studies therefore focus on the participation of Salafis in parliamentary politics (Utvik 2014; Monroe 2012), with most of these investigating the role of the members of the movement in the legislature. Researchers are particularly interested in how Salafis deal with political activism in a mostly secular environment or whether they accept democracy (Monroe 2012). With the notable exception of Drevon (2015), not many have ventured to look at the dynamics of the political organisations that Salafis establish in order to gain a presence in institutional politics. Based on their observations of the behaviour and strategies of Salafi members of parliament (MPs), academic experts often draw the conclusion that Salafism is no different from other Islamic movements when it comes to political participation (Utvik 2014).

The aim of this chapter is to analyse the organisational dynamics of Salafi parties and ask whether Salafi parties are similar to other Islamist parties or is it possible to observe specific differences rooted in the nature of Salafism? This chapter looks at the evolution and organisational structure of Kuwait's most established Salafi party, *al-Tajammu' al-Salafi al-Islami* (Salafi Islamic Group; SIG). The SIG serves as an ideal case study to observe the behaviour of a Salafi political party and analyse the dynamics that characterise Salafi political engagement in established institutions. It is the world's oldest Salafi political organisation and has been participating in parliamentary politics for more than three decades, whereas Salafi political parties in Egypt, Yemen and Tunisia were established only recently. In addition, the political circumstances in both countries have not been appropriate to inquire about the dynamics of Salafi political organisations in a relatively stable and competitive parliamentary system. In Egypt and Yemen the political process abruptly ended, while in Tunisia Salafi parties remain marginal and failed to win a single parliamentary seat in the two post-Arab Uprisings elections of 2011 and 2014.

As discussed in detail later, the SIG went through a number of splits over ideological issues, which led to a multifaceted Salafi political scene in Kuwait. Furthermore, the SIG shows weaknesses in institution building. In this it is similar to other, non-Islamic Kuwaiti parties, although unlike most of the latter, the SIG made serious attempts to create an extensive organisational framework. This chapter deals specifically with the question of why the SIG is different in this respect from the Kuwaiti Muslim Brotherhood despite the fact that Salafis and Muslim Brothers entered parliamentary politics at the same time in 1981.

This chapter argues that the establishment of the SIG was justified by the necessity to protect the *da'wa* from perceived external threats, and by the fear of marginalisation due to the lack of political representation. Therefore, the Salafis' aim in creating political organisations was not to implement a coherent political vision or agenda, but can be seen as a defensive move to protect more important priorities. It is here that one can begin to explore the contradiction of creating a Salafi political party. Participating in parliamentary politics requires the establishment of some sort of formal organisational structure, yet Salafis are most often suspicious of formal organisations and argue that they lead to *hizbiyya* (partisanship), which makes Muslims loyal to their *hizb* (party, faction), and its leader instead of God. Furthermore, Salafis strongly disagree on the legitimacy of participating in parliamentary politics. This ideological stance explains why Salafis frequently split along the lines of opposing discourses regarding politics and find it difficult to maintain strong and integrated institutional structures.

Empirical work for this chapter was conducted during multiple rounds of fieldwork in Kuwait between 2010 and 2016. Evidence consists mostly of semi-structured interviews and participant observations.

Parties and social movements

In order to understand the relationship of Salafi parties with the larger Salafi movement, two basic concepts need to be clarified. First, a number of theorists of party politics define groups and organisations that bring together individuals to capture parliamentary seats and exercise power within the state as political parties (Ware 1996; Schlesinger 1991). Such a definition is sufficiently broad to include Kuwaiti political organisations in the absence of legal regulations and institutionalisation of party politics. Second, Salafism may be conceptualised as a social movement. Diani (2000: 13) defines social movements as 'networks of informal interactions, between a plurality of individuals, groups or associations, engaged in a political or cultural conflict, on the basis of a shared collective identity'. Salafis struggle with other actors in order to change the religious identity of society according to their own understanding of Islam. For this, they engage in contentious politics in different domains, such as preaching, the media (including the Internet) and, in certain cases, institutional politics.

Broadly speaking, political parties and social movements can overlap and often are intertwined (Goldstone 2003). Parties, in fact, frequently grow out of social movements (Van Cott 2005) and this is the case of many Islamist parties. It follows that parties are in many cases the political arms of larger Islamic movements. The Lebanese *Hezbollah* is also a good example of this, whereby its political organisation was created to serve the movement's interests in the Lebanese legislature, as Daher shows convincingly in her chapter in this volume. The same can be said of Islamist parties linked to the Muslim Brotherhood, which El Kyak extensively discusses in his chapter in relation to the Moroccan Justice and Development Party (PJD).

The case of the SIG in Kuwait is similar. The party is part of the so-called *al-Jama'a al-Salafiyya* (Salafi Community; SC), an organisation that includes the majority of Salafis in Kuwait and that is active in politics, religious proselytising and charity. Because of this, the SIG is fundamentally different from mainstream Kuwaiti parties that are often no more than ad hoc interest groups, and it resembles instead Kuwait's other major Islamist party *al-Haraka al-Dusturiyya al-Islamiyya* (Islamic Constitutional Movement; ICM), the political wing of the Muslim Brotherhood.

Al-Jama'a al-Salafiyya: emergence and structure

By the early 1990s most Kuwaiti Salafis were under the umbrella of the SC. The latter possessed an elaborate and extensive institutional structure, which had been created according to the vision of the main Salafi authority in Kuwait, Shaykh 'Abd al-Rahman 'Abd al-Khaliq. This institutional structure was then employed to establish a Salafi presence in the country's parliament.

To understand the Salafis' political role in Kuwait, it is necessary to examine briefly the country's political system, although a much more detailed discussion can be found in Kraetzschmar's chapter in this volume. Michael Herb (1999) calls Kuwait – along with the other Gulf States – a dynastic monarchy, which means that the most important political and administrative positions are distributed between the members of the ruling royal family. At the same time, the Kuwait ruling family, al-Sabah, provides space for opposition movements and personalities in the form of a relatively powerful legislature (Herb 2016). In this parliament (*majlis*), most of the political parties belong to the category of elite parties (Gunther and Diamond 2003), a loose group of parliamentarians without significant organisational structure or ideology. These parties, with a few exceptions, build on patron–client relationships as their main electoral strategy (Gunther and Diamond 2003). Since the establishment of the *majlis* in 1962 and until the 1980s, the main political cleavage in the parliament pitted the al-Sabah family and its loyalists against Arab nationalist factions, with the latter openly demanding the curbing of the ruling family's power; for example, their slogan was '*izalat haybat al-sulta* (doing away with awe of the regime)' (Herb 1999: 163).

As in other Arab countries at the time, al-Sabah combined a strategy of repression, social engineering and supporting political groups willing to ally with the ruling family to counter the perceived threat coming from the Arab nationalists bloc. In 1976 the emir suspended the parliament and banned the Arab nationalists' main organisational body, *Nadi al-Istiqlal* (Independence Club) (al-Sa'idi 2016). During the 1960s and 1970s the ruling family also granted full citizenship to around 200,000 tribesmen, who previously had been excluded from political participation (Beaugrand 2016). These proved to be loyal allies of al-Sabah against its opposition, which had mostly urban origins – the *hadar* (Beaugrand 2016).

In addition to the repressive measures against the opposition and the restructuring of the demographic make-up of Kuwait, al-Sabah promoted the integration of the nascent Islamist movements into the Kuwaiti parliamentary system. As other contributors make clear, the co-optation of Islamists during the 1970s and 1980s to meet the challenges coming from leftists and Arab nationalists was a familiar strategy for Arab autocrats. The Kuwaiti ruling family first turned to the Muslim Brotherhood, represented by *Jama'iyyat al-Islah al-Ijtima'i* (Social Reform Society; SRS), to help to counterbalance Arab nationalists. After the dissolution of parliament in 1976, the rulers appointed the head of the SRS as minister of religious affairs (*wazir al-awqaf*) (al-Sa'idi 2016: 16). This hallmarked the beginning of the Brotherhood's participation in Kuwaiti institutional politics and its expansion in the country's Islamic institutional system.

Yet, al-Sabah intended from the beginning to prevent the Muslim Brotherhood's total dominance of Kuwait's Islamist scene, and the emerging Salafi movement seemed an ideal candidate to counterbalance the Brothers given the ideological animosity that traditionally characterised the relations between the two movements. Contemporary Salafism emerged in Kuwait in the 1960s due to the activities of a number of preachers who had gained their religious education in Saudi Arabia and later settled in the country. Salafis first set up informal structured networks centred in mosques and *diwaniyyas* (traditional Kuwaiti gatherings). The institutionalisation of the movement began in the 1970s mostly due to one of the main Salafi authoritative figures, the Egyptian Shaykh 'Abd al-Rahman 'Abd al-Khaliq.

Shaykh 'Abd al-Rahman, who had begun his Islamic activism with the Muslim Brothers of Egypt, urged Salafis to step out of informality and establish formal organisations in order to spread their doctrine more effectively.[1] As a result Salafis began participating in trade unions and in

Kuwait University's student organisations and got elected to the executive bodies of the cooperative societies (*al-jama'iyyat al-ta'awuniyya*).[2] Until the mid-1970s Salafis closely cooperated with the Muslim Brotherhood. In the early 1970s 'Abd al-Rahman 'Abd al-Khaliq and other prominent Salafi leaders were members of the SRS but, as a number of veteran Salafis and Brotherhood members claim, without being part of the Brotherhood's larger organisational structure.[3] In 1974 the Salafis left the organisation due to a series of ideological disagreements with members of the Brotherhood.[4] 'Abd al-Rahman 'Abd al-Khaliq and his fellow Salafis criticised the SRS because it published positive articles about Sufism in its magazine *al-Mujtama'* (The Society). This was highly problematic because Salafis generally oppose Sufism, labelling its practices harmful innovations (*bida'*) that have no basis in the scripture. In 1984 'Abd al-Rahman 'Abd al-Khaliq even wrote a book about the heretic character of Sufism.

Al-Sabah capitalised on this rift and helped the Salafi movement to become an influential actor on Kuwait's Islamic scene able to compete with the Muslim Brotherhood. The ruling family provided financial support to the Salafis so that they could create their own umbrella organisation, similar to the SRS. *Jamai'yyat Ihya' al-Turath al-Islami* (Society for the Revival of Islamic Heritage; SRIH) was established in 1981. A member of the al-Sabah family, Shaykh Fahad al-Ahmad, was among the founders of the SRIH and, according to a veteran Salafi, provided a substantial share of its start-up capital.[5] From this, it follows that it is reasonable to think that the ruling family intended to empower Salafis in order to create a considerable parliamentary force to counterbalance the Muslim Brotherhood in the *majlis* (al-Khalidi 1999). It is no surprise that Salafis first participated in parliamentary elections in 1981 and managed to send two MPs to the legislature.

'Abd al-Rahman 'Abd al-Khaliq and his followers justified this step by emphasising the necessity to protect the *da'wa* from three main dangers. The first one was the presence of secular forces that wanted to transform society according to western ideals and reduce the role of religion. The second was the perceived threat coming from the Shi'i after the 1979 Iranian revolution and Khomeini's not-so-veiled threat of exporting the revolution to the Arab world. Finally, Shaykh 'Abd al-Rahman was concerned that without political representation the Muslim Brotherhood would dominate the Islamic scene in Kuwait and Salafis would be marginalised.[6]

Interestingly, three decades later the motives of Salafis in Egypt and Tunisia were similar when they decided to stand candidates in the post-Arab Uprisings elections. In Egypt, Salafis entered parliamentary politics because they feared that in the absence of a clear institutional engagement they would become irrelevant in Egypt's public sphere. Muhammad Nur, former spokesman of the *Hizb al-Nur* (Party of Light), justified political participation as an attempt to 'protect Egypt's Islamic identity' (al-Anani 2017: 34–5). In Tunisia, Salafis decided to participate in the elections after the fall of the regime of Ben Ali because they feared that the mainstream Muslim Brotherhood oriented party *Ennahda* had adopted a 'liberal' stance on a number of issues, thus endangering the country's Muslim character (Torelli 2017).

In any case, the decision to participate in the Kuwaiti elections in 1981 became the first issue that caused a split in the Salafi movement. When Shaykh 'Abd al-Rahman 'Abd al-Khaliq and his associates suggested considering standing candidates for the elections, a group of Salafis harshly rejected the idea. As Ahmad Baqir, a senior Salafi politician, recalls, this group of dissidents travelled to Saudi Arabia to ask the, perhaps, most renowned Salafi scholar of the time, Ibn Baz, what to do.

The dissident Kuwaiti Salafis expected Shaykh Ibn Baz to confirm their stance and issue a fatwa that would forbid electoral participation. However, the opposite occurred. Ibn Baz told them it was obligatory to participate in the elections and get as many parliamentary seats as possible. This was in order to counterbalance the Arab nationalist forces of the Kuwaiti political scene and secure the nascent *da'wa*.[7] Ibn Baz's opinion was sufficient for the majority of Kuwaiti Salafis to support electoral participation, but a minority was not satisfied and argued that Ibn Baz did not sanction the establishment of political parties and agreed only on individual candidatures. Yet the Salafis, just like the Muslim Brotherhood, had already created an electoral machine and organised electoral campaigns. Thus they had already established a political party and committed the sin of *hizbiyya*. Most of these rejectionist Salafis relied on al-Albani's opinion. This leading Salafi scholar disapproved of both individual candidatures and the establishment of political organisations.[8] Subsequently this group split from the main body of Kuwaiti Salafism and continued its activities separately. Today they are widely known in Kuwait as *Jamis* or *Madkhalis* in reference to two of their main religious authorities, the Ethiopian Muhammad Aman al-Jami (1930–95) and the Saudi Rabi' al-Madkhali (1932).[9]

The reason why the majority of Kuwaiti Salafis did not see the creation of political organisations as a sin is to be found in the influence that Shaykh 'Abd al-Rahman 'Abd al-Khaliq exerted. He argued that the Prophet himself used the most advanced tools available in his time for his *da'wa*. According to 'Abd al-Rahman ('Abd al-Khaliq 1985), at the present time political parties are among the most advanced tools to spread the Salafi call. Without organisational structures and parties, Salafis would not be able to face the danger coming from the secularists and the tyrants of the Middle East. For Shaykh 'Abd al-Rahman the argument that forming parties is *hizbiyya* because they fragment the *Umma* is insufficiently convincing. In fact, he suggests, members of parliament who do not belong to any party and do not have to follow party discipline contribute more to the fragmentation of Muslims than elected representatives affiliated to political parties. The reason is that without the control of an organisation there is always a danger that they would be bribed by either the ruler or the secularists to work against Muslims.[10] Shaykh 'Abd al-Rahman's arguments show considerable pragmatism and demonstrate that Salafis usually are able to find precepts in the scripture that justify their positions and choices when circumstances make it necessary to seemingly deviate from traditional stances. Thirty years later, when Egyptian Salafis created political parties, they also simply called them tools for furthering the *da'wa* in the absence of an Islamic state (Olidort 2015).

Following its entry into institutional politics in the early 1980s, Salafism in Kuwait gained greater political prominence after the end of the 1990/1 Iraqi occupation. The emir reinstalled parliament after it had been suspended since 1986. This decision was part of a political bargain made in exile in Saudi Arabia between the various Kuwaiti political forces and the ruling family (Tétreault 2000: 85). In the 1990s and 2000s, Salafis often constituted an influential parliamentary bloc with usually five or six MPs (al-Sa'idi 2010).[11] The Salafis' electoral successes are the result of a number of factors. First, the number of committed Salafis significantly grew since the 1980s. In particular, the 1990/1 Iraqi invasion of the country and the subsequent Gulf War led to a general increase in religiosity in Kuwaiti society. Large numbers of Kuwaitis sought refuge in Saudi Arabia where they received the message of religious scholars who argued that the invasion was God's punishment for the ostensibly un-Islamic lifestyle Kuwaitis led.[12] Second, the Salafis enjoyed widespread popularity among the tribes, as many of the Kuwaiti tribesmen have primordial connections to Najd, one of the centres of the Salafi *da'wa*.

Furthermore, Arab nationalism as an alternative ideological and political programme historically held little appeal for Kuwaiti tribesmen, as it was mostly associated with the *hadar* (Herb 1999), and the tribal population of Kuwait by the 1990s had outgrown those whose ancestors were city dwellers (al-Nakib 2014). Finally, the 1981 redrawing of the electoral districts also favoured tribal voters (Beaugrand 2016). Given all this, it is no wonder that during the 1992 elections both the Muslim Brotherhood and the Salafis did rather well (al-Najjar 1995).[13]

The post-invasion period also saw the creation of Islamist political organisations officially separate from the charities that served as umbrella organisations for the Muslim Brotherhood and the Salafis. The former established the Islamic Constitutional Movement (*al-Haraka al-Dustriyya al-Islamiyya*; ICM) to serve as the Brotherhood's political arm, and which is legally separate from the SRS. The Salafis established the Popular Islamic Gathering (*al-Tajammu' al-Islami al-Sha'bi*), renamed the SIG in 2000, as a different organisation from the SRIH (al-Sa'idi 2010).[14]

The structure of *al-Jama'a al-Salafiyya*

Although officially a separate organisation, the SIG is fully integrated into a larger organisational structure created according to the vision of 'Abd al-Rahman 'Abd al-Khaliq, and which was modelled on the Muslim Brotherhood. In fact, establishing such an organisational structure is rather exceptional, as in most other places Salafis largely rely on informal and interpersonal networks. Although this organisational structure (*tanzim*) has never been revealed openly and most Salafis deny its existence, it is a well-known secret in Kuwait. During my fieldwork I managed to interview a number of Salafis who were able to give me a detailed picture what the *tanzim* looks like. These people were either former members who had left the SC for ideological reasons, or internal dissidents who believed that the analysis of a western researcher might help breathe new life into an increasingly fragmented and malfunctioning organisation.

The main governing body of *al-Jama'a* is the fifty-member *al-Jama'iyya al-'Umumiyya* (General Assembly; GA) and it consists of the most influential Salafi politicians, leading members of the SRIH and the most influential *ulama*. The GA is responsible for electing the Salafi emir and it makes the most important decisions. This governing body also supervises the other institutional bodies of *al-Jama'a al-Salafiyya*, such as the SIG, the SRIH and the so-called *Tanzim al-Manatiq* (The Organization of the Regions). The political wing of *al-Jama'a al-Salafiyya*, the SIG, also has an elaborate institutional structure. Its *shura* (council) consists of the MPs and a number of ex-MPs (seven to ten members). The *shura* elects *al-amin al-'amm* (the secretary general) and approves the SIG's policies. Yet, the most important political decisions, such as questioning a minister or proposing a new law, have to be approved by the GA. Furthermore, the SIG has a sharia council (*lajna shara'iyya*) that supervises the day-to-day policy-making of the SIG through the lens of the rulings of Salafism. The SIG is also closely connected to *Tanzim al-Manatiq*. The latter includes *majalis manatiq* (regional councils) in each electoral district (currently five, previously twenty-five). These *majalis* are intended to be responsible for *da'wa* activities, such as religious lessons and programmes for the youth. Yet, they are also employed for facilitating *al-Jama'a*'s political participation. *Majalis al-manatiq* carry out electoral campaigns, for example, and have the right to offer their opinion about the candidates.

Al-Jama'a's student organisation, *al-Ittihad al-Islami* (Islamic Union; IU) is directly responsible to the GA, but coordinates its activities and stances with the political party, the SIG. The student organisation competes in the elections of Kuwait University's student union (*Ittihad al-Talaba*). Having a strong presence in the student union is important because it can facilitate the *da'wa* on campus, as the union has the right to organise events and programmes for the students. In addition to preaching, IU is important for the SIG due to its role in the political socialisation of Salafis. Most Salafi politicians start their political activism in the IU. Those who have proved to be successful student leaders become candidates at the elections of Kuwait's cooperative societies (*jama'iyya ta'awuniyya*) or jump directly to contesting seats in municipal councils (*baladiyya*). The end stage of this process is getting elected to parliament. Students can also constitute a considerable voting bloc in parliamentary elections. Kuwait University has more than 40,000 students and the majority is Kuwaiti citizens over the age of twenty-one. Therefore, the IU plays a role in the SIG's political campaigns among students, despite the fact that this is technically forbidden according to the university's regulations.[15]

The above discussion shows that the SIG cannot be separated from *al-Jama'a*; rather, it has to be regarded as an integral part of the latter. Other organisational bodies of *al-Jama'a* play indispensable roles in organising its political campaign and in the socialisation of its future members. Furthermore, the SIG is subordinate to the GA, the governing body of *al-Jama'a*.

Among the few examples when Salafis created a similarly extensive organisational structure to Kuwait's *al-Jama'a* is the Egyptian *al-Da'wa al-Salafiyya* (Salafi Call). *Al-Da'wa* in the 1980s, inspired by 'Abd al-Rahman 'Abd al-Khaliq, established a main governing council (*shura*), a leadership hierarchy and several regional sections (Lacroix 2016). The largest Salafi party in Egypt, *al-Nur*, grew out of this organisation, and currently serves as *al-Da'wa*'s political arm after serious internal debates and schisms (Lacroix 2016).

While Salafis tried to create organisations elsewhere as well, their structures are much more rudimentary, due either to a lack of resources and/or ideological disagreements, and the repressive political environment. In Tunisia, for example, the largest Salafi organisation, *Ansar al-Shari'a*, faced considerable difficulties in transforming its loose and informal networks into an effective top-down organisation due to the resistance of many of its members who believe that such organisations oppose the teachings of Islam (Merone and Cavatorta 2013).

The fragmentation of *al-Jama'a al-Salafiyya*

Despite its solidity and complexity, this organisational structure never really worked perfectly and consequently Salafis in Kuwait are not able to create a unified political project. The *tanzim* could contain neither ideological disagreements nor tensions stemming from the members' different social backgrounds. A member of the Muslim Brotherhood, who started his Islamic activism among the Salafis in the early 1990s, compared *al-Jama'a*'s structure to that of the Brotherhood. In his view, while the shape of the two organisations was almost the same in theory, *al-Jama'a*'s was far less efficient:

> The Ikhwan had a lot of personal and religious disagreements. Among them there are Salafis in their religious practice (*'ibadat*), and there are those who even sympathise with Sufism ... There are opposing views regarding major political issues. Yet, in the end everybody obeys the decision of the organization.[16]

This did not occur in the Salafi organisation and when a group of Salafis has a different opinion on a specific issue, it often disregards the *tanzim*. The former member gave an example from 1994, when a group of Salafis who called themselves *Shabab Salafiyyu Kifan* (Salafi Youth of Kifan district) sent an open 'letter of advice' to the Salafi infrastructure minister, Jasim al-'Awn, accusing him of not behaving according to the teachings of Islam. They blamed al-'Awn for allegedly shaking hands with women, something strictly forbidden according to Salafism, and having patronised the arts – painting and music.[17] According to the rules of the *tanzim*, the issuers of the letter should have brought their complaints before the *shura* of the SIG, but, instead, they directly published the letter in the press causing embarrassment for both al-'Awn and *al-Jama'a* in general.

Unlike the Muslim Brotherhood, *al-Jama'a al-Salafiyya* has undergone a series of splits during the past two decades. The most important one occurred in the mid-1990s and reflected the Kuwaiti Salafis' ideological and social fragmentation. The transnational ideological dimension of the Salafis' division was perhaps the most visible. It occurred along the lines of the ideological debates that emerged between Salafis in Saudi Arabia during and after the Iraqi invasion of Kuwait over the permissibility of seeking military help from the US against Iraq, and whether Muslims should obey the ruler if he makes obvious mistakes.

As a result of these debates two factions emerged. The so-called *harakis* (or activists) argue that the purity of the religion can be achieved if the state's institutions are Islamised as much as possible. For the sake of this objective Muslims are allowed to openly question and criticise the ruler. Those who belong to the second group stress that the Salafi *da'wa*'s main task is purifying the belief and religious practices of people, hence they are referred to as purists. According to them, the task of governance should be left entirely to the ruler, who deserves obedience as long as he is not openly an apostate. In addition, subjects should not openly criticise the ruler. Many of these people naturally harshly criticise the *harakis* for their political involvement, accusing them of distorting *da'wa*.

In 1996, after an open feud between *harakis* and purists, the latter took over the SRIH, causing the *harakis*, who sympathised with the ideas of Abd al-Rahman 'Abd al-Khaliq, one of the founders of activist Salafism, to leave and establish their own group, *al-Haraka al-Salafiyya al-'Ilmiyya* (Scientific Salafi Movement; SSM) (Pall 2017). The discourse of the organisation radically changed compared with the era when 'Abd al-Rahman 'Abd al-Khaliq dominated it and the SRIH even stopped publishing the latter's works. Instead, it published booklets, mostly written by Saudi purist *ulama*, stressing the necessity of obeying the *hakim*. These booklets present scores of citations from the scripture that supposedly prove that obedience to the Muslim ruler is obligatory for the believers, even if he is unjust. Purists often refer to a hadith that says that Muslims should be patient even if the ruler 'beats your back and takes your property'.

However, even after most of the *harakis* left, *al-Jama'a al-Salafiyya* could not preserve its unity. In 2003, purist Salafis who left the *al-Jama'a* set up another Salafi political party. The group split from the organisation after the SIG did not vote in favour of removing the finance minister Yusuf Ibrahim during a no-confidence vote. The latter is considered a liberal, and often the target of the criticism of the Islamists. Therefore many Salafis considered supporting him a betrayal, which sacrificed the principles of Islam for political interest. A group of secessionists set up a new political organisation under the name of *Tajammu Thawabit al-Umma* (Gathering for the Umma's Principles; GUP). Muhammad Hayif al-Mutayri, the former director of SRIH's *da'wa* department (*hay'at al-da'wa*), became the head of the organisation.[18]

The new party remained ideologically purist. In an interview with the author, Muhammad Hayef profoundly disagreed with those who criticise the *hakim* or organise demonstrations. Yet, he thinks that Salafis should participate in institutional politics and use their political influence to cement the principles of Islam in society, by, for example, promoting laws that forbid *ikhtilat* (the mixing of the sexes) in public institutions. By supporting Yusuf Ibrahim, according to him, the MPs of the SIG stood behind the reviled liberal project, which is the antithesis of what the Salafis are standing for.

Ideological disagreements also played crucial role in the most recent split of the SIG. In December 2010, six members of the party decided to go into opposition, reversing their previous pro-government stance.[19] The immediate reason for this was the government's crackdown on an opposition meeting organised by the ICM politician Jama'an al-Harbash. The security forces beat up some of the MPs who were present at the event, fuelling increasing anti-government sentiment.[20] As one of the MPs, 'Abd al-Latif al-'Umayri, recounted, Khalid Sultan bin 'Issa, the most senior member of the SIG and a former head of the SRIH, proposed that the party could not support the government after that event without losing its credibility. Others, such as Ahmad Baqir, opposed this stance, arguing that openly siding with the opposition was equal to revolting against the ruler (*khrurj 'ala al-hakim*), which is forbidden according to purist Salafis.[21] The rift within the SIG was deepened with the outbreak of the Arab Uprisings in 2010/11.[22] The pro-government faction issued statements that condemned the uprisings, while the others openly supported them.[23]

In 2011 after a series of popular demonstrations, the government of Shaykh Nasir Muhammad al-Sabah resigned, and in February 2012 a pro-opposition parliament, consisting of both Islamic and secular forces, was elected (Ulrichsen 2014). When the Constitutional Court dissolved the parliament in the same year and reinstated the previous one, the opposition decided to boycott the elections. The pro-opposition faction of the SIG left the party and joined the boycott, while the pro-government faction ran in the December 2012 elections.

The fragmentation of the SIG mirrored the ideological disagreements within the *Jama'a* that came to the surface after the Arab Uprisings. A number of shaykhs within *al-Jama'a*, such as Nazim al-Misbah and Nasir Shams al-Din, showed sympathy for both the uprisings in the wider region and the popular demonstrations in Kuwait. They argued that obeying the ruler does not mean that the subjects have no right to participate in decision-making. These shaykhs argued that the emir of Kuwait permits politicians to go into opposition and, therefore, merely siding against the government does not mean revolting against the ruler.[24] Yet purists, who believe that the rulings of Islam oblige Salafis to defend the ruler, maintained the control of *al-Jama'a*. Due to the pressure of *al-Jama'a*'s leaders, Nazim al-Misbah therefore had to change his stance. Nasir Shams al-Din, along with a number of others, instead left *al-Jama'a* altogether.

After this latest split, *al-Jama'a* completely sided with the government. As a reward the SIG member 'Ali al-'Umayr received ministerial positions,[25] while cadres of *al-Jama'a* were allowed to gain more influence in Kuwait's Islamic institutions, such as the Ministry of Religious Affairs and the Bayt al-Zakat, Kuwait's main authority for managing religious taxes. All this happened at the expense of the Muslim Brotherhood, which had previously controlled these institutions. Beyond that, though, the SIG did not seem to benefit much from its close relationship with the rulers. The SIG's traditional constituency saw the party as opportunistic, using Islam as vehicle to gain positions and influence, and this is most probably one of the reasons why the SIG did not win a single seat in the 2016 parliamentary elections (al-Khalidi 2016). Furthermore, a number of Salafis openly broke with the SC, arguing that obedience to the ruler is not equal to infiltrating state institutions, which is the Muslim Brotherhood's strategy.

Accordingly, Shaykh Faysal Quzar, one of Kuwait's most influential Salafi scholars, left the SC in 2013 along with dozens of his associates, and created his own group, informally organised and based on his relationship with his students.[26] Al-Quzar has thousands of sympathisers in Kuwait and his departure might have affected the electoral base of the SIG. The discussion above shows that Salafis can be pragmatic in making political decisions and shape their discourse to match their political interests. Yet the split of Faysal Quzar highlights how ideology constrains pragmatism. When Salafis see that their leaders use the text to further their positions in the state's institutional structure, they secede and form new groups.

In other places where Salafis step out of informality and participate in institutional politics similar debates occur and they often lead to schisms. In Egypt, for example, *Hizb al-Nur* split in 2012 over disagreements about the party's relationship with *al-Da'wa al-Salafiyya*. Two factions emerged within the party. The first one wanted it to become a regular political party independent in its decision-making from *al-Da'wa*. The other faction saw *Hizb al-Nur* only as the lobbying arm of *al-Da'wa* in Egypt's state institutions. The latter faction attacked the former on ideological grounds, criticising, for example, the former's willingness to support Christian candidates during elections. According to them, electing Christians would provide *wilaya* (authority) to non-Muslims over Muslims, which the scripture explicitly forbids. This faction also argued that Islamisation of society would come only through proselytisation (*da'wa*), and not politics. Therefore, the party should use its political presence to further the *da'wa* and not to seek power by making alliances (with seculars, for instance) that are questionable according to specific interpretations of religious injunctions (Lacroix 2016). Ultimately, the first faction seceded from the *Hizb al-Nur* and established a new party, *Hizb al-Watan* (Homeland Party).[27]

In Tunisia similar debates emerged among the members of *Ansar al-Shari'a* networks. The group had the potential to eventually transform itself into a party through the creation of a more integrated institutional structure. However, the camp that opposed the idea argued that establishing a formal organisation would cause further divisions among Muslims instead of unifying them under the flag of their uncorrupted form of Islam (Merone and Cavatorta 2013). Ultimately, state repression solved the group's internal dilemma and *Ansar al-Shari'a* was banned in August 2013. Since then, smaller groups have evolved from the movement's various factions (Merone 2017).

Why do Salafis fragment and the Brotherhood does not?

Here the question is why the trajectory of Salafis in Kuwaiti party politics is so different from that of the Muslim Brotherhood. Specifically, why the SIG experienced so many splits while the ICM managed to keep its unity. As mentioned, the Salafis established similar organisational structures to those of the Muslim Brotherhood. The social make-up of the cadres and supporters of the SIG are also not very different from those of the ICM. The leadership of both parties is predominantly *hadar*, while the majority of the voting base comes from tribal areas. The argument here is that ideology and the Salafis' discourses regarding the permissibility of forming organisational structures play a key role in their fragmentation. This is a point worth exploring further because it places Salafi parties – not only in Kuwait – on a different trajectory from the ones that the Muslim Brothers have created.

The necessity of establishing an extensive organisational structure has been at the centre of the discourse of the Muslim Brotherhood since its inception. The movement's founder, Hasan al-Banna was inspired by the structure of Sufi orders, and imagined Islamic activism carried out through a hierarchical organisation (Krämer 2010). Members of the Brotherhood go through a process of socialisation from childhood and this strengthens their organisational culture (Elshobaki 2012). Just as elsewhere, in Kuwait the Brotherhood is far from monolithic when it comes to ideological views or political stances. In fact, within the movement, there are two main broad ideological directions. The first one is socially conservative. Those who belong to this trend are Salafis in religious practices, and emphasise enforcing conservative social norms in Kuwait, such as gender segregation. Its followers often label the second trend as *munfatih* (open minded). The *munfatihun* (pl. of *munfatih*) argue that the Brotherhood should not focus as much on symbolic issues and the Islamisation of the legal system. For them it is more important to establish a government that is accountable to citizens, and abolish nepotism and corruption in business or in the job market. As members of the Brotherhood have declared, an Islamic state is first and foremost a state based on social justice and accountability.[28]

Political opinions are also diverse within the Kuwaiti Muslim Brotherhood, and even within its political party, the ICM. The ICM politicians disagreed, for instance, on whether they should contest the

2017 elections after the party boycotted electoral participation in 2012, or whether they should renew the boycott. At the ICM's general assembly in May 2016 members voted for participation. Despite the fact that almost half of the participants strongly opposed giving up the boycott, they did not split to form a different group, but accepted the decision of the majority. The way in which this so-called democratic centralism works is analysed in detail in El Kyak's chapter in this volume. In similar fashion, other differences and conflicts are resolved within the organisation of the Brotherhood, as most of the members accept the decision made either by the leadership or by the majority.

The Salafi discourse about establishing organisational structures is radically different. The most prominent of the Salafi *ulama*, such as Ibn Baz, Ibn 'Uthaymin and al-Albani, looked at creating formal organisa-tions of any kind – be they NGOs or political parties – with suspicion, despite Ibn Baz not opposing electoral participation if the candidates are independent, and not party members. The great Salafi *ulama* argued that establishing organisations (*tanzim*) or working within them carries the danger of *hizbiyya*.[29] Al-Albani even went as far as calling political parties tools of the unbelievers, which Muslims cannot use to build an Islamic society.[30] The opinion of these *ulama* is crucially important because purist Salafis in particular regard them as one of their main references. Thus, after the purist takeover of *al-Jama'a* in 1996, many members felt uneasy that the new leadership kept in place the organisational structure that had been established by 'Abd al-Rahman 'Abd al-Khaliq. As former purist members of *al-Jama'a* recount, they found it contradictory that the SRIH published books condemning *hizbiyya* while being linked to a partisan organisation.[31] The aforementioned Shaykh Faysal Quzar, in one of his books, argued that the SC commits *bida'* by maintaining a hierarchical organisation. According to his reasoning, the pious ancestors (*Salaf*) were capable of establishing hierarchical organisations to facilitate the spread of Islam, yet they never did, precisely to avoid *hizbiyya* (al-Jasim 2015).

Shaykh Ahmad Abu Mus'ab, a scholar from the al-Hadiya region, was among those who left *al-Jama'a* due to his concerns about the existing organisational structure and especially due to its links to the SIG. In the late 1990s he used to be the imam of a mosque controlled by *al-Jama'a*. As he recalled, his superiors gave him the order to participate in the 1998 electoral campaign for the SIG in al-Hadiya. He had to campaign for the SIG candidates during religious lessons, visit *diwaniyyas* and organise various campaign events. As he explains:

> this is not the task of an imam. I need to take care of the religious activities in my mosque and provide answers if Muslims in my region have questions related to Islam ... and what if I think that the candidate is not a good Muslim or he would not serve the interest of Muslims? The SC does not give me the choice to campaign for someone else.[32]

In Shaykh Ahmad's perspective this is precisely *hizbiyya* because he would have to support a candidate who might harm Muslims out of loyalty to the organisation.

A more recent case demonstrates the SIG's organisational ineffectiveness. In February 2016 a by-election was held in Kuwait's third electoral district.[33] Although there were no Salafi candidates, the SIG played a significant role in the campaign because its leaders wanted to avoid the victory of a Shi'i candidate. The party endorsed one of the Sunni candidates, 'Ali al-Khamis. Yet, a few days before the voting a rift erupted between the members of *al-Jama'a*'s regional council in the third electoral district. Some of the members refused to support 'Ali al-Khamis, questioning his moral qualities and arguing that there were other Sunni candidates who were better individuals. The SIG's stance was that al-Khamis had the best chance of winning and should therefore be supported. The *mus'ul siyasi* of the district argued that al-Khamis might be morally corrupt (*fasiq*), but he had good qualities as a leader. He cited the stance of the medieval Hanbali scholar Ibn Taymiyya whom the Salafis greatly value. According to Ibn Taymiyya (1997: 35), a strong leader is better than a righteous one, because 'his moral corruption goes back to him while his strength serves the Muslims'. Those who opposed the election of al-Khamis argued that Ibn Taymiyya meant kings or sultans facing external enemies. If an MP is *fasiq*, he might vote for laws that contradict Islam. If this happens, those who assisted him in winning over someone who is righteous are also responsible before God. In the end 'Ali al-Khamis won, but it is not clear whether the Salafis who opposed him changed their opinion or not. Nevertheless, this story shows that for Salafis ideology comes before party discipline. While the Muslim Brotherhood is open to compromises for the sake of a greater goal, Salafis are prone to sink the ship over seemingly minor issues.

The Salafis' lack of organisational culture makes them susceptible to other divisive factors stemming from the broader socio-political environment. For example, while ideology played a key role in the 1996 split of *al-Jama'a* and the SIG, accounts of some of the Salafi leaders suggest that personal ambitions might have played a role as well. According to Dr Sajid al-'Abdali, a former leader of *al-Haraka al-Salafiyya*, the leading figures of the *harakis*, such as 'Abd al-Razzaq al-Shayiji and Hakim al-Mutayri, aspired to higher positions in *al-Jama'a*. When they could not realise their ambitions they split from the main Salafi organisation and established their own.[34] Some even argue that there is a tribal dimension behind the split, as many of the cadres of *al-Haraka al-Salafiyya* have a tribal background, while the leading figures of *al-Jama'a* and the politicians of the SIG are mostly *hadar*. Tribes in Kuwait constitute more than half of the population and often feel socio-economically disadvantaged compared with the *hadar*. Their role in party politics is explored in detail in Kraetzschmar's chapter in this volume.

Members of *al-Jama'a* also suggested that beyond ideological debates and personal rivalries there was an internal power struggle between Khalid Sultan and other high-ranking leaders of *al-Jama'a* behind the former's decision to leave the SIG along with his allies. Furthermore, Khalid Sultan's business disputes with some members of the al-Sabah family who are close to the emir also played a role in pushing him into opposition.[35]

The above-mentioned factors are similar to the ones that tear apart non-Islamist Kuwaiti parties as well. The reason why urban–rural (tribal) cleavages, power struggles and personal rivalries can break up the unity of a party lies in part in the nature of the Kuwaiti electoral system. Since political parties are not formally legalised in Kuwait, people vote for individual candidates and not party lists. Furthermore, due to the relatively low number of voters and the small size of the electoral districts the social standing and networks of the candidate are often more important than his or her party affiliation.

Conclusion: how the case of the SIG helps us to understand Salafi parties in general

In this chapter we have seen that the SIG, Kuwait's oldest Salafi political party, has gone through a series of splits. Furthermore, party discipline among its members can be characterised as low, which leads to weak institutional efficiency. The main reasons for this are to be found not only in the Kuwaiti political system, which makes it hard to establish unified political parties with a sophisticated institutional structure, but also in the nature of Salafi ideology, which remains deeply suspicious of party politics and institution building.

Since the SIG is integrated into the larger institutional structure of the SC, the historical cleavages and tensions among Salafis have been carried over into the party. This is why, despite entering parliament at the same time as the Salafis, the Muslim Brotherhood has gone through far fewer internal conflicts, and no splinter group has emerged from the ranks of the ICM.

This case study on the SIG and Kuwaiti Salafism contributes to a better understanding of the nature of Salafi political parties elsewhere in the Arab world. While in Egypt, Tunisia and Yemen the socio-political conditions are not favourable to observe the dynamics of Salafi parties, some developments might indicate similarities to what we have seen in Kuwait. In Tunisia and Egypt, the Salafi political scene has been fragmented from the beginning, and multiple Salafi parties and groups emerged right after the Arab Uprisings of 2010/11. For instance, Egypt's largest Salafi party, *Hizb al-Nur*, split in 2012. The reason for the split was a power struggle between two factions that involved the question of how to do politics within the framework of the Salafi interpretation of the rulings of Islam, a situation similar to that which led to the split of the Tunisian *Ansar al-Shariʿa*.

In light of the discussion on the political dynamics, rifts and organisational failure of the SIG, and the comparisons with Egyptian and Tunisian Salafi groups, it can be concluded that while Salafis show considerable pragmatism, this pragmatism has limits. Ideological purity plays a crucial role in Salafi parties, and in many cases overwrites mundane political interests. This also makes it difficult for Salafis to cooperate with non-Salafis, and especially with secular political forces. In Kuwait Salafis have often revolted and split if the leaders of their groups seemed to make political compromises at the expense of the purity of the doctrine. In light of this, there is no reason to believe that Salafis elsewhere would behave differently.

Notes

1. His older brother and father were members of the Egyptian Muslim Brotherhood. Interview with the author, Kuwait, 11 March 2012.
2. Kuwait's cooperative societies are department stores that local communities of a specific area manage. Members elect the administrators, and election results often predict the outcome of the next parliamentary elections.

3. Interview with Muhammad Ibrahim al-Shaybani, Kuwait, 2 February 2016.
4. Interview with Muhammad Ibrahim al-Shaybani, Kuwait, 2 February 2016.
5. Interview, Kuwait, 21 April 2016.
6. Interview with Shaykh 'Abd al-Rahman 'Abd al-Khaliq, Kuwait, 11 March 2012.
7. Interview with Ahmad Baqir, Kuwait, 9 February 2016.
8. Interview with Shaykh Salim al-Tawil, Kuwait, 2 February 2012.
9. Both shaykhs were active in Saudi Arabia and were known as strong critics of Islamic movements that engaged in institutional politics. They also fiercely opposed the creation of formal organisations such as parties or associations (*jama'iyya*).
10. Interview with 'Abd al-Rahman 'Abd al-Khaliq, Kuwait, 11 March 2012.
11. Five or six MPs are usually enough to form coalitions with others and influence the outcome of parliamentary decisions, as there are fifty MPs in the Kuwaiti parliament.
12. During my fieldwork in 2012 in Kuwait I had informal conversations with several Salafis who claimed to have joined the movement as a result of the shock they experienced during the Iraqi occupation.
13. The ICM secured six seats in comparison with the SIG's three.
14. The reason is that the government started to enforce a 1962 law that forbids the political involvement of charities.
15. Interview with a former head of IU, Kuwait, 11 March 2016; interviews with a number of student activists from various student organisations, 26 March 2016.
16. Interview, Kuwait, 11 March 2016.
17. *al-Tali'a* newspaper, 1 June 1994.
18. Conversations in Muhammad Hayif al-Mutayri's diwaniyya, Kuwait, 15 February 2016 and 20 April 2016; interview with a former member of GUP, 26 April 2016.
19. *Al-an* news portal, 30 March 2011, available at <http://www.alaan.cc/pagedetails.asp?nid=70946&cid=30#.V7qiLmXAX7Y> (last accessed 10 July 2016).
20. 'Istinkar Niyabi li-Ahdath al-Harbash', *al-Jarida*, 10 December 2010, available at <http://www.aljarida.com/articles/1461907960344565500> (last accessed 11 December 2010).
21. Personal conversation with Ahmad Baqir, Kuwait, 9 February 2016; personal conversation with 'Abd al-Latif al-'Umayri, Kuwait, 11 February 2016; interview with Khalid Sultan bin 'Isa, Kuwait, 3 July 2014.
22. See my analysis in Pall (2017).
23. 'Al-Jiran li-l-Ra'y: "al-Salafi" lam wa lan-Yu'ayyid al-Khuruj 'ala Bashshar', *al-Ra'y*, 27 October 2013, available at <http://www.alraimedia.com/ar/article/local/2013/10/27/461729/nr/nc> (last accessed 25 November 2016).
24. Interview with Shaykh Nazim al-Misbah, Kuwait, 11 November 2013; al-Din (2014).
25. First he became Oil Minister then Minister of Public Works.
26. Faysal al-Quzar used to be the president of League of Europe in the SRIH, a division that is responsible for allocating the donations destined for European Muslim communities.
27. *Al Arabiya*, 25 December 2012, available at <http://www.alarabiya.net/articles/2012/12/25/257011.html> (last accessed 20 November 2016).
28. Series of interviews and informal conversations, Kuwait, January–May 2016.

29. 'Abd al-'Aziz bin Baz, "Hukum al-Intima" ila al-Ahzab al-Diniyya', available at <http://www.binbaz.org.sa/fatawa/177> (last accessed 22 August 2016); Muhammad bin Salih al-'Uthaymin Sharah al-'Arba'in al-Nawawiyya', available at <https://www.youtube.com/watch?v=YafW6KTXejE&list=PL4J7e34bwb6Rd2c mxqCBIC-NNsAIyr1r1> (last accessed 22 August 2016).
30. See <https://www.youtube.com/watch?v=JxbRvAKNq60> (last accessed 22 August 2016).
31. Series of informal talks, Kuwait, January–June 2016.
32. Interview, Kuwait, 16 February 2012.
33. There are five electoral districts in Kuwait today.
34. Interview with Dr Sajid al-'Abdali, Kuwait, 4 March 2012.
35. Informal conversations with Salafis from *al-Jama'a*, Kuwait, April 2016.

Bibliography

'Abd al-Khaliq, 'Abd al-Rahman (1984), *Fada'ih al-Sufiyya*, Kuwait: Dar al-Salafi.

'Abd al-Khaliq, 'Abd al-Rahman (1985), *al-Muslimun wa-l-'Amal al-Siyasi*, Kuwait: Dar al-Salafi.

Aldrich, John (1995), *Why Parties? The Origin and Transformation of Party Politics in America*, Chicago: Chicago University Press.

al-Anani, Khalil (2017), 'Unpacking the Sacred Canopy: Egypt's Salafis between Religion and Politics', in Francesco Cavatorta and Fabio Merone (eds), *Salafism after the Arab Awakening: Contending with People's Power*, London: Hurst, pp. 25–42.

Beaugrand, Claire (2016), 'Deconstructing Minorities/Majorities in Parliamentary Gulf States (Kuwait and Bahrain)', *British Journal of Middle Eastern Studies* 43: 2, 34–49.

bin Taymiyya, Taqi al-Din (1997), *Al-Siyasa al-Shara'iyya*, Riyadh: Wizarat al-Shu'un al-Islamiyya wa-l-Awqaf wa-l-Da'wa wa-l-Irshad.

Diani, Mario (2000), 'The Concept of a Social Movement', in David Snow, Sarah Soule and Hanspeter Kriesi (eds), *Readings in Contemporary Political Sociology*, Oxford: Blackwell Publishers, pp. 1–25.

al-Din, Nasir Shams (2014), 'Khuruq al-Tawil . . . fi-l-Manhaj al-Salafi al-Asil', *al-Watan*, 22 August.

Drevon, Jérôme (2015), 'The Emergence of Ex-Jihadi Political Parties in Post-Mubarak Egypt', *Middle East Journal* 69: 4, 511–26.

Elshobaki, Amr (2012), 'The Muslim Brotherhood – between Evangelizing and Politics: The Challenges of Incorporating the Brotherhood into the Political Process', in Samir Shehata (ed.), *Islamist Politics in the Middle East: Movements and Change*, London: Routledge, pp. 107–19.

Gauvain, Richard (2013), *Salafi Ritual Purity: In the Presence of God*, London: Routledge.

Goldstone, Jack (2003), 'Introduction: Bridging Institutionalized and Non-institutionalized Politics', in Jack Goldstone (ed.), *States, Parties, and Social Movements*, Cambridge: Cambridge University Press, pp. 1–24.

Gunther, Richard, and Larry Diamond (2003), 'Species of Political Parties: A New Typology', *Party Politics* 9: 2, 167–99.

Haykel, Bernard (2009), 'On the Nature of Salafi Thought and Action', in Roel Meijer (ed.), *Global Salafism: Islam's New Religious Movement*, New York: Columbia University Press, pp. 143–68.

Herb, Michael (1999), *All in the Family: Absolutism, Revolution, and Democracy in the Middle Eastern Monarchies*, Albany: State University of New York Press.

Herb, Michael (2016), 'The Origins of Kuwait's National Assembly', LSE Kuwait Programme Paper Series 39, March, <http://eprints.lse.ac.uk/65693/1/39_MichaelHerb.pdf> (last accessed 1 September 2017).

Hoigilt, Jacob, and Frida Nome (2014), 'Egyptian Salafism in Revolution', *Journal of Islamic Studies* 25: 1, 33–55.

al-Jasim, Faysal Quzar (2015), *Al-Tanzimat al-Da'wiyya – Anwa'ha wa-Hukmuha: Tanzim Jama'iyyat Ihya' al-Turath al-Islami Anmudhajan*. No place and publisher provided.

al-Khalidi, Khalid (2016), 'Mufaja'at Intikhabat al-Kuwait: al-Ikhwan wa-l-Shabab 'ala Hisab al-Salafiyyin wa-l-Qaba'il', *al-'Arabi*, 27 November, <https://www.alaraby.co.uk/politics/2016/11/27/مفاجآت-انتخابات-الكويت-الإخوان-والشباب-على-حساب-السلفيين-والقبائل> (last accessed 3 March 2017).

al-Khalidi, Sami Nasir (1999), *Al-Ahzab al-Islamiyya fi-l-Kuwayt: al-Shi'a, al-Ikhwan wa-l-Salaf*, Kuwait: Dar al-Naba'.

Krämer, Gudrun (2010), *Hasan al-Banna*, Oxford: One World Publications.

Kuschnitzki, Judit (2014), 'Salafism in Yemen and the 2011 Uprising: A Religious Movement at the Crossroads of Continuous Quietism and Politicisation', *Middle East Insights* 119, 1–5.

Lacroix, Stéphane (2016), 'Egypt's Pragmatic Salafis: The Politics of Hizb al-Nour', *Carnegie Endowment for International Peace Report*, November, <http://carnegieendowment.org/2016/11/01/egypt-s-pragmatic-salafis-politics-of-hizb-al-nour-pub-64902> (last accessed 1 September 2017).

Merone, Fabio (2017), 'Between Social Contention and Takfirism: The Evolution of the Salafi-Jihadi Movement in Tunisia', *Mediterranean Politics* 22: 1, 71–90.

Merone, Fabio, and Francesco Cavatorta (2013), 'The Salafist Movement and Sheikh-ism in the Tunisian Democratic Transition', *Middle East Law and Governance* 5: 2, 308–30.

Monroe, Steve (2012), 'Salafis in Parliament: Democratic Attitudes and Party Politics in the Gulf', *Middle East Journal* 66: 3, 409–24.

al-Najjar, Ghanim (1995), 'Al-Intikhabat al-Barlamaniyya fi-l-Kuwayt 1992', *Majallat al-Shu'un al-Ijtima'iyya* 47, 138–90.

al-Nakib, Farah (2014), 'Revisiting Hadar and Badu in Kuwait: Citizenship, Housing and the Construction of a Dichotomy', *International Journal of Middle East Studies* 46: 1, 5–30.

Olidort, Jacob (2015), 'Why Are Salafi Islamists Contesting Egypt's Election?', *The Washington Post*, 12 November, <https://www.washingtonpost.com/news/monkey-cage/wp/2015/11/12/why-are-salafi-islamists-contesting-egypts-election/> (last accessed 1 September 2017).

Pall, Zoltan (2017), 'Kuwaiti Salafism after the Arab Awakening', in Francesco Cavatorta and Fabio Merone (eds), *Salafism after the Arab Awakening: Contending with People's Power*, London: Hurst, pp. 180–5.

al-Sa'idi, Salih Baraka (2010), *Al-Sulta wa-l-Tayyarat al-Siyasiyya fi-l-Kuwayt: Jadaliyyat al-Ta'awun wa-l-Sira'*, Kuwait: Dar al-Qabas.

al-Sa'idi, Salih Baraka (2016), 'al-Islamiyyun fi-l-Kuwayt', unpublished working paper, Kuwait.

Schlesinger, Joseph (1991), *Political Parties and the Winning of Office*, Ann Arbor: University of Michigan Press.

Tétreault, Mary-Ann (2000), *Stories of Democracy: Politics and Society in Contemporary Kuwait*, New York: Columbia University Press.

Torelli, Stefano (2017), 'The Multi-faceted Dimensions of Tunisian Salafism', in Francesco Cavatorta and Fabio Merone (eds), *Salafism after the Arab Awakening: Contending with People's Power*, London: Hurst, pp. 155–68.

Ulrichsen, Kristian Coates (2014), 'Politics and Opposition in Kuwait: Continuity and Change', *Journal of Arabian Studies* 4: 2, 214–30.

Utvik, Bjørn Olav (2014), 'The Ikhwanization of the Salafis: Piety in the Politics of Egypt and Kuwait', *Middle East Critique* 23: 1, 5–27.

Van Cott, Donna Lee (2005), *From Movements to Parties in Latin America*, Cambridge: Cambridge University Press.

Ware, Alan (1996), *Political Parties and Party Systems*, Oxford: Oxford University Press.

Wiktorowicz, Quintan (2006), 'Anatomy of the Salafi Movement', *Studies in Conflict and Terrorism* 29: 2, 207–39.

Part 2

International constraints

Chapter 6

Shi'ism, national belonging and political Islam: the *Hezbollah* and the Islamic Resistance in Lebanon

Aurélie Daher

More than thirty years after its creation, the *Hezbollah* remains something of an enigma as a party. Most observers and analysts tend to view it either as a regional player (Cambanis 2010; Devenny 2006; Hirst 2008; Jorisch 2004; Karmon 2005; Leenders 2006; Levitt 2013; Shay 2005; Sobelman 2004) – because of its history of military face-offs with Israel and now the anti-Assad forces in Syria – or as a proxy of the Iranian and/or Syrian regimes in Lebanon, supposedly under their decision-making thumbs (Fuller 2007; Gambill and Abdelnour 2002; Haji and Touma 2006; Hemmer 1999; Olson 2003; Ranstorp 1996). In contrast, studies and commentaries that concede the party a degree of manoeuvring room, if only on the Lebanese political scene, and which study it as an autonomous actor have been in shorter supply (Charara and Domont 2004; Chevalerias 1997; Daher 2016a, 2016b; Hamzeh 1997; Harik 2004; Qassem 2010).

This chapter fills a gap, at least partially, by focusing the analysis on the *Hezbollah* as a political actor on the Lebanese national scene, highlighting the evolution of its relationship to the state. In order to do so, an analytical distinction is made between the Islamic Resistance in Lebanon (IRL) and the *Hezbollah*. The former is the Shi'i military organisation created in 1982 to repel the Israeli assailant, while the latter is the civil/political wing of the IRL, set up a few months later, dedicated at first to mobilising the Shi'i community in favour of the resistance cause, but also in charge, a few years later, of lobbying the Lebanese state to protect the IRL's best interests in parliament as well as from within the government.

The goal of this chapter is to shed as much light as possible on the *Hezbollah*'s understanding of politics and to identify what is key to its political strategies and practical choices. Without downplaying the significance of its regional connections, they will only be delved into as necessary to illustrate how they function less as drivers of the *Hezbollah*'s positioning than boundaries of a 'zone of possible action' within which the party is able to move and act freely.

As for methodology, understanding the *Hezbollah*'s so-called political style is achieved mainly through inductive arguments. Notoriously averse to granting observers wide access to its organisational life, the party is less than forthcoming about its political strategies. If referring to the party's political speeches and declarations is essential to retracing these strategies, it is nevertheless also not enough. This chapter hence approaches a reading of the *Hezbollah*'s official political discourse with caution and instead places more emphasis on re-examining its history, on revisiting the reasons that led to its creation, on closely assessing its practices on the Lebanese scene and the *modus vivendi* that it has achieved with Lebanon's other political parties, all the while not losing sight of the ever-changing context of the party's environment. The chapter also builds on interviews and observant participation conducted in the pro-*Hezbollah* political sphere, within but also outside the *Hezbollah*'s milieus.

Preliminary, structuring remarks on 'the politics of the *Hezbollah*'

Does the *Hezbollah* have a philosophy of the (Islamic) state?

Contrary to what many studies on the *Hezbollah* have suggested, the party's discourse on power and its relationship to the state have been relatively constant over the years. The party has always acknowledged its 'Islamic commitment' (*iltizam islami*), seeing an Islamised regime as an ideal. Nonetheless, it needs to be stressed that, first, the *Hezbollah*'s intellectuals, unlike those of other Islamic groups, so far have not developed any ideological or institutional Islamic ruling party philosophy. Nor have they ever elaborated a theory of the forms such a regime's institutions and governing style would take. Indeed, there is no Tarek al-Bishri[1] (2005) in the party's leadership or among its intellectuals. Instead, its leaders and cadres have always spoken of a 'strong and just' Lebanese state. In other words, rather than developing a theoretical vision of a potential Islamic regime, they have instead continually echoed their constituencies' real aspirations for a strong state, one which, unlike the past and current Lebanese state, would be capable of protecting a mainly Shi'i south against threats posed by Israel; and for a just state, one that, unlike the current Lebanese confessional system, would prioritise aiding the most needy communities, including the traditionally neglected Shi'i communities. As such, the *Hezbollah*'s discourse owes more to the Lebanese communal and political tradition than to Islamic paradigms.

The second element to be emphasised is that the party's leadership has set two preconditions for establishing any Islamic regime in Lebanon. The first, put forth during the 1980s, argues that the entire Middle East needs to submit to Islamic rule before Lebanon does. The second condition, and one the party's leadership has always held to, evokes a Koranic admonition that 'there shall be no compulsion in [acceptance of] religion'.[2] This implies that any possible future Islamic regime in Lebanon is not to be implemented through force but through democratic means such as a referendum, which, the party's leadership insists, would need to be approved by a large majority.[3]

The *Hezbollah*'s discourse addressing the Lebanese system has also been remarkably consistent. The party has always objected to confession-alism, but has never taken any action to overturn it. Instead, especially after having accepted somewhat reluctantly the Taëf Agreement, which ended the fifteen-year-long civil war in 1990, the *Hezbollah*, like other Muslim groups (mainly the AMAL and the Social Progressive Party), repeatedly explained that it could live with it as a 'temporary regime', conceding that Lebanon was not ready yet for a 'one man, one vote' democracy.

The Hezbollah's intent to Islamise the political system

The *Hezbollah*'s intent to establish an Islamic state in Lebanon according to the formulation outlined above is all the more puzzling given the way power is structured in Lebanon. After all, the seats in parliament are allocated based on explicit constitutional rules. Since the constitution was amended in 1990 after the signing of the Taëf Agreement, and once more in 1992, 128 seats have been split equally between Christians and

Muslims. The *Hezbollah*, with other Shi'i groups, may not compete for more than 27 out of the total 64 seats reserved for Muslims. This means that the party cannot have the votes to initiate any institutional change – either through a parliamentary vote or a referendum – without potential allies also supporting Islamisation.

The party has never shied away from acknowledging this structural blockage, going as far as to admit that the religious composition of Lebanese society precludes the establishment an Islamic government in Lebanon. In practical terms, the *Hezbollah* thus has only two possible options: establish an Islamic regime by force through a *coup d'état*, which would fly in the face of its official party line, or set up localised Islamic 'states' in areas under its control, such as the northern Bekaa, the southern suburbs of Beirut, and south Lebanon. To date, the party has not moved in either direction. It has even refrained from setting up any parallel institutions to compete with those of the Lebanese state. This reality on the ground applies today just as it did when the *Hezbollah* enjoyed complete autonomy on the country's peripheries in the 1980s. Indeed, even though the *Hezbollah*'s social control over certain areas was unrivalled, no *Hezbollah* emirate or caliphate was established, and the party has regularly squashed any rumours to that effect. This contrasts sharply with the practice of the Palestine Liberation Organization (PLO), for example. The PLO, in the 1970s, established in fact what later came to be called a 'state within the state' in Lebanon. At the time the PLO exerted authority over large swathes of Lebanese territory where it issued its own identity cards, permits or licence plates.

Despite this fundamentally different behaviour from the one that other resistance parties and movements adopted, the *Hezbollah*'s intentions toward the Lebanese state and interests in the national political game still require further explanation.

A relationship with the state shaped by a historic mission

Following the Israeli invasion of Lebanon in June 1982, a number of Shi'i activists wishing to mobilise against Tel Aviv's troops created a new military organisation: *al-Muqawamah al-islamiyyah fi Lubnan* (the IRL). During the first few months, a council of five people, representing the main constituent currents within the IRL, embodied its civilian counterpart. A network of social and communication institutions dedicated to mobilisation replaced this five-people council and its name was fixed for all posterity in early 1984 as the *Hezbollah* (the Party of God). Assigned the official mission of defending the IRL's social and political interests, it was given the task of mobilising on its behalf and defusing any potential threats that might arise on the domestic front. Rather than being an Islamist party with an armed wing eager to impose Islamist social and political preferences, the *Hezbollah* was set up as the 'civilian' wing of a military unit solely dedicated to the latter's protection at the national level. The functions of the *Hezbollah* and the IRL have thus always been complementary: the former, with its social and political staff, exists to create the right environment within society to allow the latter to wage its fight against the occupying power unimpeded.

In this, the *Hezbollah* stands unique in the Middle East and North Africa. Most of the time, things usually happen the other way round: the civil party is the one that creates its military counterpart. This is true of all the Lebanese parties, which ended up creating their own armed militia during the civil war (the *Kataeb*, the AMAL and others). But it is also true at the regional level. In *Hamas'* case, for instance, the Palestinian Muslim Brothers, a civil organisation, emerged as an Islamist group right from the beginning, and it was only after some time that they felt the need to make a military addition to their civilian and political apparatus. Islamism, together with a specific understanding of the exercise of power and state-making, is at the core of the Palestinian organisation. In the *Hezbollah's* case, politics and government-related ideology come in second, and do not dictate the way the military party sets its priorities. The *Hezbollah* answers to a militarised, anti-Israeli-centred vision of the world before sustaining and referring to Islamic political objectives.

It follows that the relationship between the *Hezbollah* and the Lebanese state has always been shaped by the party's first and only duty of defending the IRL's interests, rather than by any Islamic ideological conceptualisation of power and how to exercise it. Time and again, from one context to the next, the *Hezbollah* has devised and then revised its policies toward successive Lebanese governments with the one constant, sacred aim of not seeing the IRL's position jeopardised.

The 1980s: keeping the state distant from the camps of the IRL

When the *Hezbollah* was created in the first half of the 1980s, the Lebanese state was embroiled in civil war. At the time, establishing a relationship with political institutions was not an issue for the party for two main reasons: the region where it first expanded – the northern Bekaa – was under Syrian occupation and hence controlled from Damascus; and the national legislative and communal electoral processes had been suspended, since 1972 and 1963 respectively, because of the war. The state retained few administrative institutions in the region but no real power to enforce the law. The *Hezbollah* could thus channel most of its energy and time into mobilisation strategies and *de facto* remain insulated from any real internal debate on political management.

Still, the party came into conflict with the authority of the Lebanese state several times in bloody clashes with the Lebanese army. These confrontations were not aimed at toppling the power in Beirut. Rather, the goal was to push government forces back and to keep them at a distance. So, for instance, in the summer of 1982 when the Iranian *pasdaran* wanted to set up a military base in the suburbs of Baalbeck, the *Hezbollah*'s leaders decided to create an appropriate environment for its newly formed organisation. The strategy was two-pronged. First was providing the infrastructure the IRL required for its development. This was accomplished between 1982 and 1983 by *Hezbollah*-led activists taking over Lebanese installations, such as the Lebanese army's Sheik Abdallah barracks south of Baalbeck. After the Lebanese troops had withdrawn, the barracks were converted into the *pasdaran*'s main headquarters. This was a highly strategic takeover of the largest and the best-equipped military complex in the Bekaa area. The *Hezbollah* also took over another state institution, the *École Normale* of Baalbeck, a teacher-training institute that it transformed into the Khomeini Hospital. Second, the *Hezbollah* leadership made every effort to defend the IRL against the authority of a Lebanese state categorically opposed to it. In March 1983, President Amine Gemayel, having proclaimed that he wanted to 'tame the terrorists' (1988) and re-establish the state's authority in the Bekaa, had the Lebanese army move to one of its training areas in Taybeh, near Brital (south of Baalbeck). Supporters of Sheikh Subhi al-Tufayli, one of the *Hezbollah*'s founders, prevented the army from marching into the village. The ensuing clash left several dead and wounded on both sides. For the *Hezbollah*, the aim was to keep the army away from the IRL's training camps.

During the 1980s, the *Hezbollah* thus either ignored the Lebanese state or actively kept its security forces at bay. The issue of whether to establish a relationship with the Lebanese authorities and their institutions did not become pressing until 1991/2 when the civil war had ended, Syria had imposed its tutelage over Lebanon, and the Taëf Agreement had been concluded. The new political situation called for two decisions: should the party accept the presence of state authority on 'its territories' and participate in the resumption of the country's political life? The party's answer to both questions was yes.

1990–2005: the years of Syrian tutelage over Lebanon

In 1990, the Taëf Agreement ended Lebanon's civil war. In 1992, the country's first post-war parliamentary elections took place and *Hezbollah* chose to participate. Much has been made of the *Hezbollah*'s choosing to enter parliament and its concern to legalise its activities. Many observers at the time were surprised as to why what was seen as an Islamic and anti-state party would join the state's institutions. Some saw the *Hezbollah*'s decision as signalling the beginning of the party's de-ideologisation or its institutionalisation or still its pragmatism, as it turned into a 'party just like the others' (Alagha 2001, 2006; Azani 2009; Hamzeh 1993, 2004; Khalifeh 2001; Norton 1998). In reality, the *Hezbollah*'s members of parliament just served one specific aim: to 'have the Resistance's "voice" heard inside Parliament' ('La-nwassel sawt al-Muqawamah lal-Barlamen')[4] and to fulfil – it bears repeating – what the party was created for: defending the IRL's interests. In other words, the *Hezbollah* does not conceive of its political action like a party that is intent on ruling, but instead as one that wants to be a lobbying actor.

Indeed, the party's leadership saw the Taëf Agreement, the change of regime in Teheran after Khomeini's death, and the war with the AMAL as illustrating how unpredictable circumstances can generate different types of threats needing to be neutralised. Hence, the *Hezbollah*'s participation in the national political arena must be placed in the context of its general strategy and not studied apart from it. Unable to completely and sustainably exert control over the extra-Lebanese context, the *Hezbollah* understood that it could not afford to alienate the Lebanese population. To do otherwise would open an internal front that, together with the Israeli army, would grip the IRL in a pincer. It was essential, therefore, to keep ordinary Lebanese or the state from turning against the IRL.

Beginning in the late 1980s to early 1990s, the party prioritised defusing threats potentially arising on the domestic scene. In effect, the party's aim had changed from keeping the state at arm's length to gaining its support for the IRL through concerted institutional action. In the autumn of 1992, when the first Hariri cabinet chose not to mention the right of resistance in its ministerial declaration, the party protested, accusing the government of 'doing its best not to pronounce the word' if not to 'liquidate the Resistance', and demanded official recognition for the latter's cause. MP Muhammad Raad called resistance a 'sacred right'[5] and MP Ibrahim Amin al-Sayyid proclaimed it was the 'only possible choice'.[6] It was even termed an 'indivisible part of the Lebanese national interest'[7] that needed to be raised to the status of 'complementarity with the state'.[8] The deeds of the IRL fighters were then contrasted with Lebanese politicians 'competing in corruption'.[9]

During the 1990s, Hezbollah's members of parliament (MPs) demanded that the state support and compensate the populations harmed in Israeli attacks. They championed the cause of prisoners detained in Israel or in the Khyam prison in south Lebanon, and urged the government to declare their cause a national one. The MPs also urged the government to promote the cause of the IRL in the media, at political gatherings and events, at international meetings, summits and congresses, saying that 'the state must support resistance by transforming all the governmental institutions into resistance institutions'[10] – in other words, to emulate what the party was already doing with its own institutions.

More importantly, each time a military crisis with Israel erupted, the state was urged to act in a complementary manner with the Hezbollah, by supporting the IRL's cause politically at home and by backing it diplomatically abroad against Israeli and western pressure. This role that the Hezbollah demanded of the state also explains in part the party's harsh condemnation at the time of Rafic Hariri's debt management policies, which were widely seen as generally increasing the country's debt and therefore diminishing national sovereignty by putting the country at the mercy of western and international actors. The party was concerned that any international help with the debt problem would undoubtedly come with strings attached in the guise of political action to tame the IRL. A fact worth highlighting here is that, in twenty-five years of sitting in parliament, the Hezbollah has not once used its representation in the chamber to agitate for even partial Islamisation – unlike some Arab Islamist parties, which tend to do precisely that upon joining institutional life, as some of the chapters in this volume suggest. The party has not leveraged it as a chip in negotiations or to exact concessions from other national groups.

Even outside parliament, the *Hezbollah*'s leadership and cadre have never addressed the issue publicly. Moreover, their political speeches have rarely invoked Islamic referents.[11] The sociologist Dalal al-Bizri noted that when the party condemned the government's tax policies, it would do so not in the name of Islamic principles, such as, for example, Islam's prohibition of *riba* (charging interest), but instead because the system hit the poor the hardest. Al-Bizri also remarked that the *Hezbollah*'s MPs do not use the *Basmalah*[12] and that the Sunni Islamist group *Jama'ah islamiyyah* had failed to get *Hezbollah*'s support for a bid to change the official weekly closing day from Saturday to Friday in accord with Muslim tradition.[13] As al-Bizri summed up: 'neither Islamization nor the concept of an "Islamic state", nor the issue of applying the *shari'ah* seem to be part of their major concerns' (al-Bizri 1999: 15).

In other words, the *Hezbollah*'s political practice in the 1990s shows that its principal objective in entering the domestic political arena was to fulfil the mission that it was created for: to advocate for the IRL's cause. Under the continuing Syrian tutelage over Lebanon, the party had it relatively easy, since the Lebanese regime was completely aligned with Damascus. In exchange for the state's mediatic and diplomatic support, the party kept its commitment not to destabilise the government in power – even when there were skirmishes with the army or the police. For example, during demonstrations in 1993 (against the regional peace process) and in 2004 (to protest electricity cuts in the southern suburbs of Beirut), party supporters were roughed up on both occasions by the security forces. Both times, the party's leadership systematically called for calm and forbade retaliation.

The Cedar Revolution of 2005: threats from the inside

The situation changed, however, starting in February 2005 when former Prime Minister Rafic Hariri was assassinated and the anti-Syrian March 14 coalition came to power. From then on, the IRL and the *Hezbollah* on the one hand, and the Lebanese state on the other, were on different sides in terms of ideology, regional and international alliances, and political preferences. Thus, the political dimension of the *Hezbollah*'s work on the domestic scene acquired even greater significance, as the IRL needed more than ever the *Hezbollah* to defuse any threat coming from the domestic political game against its interests.

Soon after the Hariri assassination, Syria, under international pressure, withdrew its troops from Lebanon. The March 14 coalition[14] won the legislative elections that summer, producing an internal political environment hostile to Damascus. The new Lebanese government also proceeded to ally itself with an international community determined to fight the 'war on terror' and to implement UN Resolution 1559, which was passed in September 2004 and called for disarming all Lebanese and non-Lebanese militias – including the IRL.

During the months following the Syrian withdrawal, the *Hezbollah*, cognisant of its minority status in parliament, laid the groundwork for a solid, sustainable alliance with a major Christian actor, the Free Patriotic Movement led by Michel Aoun. The political pact was concluded in February 2006. The party also tried to negotiate guarantees with the new government that would protect the IRL. Prime Minister Fouad Siniora's government seemed amenable. For the first time, the *Hezbollah* had a minister in the cabinet in the person of Muhammad Fneish. The ministerial programme did not mention Resolution 1559 and furthermore stated that 'the Lebanese government considers that the Lebanese resistance is the sincere and natural expression of the national right of the Lebanese people to defend its territory and dignity against Israeli aggressions, threats and ambitions [. . .]'.[15] At that time, people close to the party or to its allies held key positions in Lebanese institutions such as the military chiefs of staff, the military's intelligence service, and head of security at the Beirut International Airport. However, the *Hezbollah*'s relationship with the new government was soon jeopardised, both by international pressure on the Lebanese government to disarm the IRL and when the international commission then at work investigating Hariri's murder suggested that the *Hezbollah* had had a hand in the assassination.

After the summer 2006 war with Israel, the links between the party and the Lebanese state seriously deteriorated. In contrast to the former governments' discourse, which had supported the IRL in its open conflict with Israel, the March 14 coalition dissociated itself from the IRL, blaming it for the tragic July war. It was even revealed later that many members of the coalition had collaborated with Israel during the conflict.[16] This background explains why the *Hezbollah* stepped up its involvement in Lebanese politics after the war of 2006.

From then on, the *Hezbollah*'s arm-wrestling with the March 14 coalition escalated. It first peaked in January 2007, when activists from both sides clashed in the streets. The *Hezbollah*, understanding the risk that civil war would pose to the interests of the IRL, publicly called on its supporters to withdraw from the streets and not to engage in retaliation. The struggle reached its climax in May 2008, when *Hezbollah* fighters burst into Beirut's streets following a government decision forty-eight hours earlier to have the army dismantle the IRL's phone network with force if necessary. Eventually, in January 2011, the strife abruptly ended. When the March 14 coalition refused to publicly reject the anticipated indictments by the Special Tribunal convened to find Rafic Hariri's killers, the *Hezbollah*-led opposition toppled Saad Hariri's cabinet and asked Najib Mikati to form the new government. For the first time in the party's history, the *Hezbollah* turned proactive, taking the initiative in changing the domestic political landscape by itself – and for the first time in Lebanon's history, it took the reins of power in its own hands. The *Hezbollah* was no longer an opposition party: it led the coalition that ruled the country.

The Syrian War factor

2013–16: the Salam government

More than five years after first openly getting its hands on the levers of power in Lebanon, the *Hezbollah*'s political practice does not appear to have changed significantly. With civil violence erupting in Syria, the March 14 coalition wanted to see the Lebanese state intervene in the intra-Syrian war, particularly in 2012–14. The *Hezbollah*, like the government, preferred to have the Lebanese authorities stay out of the chaos across the border (Daher 2016a, 2016b, 2018).

From 2011 onwards, the war in Syria would illustrate even more the *Hezbollah*'s dedication to its role as protector of the IRL's interests – and especially the pragmatic degree to which the party is prepared to bend if necessary. Following the resignation of Prime Minister Najib Mikati in March 2013, the *Hezbollah* and its allies ultimately agreed to let March 14 form the government and name a head of the cabinet congenial to its political leanings although the March 14 coalition was still in the minority in parliament. This is how Tammam Salam, a client of the Hariri family, came to be named head of government. Better yet, after having exerted pressure during the years from 2008 until 2011, largely to keep individuals hostile to the IRL's cause from heading the national security apparatus – the army and the directorate of general security – the party agreed to relinquish the Interior, Justice and Defence portfolios to its opponents. Simultaneously, it gave up its sacrosanct 'blocking third', a governmental veto system that allowed it, with support from political allies, to dissolve the cabinet.[17] However, there is no reason to interpret all these developments as indicators of weakness.

The *Hezbollah* gained on two levels by letting March 14 steer the cabinet and withdrawing from the security ministry posts. In the first place, there is an international dimension that needs to be taken into account. Several foreign governments and international organisations that intended to support Lebanon in its fight against radical Jihadists by providing the national army with weapons and surveillance devices refused to work with the *Hezbollah*–IRL representatives in government. With the decision to withdraw from security-sensitive positions within the government, the *Hezbollah* facilitated cooperation between the international community, the western governments and the Lebanese government. The *Hezbollah* and the rest of the Lebanese political forces need the army to be in the best possible shape to protect the Lebanese national territory against a possible invasion by the Islamic State (ISIS) or *Jabhat Fateh al-Sham* (the former *Jabhat al-Nusra*), and to prevent the setting up of Islamic 'sheikhdoms' in fragile Sunni territories in Lebanon. However, since it is chronically underequipped, it needs outside aid; and any arms shipments from Saudi Arabia or the United States might be compromised if overseen by ministries headed by the *Hezbollah*. Second, the *Hezbollah* also must ensure that civil peace is maintained. To this end, letting Sunni ministers manage national security, especially the fight against Sunni Jihadist networks, is not without interest for the party. In (Sunni) areas where the security forces are necessarily called on to crack down in their hunt for dangerous elements, it deprives the Sunni community of any chance to interpret the (possibly heavy-handed) interventions of the army and police as having been planned deliberately against them by the Shi'i community. Starting in the second half of the 2000s, in fact, a number of narratives developed among a large segment of the Sunni community that blamed their Shi'i compatriots – and the *Hezbollah* in particular – for the relative marginalisation of the Sunni leadership on the national political scene. Some, especially Sunni deputies from northern Lebanon, did not shrink from talking about a conspiracy against the entire Sunni community the *Hezbollah* and its allies were orchestrating. In these narratives, the army, perceived as intervening exclusively against Sunni Islamist networks and cooperating with the IRL, is regularly accused of playing the role of subcontractor for the Shi'i allegedly harbouring all sorts of resentment against the Sunni. In addition to keeping the handcuffs of the Lebanese Leviathan out of the hands of the Shi'i parties, thereby depriving the Sunni of the chance to fan the flames of Sunni–Shi'i conflict, letting the Hariri family's Future Current manage Lebanese internal security and the Justice Ministry also means it alone stands to reap the whirlwind should the government's anti-Jihadist policies fail.

By making all these concessions to the March 14 coalition and especially to the Hariri-led Future Current, in a context of sectarian polarisation, the *Hezbollah*'s tactics proved efficient in preventing potentially dangerous frustration on the Sunni side, and hence in keeping the civil peace. With the IRL having its hands full in the Syrian conflict, and the Israeli government reflecting at the time on the relevance of a new war against the *Hezbollah* in Lebanon based on the IRL's military over-commitment on Assad's side, the last thing that the *Hezbollah*–IRL tandem needed was civil violence at home. Once again, the *Hezbollah* was up to its original task at the service of the Resistance.

2014–16: the presidential (non-)election

On 31 October 2016, Michel Aoun, leader of the Free Patriotic Movement, a party member of the March 8 Alliance and the main Christian ally of the *Hezbollah*, became president, ending twenty-nine months of void. It was not the first time: the state had remained headless on two previous occasions, for slightly more than a year after Amine Gemayel's term (1982–8) and then for another six months after Emile Lahoud (1998–2007) left office. But never had the vacancy lasted this long, had negotiations between the actors involved been as difficult, or had the regional context been as problematic as this time.

Per the constitutional amendment adopted at the end of the civil war (1975–90), the Lebanese president must be a Maronite Christian. The community's political leaders negotiate any candidacy for the post in the first instance; that other Lebanese might have a stake in the selection is secondary. It was only in December 2015 that a first likely name was finally put forward: Sleiman Frangieh, the leader of a small Christian party in the March 8 Alliance. The news caused a great stir, since the candidacy grew out of a handshake agreement he made with Saad Hariri, the Sunni leader of March 14. The deal between the two envisaged Hariri supporting the Frangieh candidacy, despite his being in the opposing camp, in return for March 8 backing Hariri's comeback as prime minister, a post reserved to the Sunni community and that Hariri, as already mentioned, had been ousted from in 2011.

However, several weeks later, in mid-January 2016, Samir Geagea, leader of the Maronite March 14, sprang his own surprise. Having refused for more than a decade to see his rival Michel Aoun step up to the presidency (Beydoun 1993; Corm 1992; Sneifer-Perri 1995), Geagea now announced that he was backing him as the official candidate. Lebanon's political scene was enthralled. With Geagea supporting Aoun, it finally looked like the impasse would end and would do so quickly: between the votes of March 8, those of the Christian March 14, and those of the Druze Walid Joumblatt (and with Hariri's followers, the March 14 Sunni deputies, abstaining), Aoun's election would be a foregone conclusion. At the same time, it would celebrate the end to several decades of bitter hatred between the two great branches of Lebanese Maronitism.

The *Hezbollah*, the election's true arbiter, proved, however, to be less than enthusiastic. True, for months its leadership had given assurances that Michel Aoun was its favourite; despite this, internally, the reaction to Geagea's move was tepid. Why did it take so long for the *Hezbollah* to endorse the happy accord? The delay was due to the *Hezbollah* being less concerned about the identity of the next chief of state than who would head the new government. The Lebanese constitution gives the president few prerogatives, while the prime minister is the true head of the executive branch. The capacity of the former to make trouble is considerably less formidable than the latter's. As things stood, electing Frangieh was unpalatable because he was part of a package: supporting Frangieh for the presidency meant putting Hariri at the head of the government – an option that did not in the least appeal to the *Hezbollah* unless some serious conditions could be agreed on. As the party's leadership saw it, Saad Hariri's term as head of the executive branch from 2009 to 2011 had been anything but convincing

(Daher 2017). The Frangieh–Hariri deal seemed unbalanced: the party would certainly get a president congenial to its interests, but at the cost of a head of cabinet from the side of its adversaries. In a context of pronounced tension between Iran and Saudi Arabia, Hariri's political family effectively vowed sincere and active loyalty to the Kingdom. It hence tried, on several occasions, to insert inflections running counter to the *Hezbollah*'s interests in the declarations and decisions of the Tammam Salam government at Riyadh's behest. Having a prime minister even more pro-Saudi than the current one was not appealing to the *Hezbollah*.

The *Hezbollah* therefore would gain everything by being patient. Its policy of attrition – at all times its preferred strategy – eventually succeeded. After a serious modification in the balance of power between Iran and Saudi Arabia in the late summer of 2016 (Daher 2016a, 2016b) Hariri decided, in late October, to back Aoun for the presidency on condition that he would be named prime minister. This time, the *Hezbollah* agreed to proceed with the election – the sole reason being that Hariri had committed not to jeopardise either the *Hezbollah*'s national or its regional interests. In a manner of speaking, the *Hezbollah* managed ultimately to get what it wanted both for the presidency *and* for the head of government.

Conclusion

To sum up, the *Hezbollah*, in twenty-five years of political involvement, has behaved neither as a typical Arab Islamist party nor as a traditional Lebanese political grouping dedicated to defending its community.

For most co-opted Islamist parties in Arab countries, like the Muslim Brotherhood in Egypt during a certain period of time, or the Brothers in Jordan today, supporting the regime in exchange for an Islamisation of some parts of state institutions, or public subsidies for their charity foundations, has frequently summarised their whole understanding of political participation. On the Lebanese domestic stage, the *Hezbollah* has so far never attempted to Islamise the state, or even to establish an Islamic regime over the regions from which it draws its support. And thanks to a parallel financing system that is independent from the state, it has never needed state money to fund its institutions. Moreover, in the face of attacks on the Shi'i community, the *Hezbollah*'s reaction has been to systematically call for calm and to reject retaliation. In other words, it has not been the best protector of the community, contrary to what most confessional parties in Lebanon are expected to do for their own constituencies.

The very nature, timing and selectivity of its interventions in parliament and the political arena more broadly all point to the same trend: that the party has constantly hewed to its goals and priorities and remains perfectly committed to its original *raison d'être* to this very day. As we have seen, the political alliances formed to guarantee, through a complex system of clientelism, that the state would never become a source of threat to the IRL have consistently remained the pillars of the party's strategy. The *Hezbollah* is not a *parti de gouvernement* (ruling party) as much as it is a *parti de lobbying* (lobbying party). This one logic remains, always and again, the matrix for the *Hezbollah*'s understanding of its political engagement.

One reason for such a continuity and steadfastness in the way the *Hezbollah* has been playing in the Lebanese institutional arena is that it was not created initially as an Islamist movement, that it did not grow out of a group ideologically motivated by the Islamisation of power – contrary, for instance, to Palestinian Hamas. Another reason is that the balance of power between the military and the civil branches of the IRL–*Hezbollah* dyad has always been, in a context of permanent conflict, to the advantage of the former. This prevents the latter from developing its independent agenda. One could see in the IRL–*Hezbollah* pattern something close to the IRA–Sinn Féin one during the years when the Provisional IRA was militarily active. In a Middle Eastern context though, the *Hezbollah*'s case remains unprecedented and unique.

Notes

1. An Egyptian political thinker, he developed detailed theories about what Islamic state institutions might be like.
2. *La ikraha fil-din* (*al-Baqarah* surah, verse 256).
3. In 1986, then Secretary General Subhi al-Tufayli declared that he was in favour of an Islamic state, but only of it was supported by the majority (interview in *Magazine*, 29 March 1986). Ten years later, his successor, Hassan Nasrallah, confirmed: 'I do not deny Hezbollah's wish to see established an Islamic Republic [. . .] Nonetheless, the establishment of an Islamic Republic cannot

take place by force or resistance. That requires a national referendum. And a referendum that would be positive at 51 per cent cannot be the solution. What is needed is a referendum positive at 90 per cent. Based on this consideration, and according to the current context, the establishment of an Islamic Republic in Lebanon is not possible for the time being' ('Al-sayyid Hasan Nasrallah: al-sirah al-dhatiyyah' [Sayyid Hassan Nasrallah: The (Auto)Biography], *Al-Mustaqbal al-Arabi* (331), September 2006, p. 118). In February 2012, Hassan Nasrallah evoked a speech that he had given in 1982 and that has been used since 2005 by the March 14 coalition as alleged evidence of 'Hezbollah's real project to establish an Islamic regime in Lebanon', by saying: 'In 1982, 1983, at the beginning, then, there were some brothers – and I am one of them – who gave speeches and talks about the choice of an Islamic republic in Lebanon [. . .] But I would like to remind you that amongst the Christian leaders today too, those who talk about a unique State, a democratic State, (sectarian) cohabitation, civil peace and living all together, at that time, they were then talking about a national Christian state, division and federalism' (<https://www.moqawama.org>, last accessed 7 February 2012).

4. Interview with a Hezbollah executive, March 2007, Beirut.
5. Muhammad Raad, 18 February 1993 (qtd in al-Bizri 1999: 12).
6. Ibrahim Amin al-Sayyid, 6 June 1995 (qtd in al-Bizri 1999: 12).
7. Muhammad Raad, 18 February 1993 (qtd in al-Bizri 1999: 12).
8. Muhammad Raad, 18 February 1993 (qtd in al-Bizri 1999: 12).
9. Ali Ammar, 22 December 1994 (qtd in al-Bizri 1999: 12).
10. Muhammad Berjawi, 29 June 1994 (qtd in al-Bizri 1999: 13).
11. Except for some speeches by Secretary General Hassan Nasrallah on religious occasions ('*Ashura*', for instance).
12. For example, they did not start their speeches with the invocation *Bismillah al-Rahman al-Rahim* ('In the name of God the Most Gracious and Most Merciful').
13. The *Hezbollah*'s institutions are open on Fridays, and usually closed on Saturdays and Sundays, or Sundays and Mondays.
14. Soon after the assassination of Rafic Hariri on 14 February 2005, two major demonstrations took place in Beirut, one on 8 March and the second on 14 March. The former asserted its loyalty to Syria and the Assad family's regional preferences, also rejecting UN Resolution 1559 that asks for the disarmament of all 'armed militias in Lebanon' – meaning the Palestinian militant groups and the IRL – while the latter protested against the Syrian tutelage over Lebanon. The political parties in Lebanon hence split between the March 8, pro-Syrian coalition (the *Hezbollah*, the AMAL, the Free Patriotic Movement) and the March 14, anti-Syrian, pro-west and pro-Saudi Arabia alliance (the Future Current of the Hariri family, the *Kataeb* of the Gemayels, the Lebanese Forces of Samir Geagea, and the Progressive Socialist Party of Walid Joumblatt).
15. *L'Orient-Le Jour*, 6 July 2005.
16. As revealed in 2011 by WikiLeaks.
17. The privilege of retaining a blocking third had been granted to March 8 by March 14 in 2009.

Bibliography

Alagha, Joseph (2001), 'Hizbullah's Gradual Integration in the Lebanese Public Sphere', *Sharqiyyat* 13: 1, 33–59.

Alagha, Joseph (2006), *The Shifts in Hizbullah's Ideology: Religious Ideology, Political Ideology and Political Program*, Amsterdam: Amsterdam University Press.

Azani, Eitan (2009), *Hezbollah. The Story of the Party of God: From Revolution to Institutionalization*, New York: Palgrave Macmillan.

Balqaziz, 'Abdul-Ilah (1993), *Hizbullah. 2000. Min al-tahrir ila al-rad' (1982–2006)* [Hezbollah. From Liberation to Deterrence (1982–2006)], Beirut: The Centre for Studies on Arab Unity.

Beydoun, Ahmad (1993), *Le Liban: Itinéraires dans une guerre incivile*, Paris: Karthala.

al-Bishri, Tareq (2005), *Manhaj al-nadhar fil-nudhum al-siyasiyyah al-mu'asirah fil-'alam al-islami* [Textbook for a Theory on Contemporary Political Systems in the Islamic World], Amman: Dar al-Shuruq lil-Nashr wal-Tawzi'.

Al-Bizri, Dalal (1999), *Islamistes, parlementaires et libanais: Les interventions à l'Assemblée des élus de la Jama'a Islamiyya et du Hizb Allah, 1992–1996*, Beirut: Les Cahiers du Cermoc 3.

Cambanis, Thanassis (2010), *A Privilege to Die: Inside Hezbollah's Legions and Their Endless War against Israel*, New York: The Free Press.

Charara, Walid, and Frédéric Domont (2004), *Le Hezbollah: Un parti islamo-nationaliste*, Paris: Fayard.

Chevalerias, Alain (1997), 'Le Hezbollah libanais: Une force politique', *Stratégique* 66/67, 145–59.

Corm, Georges (1992), *Liban: Les guerres de l'Europe et de l'Orient 1840–1992*, Paris: Gallimard-Folio Actuel.

Daher, Aurélie (2016a), 'La guerre saoudienne contre le Hezbollah libanais: répercussions locales d'une rivalité régionale', *Confluences Méditerranée* 97, 91–100.

Daher, Aurélie (2016b), 'L'Intervention de la Résistance islamique libanaise en Syrie: causes, formes et répercussions en termes de mobilisation', *Confluences Méditerranée* 96, 129–43.

Daher, Aurélie (2018), *Hezbollah: Mobilisation and Power*, London: Hurst; New York: Oxford University Press.

Devenny, Patrick (2006), 'Hezbollah's Strategic Threat to Israel', *Middle East Quarterly* 13: 1, 31–8.

Fuller, Graham (2007), 'The Hizballah–Iran Connection: Model for Sunni Resistance', *The Washington Quarterly* 30: 1, 139–50.

Gambill, Gary, and Ziad Abdelnour (2002), 'Hezbollah: Between Tehran and Damascus', *Middle East Intelligence Bulletin* 4: 2.

Gemayel, Amine (1988), *L'offense et le pardon*, Paris: Gallimard.

Haji Georgiou, Michel, and Michel Touma (2006), 'Le Hezbollah entre allégeances ambiguës et réalités libanaises', *Travaux et jours* 77, 127–51.

Hamzeh, Nizar (1993), 'Lebanon's Hizbullah: From Islamic Revolution to Parliamentary Accommodation', *Third World Quarterly* 14: 2, 321–37.

Hamzeh, Nizar (1994), 'Clan Conflicts, Hezbollah and the Lebanese State', *The Journal of Social, Political and Economic Studies* 19: 4, 433–46.

Hamzeh, Nizar (1997), 'The Role of Hizbullah in Conflict Management within Lebanon's Shia Community', in Paul Salem (ed.), *Conflict Resolution in the Arab World: Selected Essays*, Beirut: AUB, pp. 93–118.

Hamzeh, Nizar (2004), *In the Path of Hizbullah*, New York: Syracuse University Press.

Harik, Judith (2004), *Hezbollah: The Changing Face of Terrorism*, London: I. B. Tauris.

Hemmer, Christopher (1999), 'Historical Analogies and the Definition of Interests: The Iranian Hostage Crisis and Ronald Reagan's Policy Towards the Hostages in Lebanon', *Political Psychology* 20: 2, 267–89.

Hirst, David (2008), *Beware of Small States: Lebanon, Israel and Hizbullah*, London: Faber & Faber.

Jorisch, Avi (2004), *Beacon of Hatred: Inside Hizballah's al-Manar Television*, Washington DC: The WINEP.

Karmon, Ely (2005), 'En quoi le Hezbollah est-il une menace pour l'État d'Israël?', *Outre-Terre* 13, 391–415.

Khalifeh, Paul (2001), 'Le Hezbollah entre pragmatisme et idéologie', *Les Cahiers de l'Orient* 64, 27–32.

Leenders, Reinoud (2006), 'How the Rebel Regained His Cause: Hizbullah & the Sixth Arab–Israeli War', *MIT Electronic Journal of Middle East Studies* 6: 2.

Levitt, Matthew (2013), *Hezbollah: The Global Footprint of Lebanon's Party of God*, Washington DC: Georgetown University Press.

Norton, Augustus Richard (1998), 'Hizballah: From Radicalism to Pragmatism?', *Middle East Policy* 5: 4, 147–58.

Norton, Augustus Richard (2000), 'Hizballah and the Israeli Withdrawal from Southern Lebanon', *Journal of Palestine Studies* 30: 1, 22–35.

Norton, Augustus Richard (2006), 'Hizballah Through the Fog of the Lebanon War', *Journal of Palestine Studies* 36: 1, 54–70.

Olson, Steven (2003), *The Attack on U.S. Marines in Lebanon on October 23, 1983*, New York: The Rosen Publishing Group.

Pelletiere, Stephen (2004), *Hamas and Hizbollah: The Radical Challenge to Israel in the Occupied Territories*, Honolulu: University Press of the Pacific.

Qassem, Naïm (2010), *Hizbullah. Al-manhaj, al-tajribah, al-mustaqbal* [Hezbollah: Programme, Experience, and Future], 7th edn, Beirut: Dar al-Hadi.

Ranstorp, Magnus (1996), *Hizb'Allah in Lebanon: The Politics of the Western Hostage Crisis*, New York: St. Martin's Press.

Salameh, Husayn (2006), *Hizbullah fil-'aql al-isra'ili* [Hezbollah in the Israeli Mind], Beirut: Markaz al-Istisharat wal-Buhuth.

Salman, Talal (n.d.), *Sirah dhatiyyah li-harakah muqawimah 'arabiyyah muntasirah* [Biography of an Arab Resistance Movement that Came Out Victorious], Beirut: n.p.

Shay, Shaul (2005), *The Axis of Evil: Iran, Hizballah, and the Palestinian Terror*, London: Transaction Publishers.

Shehadi, Nadim (2007), 'Le Hezbollah entre l'Iran et le Liban', *Maghreb-Machrek* 190, 37–43.

Sneifer-Perri, Régina (1995), *Guerres maronites 1975–1990*, Paris: L'Harmattan.

Sobelman, Daniel (2004), *Qawa 'id jadidah lil-lu'bah. Isra'il wa Hizbullah ba'd al-insihab min Lubnan* [New Rules of the Game: Israel and Hezbollah after the Israeli Withdrawal from Lebanon], Beirut: Matabi' al-Dar al-'Arabiyyah lil-'Ulum.

Zisser, Eyal (2006), 'Hizballah and Israel: Strategic Threat on the Northern Border', *Israel Affairs* 12: 1, 86–106.

Chapter 7

Party politics in the Palestinian Territories

Manal A. Jamal

Palestinian political parties operate in a precarious environment where pluralism exists in an ostensibly democratic context, but parties are heavily constrained by Israel's ongoing military occupation and the post-Oslo political framework. In this context, Palestinian political parties work to represent citizens in the West Bank and Gaza Strip (WBGS) by influencing and shaping government policy and by nominating their own candidates for office. The Oslo Accords, however, established the current Palestinian political system, and within this framework, democratic outcomes must accommodate Israel's security concerns. Given the persistence of Israeli military occupation, many of these political parties also continue to function as political movements, and therefore, are committed to furthering the struggle of a collective against Israel's military occupation and to representing all Palestinians, including those beyond the WBGS. In this context, the performance of these political parties at the polls is determined by their perceived strength vis-à-vis their confrontation with Israel and not necessarily their potential to represent citizen interests and advance democracy. Relatedly, Palestinian political parties are constrained by external meddling. Although this might not be direct, it influences and shapes democratic outcomes, it renders domestic political dynamics problematic, and it limits and skews both resource allocations and regulatory restrictions. Given the distortions associated with democracy under military occupation, the natural questions that follow are: are genuine democratic exercises involving political parties even possible under these circumstances? And if so, at what price? Far from being simply a Palestinian problem, party politics under external occupation is a feature that characterises other polities in the Middle East and North Africa. This makes an examination of Palestinian party politics particularly useful because similar dynamics can potentially be observed elsewhere.

This chapter begins with a brief background about the establishment of the current political system in the WBGS. It then provides an overview of current Palestinian political parties, tracing their origins and trajectories. It focuses on two strands: those that emerged as part of the Palestinian national liberation movement, and the more recent political parties that did not. The chapter then turns to recent Palestinian elections and sheds light on the internal and external challenges these parties face as a result of Israel's ongoing military occupation and the resultant post-Oslo political framework.

Democracy in the Palestinian Authority

Key objectives of the signatories of the Oslo Accords and their patrons were to establish the Palestinian Authority (PA) and a democratic political system, or more exactly as outlined in the Declaration of Principles (DOP):

> In order that the Palestinian people in the West Bank and Gaza Strip may govern themselves according to democratic principles, direct, free and general political elections will be held for the Council under agreed supervision and international observation, while the Palestinian police will ensure public order.[1]

Moreover, the PA would serve as an interim self-government authority for Palestinians living in the WBGS; and the interim arrangements would take place in phases and last for five years, culminating in a permanent settlement based on United Nations Security Council Resolutions 242 and 338. Per these agreements, the first redeployment would be from the Gaza Strip and Jericho, and then from the major Palestinian population centres: Ramallah, Nablus, Jenin, Qaliqilya, Tulkarem and Bethlehem.[2] A Palestinian police force would be established that would be responsible for 'internal' security and public order and would replace the Israeli military. Security coordination between the two parties would continue. As part of the redeployment, the Israeli government would transfer the civil powers for education and culture, health, social welfare, direct taxation and tourism to the PA. Within a short amount of time after the Israeli military would redeploy from the main population centres, the Palestinians in the WBGS would hold elections for a Palestinian Legislative Council (PLC) that would assume responsibility for these powers. Israel would continue to control borders, at least during the interim period.

More than twenty years later, the PLO and the Government of Israel (GoI) are no closer to concluding final status negotiations. From the outset, criticism of the accords was extensive and harsh. Although supporters of the DOP pointed out that the agreements de facto included Israel's formal recognition of the PLO and allowed the Palestinians to administer their own affairs, critics pointed out that the Palestinians had not received any guarantees for a future independent, sovereign, viable state. Moreover, there were no guarantees for a halt to Israeli settlement expansion in the occupied territories. The DOP also failed to address Israel's illegal claim to the 'occupied territories'; rather, the DOP identified the territories as 'disputed territories'. One of the most damning critiques of the PLO was that it was 'transformed' from a liberation movement to a municipal government of sorts in the occupied territories. The Gaza–Jericho agreements, which spelled out the first implementation arrangements of the interim period, undermined any semblance of Palestinian autonomy by requiring the PLC to submit all legislation to Israel for approval; Israel has veto power over all legislation.[3] Moreover, given that *Fatah* controlled the PLO and the PA, the distinction between the two entities was no longer clear. The political movements participating in the PA elections would be limited to representing the interests of WBGS residents, which created a tension in their role of representing all Palestinians and their interests, regardless of geographic location. In this context of ongoing military occupation, the political movements could not focus solely on becoming political parties.

The Palestinian nationalist movement and political parties

The political movements that emerged as part of the Palestinian national struggle dominate party politics in the WBGS today. Prominent Palestinian political figures have tried to establish new political parties, but their impact has been limited. The institutions established to function solely as political parties are unable to be serious political challengers in this context. Most contemporary Palestinian political parties – *Fatah* (the reverse acronym for the *Harakat al-Tahrir al-Watani al-Filastini*; Palestinian National Liberation Movement), the Palestinian Front for the Liberation of Palestine (PFLP) and the Democratic Front for the Liberation of Palestine (DFLP) originated as part of the national liberation movement and are key members of the PLO (Sayigh 1997). Initially, these political organisations conceived of the liberation struggle in strictly military terms. *Hamas*, now a major movement and political party in Palestinian politics, was established in 1987, and is not a member of the PLO.[4] Although they run in elections as political parties, they are self-defined as political movements. Early on, *Fatah* emerged as the dominant faction of the Palestinian nationalist movement, and it would come to control the PLO, and later the PA. Beginning in the early 1960s, Palestinian students had started to set up a number of political organisations throughout the Arab world (Abu-Lughod 1971; Smith 1996). Among these students were Yasser Arafat, Khalil Wazir and Salah Khalaf, who took over the PLO in 1969.

Historically, two different streams dominated the Palestinian nationalist movement. On one side was the *Harakat al-Qawmiyyin al-'Arab* (Arab Nationalist Movement; ANM), which was more leftist in its political orientation. On the other was *Fatah*, with a more nationalist outlook. Many of the Palestinian guerrilla and political organisations that emerged in the 1960s and thereafter trace their roots to one of these political strands. The former stream conceived of the liberation of Palestine as part of a broader process involving the social transformation of the Arab world. *Fatah*, however, solely focused on the liberation of Palestine, and advocated armed struggle, which was to be carried out autonomously from independent Arab states. These groups would come to adopt different strategies in relation to the preparation and political training of their members and to mass movement mobilisation. Although the leftist groups that emerged from the ANM would first embark on mass movement mobilisation, their selectivity in recruiting and accepting members would restrain their mass movement endeavours. *Fatah*, on the other hand, as a non-ideological party, placed little emphasis on membership training and recruited members more readily. Eventually, *Fatah* emerged as the largest and strongest of the Palestinian political factions, and it is the current-day leadership party of the PA and the PLO.

The 1967 Arab defeat spawned a number of Palestinian guerrilla organisations. The ANM's Palestinian branch, along with three other small guerrilla organisations, founded the PFLP in 1967. In 1968, the Palestine Front for the Liberation of Palestine–General Command broke away from the PFLP. Then in 1969, another group splintered from the PFLP, and called itself the Popular Democratic Front for the Liberation of Palestine (now the DFLP).[5] These groups were predominately leftist in their orientation and would come to be *Fatah*'s major opposition.[6] *Fatah*, the PFLP and the DFLP would come to represent the largest Palestinian political factions in the PLO, and play an important role in mass mobilisation in the occupied territories, amassing substantial followings. Following the Oslo peace accords and the establishment of the PA, all would also become formal political parties in the WBGS.

Until 1987, the Palestinian Communist Party (PCP) worked outside the framework of the PLO. Communist activities in the Palestinian territories date back to the early 1920s, and increased in the late 1960s and early 1970s (Lockman 1996). The West Bank Communists were firmly committed to mass mobilisation and non-violent protest (Sayigh 1997). In 1969 they reactivated the General Federation of Labour Unions, and later played a leading role in the founding of the voluntary work programmes among university and high school students (Sayigh 1997). In 1982, the West Bank communists founded the PCP, later renamed the Palestinian People's Party (PPP); this took place despite the protests of the Jordanian Communist Party.[7]

Fatah's initial key military victories, as well as its commitment to non-ideological recruitment of members, led to its ascendance as a leader of the Palestinian nationalist movement. Although the early record of *Fatah*'s military operations was quite modest, the significant losses they were able to inflict on the Israeli military during the Karameh battle of 1968[8] was a turning point for the organisation (Cobban 1984). Although both sides claimed military victory, the battle was pivotal in that it inspired tens of thousands of Palestinian and Arab volunteers to join the ranks of the *feda'iyyin* – the guerrillas (Farsoun and Zacharia 1997). The growth of the guerrilla organisation imposed its own logic on the structure of the PLO. By the fourth Palestine National Council (PNC) meeting in 1969, it was a foregone conclusion that *Fatah*, because of the seats allotted to it and the support it enjoyed from independents, would be able to elect the leader of its choice to head the PLO. During that meeting, the delegates voted for Yasser Arafat as chairperson of the organisation. During the 1970s, the internal organisation of the PLO was rationalised, enlarged and consolidated, and beginning with the Lebanese civil war until its expulsion from Beirut (1975–82), the economic and social functions of the PLO were dramatically expanded (Farsoun and Zacharia 1997). By the mid-1970s, the PLO had developed the structures of a *de facto* government in exile (Farsoun and Zacharia 1997).

In the 1980s, activists in the West Bank and Gaza Strip (WBGS) also founded a number of political organisations that would come to play a significant role in Palestinian contemporary politics and amass a significant following in the occupied territories. Although Muslim Brotherhood activities in the Palestinian territories date back to the 1940s, Islamist associations, unions and organisations became increasingly popular in the early 1980s following the Iranian revolution. In the mid-1980s, Islamic Jihad splintered from the Muslim Brotherhood and established itself as a separate organisation. Most notably, the Brotherhood Islamists founded the *Harakat al-Muqawama al-Islamiyya* (Islamic Resistance Movement; *Hamas*) in 1987. Meanwhile, following the Madrid peace process, a schism emerged in the DFLP between those who supported the peace process and those who opposed it. Subsequently, supporters of the Madrid peace process broke away from the DFLP and founded the Palestinian Democratic Union (FIDA).

Due to the differences in commitments to ideology and social programmes, these various political organisations placed different levels of emphasis on the centrality and importance related to the political training of their members and to related mass mobilisation. Because *Fatah* initially focused almost solely on the military dimensions of the struggle, and because the organisation was growing at such a rapid pace, especially after the Karameh battle, it placed very little emphasis on the political training of its members and cadres. The leftist parties, on the other hand, were much more keen to develop 'political consciousness' as well as a firm grounding in leftist ideological thought amongst their members. Hence, members of the PCP, the DFLP and the PFLP had to undergo rigid ideological and political training (Quandt et al. 1973). Given the different approach of each of these groups to membership and political training, each would come to conceive and adopt different relationships with the Palestinian territories and their members and supporters based there. In sum, the development of the Palestinian liberation movement was characterised by the emergence of a plethora of political organisations, all of which were committed to the liberation of Palestine but varied in terms of what this liberation would entail, in their relationship to the Palestinian territories, and whether and to what extent they would involve mass-based constituencies. These differences would also shape the types of political parties they would become.

Post-nationalist political parties

In more recent years, a number of key Palestinian figures have established a plethora of new political parties. *Al-Mubadara al-Wataniyya al-Filistiniyya* (Palestinian National Initiative; PNI) is the most notable of these organisations, and perhaps the only party with the potential to become an important political player. The other parties include the Third Way, *Al-Wasatia* and *Al-Muntada* (Palestine Forum) (Sharnoff 2012). To date, however, they have limited mass support and their performance in the polls has been quite poor. Despite the political stature of some of the founders, their organisations pose no serious challenge to *Fatah* or *Hamas*, the two political parties that now dominate the Palestinian political system.

Mustafa Barghouti, a former member of the PPP, founding member of the Palestinian Medical Relief Committees and other professionalised NGOs, launched the PNI in 2002 as an alternative to *Fatah's* and *Hamas'* dominance. Among the co-founders were Haider Abdel Shafi, a prominent Palestinian political figure and physician and also a former PCP member, and a number of other well-known activists and intellectuals. The organisation is a democratic coalition committed to non-violent resistance (Hazan 2005). The PNI conceives of itself as a movement committed to resisting Israeli occupation and to reforming internal Palestinian politics by combatting corruption and promoting transparency and judicial and legislative reform. Quite well known to outside audiences, the party has not amassed a significant following in the WBGS. Salam Fayyad and Hanan Ashrawi established the Third Way, a centrist party, also as a counter to *Fatah's* and *Hamas'* dominance, and to participate in the 2006 legislative elections. Salam Fayyad had served as International Monetary Fund (IMF) Director to the PA between 1996 and 2001, and as Manager of the Arab Bank in Palestine, and Hanan Ashrawi is a veteran activist, and established academic and political figure, best known for her role as spokesperson of the PLO during the Madrid peace conference and during the period before the official signing of the Oslo Accords. *Al-Wasatia* and the Palestine Forum represent more modest, less ambitious efforts. Mohammed Dajani Daoudi established *al-Wasatia* in January 2007.[9] The organisation, a moderate Islamic reformist movement, advocates a so-called true teaching of Islam as a way to counter violent extremism. Despite the noteworthy mission of the organisation, it has few followers, and many are critical of Daoudi's affiliation with right-wing foreign organisations such as the Washington Institute for Near East Policy. Munib al-Masri, a Palestinian billionaire, and founder of Engineering and Development Company (EDGO) and co-founder of Palestine Development and Investment Company (PADICO), among other institutions, established *al-Muntada* in 2007. The organisation advocated the building of a democratic modern society. Although al-Masri has been active himself, the organisation has little political clout in Palestinian society.

Exercising democracy under occupation

Palestinian elections reflect the distortions of democracy under military occupation and are reflective of more general trends in political systems that suffer from similar constraints. The 1996 legislative and presidential elections, the subsequent local elections, the 2005 presidential elections and most notably the 2006 legislative elections were genuine exercises of political contestation – similar in many ways to the Iraqi elections under US occupation (Dawisha and Diamond 2006), although *Ba'ath* participation was heavily constrained. Similar to Iraq, these elections embodied the contradictions of this paradoxical context where outcomes represent the will of a citizenry, but they also must meet other criteria. In the Palestinian case, elections had to meet the PLO's Oslo obligations, as well as the demands of Israel and international actors. In the Iraq case, the elections had to conform with US strategic interests. Initially after the signing of the Declaration of Principles, the different political movements and parties engaged in intense debates about whether to participate in elections, and if participation would translate to *de facto* support and acceptance of the Oslo Accords. Ultimately, by the 2006 elections, almost all the movements decided that failure to participate would simply lead to marginalisation. They also recognised the importance of developing democratic institutions, even if outcomes had to accommodate the Oslo political framework. Accordingly, almost all the political movements decided to run in elections and adopted key features of political parties, which include running in public office, establishing clear political platforms, and advocating for their political agendas (Broning 2014). With the exception of *Wasatia* and *al-Muntada*, almost all major Palestinian political movements have participated in recent legislative Palestinian elections.

The 1996 legislative elections were limited in scope (Andoni 1996). Only *Fatah* and FIDA formally ran in the elections, and individuals from the FPLP and DFLP contested as independents without formal party endorsement. Since the majority of candidates were *Fatah*-affiliated, running as part of either the official list or unofficial lists, some dubbed the election the *Fatah* primaries. The 1996 presidential elections were also more or less uncontested. Samiha Khalil, a prolific figure of the Palestinian women's movement, ran against *Fatah*'s Yasser Arafat in what many considered a political prop to lend credibility to the elections. In the 2005 presidential elections, the PNI's Mustafa Barghouti, with the support of the PFLP and independents, ran against *Fatah*'s Mahmoud Abbas. In the 2006 elections, however, most political currents were represented: the PPP, the PFLP, the DFLP and the Third Way all formally contested the elections. Although individuals from all the political parties have participated in local elections, the exact extent of participation is more difficult to determine since candidates are not required to indicate partisan affiliation and often run as independents. *Fatah* and *Hamas* have for the most part dominated these elections as well.

The 2006 legislative elections were the most hotly contested of these democratic exercises in the WBGS. For the first time, *Hamas* and the Palestinian leftist opposition groups formally participated on party lists. The election results were a surprise to all parties, not least *Hamas* which won 74 out of the 132 seats. *Fatah* won 45, and the leftists and liberal democrats collectively secured 9 seats.[10] The 132 seats were contested on two separate lists: the first list comprised of 66 seats was contested nationally, and the second list with the remaining 66 seats was contested at the district level in sixteen different locations. The left and liberal democrats performed even more poorly at this level, not managing to win a single seat, in contrast to *Hamas* which won 45 seats (Jamal 2013).

The dismal performance of the secular nationalist political parties reflected their weakening as political movements. Additionally, they ran poorly organised electoral campaigns, unable to capitalise on running on joint lists or coordinating their campaigns. *Fatah*'s campaign was mired by internal divisions and its failure to meaningfully include the younger generation of the movement. The leftists had failed to put in place and articulate meaningful political programmes, and their outreach and grass-roots organisation efforts had been faltering for years. The new political parties ran better organised political campaigns, but they lacked support and recognition among mass constituencies given their predominately non-movement status. Although Barghouti's PNI portrays itself as a movement, its political reach was and still is a far cry from that of its PLO predecessors. Moreover, many felt that the willingness of these parties to participate in the PA and the overt support, both material and verbal, they received from western donors discredited them. Collective action problems mired the campaigns of the left and liberal democrats, and they eventually ran on four different slates (Independent Palestine, the Third Way, the Alternative and the Popular Front), severely dividing their support base.

Ultimately, the unwillingness of *Fatah* and the international community to accept the electoral outcome of *Hamas'* decisive victory undermined the entire democratic exercise. Immediately after its electoral win, *Hamas* called for the establishment of a unity government, and *Fatah* and the leftists initially refused to join. *Fatah* eventually conceded to a unity government, but this attempt at unity failed because of the already established Oslo parameters, which left little, if any, room to manoeuvre. It became clear at this stage that external military occupation and its associated framework imposed challenges in the face of Palestine's budding democracy that were insurmountable. To accommodate the post-Oslo framework, *Hamas* was required to renounce the use of violence, recognise Israel, and accept all previous agreements and obligations, including the Oslo Accords and the Road Map.[11] *Hamas* was willing to work with these conditions but would not accept them outright, as it sought some clear commitment on the part of Israel in return. For example, *Hamas* offered a ten-year *hudna* (ceasefire) instead of an outright renunciation of the use of violence. It recognised Israel as a reality it would have to work with, but would not formally recognise it. *Hamas* also insisted that the outcome of Israeli–Palestinian final status negotiations should be put to a Palestinian national referendum. Detailed discussions of *Fatah* and the international community's response against the *Hamas*-led government is beyond the scope of this chapter, but suffice it to say that *Hamas* did not give in and the response was a brutal embargo by the international community that *Fatah* supported and exacerbated to ensure the failure of its main domestic rival.

Candidates affiliated with *Fatah* and *Hamas* have similarly dominated the local municipal elections. In early 1997, the PA appointed 'transition' mayors for the interim period; most of these mayors were either members of *Fatah* or supporters of the party. The interim period lasted over eight years. In the wake of President Yasser Arafat's death in 2004, the PA decided to hold presidential, legislative, as well as local municipal elections. It is important to note, however, that the issues that dominate these elections are usually local service provision and not national issues. Moreover, families and clans play a determining role in shaping the outcomes of these elections, and therefore, election outcomes do not necessarily reflect the strength of the actual parties participating either formally or informally. The 2004 and 2005 local government elections were held in five phases. The PA held the first round of municipal elections in December 2004, a second round in May 2005, a third round in September 2005, and a fourth round in December 2005, but the fifth and final round was never held. By the third round of elections, *Fatah* had won 712 seats, compared with 418 for *Hamas* and a few seats gained by the PFLP, the PPP and independent affiliates. Realising again the extent of *Fatah*'s weakness, on 13 August 2005, before the completion of that year's local government elections, Abbas amended the Local Council Elections Law No. 5 of 1996. The new law, Local Council Elections Law No. 10 of 2005 replaced the take-all system, and each electoral list that received 8 per cent or more of the vote would be allocated seats in the local council proportional to the number of votes it received.[12] By the fourth round, *Hamas* had won the absolute majority of seats in three of the largest West Bank towns of Nablus, Jenin and El-Bireh, again exposing the weakness of *Fatah*. The fifth and last phase was not held; this round was cancelled right before the close of the nomination period as it became apparent that *Fatah* would be unable to produce candidate lists. Local elections were subsequently cancelled in 2010 and postponed in 2011. Following the 2007 *Hamas* take-over in Gaza, several *Hamas*-led councils were closed. Many international donors also suspended assistance to municipalities headed by *Hamas* officials.

The PA finally held local elections in 2012 because it knew *Hamas* would be boycotting them. *Hamas* cited harassment of its members and the need for national reconciliation as reasons for this boycott.[13] As a result of *Hamas*' call for the boycott of the elections, only 54 per cent of the 50 per cent registered to vote participated in the elections compared with the approximately 77 per cent who participated in the 2006 legislative elections. The defining feature of this election was its lack of political pluralism. Of the 354 local government localities, contested elections took place in only 93 councils.[14] In 179 localities, only one list was submitted or was valid for elections, and in the remaining 82 localities, no valid candidate list was submitted. In the latter, elections were postponed until November of that year. Ultimately, the majority of electoral contests in the ninety-three municipalities were between *Fatah* members, former *Fatah* members, or *Fatah*-affiliated candidates who ran on independent lists, and other candidates who were independent or left-affiliated. Ultimately, *Fatah* failed to win the majority of seats in five of eleven major towns. Having won the majority in six towns (Hebron, Qalqilya, Jericho, Tulkaram, Salfit and El-Bireh) they still declared it a victory for *Fatah* (Jamal unpublished MS).

The Palestinian Authority has not held legislative elections since 2006. Local elections were scheduled for autumn 2016, but since *Hamas* decided it would run in these elections, PA president Abbas postponed local elections indefinitely. It is fair to say that the development of Palestinian political parties, and Palestinian political life more generally, has come to a halt since *Hamas*' 2006 electoral victory.

Other challenges

The structure of available funding to political parties in the Palestinian territories, as well as the legal regulatory framework also contribute to the stagnation of political parties in this context. In particular, funding to political parties is intrinsically linked to the post-Oslo political order. *Fatah* now receives much of its funding through the PA and international actors keen to promote the post-Oslo Accords. Some sources claimed that *Fatah* alone spent more than $1.9 million during the 2006 elections, much of it from Western donors (Erlanger 2006). *Hamas* receives some of its funding from internal *zakat* fundraising. And the left, most notably the DFLP and PFLP, still rely primarily on their funding allocations from the PLO, and some have also managed to access Western donor funding through professionalising their NGO operations. Similarly, the liberal democrats and the newer political parties have also succeeded in acquiring Western donor funding. Access to such funding, however, is not without a price. During the 2006 legislative elections, many perceived these groups as having received funding amounts that exceeded established campaign finance limits, and that their extravagant campaigns and elaborate posters were testament to the western donor support they enjoyed. Observers commented how their signs, publicity materials and television advertisement campaigns were far more sophisticated than those of the other parties, and that this would not have been possible without the help of considerable Western donor funding. Observers also felt that western support discredited their campaigns, despite the merits of their political platform and the candidates' qualifications, because it represented a degree of overt, outside meddling in Palestinian elections.

The post-Oslo political order also circumscribes the legal regulatory framework. In 2007, President Abbas introduced the Palestinian Political Parties Draft Law. The law was endorsed by the Council of Ministers, but it was rejected by other Palestinian political organisations and civil society groups. Critics argued that the law discriminated against the Oslo oppositions, especially *Hamas*, and it further empowered *Fatah*, the leadership party of the PA.[15] To date, the PA does not have a party law, and for all practical purposes, this state of affairs provides more flexibility to the political movements and parties. The lack of defined laws, however, does not contribute to the strengthening of democratic institutions, and leaves weaker parties at the whim of the PA.

Future prospects: where are the political movements and parties now?

Undoubtedly, Palestinian political movements today are weaker than they were a decade ago. The Palestinian territories are perhaps the only place where legislators can be imprisoned *en masse*. In 2009 a third of all members of the Legislative Assembly were political prisoners detained in Israeli prisons. By 2013 at least thirteen of the legislators were still imprisoned in Israeli jails, the majority under administrative detention.[16] In November of 2016, Fatah held its seventh party convention, which to many reified the paralysis of Palestinian political life. Celebrated as a resurrection of the Palestinian national movement, the convention did little other than reappoint a disconnected, ageing leadership, further alienating its base (Høigilt 2016). The general Palestinian public was also dismayed with the extravagance of the event and the lack of revolutionary renewal it represented. It is important to note, however, that renewal has never really been a defining feature of Fatah (Baroud 2016).

In this same vein, Palestinian leftist parties have also failed to introduce comprehensive leadership renewal. Whatever leadership changes have taken place are symbolic and not far-reaching. The left has also been unable to implement a viable long-term strategy, both in terms of representing a true opposition, and in terms of mobilising a mass base. Like leftists elsewhere, as Resta outlines in her chapter in this volume, their international supporters and patrons are few. Along with the newer Palestinian political parties, they have not articulated clearly defined political and social programmes to influence leftist-oriented social policies pertaining to social issues such as health care or women's issues. Much of the advocacy work of the political parties has focused on isolated issues, involving a few of their leaders or members. One area in which a number of members of leftist parties have sought reform is in revising the electoral system, including enacting a women's quota for legislative elections. These programmes and campaigns have not been systematic, however.

The current state of the new political parties is just as problematic. Of these groups, only Mustafa Barghouti's PNI is still quite active, though limited in scope. It is not certain whether Masri's *al-Muntada* still exists, and similarly, *al-Wasatia* may exist only in name. Hanan Ashrawi parted ways with the Third Way shortly after the 2006 elections, likely taking with her the legitimacy she bestowed on the party.

Conclusion

To return to the original questions. Obviously, democracy has its limits under ongoing military occupation, and more accurately, may simply be overrated in this context. Moreover, the post-Oslo framework by design prioritises the political accommodation of Israel and external actors over democracy. The performance of these political parties remains intricately related to their strength as movements. Where democratic exercises are perhaps necessary and will likely reap more dividends is at the local level, not only the municipal level, but in syndicates, unions and other institutions of organised political life. In this regard, university student elections have established a microcosm of robust democratic contestation that may be worthy of emulation in society at large.

External occupation hinders democratic political life and generates problematic dynamics insofar as political parties that should be responsible to citizens find themselves constrained to deal with the interests of foreign actors.

Notes

1. 'Declaration of Principles', available at <http://www.unsco.org/Documents/Key/Declaration%20of%20Principles%20on%20Interim%20Self-Government%20Arrangements.pdf> (last accessed 4 September 2017).
2. The WBGS would be divided into three distinct areas (A, B and C), each consisting of different security and civil power arrangements. Israeli checkpoints would surround each of these areas. Area A would consist of approximately 17.2 per cent of the West Bank. In this area, the PA would be responsible for internal security and have wide civil powers. Area B would consist of 23.8 per cent of the West Bank, over which the PA would have civil control, and Israel would maintain overall security control. Area C would consist of 59 per cent of the territory; in this area, Israel would be responsible for both civil and military affairs, effectively under full Israeli control. For more on this, refer to the PLO Negotiations Affairs Department website at <https://www.nad.ps/en> (last accessed 4 September 2017).
3. For more on this, refer to Article VI of the Gaza-Jericho Agreement 1994, available at <http://www.iemed.org/documents/gaza.pdf> (last accessed 6 September 2017).
4. Smaller, less influential Islamist movements, such as Islamic Jihad, do not have separate political parties.
5. Activists also established a number of smaller splinter factions during this period. These organisations included the Palestinian Popular Struggle Front (a more extremist, leftist-*Ba'ath* organisation that split from *Fatah* in 1969), the Palestinian Liberation Front (split from the Popular Front for the Liberation Front–General Command in 1977), the Arab Liberation Front (an Iraqi-sponsored leftist military faction founded in 1969 by the Iraqi *Ba'ath* party) and the Popular Liberation War Pioneers (or *Sa'iqua*, founded in 1968, which was Syrian-backed and controlled by the *Ba'athists*).
6. The leftist groups, including the PCP, placed greater emphasis on their ideological development. By 1968, the DFLP, soon followed by the PFLP, began its transformation from a pan-Arabist organisation to a Marxist–Leninist organisation. These organisations were concerned with the fundamental social and political change in Palestinian society, as well as throughout the Arab world.
7. The Jordanian Communist Party was active in the West Bank, and a separate PCP was active in the Gaza Strip. Unlike, other Palestinian factions, the PCP made no effort to participate militarily, and initially opposed joining the PLO on grounds that such an action would serve the national struggle at the expense of the class struggle. In the initial years, Jewish and Palestinian communists worked within the same Communist organisations.
8. A battle fought between the PLO and Jordanian army on one side and the Israeli military on the other in the Jordanian town of Karameh.
9. *Wasatia* homepage, 'Wasatia, A Moderate Way: New Palestinian Islamic Initiative Takes the Middle Ground', available at <http://www.wasatia.info/aboutus.htm> (last accessed 4 September 2017).
10. The leftists and liberal democrats included the Democratic Front for the Liberation of Palestine (DFLP), the Palestinian Democratic Union (FIDA), the Palestinian

Front for the Liberation of Palestine (PFLP) and the Palestinian People's Party (PPP), as well as the self-described liberal democrats the Third Way party of Salam Fayyad and Hanan Ashrawi, and the Independent Palestine Party of Mustafa Barghouti performed abysmally.

11. The Road Map was put forth by the Quartet, and agreed upon by the two parties in April 2003 as a way to move the peace process forward. Phase I required mutual recognition, renunciation of the use of violence and political institutional reform on the part of the Palestinians. On the part of Israel, the Road Map required Israel to refrain from deportations and demolitions, ease movement, improve the humanitarian situation of the Palestinians in the West Bank and the Gaza Strip, and commit to a complete settlement freeze.

12. 'Local Council Elections Law No. 10 of 2005', available at <http://www.elections. ps/Portals/0/pdf/lOCAL_ELECTIONS_LAW-EDIT-EN.pdf> (last accessed 23 September 2017).

13. 'Palestine Electoral Study Mission Urges Political Reconciliation', available at <http://www.cartercenter.org/news/pr/occupied-palestinian-territory-102112. html> (last accessed 14 December 2014).

14. 'Local Elections 2012: Facts and Figures, October 17th', available at <http:// www.elections.ps/Portals/0/pdf/LE2012/LE2012-ObserverOrientation.pdf> (last accessed 23 September 2017).

15. For more on this discussion, refer to the comments by Vlad Pran Ifes, country director in the West Bank and Gaza, available at <http://www.palestinianba-siclaw.org/documents/2007-political-parties-law-cabinet-draft> (last accessed 4 September 2017).

16. For more on Israel's detention of Palestinian legislators, see Addameer Prisoner Support and Human Rights Association (2013)

Bibliography

Abu-Lughod, Ibrahim (1971), *The Transformation of Palestine: Essays on the Origin and Development of the Arab–Israeli Conflict*, Evanston, IL: Northwestern University Press.

Addameer Prisoner Support and Human Rights Association (2013), *Palestinian Political Prisoners in Israeli Prisons*, June, Jerusalem: Addameer Prisoner Support and Human Rights Association, <http://www.europarl.europa.eu/meetdocs/2009_2014/documents/dplc/dv/palestinianpoliticalprisoners/palestinianpoliticalprisonersen. pdf> (last accessed 23 September 2017).

Andoni, Lamis (1996), 'The Palestinian Elections: Moving toward Democracy or One-Party Rule?', *Journal of Palestine Studies* 25: 3, 5–16.

Baroud, Ramzi (2016), 'Fatah, Hold Your Applause: Palestinian Body Politic Rotten to the Core', *Counterpunch*, 8 December, <http://www.counterpunch. org/2016/12/08/fatah-hold-your-applause-palestinian-body-politic-rotten-to-the-core/> (last accessed 1 September 2017).

Broning, Michael (2014), *Political Parties in Palestine: Leadership and Thought*, London: Palgrave Macmillan.

Cobban, Helena (1984), *The Palestine Liberation Organization*, Cambridge: Cambridge University Press.

Dawisha, Adeed, and Larry Diamond (2006), 'Iraq's Year of Voting Dangerously', *Journal of Democracy* 17: 2, 89–103.

Erlanger, Steven (2006), 'U.S. and Israelis Are Said to Talk of Hamas Ouster', *New York Times*, 14 February.

Farsoun, Samih, and Christina Zacharia (1997), *Palestine and the Palestinians*, Boulder, CO: Westview Press.

Hazan, Eric (2005), 'A Movement of Movements? Palestinian Defiance', *New Left Review* 32, 117–31.

Høigilt, Jacob (2016), 'Fatah from Below: The Clash of Generations in Palestine', *British Journal of Middle Eastern Studies* 43: 4, 456–71.

Jamal, Manal A. (2013), 'Beyond Fatah Corruption and Mass Discontent: Hamas, the Palestinian Left and the 2006 Legislative Elections', *British Journal of Middle Eastern Studies* 40: 3, 273–94.

Jamal, Manal A. (unpublished MS), *Democracy Promotion in Distorted Times: The Limits of Western Donor Assistance*.

Lockman, Zachary (1996), *Comrades and Enemies: Arab and Jewish Workers in Palestine, 1906–1948*, Berkeley: University of California Press.

Quandt, William, Paul Jabber and Ann Lesch (1973), *The Politics of Palestinian Nationalism*, Berkeley: University of California Press.

Sayigh, Yezid (1997), *Armed Struggle and the Search for State: The Palestinian National Movement 1949–1993*, Oxford: Oxford University Press.

Sharnoff, Michael (2012), 'Can Palestinian Third Parties Make a Difference?', *Palestine–Israel Journal of Politics, Economics, and Culture* 18: 2/3, 121–5.

Smith, Charles (1996), *Palestine and the Arab–Israeli Conflict*, New York: St. Martin's Press.

Chapter 8

Sectarian friction and the struggle for power: party politics in Iraq post-2003

Sophie A. Edwards

On the Democracy Index of 2016, Iraq is number 114 of 167 worldwide and sixth of twenty in the Middle East and North Africa, being described as a hybrid regime along the lines of Lebanon, Morocco and Palestine (The Economist Intelligence Unit 2016).

The goal for Iraq was, however, a very different one when US forces took over Baghdad in 2003. Then, one of the stated aims of the invasion was to install a functioning democracy in Iraq based on a multi-party system that included all factions of Iraq's heterogeneous society. Fifteen years on and reality falls far short of those expectations. While a party system was indeed put in place, the political party landscape in Iraq is a complicated and messy one, with name changes, coalition changes and policy changes occurring on a continuous basis. In the midst of Iraq trying to find a new identity after the fall of Saddam, the political system that has developed since is dominated by a permanent struggle to achieve self-interest and to accumulate power not only between the different political parties but also individuals as well as outside forces.

In the Iraqi political system, the various entities all have an interest in the state's survival, but, equally, in keeping it weak. The result is a state that does not deliver in the areas of the rule of law, good governance or service delivery (Wahab 2017). The population is ill-served by government services, corruption is rife, and despite being able to vote, ordinary Iraqis are alienated from the institutions of the state, although they voice their criticism (Dodge 2013).

Under the eight-year government of Nouri al-Maliki as prime minister of Iraq, the situation turned so bad that Iraq was compared to the repressive regime it had replaced eleven years earlier (Dodge 2013).

While this was prevented for the time being through the ousting of Maliki in 2014, the democratic process of Iraq remains an unstable one. The collapse of the Iraqi government has been predicted several times during the last decade, particularly during spring and summer of 2016. At the time, the *Sadrist* movement protesting in the streets, parties boycotting the Council of Representatives and ministers being ousted (Lawrence 2016) all destabilised the government. Despite all these problems, Iraqis and their hybrid democracy have proven resilient to date.

No matter how malfunctioning, the Iraqi political system and the parties representing it are of key importance, as they are the core democratic features of Iraq, which prevents a return to full-blown authoritarianism. A fear of a repeat domination by one part of society over the other is the driving factor behind the continuous democratic process in the country.

The aim of this chapter is to describe the main actors within this vast landscape of party politics in Iraq, to analyse their characteristics and to improve the understanding of their background and the environment they are operating in. Building on existing academic and expert discussions on issues encompassing Iraq's political sphere – from voting behaviour, historic accounts of party formation and the role of clerics to analyses focusing on the specific Kurdish and Sunni political spheres – this chapter systematises the existing research to present a coherent picture of the complicated state of political parties in Iraq and will enrich the knowledge of the influencing factors on Iraqi party politics.

Iraq's multi-party landscape: parliamentary alliances and sectarianism

The party system in Iraq today can be described as extremely pluralistic, although this might be an understatement of the actual situation. Self-proclaimed political parties in Iraq are so numerous that their actual number is unknown to the general population. While approximately a dozen of these parties have managed to become institutionalised and be known nationally, the sheer number of competing parties has resulted in the main political parties forming alliances with mostly smaller parties to work together on the ground and to gain votes. These alliances, far from being stable, change their names and components before each election, depending on the personal interests of the main party or political leader(s) involved in the alliance intent on securing votes and power in parliament.

The alliances established in this manner largely divide Iraq's political parties into Shi'i, Sunni, Kurdish and secular blocs, with the Islamic *Da'wa* party, headed by current Prime Minister Haider al-Abadi and home of the previous prime minister, Nouri al-Maliki, dominating the Shi'i faction, followed by the Islamic Supreme Council of Iraq (ISCI'), headed by Ammar al-Hakim, and the *Sadrist* movement. Iraq's main Sunni party is the Iraqi Islamic Party (IIP), and the Iraqi National Accord, led by Ayad Allawi, is the country's most prominent secular party. When it comes to the Kurds, the main parties are the Kurdistan Democratic Party (KDP'), the Patriotic Union of Kurdistan (PUK') and the Movement for Change Party or 'Gorran'.

The division of these parties into ethnic and religious factions has been present since their official appearance on the political stage in the aftermath of the US invasion partly as a result of the way in which US forces saw post-Saddam Iraq. Since the first post-Saddam elections in 2005, political parties have used sectarianism to gain a stronghold in national politics. Having been in exile for the previous decades though, parties were unable to use an indigenous base of support and were dependent on foreign actors to support their activities (Ismael and Ismael 2010). As a consequence, the only basis they had to attract voters was sectarianism, which they happily used (Yamao 2012). Their work was facilitated by the groundwork laid down by the US forces, which had distributed jobs and government posts according to sectarian quotas. The result was that in 2005, the majority of voters favoured party lists according to their ethnic and sectarian compositions (Dawisha 2010).

While there was a move away from sectarianism and towards a focus on forming a national unity government prior to the 2010 elections, the deterioration of the security situation and the increasing alienation of ordinary citizens from the political process led parties to revert to cooperating according to their ethnic and sectarian identity (Ali 2014: 4) as of 2014 in order to gain from the divisions on the ground. Regional actors interfering in Iraqi politics by supporting individual political parties as well as proxies strengthen the sectarian trend, which is predicted to continue for the 2018 elections. It is for this reason that this chapter will also examine party politics through the sectarian lens.

The Shi'i: religious influence and personal cults

The Shi'i political parties in Iraq constitute the bloc of parties most intensely based on religious ideology. The *Da'wa* party is Iraq's oldest Islamic party, founded in the late 1950s with the support of Grand Ayatollah Mohammad Baqir al-Sadr, Muqtada al-Sadr's cousin and father-in-law (Bayless 2012). The *Da'wa* party was created as a response to the decline in importance of religion among ordinary citizens. It developed in Najaf as a clandestine movement with the support of intellectuals and students, for whom religion was at the forefront of policy-making (Bernhardt 2011). The party's immediate aim was to work against the secularisation of Iraqi society and to revive Islamic consciousness. The 1940s and 1950s had seen the attraction of communism expand in many sectors of Iraqi society and across the Arab world more broadly, as Resta explains in her chapter in this volume. It followed that clergymen and religious intellectuals needed to create a platform to increase their voice (Batatu 1981). Over the years the party moved from clerical to non-clerical leadership, but Islam still continued to be its central ideological element (Bernhardt 2011).

In comparison with the *Da'wa* party, its offshoot, the ISCI, did not move away from its clerical leadership but remained in the hands of its founding family, al-Hakim. Mohammed al-Hakim's father, Ayatollah Muhsin al-Hakim, had participated in state affairs as well as in protests from his home in Najaf following the overthrow of the Iraqi monarchy in 1958. Decades of political activism followed, closely connected to Shi'i Islamic teachings. The clerics began to run politics from home, later continued in exile – specifically Iran – and then returned to share power in Iraq's new republic after 2003 (Corboz 2015).

Both the *Da'wa* and ISCI were established during the time of *Ba'athist* rule, with the aim of creating an agenda opposing that of the socialist *Ba'ath* regime. The majority of the Shi'i population in Iraq eventually came around to supporting their agenda and finally welcomed the re-emergence of religion in the public space after the fall of Saddam in 2003.

It is not surprising that, particularly from the Shi'i side, religious voices can be heard in party politics and the political sphere, as the Shi'i majority of Iraq base their beliefs on the doctrine of the Imam, meaning that they have a chosen religious leader to follow not only when it comes to questions requiring religious knowledge, but also when dealing with worldly affairs. As a result, clerical political activism, while not always at the forefront, has been present in Iraq throughout the modern country's existence (Rahimi 2012). Due to their prominent position in society, the authority of Shi'i clerics has always been of particular importance. As a result, Shi'i clerics have often played a crucial political role, while at the same time facing criticism within their own ranks precisely for combining religion and politics (Bernhardt 2011).

The most prominent example of a religious voice influencing the Iraqis' political decision-making without being formally involved in politics is Grand Ayatollah Ali al-Sistani. Having built his reputation as a cleric in Iraq, al-Sistani, who is originally from Iran, is described as a 'quietist'. This means that he is not officially involved in politics and is against parties using his name or image, but he makes his opinion heard whenever he deems it necessary for what he perceives to be the well-being of the country. It was al-Sistani who urged Iraqis not to resist US troops in 2003 (PBS 2003), who spoke out for democracy, who provided his advice on elections to the public (Schenker 2008), who urged Shi'i parties to build a bloc in 2005 and who pushed then Prime Minister Nouri al-Maliki to leave office (Chmaytelli 2016a, 2016b).

Closer to, but also not formally engaged in, the party political sphere is another cleric, Muqtada al-Sadr. His influence has been passed down through family connections, particularly Grand Ayatollah Mohammad Baqir al-Sadr, Muqtada's cousin and father-in-law and Muqtada's father, Grand Ayatollah Mohammad Sadiq al-Sadr, who was executed by the Saddam regime after refusing to cooperate with it (Plebani 2014). From the establishment of the Mehdi Army to the entering and leaving of party politics, Muqtada al-Sadr has successfully developed a loyal following. Larger than any individual politician in the country, he built his base primarily in the poorer areas of Najaf and Baghdad, such as Sadr city (George 2016). This has turned him into the spiritual leader of the third major force in Iraqi Shi'i politics, the *Sadrist* movement, as well as into one of the most powerful men in Iraq (Salih 2016a; al-Khoei 2014).

While religious ideology is a central element in Iraq's Shi'i parties, their shared religious beliefs have not been sufficiently potent to form the basis for genuine cooperation due to personal rivalries that led individuals to compete for power. Thus, the different Shi'i parties are ideologically estranged from each other, with a number of strong and influential personalities moving in different directions, while at the same time attempting to maintain Shi'i predominance in Iraqi politics.

This has led to a number of changing alliances between the different parties.

The Islamic *Da'wa* party and the Islamic Supreme Council of Iraq, which ran together as the United Iraqi Alliance in 2005, split before the 2010 elections, with Nouri al-Maliki forming the State of Law Coalition (SLC) in order to position himself as the head of a national, non-sectarian and multi-ethnic coalition, attempting to move thereby away from the purely Shi'i image he had. The result of the split was the formation of the Iraqi National Alliance, a coalition of the remaining parties from the old United Iraqi Alliance Shi'i list. The list was made up of thirty-two parties, groups and individuals. They had no common policy structure and included rivals such as Muqtada al-Sadr and Ammar al-Hakim, leader of the Islamic Supreme Council of Iraq, with their only common ground being their Shi'i identity. The coalition's aim was not to be swept away by Maliki's State of Law (Dawisha 2010). With some parties gaining in strength and confidence, fractures appeared in the coalition, which resulted in a further reorganisation of the parties before the 2014 elections. The *Sadrist* movement, for instance, formed its own bloc, *Al-Ahrar*. It had grown particularly strong thanks to the provision of social services, linking them to a message in support of activism, nationalism and religious piety in the poor areas of Baghdad and the south. It had also secured forty seats in the 2010 elections (Plebani 2014) and was therefore encouraged to become the leading party of its own alliance. The Badr Organization as well, a political organisation which developed out of the ISCI's military arm, the Badr corps, separated from the ISCI and the Iraqi National Alliance and moved towards Maliki's State of Law. As a result, the ISCI remained the last large organisation in the Iraqi National Alliance and renamed it the Citizen Alliance or *Al-Muwatin*. While the Shi'i factions continue to officially work together in parliament under the umbrella of the 'National Alliance' so as to retain their majority, internal disputes are rife, as demonstrated by the dispute for leadership of the National Alliance in 2016 as well as the Muqtada al-Sadr-affiliated *Al-Ahrar* bloc's declaration that it would not attend the National Alliance meetings because of its opposition to Maliki's State of Law Coalition (Naser 2016). The past and current cooperation between Shi'i parties illustrates how parties are to a certain extent forced to work together on a sectarian level, despite considerable infighting. The sect-based system created in Iraq thus forces the Shi'i to stick together to share the spoils of office, but disputes are inevitable because movements and personalities have little in common beyond that.

Considering the variety of changes different parties go through, which is as true for Shi'i parties as it is for the other parties engaged in Iraqi institutional politics, as will be seen later in the chapter, it seems important to explore the question of whom people are supposed to vote for, as party programmes are unclear and ever-changing. Two factors that remain the same from election to election are the sectarian element of the different parties and the prominence of their well-known political leaders. Voters are thus forced to vote according to their own religious or sectarian belief and affiliation notwithstanding the particular composition of the coalition in question; alternatively, they can vote for a coalition out of the belief in the ability of the main political figure representing the alliance. Thus, party politics, from the point of view of voters, is about sectarian allegiances and/or personalities.

This has led to individual politicians surpassing their political parties in importance with a consequent personalisation of party politics. Iraqi parties for now fall largely into the category of ideologically and organisationally weak parties, as described in Storm and Cavatorta's introduction to this book. They are in fact the personal vehicles of political entrepreneurs and their families. There is no interest in building a party to represent the country's citizens and there are very few clear ideological tenets underpinning what parties do. As a result of the party leader being so strong, internal democracy is weak and there is no motivation for a strong party organisation to be built.

The prime example of a top-heavy party is the *Da'wa* party and its leader, Iraq's previous prime minister, Nouri Maliki. Maliki enhanced his personal status with the aim to control Iraqi politics single-handedly and because of this he endangered the continuation of Iraq's slow democratisation process. He influenced the judiciary, controlled the security apparatus and weakened political opponents with the sole aim to ensure his political survival. He did so through a number of steps. Initially he positioned himself as a strong leader in the eyes of many amongst the Iraqi population after his successful military campaign against the Mahdi Army. He then took advantage of the shortfalls in the existing power-sharing agreements by filling available administrative and military positions with his loyalists. He also forged an alliance with the chief justice of the federal court, which allowed him in turn to enhance the powers of his own office. In addition to taking advantage of the weak structures in place, Maliki's efforts to centralise power were facilitated by Iraq's rentier economy because the money generated from oil revenue is available to the executive branch, permitting the distribution of significant patronage (al-Qawaree 2014).

Having established his power, Maliki went after his political opponents, taking steps to oust prominent Sunni officials such as Tareq al-Hashemi, vice president and leader of the IIP, Deputy Prime Minister Saleh al-Mutlak and Minister of Finance Rafi al-Issawi. As Dodge (2013) argues, both the arrest of Hashemi as well as the ousting of Issawi were Maliki's moves to silence opponents who could have disturbed his own political agenda or were likely to make gains in forthcoming elections. Maliki worked relentlessly to centralise power in Iraq (Ali 2014), resulting in commentators seeing him as the next Iraqi dictator. As part of his strategy, he worked with family members and kept other party members weak. He only lost his premiership in 2014 as a result of growing popular pressure inside Iraq as well as from international actors, such as the United States, the UN Security Council and, ultimately, Iran. Finally, Grand Ayatollah Ali al-Sistani, a religious force that could not be ignored, publicly implied that it was Maliki's time to leave, suggesting that al-Sistani was a religious force that could not be ignored, an issue that will be further discussed below.

In a similar top-heavy approach, the Islamic Supreme Council of Iraq has until now only been under the rule of one family, the al-Hakims, with Ayatollah Mohammed Baqir al-Hakim founding the party and later the ayatollah's brother, Abdul Aziz al-Hakim, leading it. The latter's son, Ammar al-Hakim, and today Sayyid Ammar al-Hakim eventually took over. The Ahrar bloc, while not officially led by Muqtada al-Sadr, would not survive without the cult around his personality, with al-Sadr having recently introduced his nephew, Ahmed al-Sadr, as his political successor.

It should be noted though that many of the current problems in Iraqi party politics can be connected to the past. Under Saddam Hussein's *Ba'athist* regime, the state became synonymous with the *Ba'ath* party, with the latter engaging in the mass suppression of all opposition. This resulted in the rise of a political elite in the diaspora, which had the tendency to represent narrow interests as well as to be influenced by external actors (Ismael and Ismael 2010). This in part undermined the birth of a strong party system following the 2003 invasion.

Iranian influence

Iranian influence has been particularly strong among the main Shi'i parties, the *Da'wa* party and the ISCI, as a result of their leading members having been forced to move into exile in Iran after confrontations with the *Ba'athist* regime. While the *Da'wa* party later tried to at least partially move away from Iranian influence, the ISCI has since its formation had strong ties to the teachings of Ayatollah Ali Khamenei in Iran. This can be explained by the fact that the party itself was established in Tehran and funded by Iran, with its military wing, the Badr Brigade, today's Badr Organization, being trained, recruited and armed by Iran's Revolutionary Guard (Katzman 2009). Since the fall of Saddam, Iran's support has been crucial in empowering Shi'i parties in Iraq. Iran has been outspoken in its support for the *Da'wa* party and the Islamic Supreme Council of Iraq, working to support friendly Shi'i factions, while at the same time trying to ensure Iraq's territorial unity, as a break-up of the country would increase regional instability, with potentially devastating effects for Iran's national security (Barzegar 2010). As a result of these two contradictory objectives, Iran has only achieved mixed results through its meddling in Iraqi politics. In general, relations to Iran are a difficult matter in Iraqi politics. While some want Iranian support, the legitimacy of parties with very close ties to Teheran, particularly the ISCI, has been questioned in some sectors of the Iraqi population as well as other political parties, such as the *Sadrist* movement. Thus, as a result of their close affiliation to Iran, these parties are perceived to represent an outside force rather than the Iraqi people (Corboz 2015: 154). As a result, Iraqi parties have accepted Iranian support when it was in their self-interest to do so, but also have sought support from other countries, if this was in their interest.

Attempts at reform

In light of the domestic and international criticism Iraqi politics has received, it is no surprise that efforts for reform have been made, but without major success. Rather than working together, the ruling alliance of Shi'i parties succumbed to personal rivalries and individual interests. Maliki's successor, Prime Minister Abadi's, attempted to reshuffle the national cabinet, but this led to a battle between the State of Law and Muqtada al-Sadr's *Sadrists*, with the former aiming to preserve the status quo and the latter demanding a change in government personnel. The process of attempting to reshuffle the cabinet can be used to provide a clear example of Iraq's current political landscape, with political blocs and parties unwilling to lose ministerial positions and parties attempting to hijack the process to protect their personal interests and to undermine their opponents.

Muqtada al-Sadr used his followers to strengthen his personal demands and at the beginning of 2016, he encouraged them to take to the streets. Claiming to be dissatisfied with the lack of technocrats in the Iraqi government and unhappy with the high levels of corruption, they staged anti-government protests in Baghdad, breaking into the Green Zone and storming parliament. While the concerns of the people who took to the streets were certainly real, it can be asked why a figure like Muqtada al-Sadr, with power both within political parties and in parliament, employed such tactics in the public sphere to raise his concerns.

As a response to public pressure, Abadi did his best to overhaul the cabinet, appointing five new ministers (Chmaytelli 2016a, 2016b), but Iraq's supreme court declared the decision unconstitutional, as a result of alleged coerced voting (Hameed and Kalin 2016). As a further move, Abadi abolished three ministerial positions to cut down on government spending, including the Minister for Human Rights and the Minister for Women's Affairs. These cuts were approved and they can only be perceived as evidence of where the priorities of the ruling parties are. As Pollack (2016) explains, the Iraqi government is effectively paralysed. According to his personal experience in Iraq, Abadi and his staff have good ideas and intentions for remodelling Iraq and making it politically and economically workable for the future. However, they are unable to fight against the byzantine bureaucracy, and the reforms they propose are opposed by other factions in parliament, in particular Shi'i rivals, such as Muqtada al-Sadr, who uses 'the street' to push for these reforms, while at the same time blocking them behind the scenes in a bid to simply increase his public profile and his bargaining power.

In addition to the public dispute between al-Sadr and Abadi, a new opposition bloc was created in the Iraqi parliament in 2016 with approximately ninety-eight members. They include forty-two members from the *Da'wa* party, all of the members of Ayad Allawi's *Wataniya* bloc and a number of individuals who defected from their parties. It means that this Reform Front is the largest bloc in the Council of Representatives, having the power to influence government policy. It is said, however, that the bloc is steered by Nouri Maliki and is being used to destabilise the CoR so Maliki will then be able to return as the unifying leader (Lawrence 2016).

While reforms might thus be on the agenda of some individual politicians and 'the street' demands them, the parties as a whole do not seem to be ready to put their own interests aside in order to look after the country's interests as a whole.

The Sunnis and the seculars: lacking representation and participation

The Shi'i parties are not the only ones operating in what has become a highly sectarian context. There are a number of Sunni parties as well as 'secular' ones that are active in the country. Iraqi Sunni Arabs face a crisis of representation, resulting from a lack of engagement in the political process. After the ousting of Saddam, the Sunnis went from being the rulers to being ruled overnight. Unlike the Kurds, they have no strong sense of ethno-nationalism and they also have no united religious leadership, like the Shi'i. Consequently, they did not immediately know how to deal with losing power and were unable to deal with the new political system being put in place. As noted previously, the US authorities upon their arrival in Iraq put in place a sectarian system, with the aim to achieve power sharing. But rather than leading to cooperation among the different Iraqi confessions, the new system inevitably gave rise to sectarian entrenchment, as part of which every faction had to fight for its survival.

There was and there still is no single authority that could unite or drive the Sunnis, who are unhappy with Shi'i rule and the perceived impunity of Shi'i militias. This disenfranchisement is not translated into political participation but, often, in the support or indifference towards Sunni extremist groups, including the Islamic State (Mansour 2016). While there are Sunni politicians who have risen to prominence, such as Osama al-Nujaifi, one of Iraq's current vice presidents, or his brother Atheel al-Nujaifi, who was the previous governor of the Nineveh province, the Sunni population is so divided that it has been unable to create one or more political parties supporting its general interests, even though, just as with the Shi'i parties, outside forces provide funds to support the different parties. Such support comes mainly from Turkey and Saudi Arabia. The IIP, led by Osama Tawfiq al-Tikriti and ideologically linked to the Muslim Brotherhood, is currently the main Iraqi Sunni party. Oppressed under Saddam, the IIP rose in power after 2003, but was unable to reach its full potential as individuals' self-interest prevailed. Under Tariq al-Hashimi, for example, the party switched to the Iraqiyyah List with the view of increasing influence and power. Al-Hashimi was chased out of the country by Maliki, however, with the party failing to side with the 2012/13 Sunni protest movement (Abdulrazaq 2015). Attempts were made to deal with the absence of representation and in the lead-up to the 2009 provincial elections Sunni and Shi'i parties mushroomed. In the case of the Sunnis that meant that while eight parties participated in the 2005 elections, there were twenty in the three main coalitions in Baghdad alone, with a further six parties running on their own in Baghdad and a number of others running only outside of Baghdad. These developments reflect Sunni diversity as well as their factionalism, but also the desire to build new groups, away from the domination of parties that were criticised for functioning predominantly as a personal vehicle for their leaders. As a result, while the number of Sunni parties continued to rise, none of them stood out. As Carroll (2011) explains, this is the behaviour that has led to political parties in the Middle East failing to contribute to democratisation processes. In short, parties do not develop effective structures to link citizens to the state and to develop an identity independent of their leader.

Equally, the existing secular parties in Iraq are unable to gain a strong foothold in the current political sphere. The communist party, which had significant political and social clout in the previous century, has taken a back seat today, and even the US's politician of choice and winner of the 2010 elections, Ayad Allawi and his Iraqi National Accord, were unable to repeat their win in the subsequent elections, following the departure of a number of Sunni politicians from the party.

Just as with the Shi'i parties, the Sunnis and seculars cannot find a lasting way of working together, as can be observed in the way their alliances are constructed and later dissolve. Iraq's main secular party, Ayad Allawi's Iraqi National Accord, established the Iraqi National List for the 2005 elections, with Iraq's main Sunni party, the Iraqi Islamic Party, running the Iraqi Accord Front or *al-Tawafuq*. The Iraqi National List evolved into the Iraqi National Movement or *al-Iraqiyya* for the 2010 election, and attracted a number of Sunni parties, as well as a party newly created by the IIP's former leader, Tariq al-Hashemi. *Al-Tawafuq* ended up participating in the elections with less support from other Sunni parties. As a result of this reshuffling, *al-Iraqiyya* achieved a landslide win in the 2010 election. The two groups separated again before the 2014 elections, with Ayad Allawi heading *al-Wataniya* or the National Coalition together with fourteen smaller parties, and the main Sunni parties uniting under the *Muttahidoon* alliance (Reform Coalition United). The result was a loss for Ayad Allawi.

Feeling underrepresented within the Iraqi political structure as well as discriminated against by the ruling Shi'i majority, Iraq's Sunnis staged several protests against Prime Minister Nouri al-Maliki in 2012/13, demanding an end to their marginalisation, the release of detainees and the abolition of anti-terrorism laws (Rabkin 2016). The violent response of the government fuelled feelings of marginalisation and contributed to the success of the Islamic State in the area a year later.

While the Sunnis manage their localities through local political parties as well as through a strong tribal system, national solutions will have to be found in the coming years to integrate Iraq's Sunni population into the national political process. Whether this will be achieved by the formation or reformation of Sunni political parties or rather through a move away from sectarianism and towards an inclusion of the Sunnis in the existing Shi'i-dominated or Shi'i-led parties, will remain to be seen.

The Kurds: competitive authoritarianism and change

At the national level, the Kurds are the only reasonably stable group in the Iraqi parliament, with a fixed number of parties being present and with the two main parties, the Kurdish Patriotic Union of Kurdistan (PUK) and the Kurdistan Democratic Party (KDP), competing as a Kurdistan Alliance in the 2005 and 2010 elections. Despite internal differences, the Kurds generally find common ground in order to assert their interests in Baghdad. At the regional level, the Kurdistan Region has its own devolved political system and this is where conflicts between parties emerge.

As a result of their ethnic and religious homogeneity, the Kurds do not have to contend with the extreme pluralism of political parties in Iraqi national politics. In fact, Kurdish politics is dominated by two main parties, the KDP and the PUK, with the Movement for Change Party or 'Gorran' having first split from and recently joined forces again with the latter.

This, however, was not always the case. The Kurds only gained their political autonomy following the first Gulf War and UN Resolution 688 from 5 April 1991 (Posch and Brown 2004: 28) when the US and Britain declared a 'safe haven' for the Kurds in northern Iraq and as such allowed for the territorialisation of Kurdish nationalism. The three main Kurdish areas of Dohuk, Erbil and Sulaimaniya were virtually separated from the central government in Baghdad and the Kurdistan Regional Government (KRG) was created. The first elections were then held (Khidir 2002). Political stability did not immediately follow the elections, as the results were contested. A violent six-year internal conflict ensued (Olson 2005). It was during this civil war that the current main political parties in the region gained their power. There had previously been several other strong entities on the local scene, such as the communist and the socialist parties, as well as various tribes. It was during the 1990s that the KDP and the PUK managed to take control and either defeated their opponents or forced them into alliances (Jabar and Dawod 2006).

While the KDP and the PUK ended the civil war by agreeing to power sharing in 1998, the KDP has arguably remained the domineering party in the region. The Barzani family runs the KDP, which had been instrumental in the nationalist fight for an autonomous or independent Kurdistan Region. Under Barzani's rule and the KDP–PUK alliance, the Kurdistan Region was long praised as the flagship for democratic development in Iraq, particularly in the west. After the 2009 elections, Kurdistan was specifically hailed as a democratic success story, with a freely elected leadership and a vibrant opposition. Gorran in fact received 24 per cent of votes and the Services and Reform List, a bloc comprised of Islamic and socialist groups, achieved 13 per cent. This meant that the KDP–PUK alliance won a majority of 'only' 57 per cent, leading some to argue that the previous 'managed democracy' – where the PUK and KDP won over 90 per cent of votes – was over (Knights 2009).

But this façade of democracy crumbles when considering that the KDP enjoys in fact absolute control over local politics. The presidency of the region is in the firm grip of the Barzani clan, with the president's nephew, Nechirvan Barzani, as prime minister, and the president's son, Masrour Barzani, as chancellor of the Kurdistan Region Security Council. In addition, local institutions such as the police do not operate independently of those in power. As of 2017, the KDP's shadow government, effectively a deep state with almost total control over security, the economy and the media, controls Kurdistan's governing coalition. The KDP is clearly clinging to its power. Massoud Barzani's presidency term expired on 19 August 2015, having been voted president for his second, and, legally, final term, with a landslide (70 per cent) in 2009. Then, in 2013, in the months leading up to the September parliamentary and presidential elections, a law was suddenly rushed through parliament allowing Barzani to retain the presidency for two more years. The KDP in 2015 wished to extend Barzani's term for a further two years, until the next parliamentary and presidential elections, but was unable to push it through with just its thirty-eight seats. Gorran and the PUK were willing to discuss an extra two years for Barzani only if the presidential system were replaced by a parliamentary one, a proposal the KDP was unwilling to accept. The outcome of this stalled negotiation over presidential terms was demonstrations in the streets with protesters being killed and the KDP preventing Gorran parliamentarians, including the parliament's speaker, Yousif Mohammed, from entering Erbil in October 2015.

Rather than describing the Kurdistan Region as a work-in-progress democracy, the ongoing events demonstrate that its party politics falls rather within the competitive authoritarian category of regimes. While free elections are held in the Kurdistan Region, the main party in power abuses state resources and harasses the opposition and journalists in order to maintain its grip on power.

The situation worsened in the Kurdistan Region with the deteriorating economy. The financial crisis in early 2016 meant that the KRG was unable to pay its civil servants. With the region's economy struggling and a financial crisis being felt on the ground, people began taking to the streets in 2016, strengthening opposition parties and moving against the regional government. Within the political parties, this led to further friction between the KDP and the PUK, which had until then done their best to cooperate, despite their differences. At the same time, Gorran and PUK moved closer again. They signed an agreement in the spring of 2016 to form a joint action platform. The agreement presents a counterweight to the KDP, and the factual termination of the 'strategic agreement' between the KDP and PUK (Salih 2016b). All this highlights how internal tensions persist in Kurdistan and shows the little agreement there is among Kurdish parties on the policies to pursue if and when the region becomes even more autonomous or independent. Overall, the Kurdish parties do not operate differently from their Arab counterparts, making it difficult to see how Kurdistan could develop a more efficient and responsive party system.

Conclusion

Political parties in Iraq mirror and at the same time reinforce the ethnic and religious divisions in Iraqi society as well as in the broader Middle East. Rather than working on unifying the country, the different political factions work against each other while at the same time having to deal with their own internal frictions and rivalries.

Shi'i parties find it difficult to have genuinely national vision as leading political forces as well as dealing with the role of religion in policy-making; the Sunni parties struggle with the lack of unified representation; and the Kurds attempt to move from their power-sharing past and find a democratic balance in the KRG while presenting a united front in Baghdad. At the same time, all the parties as well as their representatives struggle to come to terms with the mayhem of the political party structure in post-Saddam Iraq, where sectarian competition is rife, with none of the different factions truly willing to cooperate; while infightings persist, which tear apart the coalitions being set up.

Complicating the matter further is the fact that Iraq, due to its ethnic and religious composition, its natural resources and geographical location, is of such importance in the Middle East region that neighbouring countries as well as international actors, such as the US and Russia, try to assert their dominance through local actors in order to influence politics according to their self-interest. Specifically, they employ the weak political party system with its internal fault lines to do so.

But it is not only the outside forces who have a negative influence on Iraq's party politics. Iraq's economic rentier system supports the centralisation of power and favours potential renewed authoritarianism in the country. It makes Iraqi party politics into a system of political forces competing for power and consequentially monetary resources, rather than a system which has at its core the task of strengthening the rule of law and working for its citizens. While many Iraqis might not accept this state of affairs, they tolerate it in the hope that time will help Iraq find its own path to democratisation.

With the difficult security situation in Iraq, the prospect of establishing a functioning democracy seems distant, and the increased power achieved by military-based political organisations raises the possibility of Iraq turning into a garrison state. A number of political parties have their personal armed wings, and armed factions are establishing their own political parties. While both Sunni and Shi'i militias set up parties, the most successful one to date has been the Shi'i Badr Organization of Reconstruction and Development. Previously called the Badr Brigade, the Badr Organization was the armed wing of the Supreme Council for the Islamic Revolution in Iraq (SCIRI) and is considered to be an Iranian proxy in Iraq. Having formed its own political party in 2012, it has been able to propel its leader, Amiri, to serve as Minister of Transportation under Maliki, while Mohammed Ghabban, another prominent party member, previously served as Interior Minister. With the party having won twenty-two seats in the 2010 elections, experts such as Sowell (2015) predict that the elections in 2018 might see a surge of the 'militia party', depending on the outcome or progress of the fight against ISIS.

With the prospects of increased military power together with the predicted attempt of a comeback by the previous prime minister, Nouri al-Maliki, the future for Iraqi politics seems grim. However, not all is lost in Iraq and lessons can be learned from the past. The example of Iraqi party politics demonstrates the importance of building a party system without outside influence, in which individuals are unable to enrich themselves and which is not built upon sectarian lines, while at the same time recognising and supporting all parts of the population. These changes cannot be achieved overnight and considering Iraq's authoritarian past, time has to be given to people and their parties to find a form of governance fit for their individual situations. While the future of Iraqi party politics is unclear, Iraq's people have until now managed to cope with the many challenges of their national politics; and with parties having no interest in the return of one-party rule, there is a chance that multi-party politics will persist and might have the possibility to transform in the long run.

Bibliography

Abdulrazaq, Talha (2015), 'The Iraqi Islamic Party: Failing the Sunnis', *Middle East Eye*, 27 May, <http://www.middleeasteye.net/columns/failing-sunnis-iraqi-islamic-party-681053448> (last accessed 1 September 2017).

Ali, Ahmed (2014), *Iraq's 2014 National Elections*, Middle East Security Report 20, Washington DC: Institute for the Study of War.

Anagnostos, Emily, and Patrick Martin (2016), 'Political Blocs and Parties in Iraq's CoR', 6 May, Institute for the Study of War, <http://www.understandingwar.org/backgrounder/political-blocs-and-parties-iraqs-cor-may-6-2016> (last accessed 1 September 2017).

Barzegar, Kayahan (2010), 'Iran's Foreign Policy Strategy after Saddam', *The Washington Quarterly* 33: 1, 173–89.

Batatu, Hanna (1981), 'Iraq's Underground Shi'i Movements', Middle East Research and Information Project, published in *Middle East Report* 102, <http://www.merip.org/mer/mer102/iraqs-underground-shii-movements> (last accessed 11 September 2017).

Bayless, Leslie (2012), 'Who Is Muqtada al-Sadr?', *Studies in Conflict & Terrorism* 35: 2, 135–55.

Bernhardt, Florian (2011), 'The Legitimacy of Party Politics and the Authority of the "*Ulama*" in Iraq's Shi'a Islamist Movement: The Example of the Islamic Da'wah Party (1957–1988)', *Journal of Shi'a Islamic Studies* 4: 2, 163–82.

Carroll, Katherine Blue (2011), 'Not Your Parents' Political Party: Young Sunnis and the New Iraqi Democracy', *Middle East Policy* 18: 3, 101–21.

Chmaytelli, Maher (2016a), 'As Iraqi Civilian Rule Weakens, Shi'ite Clerics Call the Shots', Reuters, 20 March <http://www.reuters.com/article/us-mideast-crisis-iraq-politics-idUSKCN0WM0U2> (last accessed 1 September 2017).

Chmaytelli, Maher (2016b), 'Iraq Parliament Approves Cabinet Overhaul, Bolstering PM Abadi', Reuters, 15 August, <http://www.reuters.com/article/us-mideast-crisis-iraq-oil-idUSKCN10Q0TL> (last accessed 1 September 2017).

Corboz, Elvire (2015), 'From Najaf to Najaf: A Family at the Forefront of Iraqi Politics', in Elvire Corboz (ed.), *Guardians of Shi'ism*, Edinburgh: Edinburgh University Press, pp. 123–64.

Crisis Group (2013), 'Make or Break: Iraq's Sunnis and the State', *Middle East Report* 144, 14 August, <https://www.crisisgroup.org/middle-east-north-africa/gulf-and-arabian-peninsula/iraq/make-or-break-iraq-s-sunnis-and-state> (last accessed 1 September 2017).

Dawisha, Adeed (2010), 'Iraq: A Vote against Sectarianism', *Journal of Democracy* 21: 3, 26–40.

Dodge, Toby (2013), 'State and Society in Iraq Ten Years after Regime Change: The Rise of a New Authoritarianism', *International Affairs* 89: 2, 241–57.

The Economist Intelligence Unit (2017), *Democracy Index 2016: Revenge of the 'Deplorables'*, London: The Economist Intelligence Unit.

Eisenstadt, Michael, Michael Knights and Ahmed Ali (2011), 'Iran's Influence in Iraq, Countering Tehran's Whole-of-Government Approach', Policy Focus 111, Washington DC: Washington Institute for Near East Policy.

George, Susannah (2016), 'Under Reform Mantle, Shiite Cleric Fractures Iraqi Politics', Associated Press, 10 May, <http://bigstory.ap.org/article/ae01854f003c-4cf1a6069129ad6dbe83/under-reform-mantle-shiite-cleric-fractures-iraqi-politics> (last accessed 1 September 2017).

Hameed, Saif, and Stephen Kalin (2016), 'Iraq's Top Court Invalidates Abadi's Partial Cabinet Reshuffle', Reuters, 28 June, <http://www.reuters.com/article/us-mideast-crisis-iraq-politics-idUSKCN0ZE2FD> (last accessed 1 September 2017).

Ismael, Tareq, and Jacqueline Ismael (2010), 'The Sectarian State in Iraq and the New Political Class', *International Journal of Contemporary Iraqi Studies* 4: 3, 339–56.

Jabar, Faleh, and Hosham Dawod (2006), *The Kurds, Nationalism and Politics*, London: Saqi Books.

Katzman, Kenneth (2009), *Iran's Activities and Influence in Iraq*, Washington DC: Congressional Research Service.

Khalaji, Mehdi (2005), 'Religious Authority in Iraq and the Election', Policywatch 1063, 14 December, Washington Institute, <http://www.washingtoninstitute.org/policy-analysis/view/religious-authority-in-iraq-and-the-election> (last accessed 1 September 2017).

Khidir, Jaafar Hussein (2002), *The Kurds and Kurdistan and Recent Political Development of IKR*, Dissertation, Universität Wien.

al-Khoei, Hayder (2014), 'Can the Quiet Ayatollah of Peace Save Iraq from Collapse?', *The World Today* 70: 5, Chatham House, <https://www.chathamhouse.org/publication/twt/can-quiet-ayatollah-peace-save-iraq-collapse> (last accessed 1 September 2017).

Knights, Michael (2009), '"Managed Democracy" Gives Way in Iraqi Kurdistan', Policywatch 1563, 3 August, Washington Institute, <http://www.washingtoninstitute.org/policy-analysis/view/managed-democracy-gives-way-in-iraqi-kurdistan> (last accessed 1 September 2017).

Lawrence, John (2016), 'ISW Tracking of Iraq's 2016 Political Crisis', Institute for the Study of War, <http://understandingwar.org/backgrounder/isw-tracking-iraq%E2%80%99s-2016-political-crisis> (last accessed 1 September 2017).

Levitt, Matthew, and Phillip Smyth (2015), 'Kataib al-Imam Ali: Portrait of an Iraqi Shiite Militant Group Fighting ISIS', Policywatch 2352, 5 January, Washington Institute, <http://www.washingtoninstitute.org/policy-analysis/view/kataib-al-imam-ali-portrait-of-an-iraqi-shiite-militant-group-fighting-isis> (last accessed 1 September 2017).

Mansour, Renad (2016), 'The Sunni Predicament in Iraq', Carnegie Middle East Center, 3 March, <http://carnegie-mec.org/2016/03/03/sunni-predicament-in-iraq-pub-62924> (last accessed 1 September 2017).

Martin, Patrick, with Emily Anagnostos (2016), 'Iraq's Prime Minister Abadi Attempts to Reshuffle the Cabinet', Institute for the Study of War, <http://iswresearch.blogspot.co.uk/2016/03/iraqs-prime-minister-abadi-attempts-to.html> (last accessed 1 September 2017).

Naser, Mustafa (2016), 'Why Did Iraq's Shiite National Alliance Choose New Leader?', *Al-Monitor*, 18 September, <http://www.al-monitor.com/pulse/originals/2016/09/iraq-shiite-national-alliance-ammar-al-hakim.html#ixzz4fwsuGBGe> (last accessed 1 September 2017).

Olson, Robert (2005), *The Goat and The Butcher: Nationalism and State Formation in Kurdistan-Iraq since the Iraqi War*, Qosta Mesa: Mazda Publishers.

Parker, Ned (2009), 'Machiavelli in Mesopotamia, Nouri al-Maliki Builds the Body Politic', *World Policy Journal* 26: 1, 17–25.

PBS (2003), 'Politics and Religion in Iraq', PBS, 2 December, <http://www.pbs.org/newshour/bb/middle_east-july-dec03-iraq_12-02/> (last accessed 25 May 2016).

Plebani, Andrea (2014), 'Muqtada al-Sadr and His February 2014 Declarations. Political Disengagement or Simple Repositioning?', *Analysis* No. 244, ISPI.

Pollack, Kenneth (2016), 'Iraq Situation Report, Part II: Political and Economic Developments', Brookings, 29 March, <https://www.brookings.edu/blog/markaz/2016/03/29/iraq-situation-report-part-ii-political-and-economic-developments/> (last accessed 1 September 2017).

Posch, Walter, and Nathan Brown (2004), *Kurdische Unabhängigkeitsbestrebungen und die irakische Verfassung*, Vienna: Schriftreihe der Landesverteidigungsakademie.

al-Qawaree, Harith Hassan (2014), 'Iraq's Sectarian Crisis, a Legacy of Exclusion', *Carnegie Middle East Centre*, Washington DC: Carnegie Endowment for International Peace.

Rabkin, Nathaniel (2016), *Iraq's Imperiled Democracy: Beyond Islamists and Autocrats*, Washington DC: Washington Institute for Near East Policy.

Rahimi, Babak (2004), 'Ayatollah Ali al-Sistani and the Democratization of Post-Saddam Iraq', *Middle East Review of International Affairs* 8: 4, 12–19.

Rahimi, Babak (2012), 'Democratic Authority, Public Islam and Shi'i Jurisprudence in Iran and Iraq: Hussain Ali Montazeri and Ali Sistani', *International Political Science Review* 33: 2, 193–208.

Rizvi, Sajjad (2010), 'Political Mobilization and the Shi'i Religious Establishment (*marja'iyya*)', *International Affairs* 86: 6, 1299–313.

Sadeghi-Boroujerdi, Eskandar (2016), 'Guardians of Shi'ism: Sacred Authority and Transnational Family Networks', *Iranian Studies* 49: 3, 527–31.

Salih, Mohammed (2016a), 'Muqtada al-Sadr, the Most Powerful Man in Iraqi Politics?', *Al-Monitor*, 13 May, <http://www.al-monitor.com/pulse/originals/2016/05/iraq-shiite-cleric-muqtada-al-sadr-change-politics.html#ixzz49PiatEHy> (last accessed 1 September 2017).

Salih, Mohammed (2016b), 'The New Politics of Iraqi Kurdistan', Washington Institute, 16 August, <http://www.washingtoninstitute.org/policy-analysis/view/the-new-politics-of-iraqi-kurdistan> (last accessed 1 September 2017).

Schenker, David (2008), 'The Hidden Imam', Washington Institute, 24 September, <http://www.washingtoninstitute.org/policy-analysis/view/the-hidden-imam> (last accessed 1 September 2017).

Shanahan, Rodger (2004), 'Shia Political Development in Iraq: The Case of the Islamic Dawa Party', *Third World Quarterly* 25: 5, 943–54.

Smock, David (2003), 'The Role of Religion in Iraqi Politics', United States Institute of Peace, 23 December, <http://www.usip.org/publications/the-role-of-religion-in-iraqi-politics> (last accessed 1 September 2017).

Sowell, Kirk (2015), 'Badr at the Forefront of Iraq's Shia Militias', Carnegie Endowment for International Peace, 13 August, <http://carnegieendowment.org/sada/61016> (last accessed 1 September 2017).

Wahab, Bilal (2017), 'Rules of the Iraqi Game', Washington Institute, January, <http://www.washingtoninstitute.org/policy-analysis/view/rules-of-the-iraqi-game> (last accessed 1 September 2017).

Yamao, Dai (2012), 'Sectarianism Twisted: Changing Cleavages in the Elections of Post-War Iraq', *Arab Studies Quarterly* 34: 1, 27–51.

Chapter 9

Post-Gaddafi Libya: rejecting a political party system

Amir M. Kamel

The 17 February 2011 'Day of Rage' in Libya, with its widespread anti-government protests, sparked the North African state's experience of the so-called Arab Uprisings (England 2011). A week later, Muammar Gaddafi's state TV address urged his supporters to counter the protesting crowds, a move which purportedly incited his loyalists to join governmental forces and violently suppress anti-regime sentiment. Gaddafi stated:

> I call on the people of Libya to get out of their houses and confront this bunch of people [the protestors]. If they are not brave enough to go out and face this enemy on the street, maybe they should let their women and their daughters go out. (Adams et al. 2011)

Despite such calls to loyalty to the regime, with the help of NATO intervention, the Libyan revolution first ousted Gaddafi from power and then killed him. The 'contingency' of the revolution should not, however, obscure that the fall of the regime was also the product of the specific characteristics of the Libyan state: historical tribal, regional and elitist rivalries, the location and allocation of natural resources, the rule of the Gaddafi regime itself and its legacy, as well as the involvement of external actors, notably the NATO forces. Indeed, each of these factors left a sense of 'rejectionism' in Libya, a sentiment that outmatched attempts to forge a conventional political party system in the country. In its immediate aftermath, though, the post-Gaddafi transition period appeared to set the scene for a pluralistic-inspired political system.

Specifically, Dahl's (1967) concept of pluralism, which he developed for the American political system, identified a political structure where competing power bases with limited sovereignty mean that influence and coercion are diluted, citizen consent is promoted in the long run and conflicts are peacefully settled. From there, neo-pluralism stipulates that the state, and its aligned institutions, acts autonomously in an accepted manner (McFarland 2010), and in turn this leads to peace and stability. However, post-Gaddafi Libya rejected the potential for such progression. This meant that historical, tribal and strategic interests dictated a scenario where the Libyan 'system' was epitomised as operating with a rejection-based sentiment.

This chapter assesses how the Libyan context and developments between 2011 and 2015 meant that a pluralistic political system in the North African state remained elusive. In short, the Libyan actors rejected such a political system despite the initial hopes that newly created parties offered for the construction of a stable party-based political system. This case study serves to demonstrate that the underlying historical, tribal and strategic interests contributed to this rejectionist scenario that has led to considerable instability and chaos.

This chapter initially examines Dahl's theory of pluralism and its developments, as well as the literature supporting the rejectionist sentiment in the country (i.e. rejecting foreign presence, as well as a 'united Libya' along the state borders in which it is considered today). Both of these strands of scholarship capture the rentier nature of states in general, and Libya in particular (Luciani and Beblawi 1987). From here, the chapter examines the Libyan context and how this forged the sense of rejectionism, which ultimately led to the failure of a party system in Libya. This is accomplished by examining the features and developments that took place before 2011 in the country. Then, this chapter assesses how historical rivalries, the control of resources and the legacy of the Gaddafi regime led to the 2011 Libyan Uprising, fuelling the rejectionist sentiment at the same time. Subsequently, it examines the initial transition period in post-Gaddafi Libya, which included the role of external forces (NATO, the UK, the US, France and Italy, and towards the end of the timeframe concerned also Egypt and the UAE), the 2012 elections, the failed United Nations-sponsored (UN) attempts at brokering the creation of a government of national unity, and the penetration and existence of *Dawlat al-Islamiyyah fy al-Iraq we al-Sham* (also known as *Daish*) in the country. This chapter concludes by evaluating how each of these elements ultimately resulted in a status quo where a pluralistic political system failed to develop and points to how the Libyan context rejected such a political structure.

It is worth noting that the conventional conceptualisation of 'parties' in the Libyan case was superficial in nature. This was reflected by the fact that the 2012 elections resulted in 60 per cent of the available seats going to independents. Subsequent 'political' alliances formed around historical, tribal and strategic lines rather than on ideological ones. Therefore, in spite of what appeared to be a conventional party system emerging in post-Gaddafi Libya, with parties registering to participate and putting candidates forward for elections, the results continuously demonstrated a consistent sense of rejecting this very notion.

In order to put forward its argument, this chapter provides an analysis of the developments which took place during the timeframe concerned by consulting documents, databases, policies and speeches of governments and international organisations as well as original interviews with UK military personnel involved in the attempts of the international coalition to foster a positive outcome of the post-Gaddafi transition period. It is important to note that there is a gap in the academic literature concerning developments in Libya, specific to the timeframe concerned with this chapter. As a result, this chapter has assessed much official and primary source material, as well as tertiary sources in order to conduct its analysis.

Assessing the literature

The idea of rejecting a political party structure is supported to a certain extent in studies of Libyan affairs. It is important, though, to note that this chapter does not argue that this rejectionist sentiment was absent in Libya pre-2011. Indeed, other studies have implied this to be the case. The point here is that the focus is on the 2011–15 period, and it is based on the empirical evidence from this timeframe that the argument has been formulated.

Dahl's concept of pluralism – a united agreement by the peoples within a society, either through conflict or compromise – is born out of an examination of an American community in New Haven. Dahl (1978) argues that attempts to achieve power (or autonomy) result from conflicts and cleavages in society, and the success of these attempts (Dahl denotes success as being the most 'often' achieved outcome), results in a trend towards pluralism. Dahl (2005) bounded his seminal study by including the political, economic and primal motivations of *Homo sapiens*, and significantly, the control of resources. In his work, Dahl contends that a sense of pluralism will result from an agreement between the peoples in a society (following the aforementioned attempts to resolve conflicts and disputes), which also captures the fair distribution of resources. This point in particular does not find any substantiation in the developments that took place in the Libyan case.

The concept of pluralism was then developed further through the notion of neo-pluralism, which denotes that 'political authority [... is] decided upon through a free market of votes' (Oxhorn 2004: 29). Specifically, in the case of Libya, this notion would contend that an election (a free market of votes) would have led to a sense of (neo-)pluralism in the country, which then in turn would have led to a conventional party system. However, the very nature of the Libyan state meant that elections in post-Gaddafi Libya continued to reject this notion, as the actors involved consistently reverted to historical, tribal and strategic alliances rather than subscribing to a genuine party system to solve disputes.

Wilson (qtd in McFarland 2010: 42) extended neo-pluralism further still to argue that the 'state' and 'component institutions often acted autonomously' in a neo-pluralistic state, whilst warning that these actors may be challenged by groups outside of this frame. Whilst the case of Libya demonstrated that different groups, based on historical, tribal and strategic lines, did indeed challenge attempts to set up formal 'state' structures, the result was nevertheless one which rejected any sense of neo-pluralism.

This argument that developments in Libya rejected the notions of pluralism and neo-pluralism accords with other studies on Libyan affairs, specifically when it comes to the rejection of formal political structures. Indeed, the rejection of the interference of external powers as well as of formal Libyan political structures, whether they be along pluralistic and neo-pluralistic lines or otherwise, has been identified in the literature as a key aspect of Libyan politics. Vandewalle (2012), for instance, noted how Libyans rallied around a sense of tribal belonging and family during the twentieth century, as opposed to a united Libyan state. Bowen (2006) observed how Gaddafi carried out actions that benefited his own tribe and allies, and Gause (2011) noted how the former leader employed oil wealth to protect his regime. The radical rejection of formal political structures was also demonstrated in the peculiar institutional construction of the Gaddafi regime, which distinguished it from other Arab authoritarian countries where similar strategies for holding on to power (oil wealth, favours to one's own tribe) were also employed.

Following on from this logic and in the context of the 2011 ousting of Gaddafi, Joffé (2013: 4) noted how the autocratic nature of the former leader's regime meant that 'radical political change could only result in civil war'. Indeed, Niblock (qtd in Bawden and Hooper 2011) argued that by 2011, Gaddafi had managed to amass a personal wealth, which, 'at the very least [. . .] would be several billion dollars, in whatever form and it could potentially be a lot higher'. These points demonstrate how the divisive nature and the unequal distribution of wealth in Gaddafi's Libya fuelled the sense of rejectionism in the country. Indeed, as mentioned, whilst fellow Middle Eastern countries simultaneously experienced the Arab Uprisings, the combination of the make-up of the state, the history of said make-up, Gaddafi's rule, and the distribution of wealth led to the Libyan trajectory of unrest and conflict. Further, this Libyan context compounded the sense of rejectionism in the country, which meant that a political solution, based on conventional political party structures, became elusive.

Furthermore, Brahimi (2011) echoed this sense of rejectionism in the post-Gaddafi era by declaring that the transitional government, the National Transition Council (NTC), had an arduous task of engendering a sense of legitimacy in the country, given the fact that it was a newly formed institution which was attempting to exercise its transitional functions in a state that had traditionally rejected institutions attempting to do just that.

The uniqueness of this study lies in the fact that it links the characteristics of and developments in Libya to the sense of rejectionism, which prevented the setting up of a conventional political system. Furthermore, this study focuses on the post-Gaddafi era in a manner demonstrating how the historical make-up and foundations of the Libyan state, its rentier nature and the Libyan people's resistance to internal and external actors in determining how the state is run, all contributed to rejecting a pluralistic political system in the North African state.

The Libyan context: forging a sense of rejectionism

Four main elements contributed to the rejection of a pluralistic political system in Libya in the post-Gaddafi era. Specifically: (1) the tribal, regional and elitist rivalries which existed in Libya during the timeframe concerned, having been a trait which also existed in the country pre-2011;

(2) the location and allocation of natural resources (oil and gas) and the wealth accrued from hydrocarbons, again an element predating the 2011–15 timeframe; (3) Gaddafi's rule and the impact it had with regards to compounding the previous two elements; and (4) the involvement of external actors, from the Italian forces following the break-up of the Ottoman Empire to NATO's involvement in ousting Gaddafi and from the presence of *Daish* in the Sirte region to the UN's attempts at getting Libyan actors to form a unity government.

Tribal, regional and elitist loyalties pre-dated the borders of modern-day Libya in some form or another. The Ottoman Empire occupied the area from the sixteenth century up until Italian forces took control of the Libyan territory following the signing of the 1912 Treaty of Lausanne. Italian occupation lasted until 1943 when the Allied powers (Britain and France) took over the country. Allied control lasted until 1951 when the Kingdom of Libya was established and headed by the reluctant monarch King Idris al-Senussi (Vandewalle 2012). The sentiment of tribal fidelity was present in Libya during this whole period, including the Senussi times, as well as whilst Gaddafi was in power (Vandewalle 2012). Indeed, there were multiple examples of how Senussi abused his position in power for the benefit of his own tribal, regional and allied partners, as the King formulated and implemented policies favouring his Cyrenaican homeland. Specifically, Senussi's allies (individuals, businesses and entrepreneurs) benefited from a steep reduction in taxes, which created elitism in the country, and later foreign private companies also reaped the benefits of the King's policies (Sandbakken 2006). The fact that it was a foreign actor, namely the Allied powers, that placed Senussi onto the Libyan throne in 1951 meant that the feeling of external actors dictating who the power holders in the country should be prevailed (Sharp et al. 2000). Each of the developments leading up to and including Senussi's rule fed into the rejectionist notion in Libya, which continued up until the period 2011–15.

These cleavages in Libyan society were further exacerbated by the discovery, location, production and export of hydrocarbon resources, and the distribution of the wealth accrued from these fossil fuels. Furthermore, the industry was developed using the expertise and capabilities of foreign private companies, meaning that the actions of external powers played a key role in commanding the distribution of resource-accrued wealth in Libya, something which further exacerbated the negative sense associated with foreign influence in the country (Sandbakken 2006).

Traces of Libyan oil were incidentally discovered whilst Tripoli's water wells were being drilled in 1914 (McLachlan 1989). The sector was slow to develop and further exploration took place only in 1940 before being put on hold again during World War II (St John 2015). In 1947, however, the US oil company Esso Standard carried out an expedition in the country and rated Libya's potential of having commercial quantities of the resource as 'good' (Gurney 1996: 21). This represented yet another example of an external actor determining and controlling aspects of Libyan domestic affairs. Oil exploration intensified when the 1955 Libyan Petroleum Law was implemented, which provided for the state to attain 12.5 per cent of royalties accrued from any oil that was produced and stored, and for the profits from the resource to be shared equally between the exploration company and the state on realised and unposted oil prices. This favourable framework for private companies led to the rapid development of the oil sector, and prompted a 1961 amendment to the law which determined that the equal share of profits was to be administered based on posted prices along with more stringent conditions (Clarke 1963).

The fact that the resources were being discovered and extracted by foreign companies added to the sense of external actors having a presence in the country, as technocrats ran the industry (Vandewalle 2012). The Petroleum Law strengthened this notion by allowing foreign oil companies to profit from the process whilst demoting the Libyan government to a 'tax collector' role (St John 2015: 101). The fact that the majority of the resources being discovered were located in an area which overlapped the Tripolitanian and Cyrenaican regional borders, in the Sirte Basin, further compounded rivalries because the development of the hydrocarbon sector brought to the fore the historical regional fissures in society. The result was, of course, a continued sense of rejectionism of Libya as a country.

The Gaddafi regime, in place following the 1969 Revolution, was ostensibly nationalist and redistributive. But the reality on the ground did not seem to change much. Indeed, whilst Gaddafi (of Sirte) proclaimed that he led the revolution in an attempt to offset the inequalities Senussi had created, he nevertheless presided over a Libya which built up security forces to protect and accrue oil wealth for himself and his allies (Ali 2011).

The implementation of Gaddafi's 1975 *Green Book* – the Third Universal Theory (TUT) – gave birth to the *Jamahiriya* regime and proved to be an additional divisive element in the cracks in the country's society. Indeed, under the *Jamahiriya*, political parties, freedom of the press and oppositional movements were banned (Vandewalle 1986), as the TUT specified that the population was to be 'divided into Basic

People's Conferences' who selected 'Professional Conferences' to execute state policy and 'People's Committees' to supersede the country's administration (Gaddafi [1975] 2005). This radical institutional set-up harmed further traditional institutional life, although it is worth noting that the hydrocarbon industry and issues concerning foreign policy decisions were ring-fenced from the TUT, enabling Gaddafi to maintain control over these two policy areas (Vandewalle 2012). This control ensured Gaddafi was able to protect his interests and those of his allies, augmenting the sense of rejectionism in the country under his tenure.

Gaddafi retained this level of control up until he rolled back the Weapons of Mass Destruction (WMD) programme in 2003 and implemented a series of reforms to quell sentiments of unrest and inequality in the country.[1] However, these reforms were not fully implemented and the Gaddafi regime did not genuinely believe in them (Thompson 2004). Indeed, following attempts at political and economic reforms, Gaddafi's son, Saif al-Islam, himself noted in 2007 that 'the next challenge for Libya is to draft a package of laws which you can call a constitution, but they must be endorsed by the people to become a contract between the people' (MEED 2007: 2). Each of these developments contributed to and demonstrated the sense of inequality and alienation of ordinary citizens persisting in the country up until Gaddafi's ousting in 2011.

The rejectionist sentiment in the country had an internal dimension (against the Senussi and Gaddafi regimes) and an external one (against the Italian and Allied powers) in a context where oil exploration and export made massive profits for oil companies and allies of the regime. This came to a head on the Day of Rage, which soon after seemed to give way to a new era of Libyan politics. However, the post-Arab Uprising period saw the rejection once again of a conventional political system in the country, as political loyalties continued building on historical, tribal and strategic linkages rather than ideology or political programmes.

The 2011 Libyan uprisings

In the run-up to the Day of Rage in February 2011, several cities in Libya experienced varying levels of protests (across the country in cities including Zawiya, Zintan, Benghazi, Derna and Bayda) and government forces loyal to Gaddafi disrupted them. That being said, even the military's reaction to Gaddafi's orders was ambivalent, with some willing to kill civilians to defend the regime, whilst others refused to shoot at the population (Bellin 2012). This was a confirmation of Anderson's point (2011: 6) that the Gaddafi regime had eaten away at any sense of trust in the government among citizens to an extent where Libyan institutions (whether they be conventional or not) and society were splintered and separated along a number of cleavages – among them, crucially, tribal ones. This point continues to further the argument that the sense of rejectionism in the country far outweighed attempts to form a conventional political structure in Libya, as the actors concerned reverted to historical, tribal and strategic groupings outside of such a conventional system.

In reaction to the crackdown on the protestors, UN Resolution 1970 referred the Gaddafi administration to the International Criminal Court (ICC), citing concerns over the mistreatment of the Libyan people. This move was prompted by the fact that large numbers of Libyan casualties were being sustained during the uprising, with an estimated 30,000 people killed between March and September 2011 (Laub 2011). The UN followed its earlier decision and implemented Resolution 1973 in March 2011, establishing a no-fly zone 'to help protect civilians' and authorised members of the UN 'to take all necessary measures to enforce compliance with the ban on flights' (UN 2011a: 3). By the end of the month, the London Conference on Libya (which saw the participation of various leaders and foreign ministers from the UN, the Arab League, the Organization of Islamic Cooperation (OIC), the EU and NATO) had taken place and established the Libya Contact Group, which, in July 2011, consequently endorsed the fact that Gaddafi was no longer considered to be the country's leader, and therefore the international community would recognise the NTC as the governing body in the country (Libya Contact Group 2011). This move was significant, as just two weeks earlier the African Union (AU) was still negotiating with both the Gaddafi regime and the NTC to resolve the issues in the country (African Union 2011). The AU did, however, formally recognise the NTC as the sole authority in the country a month later.

The role of external actors was significant in this instance, not just because the UN mandate enabled NATO to support the anti-Gaddafi cause in unseating the leader (Michaels 2011), who was ultimately killed in October 2011, but also because it represented the beginning of yet another involvement on the part of external actors in attempting to shape the political situation in the country and specifically in securing the unity of the country. This involvement manifested itself in multiple guises: additional UN Resolutions aimed at fostering peace in the country, support for various local groups, and foreign actors interested in accessing the energy resources in the country. Each of these elements is addressed in the following sections.

Before focusing on the post-Gaddafi period, it is imperative to reiterate the importance of hydrocarbons in the context of the uprising. Indeed, in 2011, 65 per cent of Libya's GDP came from energy production, and 80 per cent of the administration's revenues came from these resources (Chivvis et al. 2012). This was the case despite the fact that the country's energy exports were almost completely interrupted during this period with intermittent levels of production being focused on domestic consumption (EIA 2015). Furthermore, the IMF noted in April 2012 that the country's natural resources and the potential for the sector's recovery would lead to 'a post-revolution revival in the country's economic activity', provided the security situation was resolved (IMF 2012). This observation speaks to the notion that the control of the country's resources played a key role during the timeframe concerned. Furthermore, the location and control of resources was also identified as a potentially divisive factor in recognising the different actors in Libya by the former Libya British Petroleum (BP) head, Peter Manoogian, who noted:

> The oil is mainly on the eastern side, so if the rebels get that that's one thing. But it's hard to see how that could be sustained. Some countries would be in a very difficult position, especially Italy, where the export pipelines go. It would have to recognize the East, as well as the West. (Qtd in Nield 2011: 18)

Indeed, the historical sentiments of tribal loyalties, the struggle for the control of resources and the sentiment of detachment from state institutions and identity in Libya were evident in the run-up to and during the 2011 uprising in the country. Further, the significant role outside forces played in determining the shape of the situation on the ground (the UN's and NATO's role in supporting the anti-Gaddafi forces in removing the leader) fed into a sentiment of divisions following the fall of the regime.

The Post-Gaddafi transition: bound for failure?

The NTC's onerous task was to usher in an era of political unity, in the sense that it was charged with and aimed to foster an environment for democracy by devising a schedule for nationwide elections in July 2012 after acting as the de facto caretaker government for ten months. UN

Resolution 2009 of September 2011, which established the UN Support Mission in Libya (UNSMIL), provided for external support to the NTC in transitioning the country into a state of peace and, notably, to 'undertake inclusive political dialogue [and] promote national reconciliation' (UN 2011b: 3). The end of NATO operations in the country followed the UN Resolution 2009 (UN 2011b), after having played a crucial role in removing Gaddafi. These developments once again demonstrated how external actors shaped post-Gaddafi Libya.

Additionally, a number of UN Resolutions were passed from September to December 2011, lifting the no-fly zone (Resolution 2016), and removing (Resolution 2017) and reaffirming the removal of chemical and arms proliferation concerns (Resolution 2022). Resolution 2022 also extended the UNSMIL mandate initially until March 2012, and then Resolutions 2040 and 2095 extended the mission to March 2013 and 2014, respectively. The shadow the UNSMIL cast over the country's post-Gaddafi administrations inevitably continued to provide an environment where a pluralistic political system remained elusive in the sense that an external actor was still carrying out activities and implementing policies in the country to achieve their aims.

Indeed, the NTC continued to receive support from the UN. Further, the sense of 'enforcing pluralism' was further verified at this point when the UN reiterated in Resolution 2016 'the need for the transitional period to be underpinned by a commitment to democracy, good governance, rule of law, national reconciliation and respect for human rights and fundamental freedoms of all people in Libya' (UN 2011c: 2). Then, in early 2012, the UN unfroze roughly $100 billion worth of the Central and Foreign Banks of Libya's assets in an attempt to foster an environment for recovery (Mirza 2012: 34). This impetus, however, was not enough to prevent clashes between rebel forces in Benghazi, as the people of the city were critical of the NTC's ability to implement reforms, and demanded that the deputy NTC leader, Abdel Hafiz Ghoga, a defector of the Gaddafi regime, resign in January 2012. Clashes between militias across the country during that month were based, however, on tribal interests and lines (MEED 2012a). This came about despite the fact that it was evident to British forces on the ground that Libyans were 'elated at the fact that Gaddafi had been ousted'.[2]

Ghoga acknowledged and referred to this sense of mistrust and divisiveness in his outgoing statement, in which he noted that 'the consensus has not continued to maintain the highest national interests

[as] the atmosphere of deprivation and hatred has prevailed' (BBC 2012a). In May 2012, the NTC attempted to integrate the militias into the security apparatus of the country and set aside a $7.8 billion programme to entice rebels to either continue their education or join Libya's police. Just two weeks later, attacks were carried out against the NTC headquarters (MEED 2012b: 23). The task of including different militias in the fold of the legitimate state security apparatus was an arduous one as it was clear that following the revolution the dust had not settled (politically speaking), and so groups were unwilling to give up their arms/gains.[3]

The conflict also severely impacted the Libyan economy. Indeed, prior to the NTC receiving official recognition, oil production was estimated to have bottomed out at zero barrels per day (Neuhof 2011), having fallen from 1.80 million barrels per day before the conflict. The oil industry did, however, recover in 2012, with the country pumping an average of 1.48 million barrels per day that year (EIA 2013). That being said, the manner in which the NTC operated the industry, notably checking contracts meticulously, made it difficult for private sector firms to invest in Libya (Ballantyne 2011). Additionally, the IMF estimated that Libya's GDP fell by 60 per cent in 2011 and rose by 122 per cent in 2012, and identified how the economic health of the country was tied to the oil industry, something which was hampered by the NTC's inability to quell violence between rival militias in Tripoli and Benghazi forces.

The July 2012 elections marked the end of the NTC's caretaker government and ushered in the General National Congress (GNC), supported by UN Resolution 2095, which also faced resistance from different sectors of Libya's society. Indeed, a UK Parliamentary Paper estimated that around sixty different militias had surfaced since the fall of Gaddafi, with many of them refusing to disarm and with Benghazi forces and Gaddafi loyalists seeking to maintain control over the central Tripoli government (Smith 2012). Furthermore, there was an increased sense of frustration at the lack of GNC progress, which led to ports being seized, and it was evident that the 'state' (GNC) was attacking elements of the 'state' to force political will/decisions.[4] Additionally, this divisive nature of the GNC was compounded by the manner in which it was logistically set up.

Each of these developments meant that the actors concerned rejected any sense of a conventional political party structure in the country. Indeed, the GNC was made up of 200 seats, with 80 dedicated to political parties and 120 to independents. The poll results (60 per cent turnout) led to the National Forces Alliance led by the former interim prime minister, Mahmoud Jibril, winning 39 seats, the Muslim Brotherhood's Justice and Construction Party (JCP) securing 17 seats, and the anti-Gaddafi National Front Party, headed by Mohamed el-Magariaf (a former Gaddafi regime ambassador to India) winning 3 seats (BBC 2012b). These results demonstrated how a majority party was absent, with the largest bloc based on strategic lines (in the sense that the Muslim Brotherhood had a strategic presence in the country and indeed in the region), and the majority of the seats (120 of the 200) going to independents. Each of these aspects conveys how the rejectionist sentiment in the country was prevalent, even when the environment seemed conducive in part to the adoption of a conventional political party system.

One month after the elections, al-Magariaf was selected to be the GNC head, as the interim body was tasked with electing the new prime minister and cabinet. This, however, did not lead to a respite in violence in the country, once again demonstrating the rejectionist sentiment culminating in Libya with the September 2012 attack on the US consulate in Benghazi.

At the same time there were some encouraging signs of moderation. In May 2013, al-Magariaf resigned following a GNC law, which banned any figure who had previously worked in the Gaddafi regime from holding public office. He noted in his outgoing speech, 'I place my resignation in your hands [...] and I do so with a clear conscience [...] with a head held high' (BBC 2013). Al-Magariaf's successor, Nouri Abu Sahmein, an independent candidate who was a Berber and a victim of Gaddafi's repression, was elected a month later, with the support of the JCP.

Sahmein's tenure saw the surge of extremist Islamism, which sought to take the country away from a secular system that the international community was keen on seeing in Libya (Engel and Grada 2014). That being said, strategic blocs began to appear, as some actors moved away from tribal allegiances to benefit politically from the rise of Islamism.[5] Sahmein's rule ended when the GNC failed to achieve its mandate of forming a permanent democratic institution in August 2014. This led to a period of violent unrest in the country, which is still ongoing and sees the participation of external forces complicating matters further in Libya.

The presence and influence of NATO forces and the UN, along with the importance of resources to accruing wealth for the country, were compounded by the complex web of rivalries and conflicting interests in Libya, which were drawn on historical and tribal lines. As a result, these disparities influenced the GNC's succession of leaders and their mandate, ultimately leading to its failure.

Unrest and external forces continue to fuel rejectionism

In the run-up to the GNC's fall from power, a period of escalating violence and unrest hit the country. The control of hydrocarbon resources continued to play a key part in this process, as well as the influence, existence and actions of external forces. These elements resulted in an environment where a pluralistic political system remained elusive, as the rejectionist sentiment continued to outweigh the potential for a conventional party system to emerge.

Before the GNC's mandate expired, there were multiple instances where various actors (based broadly on tribal lines) acted to coerce the GNC into adhering to their respective aims. Indeed, in August 2013 the Petroleum Defense Force (PDF), led by Ibrahim al-Jathran, a former anti-Gaddafi rebellion leader who was charged with protecting the country's petroleum resources by the GNC in 2012, defected from GNC control and declared the right for his own region (Cyrenaica) to have much greater autonomy. He closed the Es-Sider and Ras Lanuf oil ports, citing this action as a means to force the 'corrupt and mismanaged' GNC to acquiesce to his demands (Coker 2013). This resulted in oil production being slashed in half three months later (Coker 2013). This action was significant, as this region to the east of the country is the site of 60 per cent of Libya's oil fields and thus is where the wealth is (Laessing and Shennib 2013).

Additionally, the minority Berber population in the west of Libya was also against the GNC, having criticised the transition administration for failing to recognise them in the constitution (Laessing 2013). In an attempt to force the GNC to adhere to their demands, the Berber tribes closed the Melitah complex, the gate to the oil and gas pipelines under the Mediterranean to Italy and the rest of Europe. Concurrently, the south-eastern Fezzan tribes also rejected the competence of the GNC by declaring an autonomous government in September 2013 in their stronghold (*Al Arabiya* 2013). It should be noted that the area became a breeding ground for rebels who had been kicked out of Mali by French forces. As time went on it also became apparent how the Fezzan region was deemed to be less and less important, in the sense that it was not often referred to when attempts at forging a national unity government were taking place in 2015.[6] Each of these examples demonstrates how tribal and regional allegiances and cleavages took precedence over conventional party lines and over the GNC's claim to Libyan unity.

Furthermore, the Gaddafi regime defector General Khalifa Haftar launched a military campaign against the so-called Islamist groups in May 2014. Haftar was viewed as an important figure both within the country and by outside actors, on account of his strongman manner and tribal and family links. He was also open to accepting concessions, and controlled resources and commanded a degree of support in the country (ECFR 2017). Two months later a round of elections was held to nominate the members of the new House of Representatives (HoR), also referred to as the Council of Deputies, which was to supersede the GNC. The elections were tainted, however, by a very low voter turnout (around 18 per cent), security fears and boycotts, and led to the Islamist GNC parties and actors losing seats (BBC 2014). The elections sparked a further bout of violence between the GNC supporters and the newly formed HoR, which also enjoyed Haftar's support.

This violence led to the UN pulling its staff out of the country and shutting its diplomatic representations, as it called for a united political solution in Libya under UN Resolution 2174 in August 2014. The UN continued in its attempts to forge a unity government when the UN Secretary General Ban Ki-moon aimed at brokering talks between the two rival governments, the HoR in Tobruk and the GNC in Tripoli, also termed Libya Dawn. Additionally, the unstable situation of the country led to *Daish* gaining a foothold in Derna and Sirte. The presence of *Daish* in Libya led to further external intervention, which in turn further undermined any notion of Libyan unity and independence. Thus, in February 2015 Egyptian jets bombed *Daish* targets in Derna and Sirte after twenty-one Egyptian Christians were beheaded by the terrorist organisation (Malsin and Stephen 2015). Furthermore, the UN passed Resolution 2238 in September calling 'for the immediate formation of a Government of National Accord, and agreement on interim security arrangements necessary for stabilising Libya through the UN-facilitated Libyan Political Dialogue' (UN 2015a: 3). A month later, the UN noted that the Libya Sanctions Committee, the body in charge of levying sanctions on the country, was:

prepared to designate those who threaten Libya's peace, stability
and security or who undermine the successful completion of its
political transition. The members of the Security Council reaffirmed
their strong commitment to the sovereignty, independence,
territorial integrity and national unity of Libya. (UN 2015b)

The language used ('prepared to designate') demonstrates that
attempted external enforcement of rules in the country clashed with
the Libyan rejectionism of outside interference. This contributed to
an environment where a pluralistic political system remained elusive
because domestic actors that might have had an interest in securing
a deal under the patronage of external actors were easily swayed to
refrain from doing so because of the fear of being accused of betraying
their own constituencies. The latter, in fact, seemed more interested in
securing localised interests than in unifying the country. At group level,
it meant that different actors in Libya who may find themselves in a more
privileged position as a result of dealing with external actors, might be
seen as privileged and therefore somehow 'illegitimate' in the eyes of
many ordinary citizens. Additionally, this situation led to an unequal
distribution of political power – curbing the potential for the targeted
individuals to come forward and engage in a dialogue aimed at finding a
resolution to the ongoing conflict – and economic wealth, which would
also more than likely be channelled towards the individuals who were not
on the sanctions 'hit list'. Finally, the continued failures of the successive
UN attempts were viewed as being counterproductive to what the UN was
attempting to do.[7] The subsequent environment was not too dissimilar to
the one Libya epitomised under Gaddafi and even Senussi (Kamel 2015),
with high levels of political and economic inequality.

Conclusion

It is clear that the developments in Libya in the period this chapter is
concerned with (2011–15) have deeper and fundamental links to the
foundation and evolution of contemporary Libya. Indeed, the historical
tribal, regional and strategic ties between the different actors in the country
provided barriers to a successful move from a post-Gaddafi transition era
into a peaceful resemblance of a pluralistic political system. It is clear that
the resistive nature of the country to a conventional pluralistic political
system evolved into a more rejectionist and conflictual sentiment. The
unequal control and distribution of wealth accrued from the hydrocarbon

sector, which made and still makes up the majority of the rentier state's income, as well as the continued and continuing attempts by external actors to pursue their goals in the country, exacerbated these sentiments.

After the timeframe this chapter is concerned with the situation in Libya has worsened even further. Indeed, in December 2015 the Government of National Accord (GNA) – a UN-sponsored body – stipulated that Fayez Serraj would be the country's new prime minister, tasked with the mandate of uniting the HoR and the GNC (Stephen 2016). This effectively led to a scenario where three governments resided in the country (Stephen 2016). The fact that Serraj was an externally imposed leader based in Tunisia further added to the HoR's and the GNC's rejection of the plan. Additionally, Serraj was not viewed as a 'strongman' among Libyans, leading elements of the UK MoD to surmise that this was a failing in the eyes of citizens and that it was as though a strongman was what was required to rule the country.[8] Furthermore, the imposition of the GNA saw *Daish* expanding its regional reach, as it moved towards Ras Lanuf in January 2016.

Each of these developments demonstrates how the role of external actors (the UK, Egypt, the UN and *Daish*) exercised their interests in an environment where the country went from having one government (the GNC) to three, with the emergence of the HoR and the GNA between 2014 and 2015. The splintering of the country and the control of hydrocarbon resources demonstrated once more how the case of Libya presents an example of a continued rejectionist attitude towards a pluralistic political system.

Notes

1. For example, the distribution of foreign newspapers was permitted in the country in 2009 (EU 2011).
2. Personal interview with Amir M. Kamel at the Defence Academy of the UK, 23 February 2016.
3. UK military personnel no. 1, personal interview with Amir M. Kamel at the Defence Academy of the UK, 23 February 2016.
4. UK military personnel no. 2, personal interview with Amir M. Kamel at the Defence Academy of the UK, 23 February 2016.
5. UK military personnel no. 2, personal interview with Amir M. Kamel at the Defence Academy of the UK, 23 February 2016.
6. UK military personnel no. 3, personal interview with Amir M. Kamel at the Defence Academy of the UK, 3 March 2016.

7. UK military personnel no. 3, personal interview with Amir M. Kamel at the Defence Academy of the UK, 3 March 2016.
8. UK military personnel no. 3, personal interview with Amir M. Kamel at the Defence Academy of the UK, 3 March 2016.

Bibliography

Adams, Richard, Paul Owen, David Batty and Matthew Taylor (2011), 'Gaddafi Speech and Libya Turmoil – Thursday 24 February', *The Guardian*, 24 February, <https://www.theguardian.com/global/blog/2011/feb/24/gaddafi-speech-libya-turmoil-live-reaction> (last accessed 1 September 2017).

African Union (2011), 'Decisions, Declarations and Resolution', Assembly of the Union, Seventeenth Ordinary Session (Malabo, Equatorial Guinea: 30 June–1 July 2011), Dec.385, <http://www.au.int/en/sites/default/files/decisions/9647-assembly_au_dec_363-390_xvii_e.pdf> (last accessed 19 February 2016).

Ali, Tariq (2011), *The Obama Syndrome: Surrender at Home, War Abroad*, New York: Verso.

Anderson, Lisa (2011), 'Demystifying the Arab Spring: Parsing the Differences between Tunisia, Egypt, and Libya', *Foreign Affairs* 90: 3, 2–7.

Al Arabiya (2013), 'Libya's Southern Fezzan Region Declares Autonomy', *Al Arabiya*, 26 September, <http://english.alarabiya.net/en/News/middle-east/2013/09/26/-Libya-s-southern-Fezzan-province-declares-autonomy.html> (last accessed 21 February 2016).

Ballantyne, Bernadette (2011), 'Contractors Await Project Revival', *MEED* 55: 46.

Bawden, Tom, and John Hooper (2011), 'Gaddafis' Hidden Billions: Dubai Banks, Plush London Pads and Italian Water', *The Guardian*, 22 February, <https://www.theguardian.com/world/2011/feb/22/gaddafi-libya-oil-wealth-portfolio> (last accessed 19 February 2016).

BBC (2012a), 'Libya: NTC Deputy Chief Abdel Hafiz Ghoga Resigns', BBC, 22 July, <http://www.bbc.co.uk/news/world-africa-16671590> (last accessed 20 February 2016).

BBC (2012b), 'Libya Election Success for Secularist Jibril's Bloc', BBC, 18 July, <http://www.bbc.co.uk/news/world-africa-18880908> (last accessed 20 February 2016).

BBC (2013), 'Libya GNC Chairman Muhammad al-Magariaf Resigns', BBC, 28 May, <http://www.bbc.co.uk/news/world-africa-22693963> (last accessed 20 February 2016).

BBC (2014), 'Libyan Elections: Low Turnout Marks Bid to End Political Crisis', BBC, 26 June, <http://www.bbc.co.uk/news/world-africa-28005801> (last accessed 21 February 2016).

Bellin, Eva (2012), 'Reconsidering the Robustness of Authoritarianism in the Middle East: Lessons from the Arab Spring', *Comparative Politics* 44: 2, 127–49.

Bowen, Wyn (2006), 'Chapter One: Nuclear "Drivers"', *Adelphi Papers* 46, 11–24.

Brahimi, Alia (2011), 'Libya's Revolution', *Journal of North African Studies* 16: 4, 605–24.

Chivvis, Christopher, Keith Crane, Peter Mandaville and Jeffrey Martini (2012), 'Libya's Post-Qaddafi Transition: The Nation-Building Challenge', RAND Corporation,

RR-129-SRF, <http://www.rand.org/pubs/research_reports/RR129.html> (last accessed 1 September 2017).

Clarke, John (1963), 'Oil in Libya: Some Implications', *Economic Geography* 39: 1, 40–59.

Coker, Margaret (2013), 'Ex-Rebel, with Militia, Lays Claim to Libyan Oil Patch', *The Wall Street Journal*, 3 October, <http://online.wsj.com/news/articles/SB10001424 052702303643304579109010913025356> (last accessed 1 September 2017).

Dahl, Robert (1967), *Pluralist Democracy in the United States*, Chicago: Rand McNally.

Dahl, Robert (1978), 'Pluralism Revisited', *Comparative Politics* 10: 2, 191–203.

Dahl, Robert (2005), *Who Governs? Democracy and Power in the American City*, New Haven, CT: Yale University Press.

Engel, Andrew, and Ayman Grada (2014), 'Libya's other Battle', Policywatch 2295, 28 July, Washington Institute for Near East Policy, <http://www.washingtoninstitute. org/policy-analysis/view/libyas-other-battle> (last accessed 1 September 2017).

England, Andrew (2011), 'Libya Crushes "Day of Anger"', *The Financial Times*, 17 February, <http://www.ft.com/cms/s/0/221bc38c-3a0b-11e0-a441-00144feabdc0. html#axzz40QLXMAtA> (last accessed 17 February 2016).

European Council on Foreign Relations (ECFR) (2017), 'A Quick Guide to Libya's Main Players', <http://www.ecfr.eu/mena/mapping_libya_conflict> (last accessed 3 February 2017).

European Union (EU) (2011), *Libya Strategy Paper and National Indicative Programme 2011–2013*, Brussels: European Neighbourhood and Partnership Instrument, <http://eeas.europa.eu/enp/pdf/pdf/country/2011_enpi_csp_nip_libya_ en.pdf> (last accessed 18 February 2016).

Gaddafi, Muammar [1975] (2005) *The Green Book*, Reading, MA: Ithaca.

Gause III, F. Gregory (2011), 'Why Middle East Studies Missed the Arab Spring: The Myth of Authoritarian Stability', *Foreign Affairs* 90: 4, 81–90.

Gurney, Judith (1996), *Libya: The Political Economy of Oil*, Oxford: Oxford University Press.

International Monetary Fund (IMF) (2012), 'Libya on Recovery Path but Faces Long Rebuilding Effort', Washington DC: IMF Middle East and Central Asia Department.

Joffé, George (2013), *North Africa's Arab Spring*, Abingdon: Routledge.

Kamel, Amir (2015), 'Libya: Some Context behind the Ongoing Unrest', Defence-in-Depth Blog, 16 November, <http://defenceindepth.co/2015/11/16/ libya-the-context-behind-the-ongoing-unrest/> (last accessed 1 September 2017).

Laessing, Ulf (2013), 'Libya's Berber to Boycott Committee Drafting Constitution', Reuters, 13 November, <http://www.reuters.com/article/us-libya-politics-idUSB-RE9AC0A120131113> (last accessed 21 February 2016>.

Laessing, Ulf, and Ghaith Shennib (2013), 'In Libya's east, a Former Rebel Commander Tests Tripoli', Reuters, 28 October, <http://www.reuters.com/article/2013/10/28/ us-libya-oil-protests-idUSBRE99R0LI20131028> (last accessed 1 September 2017).

Laub, Karin (2011), 'Libya: Estimated 30,000 Died in War; 4,000 Still Missing', *The Huffington Post*, 9 October, <http://www.huffingtonpost.com/2011/09/08/libya-war-died_n_953456.html> (last accessed 19 February 2016).

Libya Contact Group (2011), 'Chair's Statement', Fourth Meeting of The Libya Contact Group, Istanbul: NATO, 15 July, <http://www.nato.int/nato_static/assets/pdf/pdf_2011_07/20110926_110715-Libya-Contact-Group-Istanbul.pdf> (last accessed 19 February 2016).

Luciani, Giacomo, and Hazem Beblawi (1987), *The Rentier State*, London: Croom Helm.

McFarland, Andrew (2010), 'Interest Group Theory', in L. Sandy Maisel and Jeffrey M. Berry (eds), *The Oxford Handbook of American Political Parties and Interest Groups*, New York: Oxford University Press, pp. 37–56.

McLachlan, K. (1989), 'Libya's Oil Resources', *Libyan Studies* 20, 243–50.

Malsin, Jared, and Chris Stephen (2015), 'Egyptian Air Strikes in Libya Kill Dozens of Isis Militants', *The Guardian*, 17 February, <http://www.theguardian.com/world/2015/feb/16/egypt-air-strikes-target-isis-weapons-stockpiles-libya> (last accessed 19 February 2016).

MEED (2007), 'Saif al-Islam Calls for Reform', *MEED* 51: 34.

MEED (2012a), 'Special Report Libya', *MEED* 56: 3.

MEED (2012b), 'Mustafa el-Huni: Deputy Chairman, National Transitional Council', *MEED* 56: 21.

Michaels, Jeffrey (2011), 'NATO after Libya', *The RUSI Journal* 156: 6.

Mirza, Adal (2012), 'Steering an Economic Recovery', *MEED* 56: 3.

Neuhof, Florian (2011), 'Cost Analysis Drives Libya's Oil Reconstruction', *MEED* 55: 36.

Nield, Richard (2011), 'Libya's Divided Future', *MEED* 55: 12.

North Atlantic Treaty Organization (NATO) (2015), 'NATO and Libya (Archived)', *Online Topics*, 9 November, <http://www.nato.int/cps/en/natolive/topics_71652.htm> (last accessed 20 February 2016).

Oxhorn, Philip (2004), 'Neopluralism and the Challenges for Citizenship in Latin America', *Soundings: An Interdisciplinary Journal* 87: 1/2, 27–58.

St John, Ronald Bruce (2015), *Libya: Continuity and Change*, London: Routledge.

Sandbakken, Camilla (2006), 'The Limits to Democracy Posed by Oil Rentier States: The Cases of Algeria, Nigeria and Libya', *Democratization* 13: 1, 135–52.

Sharp, Joanne, Paul Routledge, Chris Philo and Ronan Paddison (2000), *Entanglements of Power: Geographies of Domination/Resistance*, London: Routledge.

Smith, Ben (2012), 'Libya's General Assembly Election 2012', UK Parliament House of Commons Paper, SNIA/6389 18 July, <http://researchbriefings.files.parliament.uk/documents/SN06389/SN06389.pdf> (last accessed 1 September 2017).

Stephen, Chris (2016), 'Libya Unveils UN-Backed Government . . . Based in Tunisia', *The Guardian*, 19 January, <http://www.theguardian.com/world/2016/jan/19/libya-unveils-un-backed-government-but-divisions-remain> (last accessed 1 September 2017).

Thompson, Richard (2004), 'More than Words Needed', *Middle East Economic Digest* 48: 44.

United Nations (UN) (2011a), 'Resolution 1973 (2011)', Adopted by the Security Council at its 6498th meeting, S/RES/1973, 17 March 2011, <http://www.un.org/en/ga/search/view_doc.asp?symbol=S/RES/1973(2011)> (last accessed 19 February 2016).

United Nations (UN) (2011b), 'Resolution 2009 (2011)', Adopted by the Security Council at its 6620th meeting, S/RES/2009, 16 September 2011, <http://www.un.org/en/ga/search/view_doc.asp?symbol=S/RES/2009(2011)> (last accessed 19 February 2016).

United Nations (UN) (2011c), 'Resolution 2016 (2011)', Adopted by the Security Council at its 6640th meeting, S/RES/2016, 27 September 2011, <http://daccess-dds-ny.un.org/doc/UNDOC/GEN/N11/567/10/PDF/N1156710.pdf?OpenElement> (last accessed 20 February 2016).

United Nations (UN) (2015a), 'Resolution 2238 (2015)', Adopted by the Security Council at its 7520th meeting, S/RES/2238, 10 September 2015, <http://www.un.org/en/ga/search/view_doc.asp?symbol=S/RES/2238(2015)> (last accessed 19 February 2016).

United Nations (UN) (2015b), 'Security Council Press Statement on Libya', SC/12084-AFR/3247, 17 October, <http://www.un.org/press/en/2015/sc12084.doc.htm> (last accessed 20 February 2016).

U.S. Energy Information Administration (EIA) (2013), 'Libya', *Country*, 23 October, <http://www.eia.gov/countries/country-data.cfm?fips=ly#pet> (last accessed 20 February 2016).

U.S. Energy Information Administration (EIA) (2015), 'Country Analysis Brief: Libya', *Country Analysis Briefs*, 15 November, p. 2, <https://www.eia.gov/beta/international/analysis_includes/countries_long/Libya/libya.pdf> (last accessed 19 February 2016).

Vandewalle, Dirk (1986), 'Libya's Revolution Revisited', *Middle East Research and Information Project* 143, <http://www.merip.org/mer/mer143/libyas-revolution-revisited> (last accessed 1 September 2017).

Vandewalle, Dirk (2012), *A History of Modern Libya*, Cambridge: Cambridge University Press.

Part 3

Societal constituents

Chapter 10

Tribes and political parties in the contemporary Arab world: a reassessment from Yemen

Larissa Alles

Tribes and tribalism in Yemen

Yemen is often described as a country dominated by tribes. The assumption of the dominance of the tribes over the state has been supported by the close alignment between the regime of former president Ali Abdullah Saleh (r. 1978–2011) and the two dominant tribal federations, Hashid and Bakil, both from the country's north-western highlands. The tribes of Hashid and Bakil wielded great influence historically in northern Yemen under the rule of the imamate (911–1962), but tribalism has also been strong in other parts of the country, especially in the provinces of Marib and al-Jawf, east of the capital Sana'a', as well as in Hadramawt and Mahra. Yet, tribes of these regions have been less influential in Sana'a'. In the central and southern regions of Yemen, however, tribalism had less of an influence (Peterson 2008: 1) and parts of the population would not identify themselves as tribal.

In previous centuries, the tribes in the north served the imam and provided armed forces when he needed them, as the imam did not have a standing army until the early 1900s. In the south, tribes as well as feudal rulers dominated over smaller fiefdoms, yet they were not as hierarchically organised as in the north. The British authorities in the protectorate of Aden (1839–1967) forged treaties with the various rulers, sultans and sheikhs in the hinterland, until the south became independent in 1967 (Peterson 2008: 7). The overthrow of the imamate in 1962 diminished the role of tribes, before some of their leaders began playing a critical role in the political system under Saleh. Tribalism in South Yemen was supressed under the socialist-Marxist regime of the People's

Democratic Republic of Yemen (PDRY; 1967–90) after independence. The unification of North and South Yemen, and the South's defeat after the 1994 civil war, re-emphasised the role of tribal actors in the whole of the country. This, however, was only partly connected to the emergence of a multi-party system in Yemen after 1990. In general, tribesmen have been in political institutions as much as other citizens as well, given that a sizeable part of the population counts as tribal. Many of them were driven to seek a position in political parties by personal motives (ideological or otherwise) rather than tribal ones. However, there have been tensions between the government and the tribes, especially regarding the autonomy of the tribes over the past decades. Although tribalism is a strong force, it is not homogenous in its viewpoints (Peterson 2008: 1). Since unification and the spread of political parties in Yemen, 'tribal loyalties [have started to] face competition from emerging political parties and both Pan-Arab and Islamist ideologies' (Peterson 2008: 17). An overlap of regime politics and tribal interests developed for tribal sheikhs, some of whom were included in the regime's patronage network, rather than tribes themselves. Political parties served for many as a vehicle to access political and economic benefits from the power centre in Sana'a'. Their tribal constituencies in the provinces benefited relatively little from these connections.

Political parties introduced an alternative organisation of power that had not been present before in Yemen. They crosscut both traditional structures of power in local areas, such as tribes or clan elders, and the formal, authoritarian power structures of the state. Parties were more ideological than the other structures of power in Yemen and promoted particular sets of ideas. In doing so, they posed a challenge to the traditional legitimacy of tribal sheikhs, as well as to neo-patrimonial regime structures. Hence, in order to unpack the question of the relationship between tribes and political parties, this chapter puts each in its context of the overall regime, thereby explaining the interaction between the tribes and political parties. After a brief overview of tribalism and the overall role of tribes in Yemeni politics, it is important to understand the landscape of political parties in Yemen, and in particular of the two main parties, the General People's Congress (GPC) and *Islah*. Both were important tools for the regime of former president Saleh to pursue a strategy of co-optation, not least in matters of dealing with the tribes. At the same time, these political parties were vehicles for powerful tribesmen and local notables to gain access to the regime. The chapter then illustrates how the incorporation of a tribal elite into the regime (largely through parties) has eroded traditional tribal structures. The split between a tiny but rich and powerful elite, and a largely powerless but poor population for which political parties do not provide a means to articulate their demands effectively, runs equally through tribal as well as non-tribal parts of the country. Hence, political parties as well as tribes have lost their capacity of mass inclusion and effectively promoting the interests of their constituencies. The chapter concludes with the 2011 protests, during which the results of this development became particularly apparent.

Who are the tribes?

Tribalism has mattered profoundly as an identity marker because it has been a 'fundamental reference point' for many in Yemen, whether tribal or not (Peterson 2008: 1). This has been true not only for tribesmen but also for those without tribal affiliations. Over the last decade, urban intellectuals in opposition to the regime of Ali Abdullah Saleh were eager to stress that they have *no* tribal affiliation, in order to underline their support for a civil state as opposed to 'backward tribalism'.[1]

As in other parts of the Arab world, the cohesiveness and influence of tribes has decreased over the past couple of decades, yet the role of tribes in Yemen remained prominent. Sheikhly families moved to the towns and links to their constituencies were weakened (Peterson 2008: 5). The urbanisation of tribal sheikhs was a direct outcome of their incorporation into the regime's patronage network. The increasing investment of tribal sheikhs in their political and economic assets alienated them from their tribal constituencies. Whilst much of Saleh's regime depended on patronage links, this is often conflated with tribalism (*qabaliya*). However, tribalism is rather a code of manners 'that depends on the pretence of moral equality' (Dresch 1995: 38). In contrast, patronage (*mahsubiya*) ties dependents to power holders inside the country and abroad, in particular in Saudi Arabia. Both tribalism and patronage have always played a role in the relation between the power centre in Sana'a' and the northern tribes, but this simultaneity drifted apart from the 1980s onwards when major sheikhs were incorporated into the regime, and were distanced from their constituencies (Dresch 1995: 38). 'Tribal influence' as such on the regime or political parties has thus been modest at best. Instead, tribal sheikhs benefited personally from their incorporation in the patronage system, often through their membership in one of the main political parties, most notably the ruling GPC and the opposition party *Islah*, as will be detailed below. They were originally seen as representatives of their tribes to the state and expected to channel state revenues back to their tribal constituencies. At the same time, the regime hoped to exert influence on the tribes through the sheikhs, given that government presence was weak in tribal territories.

Tribes in politics: the role of the sheikhs

Much of the weakness of Yemen's bureaucracy was attributed to the prevalence of informal structures of policy-making that former president Ali Abdullah Saleh entertained; dynamics that were partly associated with tribal structures and accused of reinforcing tribalism in politics. Furthermore, Saleh used elements of the bureaucracy and political institutions as channels for co-optation. The incorporation of tribes in political institutions had been necessary for Saleh to consolidate his power and expand it via close links to tribal sheikhs. Due to the significance of tribes in Yemen's northern part, incorporating tribes in political institutions had enhanced the credibility of these institutions and the bureaucracy because parts of tribal constituencies were drawn closer to the state. On the one hand, the incorporation and co-optation of tribal sheikhs and tribesmen was necessary for Saleh in order to expand his domination, but he also exploited these alliances, on the other. They were not meant to improve the conditions in tribal areas but served to enhance the power of his regime. Whilst a few tribal notables benefited from this strategy, the majority of tribespeople did not.

It should be noted though that the incorporation of tribal notables into the ruling system was not first introduced under Saleh. After the revolution in North Yemen, tribal sheikhs for the first time occupied governmental positions and were *in* power. Tribes had always been powerful but they had not been ruling the country. Under the imam that had ruled North Yemen, tribesmen had acted as tax collectors and possessed the means of coercion that the imam summoned when needed. In the Yemen Arab Republic (YAR) after the revolution, the sheikhs were one of three pillars of the state together with the military and the merchants. President Ibrahim al-Hamdi (r. 1974–7) shifted this balance and focused on the strength of the military. Tribal sheikhs felt their influence deteriorating and thus supported a coup against Hamdi through which they halted the marginalisation of tribes in the state apparatus and reinforced their position. The influence of tribalism on state structures in the north is further represented through the administrative alignment of the *mudiriyat* (directorates) with tribal areas.

The main objective of sheikhs had always been their autonomy and their authority in policy-making in their areas. Historically, a main task of a tribal sheikh was to (economically) provide for his tribe.[2] Since tribal sheikhs were incorporated in state institutions, their legitimacy shifted to their capacity to extract revenues from Sana'a' for their tribal constituencies. Hence, the co-optation of tribal sheikhs into the elite circles was not only necessary for Saleh in order to stabilise his power (he wanted to avoid Hamdi's mistake of marginalising the tribes) but also to expand his domination into tribal areas via local notables. The need to receive revenues for their constituencies fuelled tribal sheikhs' interest in being incorporated in the ruling apparatus. As a result, their inclusion in the state apparatus made the state enforce tribal *'asabiyya* (social solidarity) and also helped spread *'asabiyya* in the southern territories.[3]

At the local level, the state was perceived as absent and powerless, with only tribal sheikhs possessing real power. Real power remained with the sheikh, not with the tribe. The tribes were armed and remained in the background to support the sheikh. Everything that concerned the tribe or the sheikh was resolved between them, and the state did not interfere. In the words of a local human rights activist from Ibb, the tribes were like a state within the state: "There are two states in one (*dawlatain fi dawla*)."[4] Although ordinary people have not supported the authority of sheikhs everywhere because it has been perceived as arbitrary, an estimated 80 per cent of the population in and around Ibb, for example, still prefer to go to a sheikh in case of disputes rather than to a state court because they experience local conflict mediation as quicker and less corrupt compared with state courts.[5] At the same time, the sheikhs' incorporation in the bureaucracy made it less necessary for the regime to expand institutions beyond the centre.[6]

The use of the term sheikh changed under Saleh's rule: 'Sheikhs are ruling even if they are not looking like sheikhs,' as one interviewee said.[7] Saleh continued to describe former president Saleh, as well as other high-ranking regime figures as 'sheikhs'. Everyone who was part of the inner circle around the president and had tribal credentials was called a sheikh.[8] The regime further legitimated the position of tribal sheikhs through the Ministry of Tribal Affairs. It helped to create sheikhs, but also instigated tribal wars (Lackner 2016).

Apart from individuals who have inherited the position of a sheikh from their father, there have been cases of individuals to whom people come if they have problems or are seeking advice. Those individuals are often charismatic figures with an armed group in their background, yet without any ancestral relations to a sheikhly family. Once having acquired a reputation of dealing with disputes, such a figure calls himself 'sheikh' and tries to extend his power and influence. According to some interviewees, people accept this person as a new sheikh. However, it seems to be a matter of armed force that influences the extent of power of a local 'sheikh', as well as his relations to the elite in Sana'a'.[9] The latter may either grant him his area of influence, or back a local adversary. In this regard, it was an economically profitable business of high-ranking members of Sana'a's elite to support local tribal wars during the last two decades of Saleh's rule. The opponents were dependent on military aid from their patrons, but were too busy to become a potential competitor for power on a larger scale (Alles 2014).[10] Hence, a number of sheikhs enjoyed the status and benefits of a sheikh but did not have any traditional authority at a grass-roots level because they were perceived as being fabricated by the regime. Yet, with the support of the regime in Sana'a', they were able to act like tribal notables and to contain other local notables or sheikhs who were at odds with Saleh. Furthermore, they served as actors for the regime in their respective regions.

The general picture of sheikhs in Yemen over the past two to three decades was largely created through the prominence of a few very powerful sheikhs with long-standing tribal credentials and considerable political dominance. This does not mean, however, that all tribal sheikhs have necessarily been powerful. Their influence, rather, depended on the individual strength of a sheikh or how powerful a sheikhly family had been. Paramount sheikhs of tribal confederations increased their power and wealth through owning land inside and outside of their tribal territory. But although patronage has increased the wealth and political power of some sheikhs and influential tribesmen, this had little impact on the hierarchy within their tribes (Peterson 2008: 2–3); neither did it increase the state's influence on tribes significantly.

Traditionally, tribes have regulated and organised their affairs independently from the state. The Saleh regime relied on some support from the tribes, especially against an urban and southern population in the early 1990s (Peterson 2008: 10). Yet, the regime also instigated tribal wars to keep tribes busy and reduce the possibility for them to establish independent power bases. The co-optation of sheikhs into the regime's patronage networks served both strategies: to secure the tribes' support for the regime on the one hand, and, on the other, to simultaneously reduce the likelihood that powerful sheikhs would establish their own power bases (and abandon their lucrative position within the regime and economic sector) that could challenge Saleh's power. This indicates that tribes have not been more integrated in the system than other groups of political players. Although Saleh played them off against each other, he could not control them. It was more important that Saleh had close allies among the most powerful sheikhs and kept everyone else at bay in order to avoid any contestation of his power. The alliance with the late paramount sheikh of Hashid, Sheikh Abdullah al-Ahmar, was thus particularly important for Saleh since al-Ahmar wielded significant influence among most of the northern tribes. Since Saleh had taken over power in 1978, the two hierarchies of power in northern Yemen, that of the sheikhs and that of the state, had merged into one (Mundy 1995: 203).

One of the most significant developments under Saleh was the fact that major sheikhs turned into clients of the regime. Once fiercely independent from any central power, they became increasingly concerned with their own benefits (political and economic). Yet, the distance between them and their constituencies increased. Sheikhs moved from their tribal territories to Sana'a', triggered by patronage and careers in the military. Running parallel to this there was a phenomenon of 'youth-sheikhs' who went abroad and returned with new wealth. They turned away from being representatives of their tribes to the state and traditional heads of their tribes, and instead developed into politicians and businessmen. Urbanisation and the stalling economy in the 2000s distanced the tribes from the state (Peterson 2008; Dresch 1995). Political parties became a major vehicle for powerful sheikhs to stay connected to the regime.

Yemen's multi-party landscape

Arab countries before the 2011 uprisings usually had been ruled through one, all-powerful ruling party, often with little or no opposition allowed. In Yemen by contrast, the two ruling parties that had existed in the YAR and the PDRY before unification, Saleh's General People's Congress

(GPC) and the southern Yemen Socialist Party (YSP), both re-emerged in unified Yemen in a ruling coalition, yet with their own, very distinct support bases (Langohr 2005). In the immediate aftermath of unification, a plethora of new parties, media outlets and civil society organisations also spread throughout the country (Schwedler 2002: 49; Carapico 1996).

Engaging in 'sudden political pluralism' (Poirier 2011: 208) upon unification and treating the GPC like a proper political party was not a deliberate choice Saleh made. He was rather forced to it by the circumstances of the new, unified Yemen, and the existence of another ruling party in the form of the YSP. Saleh thus turned the GPC into a formal political party that, up to that point, had rather been a popular congress of local leaders from across the country. When Article 5 of the constitution allowed party politics in 1991, some groups therefore left the GPC umbrella and formed their own parties (al-Yemeni 2003). Within months, up to forty different parties had sprung up all across the country (Dresch 2000). Most of these parties did not have a long life expectancy. Ultimately, the country's dominant parties were Saleh's GPC, the Islamist *Islah* and the YSP. Yet, this rather unintended process of liberalisation (Schwedler 2006) was not designed to lead towards democratisation. At the time of unification, both regimes in the YAR and the PDRY had hoped to use unification and, with it, controlled forms of liberalisation to maintain their own power, and to expand it through potential and actual constituencies in the traditional area of influence of the respective other party (Schwedler 2002; Carapico 1998).

Although party pluralism facilitated a higher degree of elite competition, the new party landscape did not develop the capacity to include broader sectors of the population, that is, to generate a higher degree of mass inclusion. Higher levels of elite competition had the potential though to threaten Saleh's domination and the exclusive power of the regime's inner elite circle. The power-sharing government with the YSP after 1990 had placed a separate elite group next to the GPC and allowed it the same access to state resources. Thus, Saleh had encouraged the creation of the *Islah* party (*at-Tajammuh al-Yemeni li-l-Islah*) under Sheikh al-Ahmar to create a counterweight to the socialists based on a traditional-conservative and religious-oriented agenda. During elections in the following decade, informal accords between the GPC and *Islah* were directly engineered to marginalise the YSP. Although both the GPC and *Islah* originally emerged out of the new pluralism, they subsequently contributed to its decline (Poirier 2011; Yadav 2010). The YSP, although the former ruling party of the south and Yemen's oldest political party since October 1978, suffered from targeted marginalisation, particularly between 1990 and 1993 when up to 150 members fell victim to assassinations (Schwedler 2006). Despite its decline as a ruling party, its very existence had a significant impact on power politics between the GPC and *Islah*.

The interesting aspect in the interplay between the regime, political parties and tribes in Yemen has been their mutual dependence. The parties needed the tribes to expand their area of influence, but they also provided access to the regime. Yet, tribal affiliation always trumped party affiliation. The regime used the parties to tie actors to the regime and channel patronage money to its dependents.

The GPC as a tool for co-optation

Upon its inception in the 1980s, one of the GPC's main functions had been political mobilisation for the state, that is, promoting greater institutionalisation over traditional local forms of governance. Furthermore, it was an important tool to co-opt a broad array of political actors. The party controlled most of the benefits, which were given to the clients of Saleh. Government officials, sheikhs and officers, who had been responsible for distributing and receiving these benefits, were also the main figures in the party, often with a military background and usually from a selection of Sanhan villages (the tribe from which Saleh originated) (Dresch 2000). Hence, the actual source of the GPC's power derived from being the party of the president, and having exclusive access to state funds and the security apparatus. In addition, it directed the support of parliament according to the will of Saleh (Alley 2010). The GPC also benefited from the perception of many that it was still the party that most accurately represented the northern population (al-Yemeni 2003), accommodating a non-sectarian, broad middle ground for tribal and non-tribal actors without strong ideological undertones. For many, however, party membership was less a question of support for the regime or the president and more a way for businessmen, military personnel or public sector servants to conduct their businesses, pursue a modest career or quite simply have a paid job at all.[11] In other words, GPC membership allowed individuals greater opportunities in the economic realm and modest freedom when it came to building small businesses. This enabled the regime to contain the risk of open challenge but also enabled those without family or tribal connections to approach members of the inner elite circle. Co-optation through the GPC was facilitated via traditional and tribal ties to Saleh (al-Yemeni 2003).

The party's offers of co-optation attracted local actors, but the party also needed to propose attractive deals in order to benefit from the local power of these actors. The GPC leadership knew that

> if a sheikh or a prominent social figure wants the nomination [for parliament], he will likely run as an independent if the GPC does not nominate him. [Hence the party] is forced to take into consideration the [...] ambitions of powerful community members. (Al-Yemeni 2003: 40)

Unless, that is, it wants to lose the potential local and financial support this individual could muster for the party. There is also the risk that he would join *Islah* instead. In sum, the success of the regime's co-optation strategies was not only contingent on what it could offer, but also whether the actor in question perceived the collaboration with the GPC as beneficial. Offering possibilities for co-optation and being able to threaten with coercion accounted for the dynamic informal structures of policy-making beyond political institutions, and although the regime was a powerful actor, other actors, especially powerful tribes in the north, used the same mechanisms of threatening the regime with coercion (for example, kidnappings, road blocks or attacks on the oil infrastructure in the east) and offering *being* co-opted in exchange for benefits from the state. In other words, ideological affinities were less significant for joining the GPC than perceived benefits from the membership. This was true for both the regime and newly co-opted members, such as tribal sheikhs. This mechanism proved to be beneficial not only for the GPC, but also for other political parties, such as *Islah*.

The GPC's lack of ideology has been presented as the party's strength, enforcing its claim to be the country's 'catch-all' party. At the political elite level after 1994, however, the GPC started using a rhetoric that was clearly dismissive of the opposition. The latter was accused of demagoguery, which threatened the stability and cohesion of the country. This was primarily directed against *Islah*. In doing so, the party's policy changed after the 1997 elections into the slogan 'those who are not with us are against us' (Poirier 2011: 211–13). Originally created as an ally, the *Islah* party pursued a similar strategy of co-optation that soon turned it into a serious rival to the GPC. Both parties were important links between tribal leaders and the regime. The parties provided a channel in particular for actors who did not traditionally have a lot of influence to seek the regime's proximity.

From ally to rival: the *Islah* party

The creation of the *Islah* party by the late Sheikh al-Ahmar occurred with the support of Saleh. Founding another party after reunification with northern credentials and a distinctly anti-socialist agenda created a counterweight to the YSP in the new political landscape and carried the potential of broadening a political coalition against it. Considerable Saudi financial backing facilitated *Islah*'s formation around key individuals: the paramount sheikh of Hashid, Sheikh al-Ahmar, the Salafi cleric Abdul Majid al-Zindani, and General Ali Muhsin. During the party's early days in the 1990s, a major recruitment strategy was to absorb members of other parties, first and foremost the GPC. They were integrated in the mid-level party bureaucracy as a form of reward (Yadav 2013), copying the GPC's strategy of co-optation from the 1980s. Hence, many early party members had close links to Saleh or other high-ranking regime officials (Yadav 2013), particularly those with an Islamist tendency from within the GPC. *Islah*'s core leadership was thus derived from an Islamist faction within the GPC that was under the main influence of the Egyptian Muslim Brotherhood (Yadav 2010; Dresch 2000). Other GPC members with a distinct tribal or Salafi background felt attracted to the new party, which ended up forming a loose umbrella of social conservatism and opposition to socialist secular ideas (Yadav 2010). Many in the south saw *Islah* as being a 'political manifestation of a number of Northern interest groups [to act as] an instrument of "retribalization" in [the south]' (Yadav 2013: 25).

In order to maintain legitimacy for its existence next to the GPC, expanding its constituencies and grass-roots support was vital for *Islah*. Yet, this process led to greater autonomy from the regime, which, in turn, increased Saleh's efforts to keep *Islah* at bay in order to avoid a potential threat to his domination from within the political elite.

Despite the rivalry between the GPC and *Islah*, Saleh maintained close connections with *Islah*'s prominent leaders on the tribal side, such as Sheikh al-Ahmar, as well as with Islamist leaders like Zindani (Alley 2010). The president wanted to decrease the influence of the party over political affairs, but he did not exclude those *Islah* members with strong personal or business ties (Alley 2010). Personal links thus trumped party affiliations even at times of electoral competition.

However, the relation between the GPC and *Islah* worsened significantly when Saleh cut down on his patronage to both the al-Ahmar family and *Islah* as a party. The death in 2007 of Sheikh al-Ahmar, who had been the most decisive physical link between the two parties, accelerated this development (Phillips 2008). Due to the presence of different factions within the party, *Islah* had been able to address a similarly broad constituency by the mid-2000s to the GPC's, which made it a serious contender for power. Furthermore, both big parties had been competing for the same electorate of tribal, conservative and religiously oriented groups (Hamzawy 2009). Yet, although both parties represented the interests of tribal constituencies, as many of their members had been tribesmen, they were not 'tribal' parties (Dresch 1995). Aspects of tribal codes of behaviour, value systems (*qabyala*, which act as a method of social organisation, but also as a complex set of values that informs how a person perceives the world and evaluates his or her actions and those of others; see Salmoni et al. 2010), or tribal law were not the motivations behind their political decisions, as well as their alignments. Pragmatic considerations for the benefit of leading party members dictated their choices instead.

When elite tensions between the al-Ahmar family and the Saleh family intensified in the early 2000s, *Islah* lost some of its benefits and began relying more strongly on Hamid al-Ahmar (one of the sons of the late Sheikh al-Ahmar, and one of Yemen's biggest business tycoons as well as a vocal critic of Saleh as early as 2006) for protection and financial support (Phillips 2011). The ties to the inner elite circle, however, enabled parts of *Islah* to have at least some influence on key political issues (Hamzawy 2009), less as a party but more due to the power of influential key members. Thus, different actors within the party were alternating between the regime and the opposition on key political issues. Moreover, individuals like al-Ahmar's sons had significant influence through their economic strength.

Due to its popularity among sectors of the population, *Islah* posed a threat to the GPC, especially with regard to support from the grass roots. The party's popularity also ensured that Saleh could not easily crack down on it or limit the party's scope significantly. Yet, similar to the GPC, the party, as an organisation, was not extremely powerful. Rather, it had some powerful members who used the party as a platform for their own interests. At the same time, these key individuals also needed *Islah* to exert their influence on policy-making through its considerable public backing. As independent individuals, they would have needed to turn to an alternative structural body to exert a comparable influence. The party also gave them access to the power circles, which was necessary to pursue their personal political and economic interests.

In sum, political parties were manipulated to secure alliances in order to enhance the regime's resilience. These alliances often cut across official party boundaries and reinforced long-standing, informal alliances. The regime undermined the party system through expanding its influence via informal structures and resorting to traditional patrimonial notables such as tribal sheikhs. Thus, Saleh managed to tie different constituencies to the regime through these actors. This does not mean that Saleh relied on the tribes, however; he relied on a tight circle of close allies, regardless of their tribal credentials (Peterson 2008; Dresch 1995). This practice also weakened political parties that served as a channel to access the centre of the regime rather than forming forums of political discussion that could independently influence and challenge the regime's policies.

Tribes in political parties

Tribes were not bound to any political faction, but were represented in the political parties and the military. Their members have pursued careers just like any other Yemeni and since they account for a significant part of the Yemeni population, they have also occupied a considerable number of seats in parliament, often especially 'reserved' for them (Peterson 2008). Tribes do not share a common political attitude towards political parties. This is not surprising, as electoral districts in western countries do not exclusively support or vote for the same political party either. Yet, tribesmen would collectively vote for a member of their tribe if he ran for political office or position, or would largely follow the recommendation of their tribal sheikh at election time. They would vote for names, not for parties (Dresch 1995).

Members of parliament affiliated to a tribe, however, were not ordinary tribesmen but predominantly sheikhs or sons of sheikhs, often turning their position in parliament over time into tools to serve their own purposes and not for the general good of their tribes. There was, for instance, a case in 2009, where a sheikh from al-Dhali dismissed the inhabitants of a whole village and confiscated their land, houses and animals. Before he would permit them to go back to their homes, the sheikh demanded they grant him tenure for all of this on the claimed grounds that this land was part of the property of his father and grandfather, both of whom had been sultans under the British protectorate. The government did not deal with this issue, let alone support the villagers, as this sheikh was an important ally for president Saleh.[12] Hence, the tribal leaders' inclusion in political structures, and enabling them access to the benefits of the state, was a strategic move Saleh made to mitigate the risk of being ousted by the tribes at the beginning of his rule. It subsequently developed into a tool to exert at least indirect control over the tribes via their sheikhs. However, the incorporation of tribal leaderships in the networks of patronage around the president gradually alienated tribal sheikhs from their constituencies. The alienation from their grass roots eventually eroded the traditional tribal system. Sheikhs went from being leaders within and of their tribes to being 'agents of Saleh' who were closer to the regime than to their tribal constituencies. Furthermore, members of the big tribal confederations did not feel equally considered. The Bakil resented to a certain extent that they were not as fully incorporated and that real power stayed with the Hashid. As one Bakili GPC member from Khawlan put it: 'Bakil is the tribe of the GPC. Hashid is the tribe of the President' (Alley 2010: 398).

Tribesmen, especially from Hashid, had better opportunities to secure jobs in the civil service and the army. Although Saleh had not based his regime on the tribes but on the army, recruitment for the military followed a certain tribal bias (Dresch 1995). Yet, the real power lay only with members of Sanhan, the tribe of the president. Since Sanhan is only a minor tribe within Hashid, its prominence under Saleh additionally upset the balance of dynamics within the broader tribal structures. Even lower positions in the civil service and the military were predominantly given to members of Hashid (Phillips 2011).

In tribal conferences, party affiliations were strictly left out of discussions. Instead, tribalism was seen as limiting the excesses of factionalism, but at the same time allowed tribesmen to participate in the broader realms of national politics. Tribal conferences did not see the need to intervene in the political allegiances of the tribesmen, but increasingly perceived the conduct of state politics under Saleh as undermining tribalism as such, for instance over the tribal code of conduct (Dresch 1995: 53, 55). Under Saleh, a number of tribal sheikhs had become clients of the regime. This undermined the autonomy of the tribes, which had been a key element of their identity. Furthermore, a small number of them had gained access to significant political and economic benefits but they started to neglect providing for their constituencies whilst keeping their new wealth for themselves. Traditionally, one of the responsibilities of tribal sheikhs had been to secure access to benefits for their whole tribe

Tribesmen as political actors

In the 'neo-tribal state' of Yemen, sheikhs were the ideal point for co-optation for the regime and a means to extend influence without having to carry out state-building projects beyond the capital. The new, elevated role of the sheikhs became apparent through their newly accumulated wealth (Fattah 2010). Yet, some of those sheikhs who had been part of the politico-military apparatus voiced their discontent with the tribal dominance of some parts of state institutions and the military. This was particularly a criticism of Bakil sheikhs with regard to the Hashid dominance in the regime. Tribal elites in the regime were increasingly perceived as working for themselves and not their tribes as a whole. With this in mind, tribesmen criticised the state for not providing durable alternatives to the tribal system's dysfunctions (Asselwi 1995). The tribes' critique hinted at the 'de facto fragmentation of territorial power outside Sana'a' (Hill et al. 2013: 11) during Saleh's final years in power and this escalated during the 2011 protests. In some sense, they used the opposite argument of urban intellectuals who dismissed the regime and the government as being dominated by tribes. In both cases, however, the root of the criticism was the concentration of wealth in the hands of the regime and its tribal associates, and the absence of any trickle-down effect and distribution of state revenues to the population, whether tribal or not. This development, in the long term, eroded tribal structures, especially in cases where regime-fabricated sheikhs accumulated wealth without distributing part of these benefits to the local population.[13]

The regime protected traditional power structures and even reinstalled tribal sheikhs who had lost their influence under previous presidents, most notably Hamdi. Instead of uprooting old affiliations (based on tribalism), the regime was tightly interwoven with these particular structures and used them to expand its power through them. Furthermore, it expanded these forms of traditional power structures in areas where tribalism was less strong, such as in the areas around Taiz and Ibb, and after the 1994 civil war in the south. For example, merchants without a tribal background often called themselves 'sheikh'. The regime encouraged or even 'fabricated' sheikhs, which initiated tensions and potential conflicts between 'real' sheikhs and regime-bred sheikhs (Fattah 2010: 252–3). Rather than expanding its own domination, the regime granted authority to and protected local notables. Sheikhs were included in all the important positions of the government and in parliament through GPC membership. However, whilst tribal sheikhs had started off as representatives of their tribes to the state after the 1962 revolution, they gradually became agents of the regime with an interest in personal benefits. In other words, the mechanism to expand the regime's power and tie constituencies to the centre eventually led to mass alienation of the tribal constituencies, and the phenomenon of 'city-sheikhs' grew (Dresch 2000), that is, sheikhs who enjoyed their benefits in Sana'a' but lost their connection with their constituencies in their home areas. These did not see any trickle-down effect of their leaders' benefits.

Hence, institutionalised participation – that is, channels of input of demands and support for policy-making such as the parliament and political parties – did not effectively address the legitimacy deficit of the government (Hudson 1977), but served as a façade for decision-making that effectively occurred outside of these forums. As a result, administrative structures remained weak so as not to obstruct the balancing acts of co-opting, incorporating and excluding elite actors. These actors were most often semi-independent in the sense that they were relevant to the regime in terms of local influence, a large following, considerable business (merchants in the area of Taiz) and coercive means (powerful tribes in the northern highlands). The regime needed these actors, who in turn could make demands or press the regime for concessions. Manipulation strategies and frequent shifts in alliances dominated the 'rules of the game'. Political parties served as tools for co-optation, as well as for marginalisation and divide-and-rule strategies. The shifting alliance between the GPC and the *Islah* party between unification and the last presidential elections in 2006 illustrates these mechanisms well. The cases of powerful local actors and political parties illustrate how the notion of 'dependency' changed over the course of Saleh's rule. After taking over power in 1978 and after unification in 1990, Saleh's regime *needed* to include tribal actors in political parties and elite circles, and to draw them closer to the regime. After the northern victory in the 1994 civil war, however, Saleh started to eliminate *his* dependency on other actors. This prevented further mass inclusion and eroded previous loyalties.

Tribes and the Arab Uprisings: tribesman, citizen, party member

The 2011 protests showed that very little of the protesters' discontent was articulated through the political parties of the opposition. People were well aware of the party leaders', and especially the al-Ahmar family's, proximity to the regime. The opposition parties were not perceived as a true alternative to the incumbent regime (Phillips 2011). They had replicated neo-patrimonial structures within their own parties and thus reflected the state system, which they were supposed to oppose, creating a fundamental dilemma for the opposition. Its parties' main demands during the uprising centred on a national unity government and progressive reforms. However, they were unable to present themselves as alternative power centres, partly because they could not allocate as much wealth as the GPC. The *Islah* and the smaller parties did not challenge the system of neo-patrimonial decision-making, although this was one of the main reasons why the parties had been excluded from the inner circle of power. In other words, as political parties, they did not have much influence on the personalised structures of policy-making. Even members from within the opposition, such as from *Islah*, criticised that.

Independent young people, who were soon joined by Yemenis from all sectors of the population, including tribesmen, drove the 2011 protests. Two aspects were noteworthy for many of the young, largely urban participants of the protests. First, tribespeople travelled to Sana'a' to join the protests unarmed and side by side with the youth protesters (carrying a weapon is an important status symbol for tribesmen, hence the significance of not carrying guns during the protests). Some tribes were said to have suspended ongoing blood feuds in order to be able to participate in the protests. Second, and just as noteworthy, is that many tribesmen joined the street protests against Saleh whilst their tribal sheikhs still sided with the regime. Seeing tribesmen unwilling to follow the orders of their sheikhs to stay away from the protests, and instead joining as citizens, fellow Yemenis rather than tribesmen, was a completely new phenomenon in the country.[14] In joining the protests, tribespeople articulated their protest against corrupt sheikhs and the neglect of their tribal areas (in fact, even the home areas of the Saleh and al-Ahmar families – Sanhan and Amran – are still underdeveloped despite the direct access to wealth these two families had; see Peterson 2008: 17). In this way, they were not any different from other Yemenis active in 2011.

The dynamics of the protests changed when established political actors, in particular the *Islah* party, began influencing the protests (Juneau 2014). Hamid al-Ahmar contributed to the protests with significant financial and material support (Hill et al. 2013). Together with his brothers Hussein and Himyar (then Deputy Speaker of Parliament), he distributed cash among tribal leaders as an incentive to back the protests. Saleh and the al-Ahmar brothers both tried to bolster existing alliances and foster new ones (Johnsen 2011). Since co-optation had been a reliable method over the previous decades, it seemed opportune for all key elite actors to exploit it. The alienation of tribes from their sheikhs made it even easier for defecting elite members to co-opt the tribes. Yet, unlike in previous years, it was about boosting one's own camp rather than keeping a balance, particularly among the Hashidi tribes. Saleh's Sanhan tribe was further down in the hierarchy as compared with the al-Ahmars' al-Usaymat tribe. Yet, due to Sanhan's occupation of relevant regime positions, Saleh could have had a similar influence on the tribes. Saleh and the al-Ahmar brothers were jockeying for the tribes' support at a time when independent actors with little partisan rhetoric still demonstrated in the streets. This indicates how early elite actors realised that the momentum in the country could be, or needed to be, used for their own future position in the elite structures. Whilst the protesters were part of their rhetoric, none of the elite actors actually took on the demands of the protesters, but rather looked for conventional alliances among the established political elite. In fact, this became further apparent during the transition period and the National Dialogue Conference (NDC) in 2012 and 2013 where established political actors struggled for their positions whilst the ordinary population had again little to no influence on the political processes in the country.

Meanwhile, large parts of the Hashid confederation declared their support for the protesters. A reason for their initial hesitation might have been negotiations over reconciliation with Hashid tribes loyal to Saleh (Abu-Rish 2012). *Islah*'s financial backing of the protests continued and was said to have come mainly from Sadiq and his brother Hamid al-Ahmar. The independent youth feared old forces from *Islah* were hijacking the protests (Day 2012: 284). They argued that *Islah* was taking over Change

Square and controlled who spoke on the stage that was used for speeches and performances (Hill et al. 2013).

Over the summer of 2011, the Yemeni elites split, including the military, with *Islah* backing the protests together with some GPC defectors. Fighting between the regime and the defectors broke out and could only be halted through a negotiated power transfer under the auspices of the Gulf Cooperation Council (GCC), the US, EU and UN. During the official transition period starting in February 2012, a number of new political parties were formed, similarly to what occurred after unification in 1990. According to the Committee for the Affairs of Parties and Political Organisations for the House of Representatives and the Shura Council, nine new political parties had been announced between the start of the uprising in early 2011 and mid-2012. Yemen's political crisis 'created a social impetus for new leaders to enter the political arena through parties that are based on new visions' (Darem 2012). Many of the parties were initially founded out of opposition to the regime's repression of the protests. By mid-2013 there were thirty-two registered parties in total in Yemen. The demands of most of these parties focused on a rather vague view of 'a better Yemen', based on peace, stability, justice and equality. Their programmes centred on education, social peace and development. Although this indicates that people wanted to engage in processes to transform their demands from the streets into a framework beyond the protests, many of these new political parties were essentially driven by (former) elite actors and could not lead to greater mass inclusion. The fragmentation of the different parties suggests furthermore that the different groups would not necessarily work together. Although people's mobilisation sparked the outbreak of and spurred the intensity of elite competition, the dynamics of the uprising were taken over by elite actors, both pro- and anti-Saleh. Together with foreign actors, they all had a stake in preserving the status quo with a defeat of their respective intra-regime rival. A comprehensive reform of the political system was not in their interest. Ordinary tribespeople, just like the rest of the population, did not benefit from this development. Their demands for economic and social enfranchisement were not addressed, with living conditions deteriorating even further during the transition period (2012–14). The outbreak of the civil war in 2015 accelerated the rapid decline of living conditions, with party politics largely being paralysed and tribesmen fighting on both sides of the conflict.

Conclusion

The overlap of categories such as tribesman, merchant, sheikh, bureaucrat, minister, Islamist and army officer, and the entanglement of positions have been the backdrop of Yemeni politics. Up until the 1970s these categories made some sense with trade on the one hand and Saudi patronage to sheikhs on the other providing for quite different sources of income. With the unification of North and South Yemen and the emergence of party politics, these categories collapsed. The main political parties, GPC and *Islah*, offered new access to wealth and benefits, and undermined long-standing tribal structures on a political, economic and social level. Yet, they did not offer clear political agendas but rather helped to foster a neo-patrimonial system with a small circle of elites benefiting from access to the country's wealth, whilst the rest of the population, whether tribal or not, was confronted with increasingly difficult living conditions. The parties failed to establish a certain degree of independence from the regime. They could have served as an alternative channel to voice discontent and express popular demands, especially at a time when tribal authorities increasingly failed to do so for their constituencies. But long-standing ties to the regime of all political parties prevented them from standing up for the population, whether with or without a tribal affiliation. After the collapse of the transitional period in the aftermath of the 2011 uprising, neither political parties nor tribal representatives were able to act as advocates for the ordinary people or contribute to reinstating some sort of stability.

Notes

1. Author interviews with various journalists and local NGO workers, Sana'a, June to September 2013.
2. There is excellent work on the nature of tribalism in Yemen that, however, goes beyond the scope of this chapter. For more on this, see Brandt (2014); Adra (2011); Weir (2007); Caton (2005); Dresch (1989, 1990).
3. Author interview with a member of the staff of the Deputy Director of the Yemen Centre for Research and Studies (YCRS), Sana'a, July 2013.
4. Author interview with civil society and human rights activist, Ibb, August 2013.
5. Author interview with civil society and human rights activist, Ibb, August 2013.
6. For other regions in Yemen, see Kambeck (2014).
7. Author interview with a professor of economics at Sana'a University, Sana'a, July 2013.

8. Author interview with a professor of economics at Sana'a' University, Sana'a', July 2013.
9. Author interview with a civil society activist, Ibb, August 2013.
10. Author interview with a senior political commentator, Sana'a', July 2013.
11. Author interview with a journalist, Ibb, August 2013.
12. Author interview with an independent political observer, Sana'a', July 2013.
13. Author interview with a professor for Political Science at Sana'a' University, Ibb, August 2013.
14. Author's observation during the uprisings in 2011. Schmitz (2011) points out this phenomenon as well. Previously, it had been unheard of for tribesmen to act against their tribal sheikhs, despite some erosion of the traditional structures, due to the respect they hold for the sheikh (Dresch 1995: 40).

Bibliography

Abu-Rish, Ziad (2012), 'Saleh Defiant', in Bassam Haddad, Rosie Bsheer and Ziad Abu-Rish (eds), *The Dawn of the Arab Uprisings: End of an Old Order?*, London: Pluto Press, pp. 200–4.

Adra, Najwa (2011), 'Tribal Mediation in Yemen and Its Implications to Development', *AAS Working Papers in Social Anthropology* 19, Vienna: Austrian Academy of Sciences.

Alles, Larissa (2014), 'Patterns of Legitimacy. A Local Examination from Ibb', *Bulletin of the British Foundation for the Study of Arabia* 19, 12–13.

Alley, April (2010), 'The Rules of the Game: Unpacking Patronage Politics in Yemen', *Middle East Journal* 64: 5, 385–409.

Asselwi, A. (1995), 'Conversations with a Bakîl Shaykh', American Institute for Yemeni Studies, *Yemen Update* 6, 6–11.

Brandt, Marieke (2014), 'The Irregulars of the Sa'ada War: "Colonel Sheikhs" and "Tribal Militias" in Yemen's Huthi Conflict (2004–2010)', in Helen Lackner (ed.), *Why Yemen Matters: A Society in Transition*, London: Saqi Books, pp. 105–22.

Browers, Michaelle (2007), 'Origins and Architects of Yemen's Joint Meeting Parties', *International Journal of Middle Eastern Studies* 39: 4, 565–86.

Carapico, Sheila (1996), 'Yemen between Civility and Civil War', in Richard Augustus Norton (ed.), *Civil Society in the Middle East Vol. 2*, Leiden: E. J. Brill, pp. 287–316.

Carapico, Sheila (1998), *Civil Society in Yemen: The Political Economy of Activism in Modern Arabia*, Cambridge: Cambridge University Press.

Caton, Steven (2005), *Yemen Chronicle: An Anthropology of War and Mediation*, New York: Hill and Wang.

Darem, F. (2012), 'Yemen Sees Surge in Political Party Activity', *Al-Shorfa*, 23 July, <http://al-shorfa.com/en_GB/articles/meii/features/2012/07/23/feature-01> (last accessed 1 September 2017).

Day, Stephen (2012), *Regionalism and Rebellion in Yemen: A Troubled National Union*, New York: Cambridge University Press.

Dresch, Paul (1989), *Tribes, Government and History in Yemen*, Oxford: Oxford University Press.

Dresch, Paul (1990), 'Imams and Tribes: The Writing and Acting of History in Upper Yemen', in Philip Khoury and Joseph Kostiner, *Tribes and State Formation in the Middle East*, Berkley, Los Angeles: University of California Press, pp. 252–87.

Dresch, Paul (1995), 'The Tribal Factor in the Yemeni Crisis', in J. S. al-Suwaidi (ed.), *The Yemeni War of 1994: Causes and Consequences*, Abu Dhabi: The Emirates Center for Strategic Studies and Research, pp. 33–55.

Dresch, Paul (2000), *A History of Modern Yemen*, Cambridge: Cambridge University Press.

Fattah, Khaled (2010), 'Contextual Determinants of Political Modernization in Tribal Middle Eastern Societies: The Case of Unified Yemen', unpublished PhD dissertation, University of St Andrews.

Hamzawy, Amr (2009), 'Between Government and Opposition: The Case of the Yemeni Congregation for Reform', Carnegie Papers 18, Washington DC: Carnegie Endowment for International Peace.

Hill, Ginny, Peter Salisbury, Léonie Northedge and Jane Kinninmont (2013), *Yemen: Corruption, Capital Flight and Global Drivers of Conflict*, London: Chatham House/ Royal Institute of International Affairs.

Hudson, Michael (1977), *Arab Politics: The Search for Legitimacy*, New Haven, CT: Yale University Press.

Johnsen, Gregory (2011), 'The Tribal Element of the Protests: A Battle between the Two Bayt al-Ahmars (Updated)', *The Big Think*, 17 February, <http://bigthink.com/ waq-al-waq/the-tribal-element-of-the-protests-a-battle-between-the-two-bayt-al-ahmars-updated> (last accessed 1 September 2017).

Juneau, Thomas (2014), 'Yemen and the Arab Spring', in Mehran Kamrava (ed.), *Beyond the Arab Spring: The Evolving Ruling Bargain in the Middle East*, New York: Oxford University Press, pp. 374–97.

Kambeck, Jens (2014), 'Land Disputes in Yemen', in Helen Lackner (ed.), *Why Yemen Matters: A Society in Transition*, London: Saqi Books, pp. 197–212.

Lackner, Helen (2016), 'Understanding the Yemeni Crisis: The Transformation of Tribal Roles in Recent Decades', *Luce Fellowship Paper* 17, Durham Middle East Papers 91, Durham University.

Langohr, Vickie (2005), 'Too Much Civil Society, Too Little Politics? Egypt and other Liberalizing Arab Regimes', in Marsha Pripstein Posusney and Michele Penner Angrist (eds), Authoritarianism in the Middle East: Regimes and Resistance, Boulder, CO: Lynne Rienner, pp. 193–218.

Mundy, Martha (1995), *Domestic Government: Kinship, Community and Polity in North Yemen*, London and New York: I. B. Tauris.

Peterson, John (2008), 'Tribes and Politics in Yemen', *Arabian Peninsula Background Notes* No. APBN-007, <http://www.jepeterson.net> (last accessed 1 September 2017).

Phillips, Sarah (2008), *Yemen's Democracy Experiment in Regional Perspective: Patronage and Pluralized Authoritarianism*, Basingstoke: Palgrave Macmillan.

Phillips, Sarah (2011), *Yemen and the Politics of Permanent Crisis*, Abingdon: Routledge.

Poirier, Marine (2011), 'Performing Political Domination in Yemen: Narratives and Practices of Power in the General People's Congress', *The Muslim World* 101, 202–27.

Salmoni, Barak, Bryce Loidolt and Madeleine Wells (2010), *Regime and Periphery in Northern Yemen: The Huthi Phenomenon*, Santa Monica, CA: Rand Corporation.

Schmitz, Charles (2011), 'Yemen without Saleh. Chaos? It Doesn't Have to Be', *Foreign Policy*, 8 June, <http://www.foreignpolicy.com/articles/2011/06/08/yemen_without_saleh?page=0,0> (last accessed DATE).

Schwedler, Jillian (2002), 'Yemen's Aborted Opening', *Journal of Democracy* 13: 4, 48–55.

Schwedler, Jillian (2006), *Faith in Moderation: Islamist Parties in Jordan and Yemen*, Cambridge: Cambridge University Press.

Weir, Shelagh (2007), *A Tribal Order. Politics and Law in the Mountains of Yemen*, London: The British Museum Press.

Yadav, Stacey Philbrick (2010), 'Understanding "What Islamists Want:" Public Debate and Contestation in Lebanon and Yemen', *The Middle East Journal* 62: 2, 199–213.

Yadav, Stacey Philbrick (2013), *Islamists and the State: Legitimacy and Institutions in Yemen and Lebanon*, London: I. B. Tauris.

al-Yemeni, Ahmed (2003), *The Dynamic of Democratisation — Political Parties in Yemen*, Sana'a' and Bonn: Friedrich-Ebert-Stiftung.

Chapter 11

In the shadow of legality: proto-parties and participatory politics in the Emirate of Kuwait

Hendrik Kraetzschmar

Unlike much of the rest of the Middle East and North Africa (MENA), political parties and party politics remain somewhat of an anomaly in the Gulf Cooperation Council (GCC) countries. Independence here was obtained largely without resorting to mass politics and the formation of political movements/parties seeking independent statehood from their colonial masters (where they existed). In the post-independence era, meanwhile, GCC rulers, unlike their monarchical counterparts in Jordan and Morocco, did not allow for the creation of limited political pluralism, nor did they eventually make way to single-party regimes, as was the case in the erstwhile monarchies of Egypt, Iraq and North Yemen. During the era of political liberalisation from the 1980s onwards, as well, GCC rulers resisted for the most part calls for the introduction of party pluralism, limiting domestic reforms to an expansion of rights and the introduction of often (partial) non-partisan elections to municipal and/or national assemblies as well as select civil organisations. Political parties, so the official canon, were seen as alien (and un-Islamic) to GCC societies and as divisive organisations threatening the societal cohesion of these countries (Peterson 2012).

There are, however, two notable exceptions to this narrative, both of which have bucked GCC-wide trends on the introduction of 'party' politics. There is the Kingdom of Bahrain, which, following a short period of constitutional post-independence politics in the 1970s and subsequent absolutist rule, introduced liberalising political reforms in the late 1990s that saw the establishment of an elected lower house of parliament and the legalisation of party-like organisations, which have since participated in national and municipal elections. Then there is the

Emirate of Kuwait, which boasts a long history of plural elections even pre-dating independence, and is widely credited with having one of the more liberal political orders in the Arab world, featuring a comparatively powerful legislature as well as a vibrant political society, as Pall notes in his chapter in this volume. Like Bahrain, this political society comprises numerous party-like organisations. These, however, differ from their Bahraini counterparts in that they do not operate on a legal footing but, as will be elaborated below, remain within the legal grey zone of national politics.

This chapter focuses on Kuwait and explores the country's landscape of party-like organisations and their workings in national politics. Expanding on extant scholarship on the Kuwaiti case, the chapter uniquely positions the study of these organisations within the broader realm of electorally relevant socio-political forces operating in Kuwaiti politics. As such, it sheds light not only on the complex scene of local participatory politics, but on the challenges faced by Kuwait's party-like organisations in becoming principal players in the country's electoral politics. Whilst some of these challenges are uniquely linked to the Kuwaiti context, many others resonate with the plight of political parties in the Arab world more broadly, highlighting yet again the many common trademarks that exist across regional party systems. As will become apparent below, these pertain to the challenging legal-political context within which parties operate, the preponderance of ascriptive identities (sectarian/ethnic/tribal) over political ones both across and within political parties (particularly in the Mashreq), and the difficulties parties face more broadly in asserting themselves as principal actors in electoral and parliamentary politics. This chapter argues that overcoming these challenges in the Kuwaiti context will require more than a mere change in legal status, and must involve a sustained transformation of conceptions of national identity and citizenship.

Proto-parties and the realm of participatory politics

Before sketching out the contours of 'party' politics in Kuwait some conceptual clarifications are in order. This need for conceptual clarity derives from the observation that within the extant literature on Kuwaiti politics we encounter a cacophony of terms to denote party-like organisations, some of which are deemed more appropriate than others. The reason for this cacophony of terms most likely resides in the fact that without formal party legislation in place (a point returned to later on) it is difficult in the Kuwaiti context to formally speak of the existence of political parties. Country experts have thus sought to deploy various designations for those political formations partaking in national politics, including most prominently terms such as proto-, pseudo- or quasi-parties, political groups, political societies, political blocs, party-like blocs, parliamentary blocs or political currents (Gavrielides 1987; Tétreault 2000; Freer 2015). Whilst some of these terms may be used interchangeably, it is proposed here that a clear conceptual distinction be drawn between proto-/quasi-/pseudo-parties and/or political societies/blocs on the one hand and parliamentary blocs on the other. I thus propose to reserve the term proto-, pseudo- or quasi-parties exclusively for those groupings that (1) self-define as such;[1] (2) fulfil some, if not all, of the functions widely associated with political parties, including most notably the selection of candidates for elected office; and (3) retain a physical presence in society outside the electoral cycle and the elected institutions of the state. The term parliamentary bloc, in turn, should be earmarked for groupings of members of parliament (MPs) formed in the aftermath of an election and with the purpose of coordinating policy positions/agendas in parliament. These blocs are hence distinct from proto-/quasi-/pseudo-parties in that they (1) usually comprise MPs from different parties and affiliated independents; (2) only form post-election; (3) have no institutional presence outside parliament; and (4) are limited in duration.

The second concept of note that requires unpacking in the Kuwaiti context is that of 'parliamentary opposition'. Whilst present to some extent, opposition politics in Kuwait is far less structured, and the opposition–government binary far more fluid, than in western-style parliamentary democracies where opposition tends to be partisan, highly institutionalised and formally recognised. For one thing, and given the lack of party legislation, in the Kuwaiti context there is no formal legislative opposition to speak of. Whatever exists in domestic politics as opposition is thus self-defined, marked by oppositional behaviour towards government initiatives and ministers, rather than by official status. Moreover, given that government is not parliament-dependent (a point returned to later), the Kuwaiti opposition also lacks the characteristic of a government-in-waiting that could present itself as an institutionalised alternative to the incumbent. What we find instead is a parliamentary opposition that tends to be loosely organised and not exclusively partisan, comprising both party-like formations as well as unaffiliated/independent (mostly tribal) MPs. When it comes to the politics of opposition, as well, high levels of fluidity mark the political reality on the ground, with issue-based opposition prevailing over in-principle opposition and with the country's key political players often shifting in stance within and across legislative periods. Indeed, it is not unheard of for Kuwait's party-like formations to declare themselves in opposition, whilst at the same time accepting government posts, and to oscillate between pro-and anti-government stances, thus blurring the line between the two. In his chapter in this volume, Pall makes a similar point when examining the Salafis' behaviour.

For the purpose of this analysis, then, party-like formations in Kuwaiti politics will be labelled proto-parties to stipulate their status as non-legalised, yet tolerated, parties-in-waiting. The term opposition, meanwhile, will be deployed, keeping in mind, however, the caveats detailed above.

Regime context

Kuwaiti proto-parties operate within a constitutional architecture that is significantly more liberal than that of any of the remaining monarchical regimes on the Arabian Peninsula. Situated somewhere along the continuum between absolute and constitutional monarchy, Kuwait features a strong executive branch of government that is held in check to some extent by an elected parliament and a semi-autonomous, yet vibrant, civil society sector. Headed by the Emir, the Kuwaiti executive remains dominated by members of the al-Sabah family who hold key posts in cabinet, including most notably that of the prime minister (PM). This executive operates, however, alongside a unicameral legislative branch – the sixty-five-seat *Majlis al-Umma* (National Assembly), of which fifty members are popularly elected and the remaining fifteen are cabinet ministers – which, by regional standards, is vested with considerable law-making and control powers, a reality that is reflected in the Kuwaiti legislature's Parliamentary Power Index (PPI) score of 0.38, which is miles better than that of the other GCC states, including Bahrain (Herb 2009; Fish and Kroenig 2009). They include, most notably, the authority to initiate and approve legislation, the power to question/interpellate members of cabinet, the right to vote ministers out of office and declare an inability to cooperate with the PM, as well as the requirement of any newly appointed Emir to obtain parliamentary consent before taking on the helm of rule (Kuwaiti Constitution 1962). These considerable powers are meaningful and widely exercised largely due to the absence of a ruling party/coalition which could rubber-stamp government appointments and legislation, and the presence of a plural, and at times oppositional, legislature, featuring blocs of MPs who are able, and willing, to draw on a wide range of statutory powers to challenge executive rule.

Despite parliament's comparative strength vis-à-vis the executive, it is not possible, however, to designate Kuwait as a full-blown constitutional monarchy within a democratic system of governance. This is for many reasons, but is largely because one key ingredient of a democratic parliamentary system is missing in the Kuwaiti context: that is, the right of the parliamentary majority party/coalition to appoint the PM. Indeed, rather than being parliament-dependent, it is the prerogative of the Emir to appoint the PM, who then appoints the members of cabinet without the need for parliamentary approval (Kuwaiti Constitution 1962). Amongst Kuwait's proto-parties, this monarchical prerogative constitutes one of two key constitutional bones of contention, with there being across the board consensus on the need for a PM chosen by parliament.

The other key bone of contention, meanwhile, concerns the absence of a political parties law. Although proto-parties have existed in Kuwaiti politics even before independence in 1961 and been able to operate relatively freely in the political arena since, they have done so within the grey zone of constitutional politics. Whilst guaranteeing the right to form civil (non-political) associations (Article 43) and freedom of public assembly (Article 44), the Kuwaiti Constitution and its explanatory memorandum carry no provisions for the establishment of political parties and the passage of a parties law (Kuwaiti Constitution 1962). Consequentially, and unlike elsewhere in the MENA region where party pluralism is permitted, to this day there is no party legislation in place to regulate the licensing and operations of the country's proto-parties. Most Kuwait experts, though not all, read this constitutional omission as signalling that political parties are ultimately compatible with the constitution and that hence they can be legalised through simple legislation (al-Mdaires 2010; al-Remaidhi and Watt 2012). This legal opinion is supported by the explanatory note accompanying Article 43 of the constitution which – whilst excluding political parties from being formed under its current provisions – explicitly states that political parties are not per se constitutionally banned.[2]

Over the past decade, proto-parties have recurrently voiced their unease with this status quo, demanding an end to legal uncertainty and the introduction of proper party legislation. Public pronouncements to this effect abound from across the ideological spectrum, including some concrete proposals for the establishment of a parties law, such as those presented by a cross-section of opposition MPs in the summer of 2012 (Kuwait Times 2012). Ultimately, this, and similar such initiatives, failed to see the light of day, however, with some observers of Kuwaiti politics questioning more broadly the extent to which there is in fact a sense of urgency amongst proto-parties to change the status quo. Indeed, whilst officially advocating legalisation, in actual practice many proto-parties appear in no haste to exit the grey zone of politics, knowing full well that any party legislation would bring with it closer governmental and public scrutiny of their internal organisation and financial affairs. Added to this must be a concern that resonates well beyond the Kuwaiti confines; namely, the deep-rooted fear prevalent amongst leftist, nationalist and liberal political forces across the Arab world that formal (democratic) politics, if/when introduced, would work to the advantage of their principal ideological adversaries: the Islamists (Abdelrahman 2009). In the Kuwaiti context this fear finds expression amongst others in the concern (particularly within the national-liberal current) that any formalisation of party politics would disproportionately benefit the ICM and Salafi proto-parties, and thus further strengthen their position vis-à-vis the government in the pursuit of a conservative socio-political agenda.[3]

Showing no sign of acceding to opposition demands on either issue, meanwhile, it is clear that the Emir and the Kuwaiti government sustain this legal limbo as part of a broader multi-pronged strategy to manage and contain the field of proto-parties. For while the regime derives both domestic and international legitimacy from facilitating political pluralism, it has taken great care to ensure the country's proto-parties do not morph into any serious challengers to the political status quo. As in monarchical regimes elsewhere in the Arab MENA, this has been achieved through a combination of legal means and the sponsorship/ co-optation of pliant pro-regime MPs and forces in parliament. So for instance, experts of Kuwaiti politics widely agree that the government has skilfully used electoral legislation (and particularly those provisions relating to the vote and districting) to engineer outcomes that favour tribal over party-political affiliations and that prevent any one proto-party from becoming a dominant force in parliament (Tétreault 2000; Herb 2013).[4] In this Kuwait is strikingly similar to neighbouring Jordan, where too the regime has fiddled with voting provisions and districting to ensure MPs from traditionally regime-loyal rural/tribal areas are over-represented in parliament and to undercut mass voting along partisan lines (Lust-Okar 2009).

The Kuwaiti government's unwillingness to legislate on a parties law, meanwhile, can also be understood as playing a part in its strategy to manage and contain formal politics in the county. Indeed, without any such law in place, it remains relatively easy for the government to disband 'unofficial' proto-parties deemed unruly without causing too much of a stir and without the need to engage in lengthy, and possibly, uncertain judicial proceedings. The mere threat of a crackdown, in fact, may well be sufficient to tame any proto-party that crosses the red lines of permissive political engagement. Significantly also, the status quo is widely perceived as enabling the government to hold sway over legislative politics. As Allarakia (2007) and al-Zumai (2007) have pointed out, the absence of legalised political parties (together with the prevalence of a candidate-based electoral system that perpetuates familial, tribal and sectarian voting behaviour) produces electoral contests that remain dominated by highly personalised campaigns and parliaments composed of weak, fragmented and often undisciplined proto-parties and parliamentary blocs that share the floor with numerous (tribal) independents and so-called service MPs who seek to extract rent from the state in return for their support of government policy. Parliaments thus fractionalised are less likely to feature a cohesive majority party/ parliamentary bloc that could present a serious and sustained opposition to the government, providing the executive instead with ample options to entice individual deputies through 'pork-barrel favours' into voting along government lines. Proto-parties as well feature prominently in this government strategy of building pro-government (ad hoc) coalitions and of thwarting opposition unity in the *majlis*. This is achieved primarily by means of co-opting select proto-parties into the government's orbit through offers of ministerial and/or other government posts. The aim thereby is not only to secure working majorities in parliament, but to foster divisions within the opposition, bind influential proto-parties and politicians closely to the government's chest and/or balance against forces deemed as politically too influential (Brown 2007). If all else fails (and the government is confronted with an intransigent opposition in parliament), finally the Emir can draw on his constitutional prerogative to dissolve parliament prematurely and call for fresh elections (Kuwaiti Constitution 1962).

The landscape of proto-parties

Although proto-parties have featured in Kuwaiti electoral politics ever since independence, it is only in the aftermath of the Iraqi invasion and subsequent liberation in 1990–1 that we see the emergence of the plethora of proto-parties operating in Kuwait today. The characteristics of this proto-party landscape are very much a reflection of both the institutional-legal context within which they operate and the socio-political cleavages prevailing in Kuwaiti society. The latter can be linked to the range of proto-parties we encounter in Kuwaiti politics today, while the former helps to shed light on key organisational trademarks. It has been widely noted, for instance, that the absence of a parties law – combined with the presence of electoral/campaign regulations and parliamentary statutes that do not account for the existence of proto-parties – contributes significantly to the prevalence of highly personalistic behaviour among proto-party candidates and MPs, and thus of party organisations marred by internal fragmentation and disunity. As concerns the latter, meanwhile, it is apparent that proto-parties broadly mirror some of the key socio-political cleavages extant in Kuwaiti society. As elsewhere in the region, Kuwaiti society is characterised by a diverse demographic, featuring cleavages along geographic (urban/*hadari* vs desert/*qabali*), ideological and sectarian lines (Sunni vs Shi'i) (Salem 2007).[5] Proto-parties, as they exist today, encapsulate this multiplicity of at times cross-cutting cleavages and feature a range of ideological currents that contain religious, populist-leftist and national-liberal tendencies. Comprising both Sunni and Shi'i-based groupings, the religious current contains the mainstream Kuwaiti Muslim Brotherhood (KMB) affiliate *al-Haraka al-Dusturiyah al-Islamiyya* (Islamic Constitutional Movement; ICM, also known locally by its Arabic acronym *Hadas*), founded in 1991, whose traditional support base is mostly, yet not exclusively, *hadari* and which pushes for far-reaching political reforms (for example, the move towards a constitutional monarchy) alongside a socially conservative agenda of Islamising society and politics (Freer 2015). *Hadas* is nowadays firmly anchored within the country's opposition, although it has at times accepted cabinet posts, seeking to present itself as a responsible and measured player in domestic politics (Brown 2009). The religious current also encompasses several Salafi proto-parties which are again most popular amongst the *hadar* in urban areas, but whose socio-religious conservatism also resonates well with voters from tribal constituencies, as Pall makes clear in his chapter in this volume. Salafi proto-parties of note include the traditionally pro-government *al-Tajammu' al-Salafi al-Islami* (Salafi Islamic Gathering; SIG), as well as *al-Haraka al-Salafiyya* (Salafi Movement; SM) and *hizb al-Umma* (Nation Party; NP), which tend to be more oppositional/confrontational towards the government. Key political demands common to all Salafi proto-parties include the amendment of Article 2 of the constitution, declaring sharia the sole source of legislation (rather than the main source). On the Shi'i side, lastly, the religious current is represented by a range of proto-parties, amongst which *al-Tahaluf al-Watani al-Islami* (National Islamic Alliance; NIA) is undoubtedly the most widely recognised (Albloshi 2016).[6] Born out of Kuwaiti *Hezbollah*, the NIA morphed in 2008 from a pro-Iranian oppositional force to one aligning closely with the government (al-Mdaires 2010). This shift in alignment took place in the wake of the Mughniyeh mourning crisis of 2008, after which the NIA was offered a ministerial post in government and realigned itself as a pro-government force.

Religious proto-parties in Kuwait are thus fragmented along Sunni–Shi'i lines as well as exposing various intra-sectarian divisions, primarily within the Salafi and Shi'i constituencies. In both instances, these divisions stem from political and interpersonal differences within the respective movements, which led to their pluralisation. Amongst the Salafi forces, as Pall analyses in detail in his chapter in this volume, one of the principal political dividing lines, yet not the only one, concerns that between so-called purists, who advocate unconditional obedience to the country's rulers and remain limited in their political activism to the defence of *da'wa* as well as the Islamisation of social practices, and more 'activist' (*haraki*) Salafi leaders and factions who espouse a more oppositional stance to the Kuwaiti regime, rejecting the country's alliance with the USA and calling for far-reaching political reforms. The Shi'i movement, in turn, is divided along demographic and political lines, featuring distinct community/political organisations for descendants from Al-Asha province in Saudi Arabia (*hasawiyin*), Bahrain (*bahrana*) and Iran (*'ajam*), as well as differences between supporters and opponents of the Iranian *Wilayat al-Faqih* doctrine. Both sets of proto-parties, moreover, expose a history of shifting divisions between those supportive of, and those taking an oppositional stance towards, the government.[7]

The populist-leftist current in Kuwaiti politics, meanwhile, is represented by *Kutla al-Amal al-Sha'bi* (Popular Action Bloc; PAB), a hybrid political formation that initially emerged in parliament but has since morphed into a proto-party of sorts with a popular base primarily within the tribal segments of society,[8] and *al-Haraka al-Taqadumiyya al-Kuwitiyya* (Kuwaiti Progressive Movement; KPM) which, founded in 2011, traces its roots to Arab nationalist/socialist forces of the 1950s and 1960s and whose key policies revolve around demands for social justice, economic equality and national independence.[9]

The national-liberal current, lastly, is historically fragmented and broadly represented by three proto-parties.[10] These comprise the more established *al-Manber al-Demuqrati al-Kuwiti* (Kuwait Democratic Forum; KDF, established in 1991), whose existence can be traced back to local Arab nationalist forces in the 1960s and 1970s, and *al-Tahaluf al-Demuqrati al-Watani* (National Democratic Alliance; NDA), which split from the KDF in 2004 (Crystal and al-Shayeji 1998; Ghabra 1997). The two proto-parties were joined in 2014 by *hizb al-Muhafizin al-Madani* (Civil Conservative Party; CCP), which has as yet to partake in national elections, however. Most popular in the urban/*hadari* constituencies, all three proto-parties are similar in outlook and advocate liberalising social and political reforms.[11]

The proto-party landscape is therefore plural and ideologically diverse, albeit dominated by religious-based forces and inter-sectarian fragmentation. In this, as other contributors make clear, Kuwait matches the preponderance of confessional politics in other parts of the region, most notably in Iraq, Lebanon and Bahrain, where sectarian cleavages have come to dominate the party-political scene and where truly cross-sectarian political parties remain marginal. In Kuwait, as well, the proto-party political scene is lacking any truly cross-sectarian forces that could advance a unifying national agenda transcending the religious (and tribal) divide. This applies as much to the country's religious current as it does to those proto-parties professing to leftist or liberal ideals, whose composition also fails to reflect Kuwait's sectarian diversity.[12]

Proto-parties, parliamentary blocs and other socio-political protagonists

One of the most noteworthy trademarks of Kuwait's proto-party landscape to date (and one that only reveals itself fully when moving from micro to macro perspective) concerns its position within the broader realm of participatory politics. Whilst proto-parties constitute meaningful protagonists within this realm, they are by no means the only, let alone predominant, players in it. On the contrary, proto-parties operate in Kuwaiti politics alongside, and at times as part of, a host of other politically active groupings and configurations, thus presenting an imagery of the domestic political scene that is dense and exceedingly complex.

Figure 11.1 attempts to map some of this complexity, depicting the socio-political field within which proto-parties operate. It shows, for instance, that, whilst proto-parties may remain unaligned, more often than not they tend to cooperate in the societal and political arenas, forging broader pre-electoral pacts (mostly in the form of localised non-competition or vote-swapping agreements) and/or coalescing around post-election parliamentary blocs as well as ad hoc issue-based coalitions. Examples of the former abound and include, for instance, the various pan-Islamist electoral tickets ICM has forged with other Salafi, and at times even Shi'i, proto-parties and independent Islamist candidates, or the attempts made in 1992 and 2008 by several, though not all, Shi'i

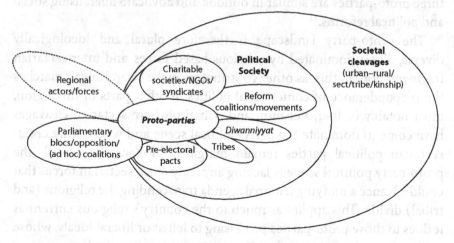

Figure 11.1 Kuwait's proto-parties in their socio-political context.

proto-parties to contest elections under the unified banner of *al-Tahaluf al-Watani al-Islami* (National Islamic Coalition). Prominent occurrences of the latter, meanwhile, include *Kutla al-Tatwir wa al-Islah* (Development and Reform Bloc), forged in the 2000s between ICM MPs and a number of independent Islamists; *Kutlat al-'Amal al-Watani* (National Action Bloc), comprising MPs from KDF and other independent liberal-leaning MPs; or the 2012 *Kutlat al-Aghlabiya* (Majority Bloc), a rather loose opposition coalition of thirty-four MPs cutting across the proto-party spectrum.[13] Outside the realm of parliament, as well, cooperation is commonplace, with proto-parties frequently joining in broader protest movements. One such example concerns *al-Haraka Nabiha Khamsa* ('We Want 5' Movement), which was formed by Kuwaiti youth in 2005/6 and whose call for an end to corruption and a reform of the country's electoral law was publicly endorsed at the time by the KDF, the NDA, the NIA and the SM (Gause 2013).

Other realities depicted in Figure 11.1 concern the myriad of inter-linkages that are known to exist between proto-parties and societal groupings and/or individuals in the country and the wider region, some of which render questionable the degree of decision-making autonomy Kuwaiti proto-parties enjoy over their internal affairs. Importantly, these inter-linkages go both ways, with proto-parties penetrating, through directorship elections or otherwise, the realm of civil society and with civil organisations forming the 'organisational bases' of certain proto-parties. The close (interpersonal) connection extant between some of the country's *diwanniytat* and proto-parties is just one such example, and so are the activities of proto-parties within, and at times their dominance over, some of Kuwait's main civil organisations, such as the professional syndicates, student and trade unions, cooperative/charitable societies and the mosques.[14] As Tétreault and al-Ghanim (2009) remark, this infiltration by proto-parties into the realm of formal civil society has rendered an ostensibly non-political environment fiercely political. It has also, it ought to be added, provided the proto-parties in question with additional mobilising sites, which is particularly useful during election times.

Other inter-linkages of note pertain to those widely thought to exist between some of the country's proto-parties and certain Islamic charitable associations and movements. Prominent cases in point include *Hadas*, which, albeit formally independent, is assumed to retain close affinities in outlook and membership base to both the KMB and its charitable branch organisation *Jam'iyat al-Islah al-Ijtima'i* (Social Reform Society; SRS), as well as the SIG, which was founded in 1992 as the 'political arm' of the Salafi *Jam'iyat Ihya' al-Turath al-Islami* (Revival of Islamic Heritage Society; RIHS) (al-Mdaires 2010).[15] *Hadas*, the SIG and some of the other Islamist proto-parties with similar such linkages to charitable associations, thus emerged from within the civil society sector, benefiting directly from their parent movements' organisational/membership base and capacity for societal outreach.

It is interesting to recall in this context as well that, prior to the formation of *Hadas* and the SIG in the 1990s, the two parent associations/movements (the KMD/SRS and the RIHS) were themselves politically active, running candidates in parliamentary elections and thus gaining valuable experience in the art of electioneering. In fact, by nominating contestants in elections as early as 1981, the RIHS constitutes the first Salafi grouping anywhere in the Arab world to abandon its rejection of plural politics in favour of electoral participation, thus long before the more recent entry of Salafi parties into the electoral fray elsewhere.

Beyond the domestic realm, lastly, there is a recognised transnational dimension to Kuwaiti proto-party politics. Indeed, many of Kuwait's proto-parties form part and parcel of the varied transnational linkages/networks that characterise identity politics in the MENA and beyond. Most widely recognised in this regard are the organisational/interpersonal connections that exist between the various national branches of the Muslim Brotherhood, but they also include those between Salafi and Shi'i Islamist groups in the region. In the Kuwaiti context, such transnational linkages are harboured, for instance, by some of the Salafi proto-parties, which are thought to retain strong (interpersonal linkages) with like-minded Salafi sheikhs and groupings in, amongst others, Saudi Arabia, Lebanon and Syria as well as by some of the Shi'i proto-parties with perceived connections to Iran and Bahrain.[16]

Proto-parties in Kuwait, it is thus evident, are embedded in, and operate as part of, a complex web of electoral alliances, parliamentary blocs and societal inter-linkages within the political arena. Moreover, they do so alongside other socio-political formations and constellations that imbue domestic politics with yet even greater complexity. These include, on the one hand, Kuwait's myriad of tribes, which, by virtue of their involvement through tribal primaries and candidacies in national elections, have been described as behaving like yet another set of proto-parties (Tétreault 1995). Within the *majlis*, meanwhile, MPs belonging to proto-parties and party-led parliamentary blocs find themselves seated alongside a diverse range of independent MPs, often with tribal background, blocs of pro-government 'service MPs', as well as the only constitutionally recognised parliamentary bloc, the fifteen-member bloc of cabinet members sitting in parliament as ex-officio MPs.

Proto-parties, elections and voters

How then can one account for the difficulty of proto-parties thus far to emerge as predominant players in Kuwaiti politics, sharing instead (as they do) the arena of electoral and parliamentary politics with a diverse range of political entrepreneurs and socio-political forces? To understand this reality, a closer look at the nature of electoral politics, and the performance of proto-parties in it, is warranted. What it reveals is this: in Kuwait the route to elected office remains varied, with proto-parties constituting only one of multiple viable avenues through which political hopefuls can seek, and have in fact sought, parliamentary representation. In other words, unlike in established party systems elsewhere, proto-parties in Kuwait do not perform a gatekeeper function to elected office. Empirically this is manifest, first and foremost, in the electoral behaviour of the proto-parties themselves, which exposes two common trademarks: first, across-the-board self-limitations on the number of officially nominated candidates and second, a reliance on, and endorsement of, so-called affiliated independents. As concerns the former, it is worth noting that there has never been a national election in Kuwait in which proto-parties put forward official candidates for all, let alone a plurality of, elective *majlis* seats. Casting one's eyes back over the past two decades it is apparent, in fact, that the total number of official proto-party candidacies witnessed a steady decline over time, so much so that by the 2000s most proto-parties barely selected a mere handful of candidates.[17] Symptomatic of this trend is the country's most prominent and best-organised proto-party, *Hadas*, which in the most recent 2016 elections nominated only four official candidates in two of the country's five electoral districts. Together with about another three dozens of contestants, official proto-party candidates in 2016 accounted, in fact, for less than 10 per cent of the over 400 registered hopefuls.[18] With so few official candidates in the race, proto-parties are ill-placed to make a forceful entry into parliament, let alone dominate its composition.

The low number of official proto-party candidacies is somewhat offset, meanwhile, by another prominent feature of Kuwaiti electoral politics: the endorsement by proto-parties of so-called affiliated candidates. In past elections, this set of candidates comprised a colourful mix of political hopefuls, including proto-party members who nonetheless sought to run outside the party umbrella – or were encouraged to do so (according to Alshayji 2009, some proto-parties, such as the KDF in 2008, even actively discouraged their members from running in elections, opting instead to support independent (affiliated) candidates with similar political views) – as well as non-affiliated candidates with tribal backgrounds and/ or Islamist, leftist or liberal leanings. As Assiri (2007: 34) explains, the decision calculus of those proto-party members running outside the party framework would usually revolve around the fact that 'voters in their designated electoral district disliked organised political associations', voting instead on the basis of a candidate's reputation, social standing and/or ability to extract government services, and that hence there was little utility, and potentially even a risk, in running as an officially endorsed proto-party candidate. As for truly non-affiliated candidates, meanwhile, it has become a norm in Kuwaiti electoral politics for proto-parties to seek out those with similar religious/ideological views and chances of victory, support their candidacies and, if successful, entice them into broader parliamentary blocs post-election. Such sponsorship would usually not materialise in the form of organisational/financial support, but revolve primarily around the encouragement of voters to cast their ballots for these 'affiliated' candidates. Examples of such arrangements abound and include a range of self-declared Salafi, liberal and Shi'i candidates who in 2012 and in preceding polls ran officially unaligned, yet also received backing from ideologically/religiously proximate proto-parties.[19]

Aside from those nominated by or affiliated to a proto-party, the vast majority of political hopefuls in Kuwaiti *majlis* elections, thus, run as fully-fledged independents. Within this group of candidates, again various types can be detected. Most prominently, they include so-called service candidates, who stake their fortunes on delivering their constituents access to government services in return for sponsoring government legislation in parliament. They also include candidates running on tribal tickets (Salih 2011),[20] and those seeking parliamentary representation simply by means of any combination of personal, kinship, professional and/or financial standing in the area. Of note in this context is the growing recourse political hopefuls have made to the NGO sector as a springboard for their political careers. Indeed, as numerous Kuwait experts have pointed out, it has become rather common for aspirants to elected office to seek leadership positions on prominent civil organisations, such as trade unions, sports clubs, the lawyers syndicate, the Kuwaiti Chamber of Commerce or the Kuwait Economic Society, as a means to build up a national reputation as competent decision-makers and prop up their electoral support base.[21]

Elections in Kuwait are thus no straightforward political battles between proto-party candidates, but remain characterised by the preponderance of independent candidacies, be they informally linked to a proto-party or not. This raises the question of why proto-party candidates remain so marginal to the country's parliamentary election process, despite the sustained presence of proto-parties in the country's parliamentary history and the relative freedom of action they enjoy in the political realm. It is suggested here that a combination of institutional and societal givens go a long way in accounting for this reality. For one, proto-parties operate in a societal context in which voters appear to remain overall sceptical of the virtues of political parties[22] and little concerned with party-political considerations in their voting intensions. According to opinion polls conducted in 2006 and 2007, for instance, over 60 per cent of respondents did not see the need for legalised political parties and most were 'unable to name a single bloc' in parliament (DRI 2008). This sentiment is also reflected in a more recent Arab Barometer poll, which asked respondents whether any of the existing proto-parties reflected their 'social, political and economic aspirations' (Arab Barometer 2013). Whilst 95.6 per cent of those consulted did not feel close to any proto-party, the most frequently cited proto-party, *Hadas*, was named by a mere 1.1 per cent of respondents. None of the other extant political forces, be they Salafi, Shi'i, leftist or liberal, crossed the 1.0 percentage mark in respondent preferences. Expert accounts, as well, have repeatedly highlighted the non-partisan decision-making calculus of Kuwaiti voters, which, with few exceptions, remains determined by kinship, tribal and/or religious affiliations as well as the benefits offered by candidates to voters, rather than by ideological considerations and proto-party programmes.[23] It is evident then that within this societal environment, a proto-party ticket in and of itself offers candidates little in terms of electoral advantage, and that hence running outside the party-political framework altogether remains not only a viable, but also an attractive, route to elected office.[24]

Further complicating matters for proto-parties, meanwhile, is the fact that these societal givens intersect with electoral rules that, in their various incarnations throughout the 1990s and 2000s, have rendered it difficult for proto-parties to advance their name recognition, entice voters to cast their ballot along ideological/policy lines and run nationwide campaigns featuring candidates in all districts. Particularly problematic in this regard are the voting systems used in 2006 and from 2012 onwards, which, by limiting voters to four and then one votes respectively in ten-seat districts, have forced proto-parties to contest only a fraction of available district seats, so as not to spread their electoral support too thinly and thus run the risk of not winning a single seat. To this must be added the gerrymandered nature of electoral districts, which perpetuates rather than undercuts ascriptive (particularly tribal) affinities and which hence ultimately also works against the emergence of national political campaigns revolving around a set of strong programmatic proto-parties (Aiko 2011).

Despite their long and illustrious presence in Kuwaiti politics, proto-parties thus evidently struggle to propel themselves to the fore of the country's electoral politics for the reasons outlined above. In this the Kuwaiti experience is of course far from unique, but mirrors the myriad struggles elsewhere in the Arab MENA of political parties to assert themselves as principal players on the electoral scene. Most obvious here is of course the case of Jordan, which bears striking similarities to the Kuwaiti scenario inasmuch as here too political parties (albeit legalised) are confronted with a societal and electoral environment that favours independent, service-oriented candidacies over party affiliation and programmatic voting behaviour.

Conclusion

Proto-parties, so much is evident, have become a permanent fixture in the Kuwaiti political system, forming part and parcel of the country's electoral and parliamentary politics. They are, moreover, unique by regional standards in that (Bahrain apart) their existence is unrivalled in the Arab Gulf monarchies and their legal status distinctive from any other party system in the Arab world. This legal status, or better the lack thereof, is frequently evoked, in fact, when it comes to highlighting some of the most persistent challenges the country's proto-parties are faced with in society and politics. As this chapter has revealed, these revolve primarily around the absence of durable voter identifications with the country's proto-parties and their lukewarm performance in national elections.

For some, the key to overcoming these obstacles resides in institutional reform, and here particularly in the passage of a parties law and far-reaching electoral reform. Putting proto-parties on a legal footing, so the assertion goes, would spur the development of their organisational capabilities, produce greater transparency of, and hence trust in, their internal activities and financial affairs, and even reduce the prevalence of ascriptive groupings and identities (religious/tribal/kinship) in Kuwaiti politics. According to Su'ud al-Mi'jil, for instance, 'tribalism and/or sectarianism is inevitable in a political system that does not allow for the formation of political parties, which could help channel personal affiliations away from tribe or sect' (qtd in Salih 2011: 156). Indeed, combined with electoral rules that foster programmatic over personalistic voting behaviours (as is likely to happen under a nationwide electoral district and/or list-based electoral rules) these reforms may go some way in elevating proto-parties to the fore of domestic politics, particularly if, as most proto-parties demand, these reforms are accompanied by the establishment of a proper parliamentary system in which the majority party/coalition gets to govern.[25]

This said, it is questionable whether, given the strength of tribal/kinship affinities and the growth of sectarianism in the region, these reforms will ultimately also succeed in producing a party system whose constituent parts are truly 'catch-all' in nature and national in programmatic outlook. Such a party system is sorely needed, of course, to improve the quality of Kuwaiti politics, where parochial interests, ascriptive identities and rent-seeking behaviour prevail over a nationally oriented public debate. Institutional engineering on its own, however, is unlikely to facilitate this development, as is evident from a cursory look across the border at nearby Lebanon and Iraq, where electoral provisions safeguarding against confessionalism and strengthening the role of political parties have done little to facilitate the emergence of truly cross-sectarian mass-based political parties. To achieve this in Kuwait, as in Lebanon and Iraq, much broader and harder-to-achieve societal debate and change is needed, one that transcends issues of constitutional design and tackles more fundamental questions about the nature of national identity, belonging and citizenship.[26]

Notes

1. On the basis of this criterion, and unlike some scholars of Kuwaiti politics, I do not consider/treat 'tribes' as quasi-/proto-/pseudo-parties.
2. Author interview with Kuwaiti civil activist, 8 July 2016.
3. Author interviews with Kuwaiti academic and former journalist, 18 June 2016; and Kuwaiti civil activist, 8 July 2016.
4. Examples include the 1981 and 2012 electoral reforms. The 1981 reform, which increased the number of electoral districts from ten to twenty-five, is widely seen as gerrymandered in favour of tribal and at the expense of urban/*hadar* representation, thus harming the prospects of proto-parties with a mostly urban electorate. The 2012 electoral reform, which reduced the number of votes per voter from four to one, is also thought to perpetuate ascriptive voting behaviour at the expense of programmatic and party-political considerations and prevent the formation of electoral lists/alliances.
5. Shi'i citizens are thought to make up between 15 and 25 per cent of the total population. The *hadari–qabali* demographic split, meanwhile, is thought to be 35 to 65 per cent.
6. The NIA was created in 1998. Other Shi'i proto-parties present in Kuwait today include, for example, *Tajamm' al-'adala wa al-Salam* (Assembly of Justice and Peace), *harakat al-Tawafuq al-Watani al-Islamiyya* (Islamic Movement of National Coalition), *al-Mithaq al-Watani* (National Covenant), *Tajamm' al-'Ulama' al-Muslimin al-Sh i'a f i al-Kuwait* (Assembly of Muslim Shi'i Clerics in Kuwait) and *Tajammu' al-Risala al-Insaniyya* (Assembly of the Humanitarian Message).
7. Author interview with Kuwaiti academic and former news columnist, 5 July 2016.
8. Author interview with ICM member and former MP, 18 August 2016.
9. For a detailed programme, see the KPM website, available at <http://taqadomi.com/> (last accessed 7 November 2016).
10. This fragmentation is not so much due to policy differences as to personal rivalries and lack of internal discipline, particularly between KDF and NDA. Author interview with Kuwaiti academic and women's rights advocate, 4 July 2016.
11. Further details on the CCP and its programme can be consulted on its website, available at <http://ccpkuwait.com/> (last accessed 7 November 2016). Author interview with Kuwaiti academic and former news columnist, 5 July 2016.
12. Further details on the CCP and its programme can be consulted on its website, available at <http://ccpkuwait.com/> (last accessed 7 November 2016). Author interview with Kuwaiti academic and former news columnist, 5 July 2016.
13. Author interview with ICM member and former MP, 18 August 2016.
14. The Salafi SIG, for instance, retains a strong presence in various cooperative and charitable societies and both Salafi proto-parties and the ICM have made strong showings in past elections to labour/student unions/organisations. Author interviews with Kuwaiti academic and political activist, 1 July 2016; Kuwaiti academic and women's rights advocate, 4 July 2016; Kuwaiti academic, 5 July 2016; and Kuwaiti academic and former news columnist, 5 July 2016.
15. Author interview with Kuwaiti academic and former journalist, 18 June 2016.

16. Author interviews with Kuwaiti academic and women's rights activist, 4 July 2016; and Kuwaiti academic and former journalist, 18 June 2016.
17. Once elected, one of the distinct advantages such affiliated MPs hold over those elected on a proto-party ticket is that they are not bound by party dictates and discipline. Author interview with Kuwaiti academic and political activist, 1 July 2016.
18. Data obtained from Kuwaiti civil activist, 8 July 2016.
19. Also author interviews with Kuwaiti civil activist, 8 July 2016.
20. Many candidates on these tickets were selected by their respective tribes in illegal, but prevailing, primary elections.
21. Author interview with Kuwaiti academic and women's rights advocate, 4 July 2016.
22. Several research respondents alluded to the fact that Kuwaitis retain an overall adversarial position towards political parties in general, citing the troubled experience of party politics in Lebanon, including the civil war, as well as the emergence of one-party dominant regimes elsewhere as reasons for rejecting the legalisation of proto-parties in their country. Author interviews with Kuwaiti academic and former journalist, 18 June 2016; Kuwaiti civil activist, 8 July 2016; and Kuwaiti academic, 5 July 2016.
23. Author interviews with Kuwaiti academic and political activist, 1 July 2016; Kuwaiti civil activist, 8 July 2016; and Kuwaiti academic, 5 July 2016.
24. Author interview with Kuwaiti academic and former news columnist, 5 July 2016.
25. Author interviews with Kuwaiti academic and political activist, 1 July 2016; and with Kuwaiti academic and former news columnist, 5 July 2016.
26. Author interview with Kuwaiti academic and women's rights advocate, 4 July 2016.

Bibliography

Abdelrahman, Maha (2009), '"With the Islamists? – Sometimes. With the State? – Never!" Cooperation between the Left and Islamists in Egypt', *British Journal of Middle Eastern Studies* 36: 1, 37–54.

Aiko, Hiramatsu (2011), 'The Changing Nature of the Parliamentary System in Kuwait: Islamists, Tribes, and Women in Recent Elections', *Kyoto Bulletin of Islamic Area Studies* 4: 1/2, 62–73.

Albloshi, Hamad (2016), 'Sectarianism and the Arab Spring: The Case of Kuwaiti Shi'a', *The Muslim World* 106: 1, 109–26.

Allarakia, Luai (2007), 'Rent Distribution as an Epiphenomenon of Regime Type: Economic Voting in Kuwait's 23th and 13th National Assembly', unpublished paper.

Alshayji, Abdullah (2009), 'The 2009 Kuwaiti Parliamentary Election: The Challenges and the Future of the Kuwaiti Democratic Paradigm', *Contemporary Arab Affairs* 2: 4, 602–17.

Arab Barometer (2013), 'Kuwait', poll, <http://www.arabbarometer.org/content/online-data-analysis> (last accessed 6 November 2016).

Assiri, Abdule Reda (2007), 'The 2006 Parliamentary Election in Kuwait: A New Age in Political Participation', *Digest of Middle East Studies* 16: 2, 22–44.

Brown, Nathan (2007), 'Pushing towards Party Politics? Kuwait's Islamic Constitutional Movement', Carnegie Papers 79, Washington DC: Carnegie Endowment for International Peace, pp. 3–20.

Brown, Nathan (2009), 'Kuwait's Islamic Constitutional Movement: A Model or a Warning for Democratic Islamism?', in M. A. Mohamed Saleh (ed.), *Interpreting Islamic Political Parties*, New York: Palgrave, pp. 117–28.

Crystal, Jill, and Abdallah al-Shayeji (1998), 'The Pro-democratic Agenda in Kuwait: Structures and Context', in Bahgat Korany, Rex Brynen and Paul Noble (eds), *Political Liberalization and Democratization in the Arab World: Comparative Experiences*, vol. 2, Boulder, CO and London: Lynne Rienner, pp. 101–25.

Democracy Reporting International (DRI) (2008), 'Assessment of the Electoral Framework: Final Report Kuwait', <http://aceproject.org/ero-en/regions/mideast/KW/kuwait-assessment-of-the-electoral-framework-dri/at_download/file> (last accessed 11 November 2016).

Fish, Steven, and Matthew Kroenig (2009), *The Handbook of National Legislatures: A Global Survey*, New York: Cambridge University Press.

Freer, Courtney (2015), 'The Rise of Pragmatic Islamism in Kuwait's Post-Spring Opposition Movement', working paper, Rethinking Political Islam Series, Washington DC: Brookings Institution, pp. 1–15.

Gause III, F. Gregory (2013), '"Nabiha 5": A Kuwaiti Youth Movement for Political Reform', *Background Paper*, Beirut: AUB Issam Fares Institute for Public Policy and International Affairs, pp. 4–10.

Gavrielides, Nicolas (1987), 'Tribal Democracy: The Anatomy of Parliamentary Elections in Kuwait', in Linda Layne (ed.), *Elections in the Middle East: Implications of Recent Trends*, Boulder, CO: Westview Press, pp. 153–213.

Ghabra, Shafeeq (1997), 'Balancing State and Society: The Islamic Movement in Kuwait', *Middle East Policy* 5: 2, 58–72.

Herb, Michael (2009), 'Kuwait: Obstacles to Parliamentary Politics', in Joshua Teitelbaum (ed.), *Political Liberalisation in the Persian Gulf*, London: Hurst, pp. 133–55.

Herb, Michael (2013), 'Kuwait's Endless Elections: The Opposition in Retreat', Project on Middle East Democracy, <http://pomed.org/wp-content/uploads/POMED-Policy-Brief-Herb-Sep-2013.pdf> (last accessed 1 September 2017).

Kuwait Times (2012), 'Opposition Announces Declaration for Nation', *Kuwait Times*, 16 July.

Kuwaiti Constitution (1962), Issued at the Seif Palace, 11 November, <http://www.wipo.int/edocs/lexdocs/laws/en/kw/kw004en.pdf> (last accessed 11 September 2017).

Lust-Okar, Ellen (2009), 'Reinforcing Informal Institutions through Authoritarian Elections: Insights from Jordan', *Middle East Law and Governance* 1: 1, 3–37.

al-Mdaires, Falah Abdullah (2010), *Islamic Extremism in Kuwait: From the Muslim Brotherhood to al-Qaeda and other Islamist Political Groups*, London and New York: Routledge.

Peterson, John (2012), 'The GCC States: Participation, Opposition, and the Fraying of the Social Contract', LSE Kuwait Programme on Development, Governance and

Globalisation in the Gulf States, <http://eprints.lse.ac.uk/55258/1/Peterson_2012. pdf> (last accessed 4 September 2017).

al-Remaidhi, Abdullah, and Bob Watt (2012), 'Electoral Constituencies and Political Parties in Kuwait: An Assessment', *Election Law Journal* 11: 4, 518–28.

Salem, Paul (2007), 'Kuwait: Politics in a Participatory Emirate', Carnegie Papers, Beirut: Carnegie Middle East Center, pp. 7–8.

Salih, Kamal Eldin Osman (2011), 'Kuwait Primary (Tribal) Elections 1975–2008: An Evaluative Study', *British Journal of Middle Eastern Studies* 38: 2, 141–67.

Tétreault, Mary Ann (1995), 'Patterns of Culture and Democratization in Kuwait', *Studies in Comparative International Development* 30: 2, 26–44.

Tétreault, Mary Ann (2000), *Stories of Democracy: Politics and Society in Contemporary Kuwait*, New York: Columbia University Press.

Tétreault, Mary Ann, and Mohammed al-Ghanim (2009), 'The Day after "Victory": Kuwait's 2009 Election and the Contentious Present', *Middle East Research and Information Project* 281, <http://www.merip.org/mero/mero070809?ip_login_no_cache=a9a474353d7539dd7402e4cb9f6cfd19> (last accessed 1 September 2017).

al-Zumai, Fahad (2007), 'Rentier States and Economic Regulation Infrastructure: Kuwait as a Case Study', *Journal of Law* 31: 3, 11–57.

Chapter 12

Transformations in the political party system in Mauritania: the case of the Union for the Republic*

Raquel Ojeda-García

This book is based on the idea that even in non-democratic political regimes, political parties are relevant, and that it is worthwhile to analyse these parties and their functions within the framework of political party systems. In the case of Mauritania, the question at hand is whether the incumbent party is an authoritarian dominant party. According to Sartori's classification of party systems in Africa (1976: 260), authoritarian dominant parties are those that win an absolute majority in three consecutive legislative elections in a non-democratic context. Sartori's classification consists of four main system types: authoritarian dominant, dominant, non-dominant and pulverised (Sartori 1976: 260). Authoritarian dominant systems are characterised by a single party that stays in power for three consecutive elections using extra-democratic strategies. This type of party system does not allow for real competition between parties on an equal footing or for power-sharing, but merely offers them as a theoretical possibility. This dominant party system can be equated with the predominant party system described for structural systems in the west. In non-dominant systems, on the other hand, several parties coexist and act as counter-weights to each other. Finally, the pulverised system is characterised by a high number of parties, where none dominates the others (Bogaards 2004: 178). Bogaards endorses Sartori's party system classification and his definition of the dominant authority, which he defends for four reasons (2004: 174): (1) it establishes a threshold to be able to speak of a 'dominant' party; (2) it considers the inclusion or exclusion of the opposition in the system; (3) it considers whether the system is presidential or collegial; and (4) it takes into consideration whether the government is divided or functions homogeneously and the length of time that the party is in power.

The question regarding the type of party that controls the government in Mauritania is closely related to both the nature of the party system and the political regime. The independent variables at play include the degree of the party system institutionalisation and the political regime's degree of democratisation. Both variables have an impact on the party typology (particularly on the party in government) although the existence of an authoritarian dominant party also perpetuates the authoritarian nature of the regime, that is, the dependent and independent variables interact and influence each other.

As a general comment, in this field of study, Mauritania may be considered a West African, North African or Maghrebi country according to different academic traditions. In any analysis of the state of play regarding the party systems and political parties, it becomes immediately clear that there are very few comparative publications on the topic for the Middle East and North Africa, while there are more studies of this type concerning the African continent (Bogaards 2004; van Cranenburgh 2003; Doreenspleet 2003).

In the introduction to this book, Storm and Cavatorta pose a question regarding the usefulness of analysing the role of a party even when the regime is non-democratic, the system is strongly presidentialist and party system institutionalisation is weak. This is the starting point for Mauritania, a party system characterised by its low levels of institutionalisation – a consequence of high volatility and fragmentation, very low competition between parties, and weak opposition parties that compete for a very small percentage of seats (Ojeda-García 2015: 110). Given that this situation is aggravated by an extremely underdeveloped economic context, a political and social context where clientelism, ethnic and tribal divisions, the consolidation of Islamist movements in the political arena and permanent political control by an Arab military establishment dominate (N'Diaye 2006; Marty 2002), the question about the functionality and nature of the party in power is fundamental. As Storm and Cavatorta note in their introduction, the difficulty lies in avoiding a priori reasoning and overstressing the specificity of the case at hand. Neither the political parties nor the party system in Mauritania differ substantially from the political parties in other countries in Africa and the Arab world in their behaviour or in the institutional weakness of the party system.

In short, if this analysis begins with the definition of the Mauritanian regime as 'restrictive hegemonic pluralist authoritarianism' (Szmolka 2011: 21), the challenge lies in discovering how the current party in government, the Union for the Republic (UPR), exercises the classic functions of representation and participation. The premise behind this chapter is that the UPR is an authoritarian dominant party, even though it has only participated in one legislative election since the current president of the republic, the coup leader and former general Mohamed Ould Abdel Aziz, set it up in 2009 (Ojeda-García 2012). Shortly thereafter, Abdel Aziz had to step down as party chairman and member in order to run in the presidential elections. In the 2013 elections, his party won 51.7 per cent of the seats in the National Assembly (Ojeda-García 2015: 120). In other words, in light of the above, the system cannot be considered an authoritarian dominant one according to Sartori. However, the surrounding context is not democratic and, thanks to the support of pro-government parties, the UPR controls more than 70 per cent of the seats in parliament. Therefore, after the brief 2005–8 transition period and the defeat of the Republican Party for Democracy and Renewal (formerly the Democratic and Social Republican Party; PRDS), created by Ould Taya to control the elections from 1991 to 2005, the UPR has been the authoritarian dominant party.

The following section explains how the weak institutionalisation of the party system and the authoritarian components of the political regime determine the nature and functions of the incumbent party.

The unbearable lightness of the Mauritanian party system

The importance of analysing party systems is due to the very essence of representative democracy. Political parties are key actors in representative democracies, exercising the functions of representation and participation. According to Rakner (2011: 1109), the essential functions performed by parties for democracy are: candidate nomination, electoral mobilisation, issue structuring, social representation, interest aggregation, forming and sustaining governments and social integration.

Party system institutionalisation refers to the continuity of political parties competing for votes and their ability to control access to political positions. In this way, the functioning of democracy depends on the voters being able to choose between different parties as real alternatives (Rakner 2011: 1109, 1110). Lindberg (2007: 241) has reflected on the degree of institutionalisation/stability of party systems and their non-institutionalisation/fluidity. For Lindberg, measuring the degree of institutionalisation of a party system may not provide all the information necessary to understand its contribution to the democratisation of the regime, but it is possible to detect nuances in the transition from stability to fluidity. A fluid system tends to be more democratic because there is a greater division of seats between parties, or more parties in competition. On the contrary, greater institutionalisation of the system gives rise to legitimacy and predictability in the party system. Lindberg (2007: 241) concludes that the danger arises when a system tends towards one of the extremes, that is, when it remains fluid or highly institutionalised, because in this situation the system is 'frozen', which acts as a barrier to multi-party politics.

Indicators of party system institutionalisation in Mauritania

Analyses of party systems in Africa and even those in Latin America and Eastern Europe (Sartori 1976; Mainwaring and Scully, cited in Lindberg 2007: 215) provide the primary indicators for the Mauritanian case: first, the strength or weakness of the party's roots in society (party legitimacy); second, personalisation and leadership within the parties, as well as their ideological platform; and third, the degree of parliamentary volatility between elections to determine the stability of the parties (Mainwaring and Torcal 2005: 141; Manning 2005: 722; Riedl 2014: 2). Other variables that affect the degree of institutionalisation of party systems include the electoral system – whether it is majority or proportional, which is better suited to more heterogeneous societies (van Cranenburgh 2003: 189) – and the type of regime (presidential or parliamentary). In this respect, the deeper the party's social roots and the better its agenda, the less important are the leader and the personalisation of relationships, both internal and external (with the voters). In addition, the lower the degree of volatility, the more institutionalised the party system.

Rakner (2011) also discusses the importance of the role of opposition parties. The degree of institutionalisation depends not only on the permanency of the winning or runner-up party in the party system, but on the other parties represented in the political institutions. The degree of freedom and fairness of an election cannot be ascertained without considering the opposition parties (Goeke and Hartmann 2011: 276). Therefore, the analysis of Mauritania also includes a fourth and fifth indicator: the degree of opposition party participation in elections or their ability to boycott elections and, finally, whether the results are accepted after the election is over (Lindberg 2006a: 128; Manning 2005).

Lindberg himself warns about the risks of abusing boycotts and the negative consequences of repeatedly resorting to boycotts or questioning official results. On the other hand, the participation of opposition parties in elections that are flawed – that is, not completely competitive, transparent and fair – helps maintain authoritarian regimes (Lindberg 2006b: 129). These assertions should be qualified and additional factors considered: the degree of participation, which always improves the quality of the regime, and the degree of competitiveness, since the winning party is forced to share the votes, if only a few, if the opposition participates. In other words, the non-participation of opposition parties does not always weaken the party in power or challenge its legitimacy in the eyes of the electorate.

There is some debate about whether these indicators, for example, volatility or fragmentation, are applicable to a situation like Africa, which is different from the west, where these concepts first emerged and were applied (Mainwaring and Torcal 2005: 142; Lindberg 2007: 219). Even if this is the case, however, this chapter is not going to focus on the difference or specificity of Africa or the Mauritanian party system, but rather on the assumption that the theoretical application of variables to other contexts may shed some 'qualified' light on their political reality (Lindberg 2007: 222). Additionally, a review of the academic literature on party systems in Africa elucidates the effects of the third wave of democratisation that began in the 1990s (Manning 2005: 707; Lindberg 2006a: 139). Interestingly, not a single regime was *de jure* controlled by only one party, which suggests that party competition took root (Manning 2005: 707). However, poorly institutionalised party systems like the Mauritanian system still exist today.

Before analysing the degree of institutionalisation in the Mauritanian party system using these indicators, some background on recent elections in the country is necessary. The last legislative elections were held in November and December 2013 and the last presidential elections in June 2014. During the democratic transition period (2005–8), legislative elections were held that were widely recognised as free and fair (MOE-UE 2007). However, despite the 2008 military *coup d'état* (won by the coup leader, General Mohamed Ould Abdel Aziz), the legitimate parliament was not renewed until 2013, even though the constitution mandated elections in November 2011 (Ojeda-García 2015: 114). Not only were the elections for the new parliament delayed by two years, but the democratically elected party was forced to coexist with a putschist president whose own election, moreover, had been seriously challenged.

The most peculiar aspect of Mauritania with regard to its party system comes down to the PRDR's loss in the 2006 election. Many authors agree (Bogaards 2000: 163; van de Walle 2003: 300; Jourde 2008: 75; Ishiyama and Quinn 2006: 318; Rakner and van de Walle 2009: 108; Manning 2005: 708) that after the third wave in Africa, the dominant parties won the first elections of the democratic transition or came in second, as leaders of the opposition. All the signs indicated that this would be the case in Mauritania as well, but it was not. The PRDR had the bottom knocked out of it in the first transparent and fair parliamentary elections held in Mauritania, coming in fourth place (Ojeda-García 2012).

Regarding the other parameters discussed in the literature for African political systems, the most significant in this context concerns the enormous division between the number of votes obtained by the winning party and the opposition parties in some elections (see Table 12.1), the intense competition between opposition parties and the high degree of fragmentation that exists between the opposition parties (Manning 2005: 724). This usually translates into a high number of parties in general, but a low number of important parties. Rakner (2011: 1207) has noted that even in parliamentary elections that are classified as democratic, the opposition does not exceed the threshold of 20 per cent of the seats (van de Walle 2003: 297, 303).

Electoral volatility is usually quite high, as is party switching. In Mauritania, party switching (changing party affiliation during one's term or deserting the party and running as an independent) is also known as 'political nomadism', but its regulation is very limited (Goeke and Hartmann 2011: 276). The main effect of party switching is that it weakens

Table 12.1 Results of the 2013 National Assembly elections (first round 23 November and second round 21 December). (Source: Commission Électorale Nationale Indépendante (Islamic Republic of Mauritania), <http://www.ceni.mr/spip.php?page=article&id_article=631> (last accessed June2014); also reproduced in Ojeda 2015: 120)

Party	Number of seats (out of a total of 147)	% seats
Union for the Republic (UPR)	76	51.70
Tawassoul	16	10.95
El Wiam	10	6.84
Popular Progressive Alliance (APP)*	7	4.8
Union for Democracy and Progress (UDP)*	6	4.1
El Karam	6	4.1
Burst of Youth for the Nation	4	2.73
Alliance for Justice and Democracy/Movement for Renewal (AJD/MR)	4	2.73
El Vadila	3	2.05
Party of Unity and Development (PUD)	3	2.05
Ravah Party	3	2.05
Republican Party for Democracy and Renewal (PRDR)*	2	1.36
Democratic Justice Party	2	1.36
Party of Mauritanian Authenticity (PAM)	1	0.68
Socialist Democratic Unionist Party (PUDS)	1	0.68
Dignity and Action Party (PDA)	1	0.68
Democratic People's Party (PPD)	1	0.68
El Islah	1	0.68
Total	**147**	**100**

* Parties represented in the 2006 National Assembly.
Population: 3,359,185; registered voters: 1,189,105; voters: 878,693; participation: 75.53 per cent.

political parties, which never truly take root in society. A large number of 'floating' politicians only endanger the stability and legitimacy of a government (Goeke and Hartmann 2011: 263–4). Strong personalism and loose membership, along with the emergence of new parties as mechanisms to resolve internal conflicts, further weaken the party system (Goeke and Hartmann 2011: 264). On other occasions in the context of multi-party elections, the leaders in power create divisions in some opposition parties and even promote independent candidates or the formation of small parties in order to divide and weaken the opposition parties in the legislative elections.

As in other Arab countries, the party system in Mauritania is subject to some prohibitions; for instance, parties with ethnic or religious bases are not allowed. These prohibitions are usually justified by the need to strengthen democracy, neutralise ethnic heterogeneity and resolve intercommunal conflicts (Moroff and Basedau 2010: 666). However, in Mauritania, the ultimate aim in limiting pluralism is to curb the consolidation of Islamist parties. The first Islamist movements began to seek legalisation as political parties in the early 1990s and were systematically rejected. This was not only the act of an authoritarian regime, but also weakened a well-established and widespread political actor. This explains why the Action for Change party was banned in 2002 because of its criticism of *bidan* oppression of the black Mauritanian population (Moroff and Basedau 2010: 668; Leservoisier 2009: 148), and why the first Islamist political party, the *Tawassoul*, was not legalised until 2007 (Ould Hamed 2008).

Parties in Africa and the Arab world are usually controlled by an elite or by a leader, and ideological positions, platforms and the party base are generally on the sidelines (Manning 2005: 718, 724). The personalism of parties cannot be understood without taking into account other features characteristic of political regimes on the continent, like clientelism and tribalism. The articulation of interests and social organisation through patronage or family or tribal networks diminishes political parties, which cannot perform these functions. This situation encourages the creation of 'fictitious' parties with no social or ideological anchor, fosters personalism and a minimal structure for the leader, and, perhaps more importantly, this 'bigmanism' converts parties into empty institutions, since the support of opposition party members is won with perks and economic and political favours (Rakner 2011: 1114). As analytic authoritarianism has observed, even if the regime returns to autocratic rule after a short period of democracy, the president's power is limited and the regime has to negotiate with the military, the opposition or tribal groups (LeVan 2014: 213). Weak candidates may control a small but very coherent mass of votes, making them 'relevant' with regard to creating winning majorities or guaranteeing the power of the majority in elections. The case of the UPR and the other parties in the Coalition of Majority Parties, comprising the Union for the Republic, the Republican Party for Democracy and Renewal (PRDR), the Union for Democracy and

Progress (UDP), Democratic Renewal (RD), the Mauritanian Party for Unity and Change (HATEM-PMUC) and the Union of the Democratic Centre (UCD), has shown how small, weakly rooted parties with little electoral strength can enter the orbit of the authoritarian dominant party and help it gain practically absolute power in parliament and, of course, in the executive branch as well.

These characteristics, in addition to cleavages that are mainly ethnolinguistic instead of ideological (van de Walle 2003: 297, 303; Kinne 2001: 615), explain the high number of candidates in presidential elections, even when they know that their chance of winning is nil. They are motivated by the possibility of obtaining benefits from the powers that be in exchange for the support of the communities that they control (Mozaffar and Scarritt 2005: 415). The markedly presidentialist Mauritanian political system favours personalist voting and populist strategies in elections, especially at the presidential level (Mainwaring and Torcal 2005: 161; Manning 2005: 711). Despite an opposition boycott, the most recent presidential election held in Mauritania in June 2014 had five candidates, while in 2007 there were twenty.

One of the initiatives that met with the most opposition in recent months, even by senators in the ruling UPR, was the proposal to eliminate the Senate. This initiative came from the president and included other controversial points like changing the anthem and the flag and creating regional councils with no legislative capacity, all of which would require a constitutional reform which was finally approved by a referendum on 5 August 2017. Critics from within the UPR and the opposition who refused to approve the reform have spotlighted the regime's drift towards authoritarianism and Abdel Aziz's ambition to run for a third term.

Legislative elections and the drift towards authoritarianism

The most recent legislative elections support all of these assertions about the party system in Mauritania, in consideration, as well, of events elsewhere in the region. The electoral results not only serve to measure parliamentary volatility, but also highlight fundamental institutional variables that explain the nature and functions of the party in power. In this respect, van Cranenburgh has criticised the low number of studies that take the institutional context surrounding competitive politics into consideration, such as the electoral system and the relationship between the legislative and executive branches (van Cranenburgh 2003: 188). Looking at the electoral system, in the last legislative elections, despite the use of a mixed (majority and proportional) electoral system, the results were those of a single-party system. Small uninominal constituencies persist whose representatives are elected by majority formulas. The UPR was the indisputable winning party, with 51.7 per cent of the seats, followed by the main opposition moderate Islamist party, *Tawassoul*, which only obtained 11 per cent of the seats. The gap between the first- and second-place parties is enormous and, moreover, a large number of parties did not even obtain 7 per cent of the seats. The importance of institutional variables cannot obviate the connection made by many authors who emphasise the relationship between the operation of the party system and the political culture in African countries (Kuenzi and Lambright 2005; Lindberg 2006a, 2007; Bogaards 2000: 163; van de Walle 2003: 300; Jourde 2008: 75; Ishiyama and Quinn 2006: 318; Rakner and van de Walle 2009: 108; Manning 2005: 708). All have theorised about elements that have a bearing on clientelisms and personalism inside parties (van Cranenburgh 2003: 189), in addition to 'bigmanism'.

Pedersen's electoral volatility index[1] highlights the first difficulty with the Mauritanian case, which is the youth of the country's political parties; neither the UPR nor the *Tawassoul* existed in 2006 and, therefore, there are no electoral results with which to compare. This obstacle has been resolved by assigning a 0 value to the percentage of seats for parties that did not participate or did not win any seats in the 2006 election. After applying the Pedersen index, the result is very high volatility: 90.75 per cent (Ojeda-García 2015: 118).

In 2006, there was a widespread call to boycott the elections from the main opposition party coalition, the Coordination of Democratic Opposition (COD), but participation was 75.53 per cent, nonetheless. This data highlights what Lindberg (2006b: 129) warned about the possible risk inherent in resorting to boycotts, because voters may tire of them, especially when the opposition does not form a consolidated bloc or provide a real alternative to power. In the end, *Tawassoul* ran in the election, pulling away from the COD, as did the Popular Progressive Alliance (APP).

In 2004, at the end of Ould Taya's authoritarian regime, volatility was a quite stable 17 per cent, which confirms that authoritarian dominant parties provide stability to systems (Riedl 2014: 1). However, the data for the transition period is completely different. In the 2006 election, the volatility index was 77.95 per cent and the effective number of parties was 4.22. In other words, the party system at that point could be qualified as 'non-dominant'. However, the party system in 2013 was clearly drifting towards instability, while the regime began to tend towards authoritarianism for a number of reasons: first, the two parties with the most votes were new, the UPR created by Abdel Aziz in 2009, and *Tawassoul* legalised during the presidency of Sidi Ould Cheikh Abdallahi in 2007; second, volatility reached almost 91 per cent; third, the winning party obtained more than 50 per cent and the runner-up only 11 per cent, due to the high fragmentation in the National Assembly and the large number of parties with very few seats; and finally, only three parties obtained seats in both the 2006 and 2013 elections: the PRDP, the APP and the UDP, although none of these won more than 7 per cent of the seats (Ojeda-García 2015: 119).

Amidst this trend of low institutionalisation and the consolidation of a new authoritarian dominant party, there was another substantial difference between the legislative elections of 2006 and those of 2013: no independent candidates were allowed to participate in the latter elections. In 2006, independent candidacies served as open channels for Islamists to run in their constituencies, as no Islamist party had been legalised at the time. At the same time, the former leaders and deputies of the PRDS found a way to shrug off the initials of the former authoritarian dominant party while maintaining control in their political spaces. In fact, the independent deputies received the most votes and after the elections, they joined together as the National Rally of Independents (RNI) (Ojeda-García 2015: 119).

Party rootedness, personalism and accepting the outcome of elections

The second criterion in an analysis of the degree of institutionalisation of the party system is whether the parties have strong or weak roots. The political parties attend to the articulation of interests in

Mauritania's rarefied circles, but close tribal links among the Arab *bidan* population and ethnic ties between the black Mauritanians relegate party intervention to the background, even with regard to renewing the elites (Manning 2005: 715; Lindberg 2007: 215; Riedl 2014: 7). Having said this (Jourde 2001: 28), while ethnicity is an important question in Mauritania, relationships do exist between communities and tribes, and the elites in some black Mauritanian communities accept the existence of the authoritarian regime. This reflects the fact that there is no ethnic homogeneity and that differences between both the elites and the tribes persist (Jourde 2001: 29). Leservoisier (2009) goes further, concluding that ethnicity is not a question of genealogy, but of acceptance by the community, and that the creation of identity is a more complex process. For example, while the *Haratin* occasionally demand social justice and equal status among groups, they nevertheless reproduce hierarchical principles in their own communities (Leservoisier 2009: 150).

It is clear from the above discussion that Abdel Aziz created the UPR ad hoc for the 2009 presidential election. The line officially declared by this catch-all party is centrism and moderation,[2] but it is totally absorbed by the personalism of the president, although he is no longer a member of the party. Members of the former authoritarian dominant party, the PRDS, quickly joined the ranks of the new UPR, which offered the best guarantee of being able to continue to control the mechanisms of power. In fact, the UPR has come to occupy the space left by the PRDS (Ould Khattat 2011), which has been renamed the Republican Party for Democracy and Renewal and is a party in its own right. However, although it has not totally disappeared from electoral competition, it is completely amorphous. *Tawassoul*, on the other hand, is more strongly rooted both socially and spatially, since some of its leaders like Mohamed Jemil Ould Mansour come from former Islamist movements (although they were never recognised as political parties). Both Mansour and Ould Dedew, the spiritual leader of *Tawassoul*, have been on the political scene campaigning since the 1990s with movements like the failed *Umma* party and Mansour's Party of Democratic Convergence (PDC), with which he became mayor of one of the most populous districts in Nouakchott in 2003 (Cavatorta and Ojeda-García 2017: 313). In any case, from a formal point of view, *Tawassoul* is only ten years old.

With regard to the third indicator, Rakner has shown (2011: 1111) that in Africa, political parties tend to become either dominant movements or a multitude of personalist organisations with weak social roots. The personalisation of the UPR is clearly visible both in the party's campaigns and in the official party speeches and documents. During the entire legislative campaign, the constant references to the leader, President Abdel Aziz, were indicative of this intense personalisation. The figure of the leader and tales of his achievements were omnipresent. The opposition party campaign speeches also revolved around the leader and were strongly personalised, although in their case, they chose to criticise and oppose Abdel Aziz.[3] It is striking that in a very short period of time the UPR has managed to place a large number of representatives in every national and local institution across the country.[4] However, given the ideological heterogeneity, the different party backgrounds of many of its members and the short amount of time that has elapsed, it is clear that the party is not a product of the citizens or of social mobilisation. Neither does it aim to defend the interests of a particular sector of the population or a defined ideology. The party has won not because of some spontaneous mass conviction on the part of the citizens, but because it is the visible and institutional tool that the former coup leader and general uses to control power.

In short, this personalisation is progressively producing a symbiosis between the president, the party behind the president and, finally, the government (Jourde 2008: 83). When Manning (2005: 714) talks about one-party states in Africa, she emphasises the fact that the state becomes the sole actor capable of guaranteeing the provision of economic and political needs. The more strongly rooted parties are based on a social ideology, particularly related to anti-slavery, ethnic and religious demands. In the case of Mauritania, the Initiative for the Resurgence of the Abolitionist Movement (IRA) and the *Touche Pas à Ma Nationalité* (Hands Off My Nationality) Movement (TPMN) led the electoral campaigns along with the president, backed by the UPR. The leader of the IRA, Biram Dah Abeid, was even a candidate for the presidential election (as an independent candidate, since his party was not legalised) (Hill 2016: 194), although he was arrested shortly thereafter. He has been one of the most high-profile leaders in the battle against slavery in Mauritania with broad support and recognition abroad and a high mobilisation capacity, just like the Islamist movements. In fact, the leader of *Tawassoul*, Ould Mansour, lent him his support after his arrest, once the presidential election was over.

Calls to boycott elections serve as an indicator to analyse the fundamental role of the opposition in the party system. In the November and December 2013 elections, the opposition formed blocs in support of or against the president. During the Ould Taya dictatorship and up to 2005, this was the cleavage that dominated the party system in Mauritania. Today, this line determines the position taken by the current parties. In 2013, the blocs were as follows: the revamped opposition COD,[5] the governmental or pro-government Coalition of Majority Parties[6] and, finally, the Coalition for Peaceful Alternative (CAP).[7] The third bloc was the result of a division within the COD when one of the most important opposition leaders, Ould Boulkheir, who at that moment was president of the National Assembly as a member of the Popular Progressive Alliance (APP), decided to join some other parties in an attempt to prevent high polarisation in the party system and to negotiate free elections with the UPR within the framework of 'national dialogues'.

The last indicator related to the role of the opposition concerns the delicate question of accepting the election results. After the second round of the parliamentary elections was held in 2013, the COD reported several cases of voter registration card buying and voter registration constraints among the black Mauritanians. This racist slant affecting the census and the ability to register among some ethnic and black communities had already been reported by the TPMN. In addition to complaints filed by the black Mauritanian communities, *Tawassoul* and *El Wiam* also reported a lack of transparency and other types of irregularities during the elections. However, this did not prevent the two parties from keeping the seats they had won in the elections and continuing to play as participants in the institutional game.

The party system in Mauritania, then, is poorly institutionalised as it does not have strongly rooted structures in society and there is no real competition between the parties. What competition there is involves a high number of opposition parties that are not able to win even 10 per cent of the seats and pose no threat to the overwhelming winner, the UPR. The volatility index of 90.75 per cent between the 2006 and 2013 elections reflects not only the fluidity of the system, but also the difficulty of applying indicators to complex realities with parties created for each election that do not then carry on. Only three parties, which won less than 10 per cent of the seats, were in the National Assembly in 2006. In 2013, the Assembly contained eighteen parties, but fourteen of them held less than 4 per cent of the seats. Despite forming a coalition against the UPR and the president before the elections, the opposition was not able to form single lists, let alone boycott the elections, since two of the main parties, the *Tawassoul* and the APP, ran in them. On the other hand, for the presidential election, the National Front for Democracy and Unity (FNDU) was created and the opposition parties presented a united front, but no candidate from the parties in the coalition ran, and they did not accept the results, which delegitimised both the process and, of course, the results themselves. The only exception to this boycott came from the leader of the IRA, Biram Dah Abeid, who ran and came in second with 8.67 per cent of the vote after Abdel Aziz's 81.89 per cent, but was then arrested and sentenced to two years in jail.

Authoritarian persistence

The second part of this analysis must begin with a definition of the very concept of democracy, which at a minimum is 'a form of political regime in which citizens choose, in competitive elections, the occupants of the top political offices of the state' (Bratton and van de Walle 1994: 13).

According to Szmolka (2010: 115), the variables to consider when classifying a political regime are: the existence of real pluralism with respect to both parties and social groups; competitive, free and transparent elections; no veto players without political responsibility or reserved domains; autonomy of representative institutions; and respect for and guarantee of public freedoms and rights. By evaluating these variables, it becomes possible to grade political regimes from democratic to authoritarian. An authoritarian regime does not include the conditions of pluralism, free elections, no veto players, an independent legislative power, and guarantee of public freedoms and rights.

In 2012, Mauritania was classified as having a 'restrictive hegemonic pluralist authoritarianism' (Szmolka 2011: 21). Specifically, the military is the main decision-maker (Marty 2002; N'Diaye 2006). Mauritania only experienced a short democratic transition period from 2005 to 2008 (Zisenwine 2007; Ojeda-García and López 2012; Aghrout 2008; Hochman 2007). According to some (Rakner 2011: 1106; Manning 2005: 716), international donors, who imposed their conditions to initiate an economic and political process of liberalisation in the country, were largely responsible for this opening. During the democratic transition period, pressure from the European Union (Hill 2016: 190) was decisive in convincing the military junta, the so-called Military Council for Justice and Democracy (CMJD), led by recently deceased General Ely Ould Mohamed Vall, to adopt a series of measures that would allow some democratically elected representative institutions, including the presidency, to be established. As noted by Chacha (2016: 2), coups can become a window of opportunity for democratic transition under pressure from the international community.

International pressure and the façade of political opening

Under international pressure and in the midst of political isolation, the Ould Taya government began to hold multi-party elections in 1991, another turning point in the political history of Mauritania and a moment of opening for the regime. However, this in no way meant that authoritarianism or the authoritarian dominant party were coming to an end; quite the opposite, in fact. In the Arab as well as African context, the fact that elections have systematically been held for decades does not mean that opposition parties in the legislature have become stronger, which is a serious handicap for democratisation. The weakness of opposition parties is a consequence of the lack of democracy, but also the reason that it persists (Rakner and van de Walle 2009: 109). Three indicators reveal the weakness of the opposition parties: their small size; their short political life (they appear and disappear from one election to another), which highlights the fragile institutionalisation of the party system; and the phenomenon of independent candidates. Rakner and van de Walle (2009: 112) cite the following factors as contributors to party weakness: the advantages of incumbency; the opposition's limited access to state and economic resources; and the low level of legitimacy that opposition parties have among the citizens. One additional factor that is extremely influential is the hyper-presidentialism that characterises African regimes, one result of which is less separation of powers (van Cranenburgh 2009: 51). The weakness of local and regional entities is not helpful either, since there are no other authentic political arenas where decisions can be made and implemented that differ from those adopted by the central executive branch. The weakness of opposition parties is balanced by financing opposition leaders (which satisfies their personal ambition) and with rhetoric that instrumentalises the danger of emerging radical Islamism.

Mechanisms like gerrymandering, the manipulation of voter registration, harassment of the opposition and even the violation of human rights and civil liberties are some of the elements that indicate a lack of democracy in a regime (van de Walle 2003: 306; Handlin 2017: 42). In the last elections, accusations by some movements regarding these issues were constant. The TPMN was quite visible in the media as the voter registration lists (*Recensement Administratif à Vocation Électorale*; RAVEL) were being drawn up, and the group was open about its opposition to the system used, calling it degrading and unfair to black Mauritanian communities with respect to the *bidan* (Arab) population. Interest in this area has grown thanks to the steady, protracted battle being fought by *SOS-Esclaves Mauritanie* and its best-known leader, Boubacar Ould Messaoud, who is not only a pioneer of speaking out against slavery in Mauritania, but also a critic of the use of religious interpretations to support this practice.

The presence of the military, which has used *coups d'état* to make changes in the presidency and interrupt political processes, makes it impossible to speak of a process of democratisation in Mauritania. The most recent coup was in August 2008 and the general who led the uprising against legitimate President Abdallahi is still in power after two presidential elections, in 2009 and 2014. Moreover, it seems likely that his current attempts to reform the constitution are aimed at giving him the option to run for a third term. In any case, the low level of competition between the parties is fomenting the emergence of an illiberal democracy controlled by an authoritarian dominant party (van de Walle 2003: 209). Furthermore, the more the military intervenes, the more the belief grows that it must continue to intervene. The military's image as a guarantor of stability in the face of dangerous ethnic divisions and other risks like radicalised Islamism bolsters the institution (Kalu 2004: 531).

The centralisation of power in the figure of the president is also causing clientelism to converge around his person, since he largely controls state resources. Van de Walle (2003) uses these factors to explain the fragmentation in Africa. The combination of hyper-presidentialism and clientelism crushes incentives to consolidate opposition parties; instead, it reinforces individualism, resulting in the personalisation of parties around a bigman (van de Walle 2003: 313). During the era of

Ould Taya, the PRDS was already trending this way (Marty 2002: 94), but under the UPR government, there are few signs that this recourse to tribal division has disappeared. This type of division can even be traced back to the crises that have afflicted the various governments since 1991, and is primarily due to the redistribution of power between the different tribes rather than to a popular election movement or a response to demands for change. The use of tribal divisions has been accompanied by the persecution of the already weakened opposition through the illegalisation of parties like Action for Change (AC), the Islamist party and the Union of Democratic Forces (UFD) (Marty 2002: 94), and through the imprisonment of their leaders. In short, winning the presidential elections became, and still is, the top prize in political life, since the strong institutionalisation of the presidency and the office's broad powers give the president the necessary resources for patronage (Mozaffar and Scarritt 2005: 415).

In the same respect, the concept of neo-patrimonialism is still valid in Mauritania where the UPR has taken over the spaces left by the former PRDS. Neo-patrimonialism consists of controlling the production and distribution of most of the economic resources by the state elite. Access to these resources is done through tribal quotas. After privatising the large national monopolies in the 1980s and 1990s under pressure from the International Monetary Fund, the military oligarchy (Marty 2002: 96) managed to take control of the principal public companies. The favour was returned with funds from the PRDS, the architect of the concession with jurisdiction over all levels of the state. This maintained the inseparable union with the military oligarchy, which was teeming with tribal balancing acts. Everything was orchestrated through the authoritarian dominant party, which permeated every crack and crevice in the state. The same has occurred in the administration. The positions in the state administration are largely filled not according to the criteria of merit and skill, but to personal proximity, ethnicity and politics, for which reason it is very difficult to replace the administrative staff, even when the government changes hands. The little room to manoeuvre given a new party in the executive branch, especially in key sectors like security and intelligence, is usually used to appoint trusted political allies. The other priority is to win the loyalty of appointees under previous governments, which, in the end, preserves neo-patrimonial practices, generating an institutional inertia that is very difficult to break and a closely knit network of patronage. The essence of neo-patrimonialism consists of rewarding personal favours through positions in the public administration or through licences or the concession of contracts and projects. In other words, neo-patrimonialism is a mixture of bureaucratic norms and patrimonialist behaviour (Marty 2002: 103).

The Arab Uprisings of 2010/11 also affected Mauritania, but they did not receive the same media coverage as in neighbouring countries. These protests did not result in greater democratisation of the regime, as occurred in other countries in the Maghreb like Tunisia, but quite the contrary; the outcome was the restoration of a competitive authoritarian regime by Abdel Aziz (Hill 2016: 191), defined as – according to Handlin (2017: 45) – 'electoral regimes in which incumbents received less than 75% of the vote in either the most recent legislative or executive election'.

Finally, the weakness of the state is an institutional deficit that sullies the election processes and the development of a democratic government. Control of the state is the result of a three-way pact between the indigenous political elites (the tribes), corporate capital and the military aristocracy (Kalu 2004: 527, 537). The institutions and, therefore, the consolidation of the state, play a fundamental role in establishing democratic values. In other words, it is not possible to have a democratic regime in a weak state, and the two processes of democratisation and the consolidation of the state are inseparable (Bratton and Chang 2006: 1061). Additionally, there is practically no external pressure to promote greater democratisation (Jourde 2008: 78). Western countries have chosen to guarantee the security of the area and therefore prefer to support (or, at least, not put pressure on) the governments in power since, as in the case of Mauritania, they have become essential allies of the great powers in the fight against terrorism and transnational radical Islamism (Jourde 2007).

Conclusion

Citing Richard Joseph, Jourde (2008) reflects on the capacity for authoritarian dominant parties to survive in a context of multi-party elections. These parties are able to remain in power thanks to a process of learning how to submit without succumbing. Obviously, the parties also resort to marginalising the opposition and dividing it in order to weaken it (van de Walle 2003: 30). The election campaigns of both Abdel Aziz and the UPR have been dominated by populism and, as the literature of analytic authoritarianism indicates (LeVan 2014: 213), a greater concern for providing services directly to citizens than for responding to criticisms about the lack of democratisation. For this reason, both the electoral and governing strategy in Mauritania are based on ending corruption, extreme poverty and unsafe housing, while 'political' questions do not appear to matter.

With regard to external factors, the preference of the great international powers for stable governments to the detriment of democratisation has also contributed to the continued existence of these authoritarian systems (Hill 2016: 194–5). In West Africa, Mauritania has been a great bastion against transnational Islamism, which has won open international support for the authoritarian regime, with the primary consequence being the repression of opposition movements (Jourde 2008: 77).

Therefore, to answer the question of what functions authoritarian dominant parties can perform in a non-democratic context, following Golosov, it seems that they exercise symbolic functions in authoritarian elections like projecting an image of invincibility (Golosov 2016). In restrictive hegemonic authoritarian regimes like the Mauritanian one, the participation of opposition parties is tolerated and there is even some freedom of the press (in 2011, the state monopoly over television and radio stations was abolished) (Hill 2016: 195). However, considering the degree of institutionalisation in the party system, which is low, there can be no real competition between the authoritarian dominant party and the other parties. On the contrary, an institutionalised party system would have offered opportunities for participation, representation, accountability and alternation; in other words, the chance to make a real impact on democracy (Riedl 2014: 3).

Notes

* This work was supported by the Research Project 'Authoritarianism persistence and political change processes in North Africa and Middle East: consequences on political regimes and international scene', Juanta de Andalucía 2012–16 (SEJ-3118).
1. The calculation is made on the basis of the sum of the vote (or seat) percentage change for each party between the most recent and the previous elections, divided by two (Lindberg 2007; Mozaffar and Scarritt 2005).
2. 'Présentation du Parti de l'Union Pour la République (UPR)', available at <http://upr.mr/fr/wp-content/uploads/2017/01/La-Presentation-du-Parti-UPR.pdf> (last accessed 17 June 2017).

3. 'Mauritanie: La campagne vire en duel entre pouvoir et islamistes', available at <http://cridem.org/C_Info.php?article=649866> (last accessed 19 November 2013); 'Awoynatt Sitre (Ould Yengé): Les candidats d'APP accusent l'UPR de corruption', available at <http://cridem.org/C_Info.php?article=649827> (last accessed 18 November 2013).

4. The UPR has 76 deputies out of 147 in the National Assembly, 41 senators out of 56, 141 mayors out of 218 in the entire country and 1,955 municipal counsellors out of 3,722. See 'Présentation du Parti de l'Union Pour la République (UPR)', available at <http://upr.mr/fr/wp-content/uploads/2017/01/La-Presentation-du-Parti-UPR.pdf> (last accessed 17 June 2017).

5. The COD was created in 2012 and comprises the following parties: Rally of Democratic Forces (RFD); Union of Progress Forces (UFP); *Tawassoul*; National Pact for Democracy and Development (PNDD-ADIL); and the Alternative (*Al-Badil*). See 'Mauritania Government 2017', available at <http://www.theodora.com/wfbcurrent/mauritania/mauritania_government.html> (last accessed 4 September 2017).

6. Union for the Republic; the Republican Party for Democracy and Renewal (PRDR); the Union for Democracy and Progress (UDP); the Democratic Renewal (RD); the Mauritanian Party for Unity and Change (HATEM-PMUC); and the Union of the Democratic Centre (UCD). See 'Mauritania Government 2017', <http://www.theodora.com/wfbcurrent/mauritania/mauritania_government.html> (last accessed 4 September 2017).

7. The most important parties in the CAP, created in 2012, were the Popular Progressive Alliance (APP), *El Wiam* and the *Sawab*. See 'Mauritania Government 2017', <http://www.theodora.com/wfbcurrent/mauritania/mauritania_government.html> (last accessed 4 September 2017).

Bibliography

Aghrout, Ahmed (2008), 'Parliamentary and Presidential Elections in Mauritania 2006 and 2007', *Electoral Studies* 27: 2, 385–90.

Bogaards, Matthijs (2000), 'Crafting Competitive Party Systems: Electoral Laws and the Opposition in Africa', *Democratization* 7: 4, 163–90.

Bogaards, Matthijs (2004), 'Counting Parties and Identifying Dominant Party Systems in Africa', *European Journal of Political Research* 43, 173–97.

Bogaards, Matthijs (2008), 'Dominant Party Systems and Electoral Volatility in Africa', *Party Politics* 4: 1, 113–30.

Bratton, Michael, and Eric C. C. Chang (2006), 'State Building and Democratization in Sub-Saharan Africa. Forwards, Backwards, or Together?', *Comparative Political Studies* 39: 9, 1059–83.

Bratton, Michael, and Nicolas van de Walle (1994), 'Neo-patrimonial Regimes and Political Transition in Africa', *World Politics* 46: 4, 453–89.

Cavatorta, Francesco, and Raquel Ojeda-García (2017), 'Islamism in Mauritania and the Narrative of Political Moderation', *Journal of Modern African Studies* 55: 2, 301–25.

Chacha, Mwite (2016), 'Economic Interdependence and Post-Coup Democratization', *Democratization* 1: 20, 1–20.

Doreenspleet, Renske (2003), 'Political Parties, Party Systems and Democracy in Sub-Saharan Africa', in M. A. Salih (ed.), *African Political Parties*, London: Pluto Press, pp. 169–87.

Goeke, Martin, and Christof Hartmann (2011), 'The Regulation of Party Switching in Africa', *Journal of Contemporary African Studies* 29: 3, 263–80.

Golosov, Grigorii V. (2016), 'Why and How Electoral Systems Matter in Autocracies', *Australian Journal of Political Science* 51: 3, 367–85.

Handlin, Samuel (2017), 'Observing Incumbent Abuses: Improving Measures of Electoral and Competitive Authoritarianism with New Data', *Democratization* 24: 1, 41–60.

Hill, J. N. C. (2016), *Democratization in the Maghreb*, Edinburgh: Edinburgh University Press.

Hochman, Dafna (2007), 'Divergent Democratization: The Paths of Tunisia, Morocco and Mauritania', *Middle East Policy Council* 14: 4, 67–83.

Ishiyama, John, and John James Quinn (2006), 'African Phoenix? Explaining the Electoral Performance of the Formerly Dominant Parties in Africa', *Party Politics* 12: 3, 317–40.

Jedou, Ahmed (2014), 'Democracy Deadlocked Yet again in Mauritania', *Fikra Forum*, <http://fikraforum.org/?p=5042> (last accessed 4 September 2017).

Jourde, Cédric (2001), 'Ethnicity, Democratization, and Political Dramas: Insights into Ethnic Politics in Mauritania', *African Issues* 29: 1/2, 26–30.

Jourde, Cédric (2007), 'Mauritania: Clash of Authoritarianism and Ethnicity', in William F. S. Miles, (ed.), *Political Islam in West Africa: State–Society Relations Transformed*, London: Lynne Rienner, pp. 101–27.

Jourde, Cédric (2008), 'The Master Is Gone, but Does the House Still Stand? The Fate of Single-Party Systems after the Defeat of Single Parties in West Africa', in Edward Friedman and Joseph Wong (eds), *Political Transition in Dominant Party Systems: Learning to Lose*, London and New York: Routledge, pp. 75–90.

Kalu, Kalu N. (2004), 'Embedding African Democracy and Development: The Imperative of Institutional Capital', *International Review of Administrative Sciences* 70: 3, 527–45.

Kinne, Lance (2001), 'The Benefits of Exile: The Case of FLAM', *The Journal of Modern African Studies* 39: 4, 597–621.

Kuenzi, Michelle, and Gina Lambright (2001), 'Party System Institutionalization in 30 African Countries', *Party Politics* 7: 4, 437–68.

Kuenzi, Michelle, and Gina Lambright (2005), 'Party Systems and Democratic Consolidation in Africa's Electoral Regimes', *Party Politics* 11: 4, 423–46.

Leservoisier, Olivier (2009), 'Contemporary Trajectories of Slavery in Haalpulaar Society (Mauritania)', in Benedetta Rossi (ed.), *Reconfiguring Slavery: West African Trajectories*, Liverpool: Liverpool University Press, pp. 140–51.

LeVan, A. Carl (2014), 'Analytic Authoritarianism and Nigeria', *Commonwealth & Comparative Politics* 52: 2, 212–31.

Lindberg, Staffan (2006a), 'The Surprising Significance of African Elections', *Journal of Democracy* 17: 1, 139–51.

Lindberg, Staffan (2006b), 'Opposition Parties and Democratization in Sub-Saharan Africa', *Journal of Contemporary African Studies* 24: 1, 123–38.

Lindberg, Staffan (2007), 'Institutionalization of Party Systems? Stability and Fluidity among Legislative Parties in Africa's Democracies', *Government and Opposition* 42: 2, 215–41.

Mainwaring, Scott, and Mariano Torcal (2005), 'La institucionalización de los sistemas de partidos y la teoría del sistema partidista después de la tercera ola de democratización', *América Latina Hoy* 41, 141–73.

Manning, Carrie (2005), 'Assessing African Party Systems after the Third Wave', *Party Politics* 11: 6, 707–27.

Marty, Marianne (2002), 'Mauritania, Political Parties, Neo-patrimonialism and Democracy', *Democratization* 9: 3, 92–108.

Mission d'observation électorale-Union Éuropéenne (MOE-UE) (2007), *Mauritanie 2006–2007: Elections municipales, législatives 2006 et présidentielles 2007. Rapport final*, <http://www.eods.eu/library/FR%20MAURITANIA%202006-2007_fr.pdf> (last accessed 4 September 2017).

Moroff, Anika, and Matthius Basedau (2010), 'An Effective Measure of Institutional Engineering? Ethnic Party Bans in Africa', *Democratization* 17: 4, 666–86.

Mozaffar, Shaheen, and James Scarritt (2005), 'The Puzzle of African Party Systems', *Party Politics* 11: 4, 399–421.

N'Diaye, Boubacar (2006), 'Mauritania, August 2005: Justice and Democracy, or Just another Coup?', *African Affairs* 105: 420, 421–41.

Ojeda-García, Raquel (2012), 'La derrota del antiguo partido autoritario dominante (PRDR) en las elecciones legislativas de 2006 en Mauritania', *Revista de Investigaciones Políticas y Sociológicas* 4, 31–54.

Ojeda-García, Raquel (2015), '¡Mauritania: régimen autoritario y reconfiguración del sistema de partidos!', in Inmaculada Szmolka (ed.), *Escenarios post-primavera árabe: actores y dinámicas de cambio, Revista CIDOB d'Afers Internals* 109, pp. 109–31.

Ojeda-García, Raquel, and Alberto López Bargados (2012), '¿E Pur Si Muove? Logics of Power and the Process of Transition in the Islamic Republic of Mauritania', in Ferrán Izquierdo Brichs (ed.), *Political Regimes in the Arab World: Society and the Exercise of Power*, London: Routledge, pp. 104–21.

Ould Hamed, Moussa (2008), 'Menace terroriste en Mauritanie: Un cas d'école', *L'Année du Maghreb* IV, 337–43, <http://anneemaghreb.revues.org/462> (last accessed 19 September 2017).

Ould Khattatt, Mohamed (2011), 'Pourquoi, à l'UPR, rien ne va plus ou presque?', *Chroniques politiques mauritaniennes*, 8 July, <http://chroniques-politiques-de-mkhattatt.blogspot.co.uk/2011/07/pourquoi-lupr-rien-ne-va-plus-ou.html> (last accessed 19 September 2017).

Rakner, Lise (2011), 'Institutionalizing the Pro-democracy Movements: The Case of Zambia's Movement for Multiparty Democracy', *Democratization* 18: 5, 1106–24.

Rakner, Lise, and Nicolas van de Walle (2009), 'Opposition Weakness in Africa', *Journal of Democracy* 20: 3, 108–21.

Riedl, Rachel Beatty (2014), *Authoritarian Origins of Democratic Party Systems in Africa*, New York: Cambridge University Press.

Sartori, Giovani (1976), *Parties and Party Systems: A Framework for Analysis*, Cambridge: Cambridge University Press.

Szmolka Vida, Inmaculada (2010), 'Los regímenes políticos híbridos: democracias y autoritarismos', *Revista de Estudios Políticos* 147, 103–35.

Szmolka Vida, Inmaculada (2011) 'Democracias y autoritarismos con adjetivos: la clasificación de los países árabes dentro de una tipología general de regímenes políticos', *Revista Española de Ciencia Política* 26: 11–62.

van Cranenburgh, Oda (2003), 'Power and Competition: The Institutional Context of African Multi-party Politics', in M. A. Salih (ed.), *African Political Parties*, London: Pluto Press, pp. 188–206.

van Cranenburgh, Oda (2009), 'Restraining Executive Power in Africa: Horizontal Accountability in Africa's Hybrid Regimes', *South African Journal of International Affairs* 16: 1, 49–68.

van de Walle, Nicolas (2003), 'Presidentialism and Clientelism in Africa's Emerging Party Systems', *Journal of Modern African Studies* 42: 2, 297–321.

Zisenwine, Daniel (2007), 'Mauritania's Democratic Transition: A Regional Model for Political Reform?', *Journal of North African Studies*, 12: 4, 481–99.

Chapter 13

Women's political inclusion and prospects for democracy in North Africa

Loes Debuysere

Globally speaking, women are not prominently present in formal politics. To give just one example, women occupy on average 22.62 per cent of the seats in parliaments worldwide, which means that only one in five parliamentarians in the world are women today (IPU 2016). More than in formal politics, women generally predominate in civil society, through political participation in voluntary associations or labour unions and through their mobilisation in all kinds of social and economic protests. Given women's importance in civil society (in contrast to men who are generally more active in formal politics) it is important to broaden our understandings of what politics and democratic participation exactly are (Bell et al. 2004). Indeed, women's political participation cannot be narrowed down to women's formal political inclusion in elections, political parties or political institutions like government or parliament. However, it is important not to neglect what takes place within formal institutions, given these institutions' major role in a country's decision-making and law-making processes. Therefore, this chapter will specifically zoom in on women's *formal* political participation in the region of North Africa.

Equal formal political participation matters, especially in democracies. Since women constitute at least half the population of the world, gender justice requires their equal presence in politics and in the representative body (Jožanc 2011; Dahlerup, qtd in Mervis et al. 2013). Of course, a demand for gender parity in political institutions needs to avoid the trap of essentialism; attention needs to be paid to multiple differences between women (and men for that matter). Gender intersects with other categories, such as race, class, ethnicity or sexuality, which all equally weigh on the formation of interests, preferences or values of individuals (Jožanc 2011: 9). However, since gender is one of the categories that influence social perspectives that, in turn, shape the political debate, women's perspectives, which proceed from women's (unequal) social and structural position, must be taken into account (Young 2000: 136). While not the focus of this chapter, the debate on essentialism and anti-essentialism has been a crucial one in feminist philosophy. For a more in-depth discussion of the debate, see the work of Alison Stone, Gayatri Spivak and Iris Marion Young, amongst others. Moreover, since participatory parity (equal participation in all spheres of life) is a necessary condition for political democracy and justice, as Nancy Fraser (1990, 2013) rightly argues, gendered effects of domination and subordination need to be overcome in any democracy. Of course, if one settles for a scant definition of democracy, in which only free and fair elections every four years are required, then it is possible to end up with a gender-blind form of democracy. However, a broader, feminist take on democracy would define the quality of a democracy

> not only by the presence or absence of political institutions or the regularity of elections, but also by pointing towards the importance of equal rights and equal participation of citizens, be it in political parties, elections, parliaments or other decision-making bodies. (Moghadam 2011)

If one takes this broader definition of democracy as a starting point, a country cannot be fully democratic if it does not offer equal chances and representation of women in its political institutions. Conversely, it is expected that in democracies or in transitions towards democracy the rights and participation of women will improve. Indeed, gendered democratisation literature (Waylen 2007; Viterna and Fallon 2008), which looks at gendered processes underpinning democratic political change, argues that 'there are strong theoretical reasons to anticipate that democratic transitions will create more gender equitable states' (Viterna and Fallon 2008: 668), since democracies, for example, open up new opportunities for political participation for women (and men). However, empirical work on democratic transitions in Latin America in the 1970s or Eastern Europe in the 1990s shows how a majority of these regions' countries debunk this theoretical hypothesis or assumption. In many transitional countries, even so-called democratic success stories, women did not enjoy more formal political inclusion in democratic institutions.

Many authors working on engendering democratisation (Waylen 2007; Viterna and Fallon 2008; Fallon et al. 2012) therefore highlight the ubiquity of gendered 'democracy paradoxes' during transitions towards democracy: increasing levels of democracy often do little to improve women's legislative representation or women's political influence. Kunovich and Paxton (2005) identify two sets of factors that can explain this lack of women's political inclusion in any given country. On the one hand, there are structural, political or ideological factors at the country level that possibly hinder women's representation (for example, the number of women in the labour force, (a lack of) quota systems, a region's culture or beliefs). On the other hand, there are factors relating to the political parties in power (for example, their ideology, number of leading women) that enable, or hinder, women's political representation.

Indeed, Kunovich and Paxton (2005) believe that political parties, in their important function as gatekeepers, mediate the relationship between the more structural, country-level factors and the eventual political outcomes for women. This concurs with Viterna and Fallon's observation (2008: 668) that during democratic transitions political parties are one of the key factors that 'shape the political openings and ideologies available to women' in order to obtain (positive or negative) gendered outcomes at the level of the state. More concretely, literature on the role of political parties during democratic transitions has found that conservative parties are often responsible for the previously described 'democracy paradox': thanks to the opening up of the political space, fundamentalist and conservative political parties can get elected and pose threats to gender equality and representation (Arat 2010; Moghadam 2011). Conversely, there is an assumption in gendered democratisation literature that when leftist parties come to power during transitions, it will be more likely to find women in political decision-making positions (Waylen 2007).

This chapter seeks to verify, in the specific context of post-2011 North Africa, the two hypotheses that have been introduced thus far: first, the hypothesis that there exists a positive correlation between levels of democracy and women's formal political participation and second, the hypothesis that the ideology of political parties determines women's formal political participation. The North African region has faced political change in the aftermath of massive popular uprisings in 2011 that called for more 'bread, freedom and human dignity'. In response to these uprisings, most states in the region initially embarked on processes of democratisation, with some launching some cosmetic (Morocco, Algeria) and others more comprehensive (Tunisia, Egypt until 2013) democratic reforms. Six years since the uprisings, however, some argue that only Tunisia achieved a successful democratic transition (Stepan 2012). It is therefore fair to say that the democratisation literature can only explain so much about Arab politics today (Valbjørn 2015).

However, since not much has been written about the gendered nature of the Arab Uprisings and subsequent transitions (Moghadam 2014), this chapter takes the hypotheses of the existing gendered democratisation literature as a starting point to analyse the Arab (and especially the Tunisian) Uprisings. Two concrete research questions are being looked at against the renewed North African context: *Does the region witness any gendered democracy paradoxes with regard to women's formal political representation? And what is the importance of the ideology of the political parties in power for this representation?* To answer these questions, the chapter first pays attention to *country-level* differences that can explain different trajectories of women's political participation in the North African countries, in order to verify the first hypothesis about a positive correlation between levels of women's participation and levels of democracy. After this quantitative discussion of regional data on women's political inclusion, the chapter then focuses on the alleged success story of Tunisia, to test, based on qualitative data obtained during semi-structured interviews in Tunis between 2012 and 2016, what role political parties play in enabling women's political participation. The focus on one country, Tunisia, allows digging into the impact of party-level differences (for example, different party ideologies) and as such, the analysis seeks to verify the second hypothesis that leftist (or, in the Tunisian context, so-called 'modernist' or democratic) parties are more likely to pay attention to women's political inclusion and representation.

Women's formal political participation in North Africa

It is sometimes claimed that while women are well represented in civil society, men are more active in formal politics (Bell et al. 2004). Most countries in North Africa are no exception to this. Figure 13.1 shows how the levels of women's civil society participation vary between North African countries, with women in Tunisia and Morocco among the most active (the V-Dem dataset measures civil society participation in terms of women's freedom of discussion, women's participation in civil society organisations and the percentage of female journalists). When discussing women's formal political activism throughout the region, Figure 13.2 illustrates that Algerian and Tunisian women are among the most represented in formal political institutions (the V-Dem dataset measures formal political activity in terms of women's share in the overall distribution of power and their descriptive representation in the legislature). In order to understand the different trajectories of different North African countries in terms of women's formal political activism, the focus of this chapter, it is important to look at both country-level and political party-level differences (Kunovich and Paxton 2005).

While political parties are the principal actors that eventually mediate openings for women into politics, they do, however, always act in and against a certain country-specific context. There are several factors at the country level that can have an impact on women's inclusion in politics (Kunovich and Paxton 2005; Paxton et al. 2010). There are structural factors like women's share in the workforce or a country's level of education; political factors like a country's electoral system, presence or absence of gender quota, levels of democracy; and ideological factors relating to a certain region, with a certain culture, religion, beliefs or attitudes. Given the fact that only countries of the same region (North Africa) are under scrutiny here, the focus will be on the importance of

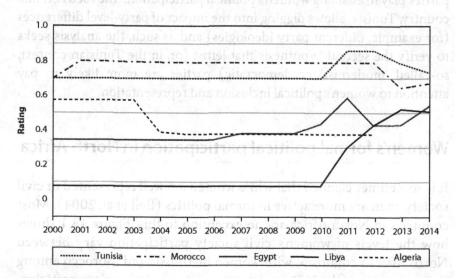

Figure 13.1 Women civil society participation index. (Source: Varieties of Democracy (V-Dem) 2015, <https://www.v-dem.net/en/>, last accessed 14 September 2017)

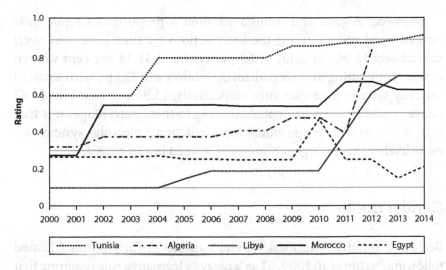

Figure 13.2 Women political participation index. (Source: Varieties of Democracy (V-Dem) 2015, <https://www.v-dem.net/en/>, last accessed 14 September 2017)

political factors (electoral system, quota, democracy) and especially on whether and how levels of democracy shape women's access to political positions in North African countries. Such discussion allows to detect potential gendered democracy paradoxes in the region.

Electoral system

Paxton et al. (2010: 26) argue that 'the importance of an electoral system to women's political representation is the most consistently demonstrated finding in the cross-sectional literature'. Scholars generally agree that a proportional representation system is most beneficial for women's representation (Paxton et al. 2010: 34). More than a plurality-majority system, a proportional representation system (in which citizens vote for a party list rather than for individual candidates) helps women to gain access to the political system. Table 13.1 shows the electoral system of all five North African countries under scrutiny.

Table 13.1 Electoral systems in North Africa. (Source: IPU 2015)

Morocco	Algeria	Tunisia	Libya	Egypt
Proportional	Proportional	Proportional	Mixed	Mixed

Morocco, Algeria and Tunisia adopted a proportional representation electoral system during the last elections for their lower chamber; respectively 16.96 per cent, 31.60 per cent and 31.34 per cent women are currently sitting in their parliaments. Libya and Egypt, with a partial majority system, have currently, respectively, 15.96 per cent and 14.93 per cent women in parliament. According to these percentages it is true that countries with proportional representational electoral systems are more likely to have a higher number of women in parliament.

Gender quota

Besides a country's electoral system, national gender quotas (defined following Paxton et al. 2009: 31 as 'a party or legislative rule requiring that women make up a certain percentage of a candidate list, a parliamentary assembly, a committee, or a government') can also have a positive impact on women's political inclusion. Table 13.2 illustrates which national gender quotas have been adopted during parliamentary elections in the five North African countries under scrutiny, both before and after the 2010/11 Arab Uprisings. It shows how most countries have expanded their gender quotas since 2011, except for Egypt.

Table 13.2 Gender quota in North Africa. (Source: IDEA 2015)

Morocco	Algeria	Tunisia	Libya	Egypt
Last parliamentary election before the 2011 Arab Uprisings				
Yes Reserved seats (30 seats)	No	Yes Reserved seats (30%)	n/a[1]	Yes Reserved seats (64 seats)
Elections since 2011 uprisings				
Yes Reserved seats (60 seats)	Yes Reserved seats (variable, between 20% and 50%)	Yes Legislated Candidate quota (Vertical parity on electoral lists)	Yes Legislated Candidate quota (Partial parity on electoral lists)	2011/12 elections No[2] 2015 elections Yes Reserved seats (56 seats)

[1] Since the bloodless coup that brought Colonel Muammar Gaddafi to power in 1969, Libya has known a unique political system called the *Jamahiriya* (State of the Masses). Under this system every Libyan citizen participates nominally in the ruling structure through membership in local congresses (Pargeter 2010). In reality, however, it was Gaddafi who held complete control over the state apparatus.
[2] Even though parties were obliged to nominate at least one woman as part of their district candidate lists.

Levels of democracy

The last (and for our purposes most interesting) country-level political variable that can have an impact on the number of women in parliament is a country's democratic growth. As mentioned in the introduction to this chapter, theoretically speaking, it is expected that higher levels of democracy will coincide with higher levels of women's parliamentary representation.

In what follows, Morocco, Algeria, Tunisia, Libya and Egypt's 'growth of democracy' is discussed in relation to women's parliamentary representation in these countries, in order to compare different trajectories in women's political inclusion across them. Although women's representation in parliament reflects only one aspect of women's formal political inclusion, it is the most used parameter in quantitative literature to discuss women's political participation, and the number of women in legislatures has been neither too small and homogenous nor too large and heterogeneous to prohibit research from being either practical or meaningful (Cammisa and Reingold 2004: 182). Table 13.3 shows the different

Table 13.3 Levels of democracy in North Africa. (Source: IPU 2015 (W.i.P. in %); EIU 2015 (D.I.))

	Morocco		Algeria		Tunisia		Libya		Egypt	
	W.i.P.	*D.I.*	*W.i.P.*	*D.I.*	*W.i.P.*	*D.I.*	*W.i.P.*	*D.I.*	*W.i.P.*	*D.I.*
2005	10.77	n/a	6.68	n/a	22.75	n/a	n/a	n/a	1.98	n/a
2006	10.77	3.9	6.68	3.17	22.75	3.06	n/a	1.84	1.98	3.9
2007	10.46	n/a	7.71	n/a	22.75	n/a	n/a	n/a	1.98	n/a
2008	10.46	3.88	7.71	3.32	22.75	2.96	n/a	2.00	1.98	3.89
2009	10.46	n/a	7.71	n/a	27.57	n/a	n/a	n/a	1.98	n/a
2010	10.46	3.79	7.71	3.44	27.57	2.79	n/a	1.94	12.70	3.07
2011	16.96	3.83	7.71	3.44	26.27	5.53	n/a	3.55	1.97	3.95
2012	16.96	4.07	31.60	3.83	26.27	5.67	16.5	5.15	1.97	4.56
2013	16.96	4.07	31.60	3.83	26.27	5.76	16.5	4.82	1.97	3.27
2014	16.96	4.00	31.60	3.83	31.34	6.31	15.96	3.80	1.97	3.16
2015	16.96	4.66	31.60	3.95	31.34	6.72	15.96	2.25	14.93	3.18

W.i.P. = Women in Parliament.
D.I. = The Economist Intelligence Unit's Democracy Index.

percentage of women in parliament (W.i.P. in %, lower chamber) per country over the last decade (2005–15).

Generally speaking, women's political participation in parliament has been gradually increasing in almost all North African countries over the last ten years, with especially high levels today in Algeria (31.6 per cent) and Tunisia (31.34 per cent). It must be noted that the widespread violence and insecurity in Libya impedes all genuine progress in women's rights and representation, as Kamel discusses in his chapter in this volume.

In order to verify whether the countries' different trajectories in women's legislative representation can in any way be explained by these countries' levels of democracy, Table 13.3 also provides the Economist Intelligence Unit's (EIU) Democracy Index (D.I.) for all five countries over the last ten years. The EIU uses five different variables to measure a country's democracy level: free and fair elections, civil liberties, efficient government, sufficient political participation and a supportive democratic political culture.[1] The D.I. of each country is the average score of all five variables of democracy on a scale of 0–10 (with 0 being not democratic at all and 10 being very democratic).

The indices of the North African countries illustrate how Tunisia has made the most progress in terms of democratisation over the last years, making Tunisia the first Arab country to be labelled a flawed democracy by the EIU. Morocco, referred to as a hybrid regime by the EIU, also improved its index, albeit in a less spectacular way than Tunisia. The indices of the other three countries (Algeria, Libya and Egypt) have remained rather stable when comparing 2010 and 2015, meaning that these three states are still highly authoritarian in nature, or, in the case of Libya, mired in civil war. The case of Egypt illustrates how democracy, like women's representation, is not static or teleological over time, with its index changing considerably over the course of the last five years.

A comparison between a country's D.I. and its percentage of women in parliament illustrates the following: those countries that have become (slightly) more democratic, principally Tunisia and Morocco, have seen an increase in the number of women in parliament over the last years. Inversely, however, an increase in women's political participation in parliament does not necessarily mean that a country has become more democratic. For example, Algeria's high levels of women's representation in parliament since 2012 have coexisted with low levels of democracy; and pre-uprising Tunisia, a highly authoritarian country at the time, also witnessed high numbers of women in parliament. To understand why high levels of women's representation sometimes characterise highly authoritarian regimes, it is important to understand the widespread phenomenon of state feminism in North Africa. Amira Mhadbi (2012) defines state feminism as 'the systematic and explicit governmental exploitation of the feminist cause for political reasons narrowly linked to enhancing the image, prestige and ideological sustainability of the autocratic regime'. Indeed, throughout the region, women have been and are still being used by authoritarian (and less authoritarian) regimes to negotiate and maintain power (Elliott 2014; Jomier 2011; Pratt 2015).

State feminism explains why the first theoretical hypothesis about a positive correlation between levels of democracy and levels of women's political participation only proves partially true in the North African context. While those countries that have become more democratic since the Arab Uprisings (excluding Egypt's initial democratisation process) have indeed seen progress in women's political participation, higher levels of women's political representation are by no means a guarantee or an indicator for democratisation. There thus exists no direct correlation between democracy levels and increased participation of women in politics (Mervis et al. 2013). In fact, this finding is also applicable beyond the North African region. The allegedly most democratic countries in the world today, that is, the Nordic countries, have the highest levels of women's equality. Inversely, the country with the highest share of women in parliament (63.8 per cent, according to IPU 2015), Rwanda, can hardly be considered democratic (D.I. 3.07 in 2015). In terms of gendered democracy paradoxes in post-Arab Uprising North Africa, Table 13.3 shows how only Egypt, during the democratic efforts made in the early days following the fall of Hosni Mubarak, has experienced such paradox in terms of parliamentary representation of women. In Morocco and Tunisia, which also saw a rise in their D.I., no such paradox occurred.

Egypt

When Egypt was considered the most authoritarian (whether under ousted President Mubarak just before the popular uprisings in 2010 or under current President Abdel Fattah el-Sisi who came to power in 2013), the country witnessed the highest levels of women's participation in its parliament. This can be understood in the light of an authoritarian top-down state feminist project (visible under both Mubarak and today's regime of el-Sisi) that implemented a women's quota. Conversely, when Egypt was at the height of its democratisation process, immediately after the uprisings in 2011, it had the fewest women (2 per cent) elected in parliament. Thus, under democratically elected President Morsi (2011–13), one of the figureheads of Egypt's Islamist Freedom and Justice Party (FJP), Egypt displayed a gendered democracy paradox in its share of women in the legislature.

Indeed, the opening up of the political sphere in Egypt after the fall of authoritarian President Mubarak coincided with very low levels of women's representation. While Mubarak had introduced a quota of 12 per cent women for parliament in the 2010 pre-uprisings elections, those were abolished after the uprisings because they were associated, like some other so-called women-friendly laws (often referred to as Suzanne's laws in reference to Suzanne Mubarak, wife of the former president), with the authoritarian regime of Mubarak (Pratt 2015). The conservative ideology of the FJP (which won 40 per cent of the seats during the first parliamentary elections in 2011/12) and of the Salafi coalition can be seen as a cause for Egypt's low levels of women's representation. However, without the top-down reintroduction of a quota in 2015 by Egypt's new military regime, women's representation would not have been strong in the 2015 parliamentary elections (from which the Islamist FJP was banned) as most participating political parties barely nominated women for individual seats (Fouad 2015).

Morocco

Like today's Egypt, Morocco also demonstrates top-down state feminist tendencies. Morocco is often hailed in the international media and forums as a trendsetter in the realm of women's rights in the developing world. Under King Mohammed VI, a progressive reform of the personal status code (*moudawana*) was passed in 2004, which the King promoted as an indispensable ingredient of his democratisation project. However, underneath the liberal veneer of the new *moudawana*, the regime still reaffirms and sanctions patriarchal gender relations entrenched in many communities across Morocco (Elliott 2014). In the aftermath of popular protests in 2011, Morocco has witnessed slightly higher levels of democracy because of some reforms and constitutional amendments introduced by the monarch. The limited democratisation in Morocco has coincided with a slight increase in women's parliamentary representation, thanks to the successful lobbying for a higher national women's quota by prominent Moroccan women's groups (Darhour and Dahlerup 2013). Also, Morocco's Islamist Justice and Development Party (PJD), which won both the 2011 and 2016 elections, respected the quota, with currently 18 PJD women represented in parliament (out of 125 PJD seats). Thus far, Morocco has not displayed a gendered democracy paradox in terms of women's parliamentary representation.

Tunisia

As Tunisia has seen the most progress in terms of democratisation, its percentage of women in parliament has not dropped since 2011. Indeed, Tunisia has thus far not experienced a gendered democracy paradox regarding women's legislative representation, even though, like in Morocco and Egypt, an Islamist party (the *Ennahda*) won the first democratic parliamentary elections and led the first government. The high numbers of women in the Tunisian parliament are due to the parity principle in the 2011 and 2014 electoral law, according to which men and women have to alternate on all electoral party lists. The new quota system for electoral parity was adopted after intensive lobby work by women's associations (Debuysere 2016b).

This chapter has thus far made only superficial references to the role of political parties. In order to better understand what role (the ideology of) political parties play in enabling or preventing women's formal political inclusion, the second part of the chapter will specifically focus on the Tunisian case, the most progressive of the North African states. A focus on one case study allows for a more meticulous examination of the party dynamics at work. As already mentioned, political parties are believed to interact with some of the previously discussed country-level factors (for example, quotas) and mediate, at least partially, the effects of these national-level factors in producing outcomes for women. Based on qualitative data collected during interviews in Tunis with politicians of all ideological backgrounds, the gate-keeping role (Kunovich and Paxton 2005: 513) of Tunisian political parties will be scrutinised in order to verify whether the second hypothesis, according to which the ideologies of political parties in power matter for women's political inclusion, holds true.

Political parties and women's participation in Tunisia

Tunisia has been labelled the success story of the Arab world, as it is the only country in the region that has succeeded in organising free and fair elections in two consecutive instances while also concentrating power in the hands of the elected representatives. The first democratic elections, which took place in October 2011, brought an Islamist-led coalition government (commonly referred to as 'the troika') to power. The *Ennahda*, the winning party, but without an absolute majority, agreed to govern in coalition with two smaller centre-left parties (the *Congrès Pour la République* (CPR) and the *Ettakatol*), while the elected deputies were tasked with drafting a new constitution in Tunisia's National Constituent Assembly (ANC). A major political crisis, a National Dialogue and a new constitution later (Zemni 2015), Tunisia organised new elections in late 2014, which this time brought the so-called secular *Nidaa Tounes* alliance to power. Following negotiations, *Nidaa Tounes* entered into a coalition government together with three other parties (the *Ennahda*, the UPL and the *Afek Tounes*); those elected for parliament in 2014 took a seat in the new Assembly of People's Representatives (ARP).

While Tunisia certainly made progress in terms of democratic rule, as illustrated by the steady increase of its D.I. from 2010 to 2015, challenges remain numerous for the country. In a region where terrorism and insecurity are the order of the day, Tunisia also experiences economic difficulties and struggles to reform some key institutions, like the judiciary and the security sector. Corruption is still widespread and some say even getting worse (Aliriza 2016). It is therefore important to remain cautious about labelling Tunisia a success story (Marzouki and Meddeb 2015). Nonetheless, Tunisia's attempts at democratisation make it an interesting case to study (new) tendencies in women's participation in political institutions like political parties.

In general, Tunisian women have been and still are a lot less active in political parties than in Tunisia's civil society.[2] Tunisia's women's movements generally agree that women's formal political participation remains difficult, facing many obstacles. First and foremost, there is a widespread mentality in Tunisia that women are not fit for top political positions, as political science professor Jinan Limam asserts:

> It's the profile of the dominant masculinity. The profile of what a leader must look like is always a man. Leadership is masculine. That's the main reason why Tunisians are less inclined to vote for a woman who heads an electoral list and why political parties are reluctant to put women in top positions.[3]

Table 13.4 Female political leadership in Tunisia. (Source: Arab Women's Leadership Institute 2015)

	November 2013 (%)	February 2015 (%)	
		Men	Women
Male support for women candidates in Tunisia	6	66	
Tunisians who say the country is headed in the right direction for women's political participation	n/a	63	67
Tunisians who actually voted for a woman	n/a	5	4

The discrepancy between alleged support for women candidates and actual voting behaviour, as Table 13.4 illustrates, is telling in this regard.

Moreover, Tunisian women face the universal problem of balancing work-life and home-life, paid and unpaid work. Rather strict traditional gender roles hold women responsible for managing family life, which leaves little time for a public or political life.[4] Fattoum Lassoued, a former *Ennahda* member of the National Constituent Assembly (ANC), gives an account of that difficulty:

> I am a lawyer, I have two small children and I'm married. My husband really encouraged me to take the post. That's why I now live in this hotel in Tunis [in order to be close to the National Assembly], while I normally live in Sfax. If my husband had not encouraged me, I would not have been here.[5]

Even though Tunisia scores high in terms of women's parliamentary representation and even though most political parties have expressed support for women's rights, female politicians complain about the instrumentalisation of women at the political level. As Saida Ben Garrach, a well-known feminist and president of the women's commission of *Nidaa Tounes*, puts it:

> Women are mentioned in the discourse of all political parties, that is to say, they are seen as a factor of mobilisation. But at the same time, they are forgotten as political actors, they always end second. It's clear that the position of women in political parties is always one of instrumentalisation, even in parties that have put most women on top of their electoral lists [*tête de liste*].[6]

To increase their political weight, women have to a certain extent engaged in cross-party cooperation in parliament. For example, in the aftermath of a brutal rape of a young woman by several policemen in 2012, an informal women's commission was set up in the ANC, uniting women of all ideological tendencies.[7] Although issues relating to women and their rights have been discussed in this commission, its impact must not be overstated, as many women put their partisan affiliation before what can be considered collective women's causes.[8] In the ARP that came into being after the 2014 parliamentary elections a new initiative for a women's caucus was launched. This initiative, however, quickly failed because of disagreements about who should take the lead.[9]

Before digging into the ideological party-level differences between Tunisia's most important political formations, it is important to point out the regional aspect to women's political participation in Tunisia; an aspect that transcends partisan ideology. During the 2014 elections, for example, women figured a lot less as *tête de liste* (regardless of political party of affiliation) in the poorer south and interior regions than in the richer coastal districts and the capital. Mouna Mathari, member of Tunisia's leftist Popular Front, explains:

> We know that a woman who leads a party's electoral list does not have any chance to win south of Sfax. It really is a problem. These are very nationalistic, Arab, Islamist, conservative regions. It is not easy.[10]

Turning to the hypotheses about political parties that were mentioned in the introduction to this chapter, the following questions arise: are leftist or self-declared democratic parties in Tunisia more willing to give women important positions in the party? Are conservative, right-wing or Islamist parties inherently more hostile to the idea of women's political inclusion? Is there a link between a party's internal democracy and its internal policies on women's inclusion? In what follows, these questions are addressed through a discussion of the gendered dynamics within three principal political formations in Tunisia: the Islamist, conservative *Ennahda* party, the 'secular' neo-liberal *Nidaa Tounes* and the leftist Popular Front.

Women's participation within the Islamist *Ennahda* party

Women figure quite prominently in Tunisia's Islamist *Ennahda* party, led by Rachid al-Ghannouchi. Although the executive bureau of the party only counted two women out of a total of twenty-six members before the latest party conference,[11] the *Ennahda* enforces a gender quota in its *majlis al-shura* (consultative council) and the *Ennahda* women have been visibly present in Tunisia's parliament. In the 2011 constituent elections, the *Ennahda* won 90 of the 217 seats in the ANC, 42 of which (47 per cent) went to women. In 2014, when the *Ennahda* came second in the parliamentary elections, the *Ennahda* women secured 27 of the party's 69 seats (39 per cent) in the ARP. According to the young Sayida Ounissi, this significant presence of women in the parliament is helping the *Ennahda* women to also gradually obtain key positions in the party:

> Women have high positions, especially at the parliamentary level. In fact, it is much easier for us to get a position at the state-level, in the institutions, than at the party-level. Nonetheless, it is becoming easier to advocate for us in the political party too. Now we can say, 'Look, we did a great job in the parliament, so it means we can do a great job within the party too.'[12]

The relatively high numbers of *Ennahda* women elected to parliament are to be explained with the legal obligation for all political parties to implement vertical parity (in both the 2011 and 2014 elections) on their electoral lists. Vertical parity forces all political parties to alternate between men and women on their electoral lists and although Tunisia's closed-list proportional electoral system implies that often only the (often male) *tête de liste* gets elected (see Table 13.5), vertical parity has ensured higher levels of women's political participation in parliament when the same party wins more than one seat in a given constituency.

The parity principle was first adopted in 2011 after discussions in Tunisia's Higher Authority for Realisation of the Objectives of the Revolution, Political Reform and Democratic Transition, led by jurist

Table 13.5 Female chief candidates (*tête de liste*) in Tunisian political parties.

Percentage of women tête de liste *for Tunisia's three major political parties*			
	Ennahda	**CPR**	**Ettakatol**	**Total of all parties**
Constituent assembly elections 2011	3 (1 woman)	6 (2 women)	9 (3 women)	7
	Ennahda	**Nidaa Tounes**	**Front Populaire**	**Total of all parties**
Parliamentary elections 2014	9 (3 women)	9 (3 women)	15 (5 women)	12

Yadh Ben Achour. While secular feminists took the lead in lobbying for this vertical parity clause, the parity rule did not harm the *Ennahda* party. As one member of the *Ennahda*'s Bureau of Women and the Family in Ben Arous recalls:

> You know, this parity rule, it was [initially] made by people who thought that the *Ennahda* would not have enough women to alternate between men and women. In fact, they set it up as a trap. But this trap was reversed because the *Ennahda*, in fact, has many women. They wanted to set up a trap, but didn't know that the *Ennahda* has women at all levels, we don't have any problem with that.[13]

Indeed, Mouna Mathari of the leftist Popular Front, explains how secular and leftist political parties miscalculated the emphasis they placed on the idea of a quota before and after the 2011 elections:

> We didn't analyse the Islamist phenomenon well. It was a big wake-up call that the Islamists won the 2011 elections. [...] What is interesting is that there exists a very strong Islamist women's movement. It was wrong of us to think that Islamist women were submissive to their party and wouldn't do anything.[14]

In general, most members of the *Ennahda*, men included, are convinced that women should play an important role within the party. The reason for this acceptance is embedded in the *Ennahda*'s history of repression during the Ben Ali regime. Women, who suffered considerable hardship and humiliation, played a crucial role in holding the family together while their husbands were in prison. Therefore, members argue, women deserve to be present in political life today.[15] However, opinions about how (many) women should represent or participate in the party vary among members of the *Ennahda*. While Sayida Ounissi points out that there is not necessarily a generational fault line, she invokes the necessity of positive discrimination as the main point of divergence between the *Ennahda* members:

> It's not really a generation issue. There are old people in the party who are convinced that women should be represented and then there are a lot of young people for whom it is no issue. There is nobody who believes that women should not be represented, but the difference inside the party is between those who believe that we should bring tools or positive action towards women, you know, positive discrimination. On the other hand, you have people who say things should go naturally, let people do the way they do it, we

> should not create this positive action. I personally am convinced,
> however, that inequality is very difficult to tackle if you don't take
> clear action, it doesn't go away naturally.[16]

That not everyone agrees on the importance of a quota or positive discrimination was illustrated when the ANC had to vote for Tunisia's 2014 electoral law. The issue of horizontal parity, which demands that women and men not only alternate on the lists but also as *tête de liste*, divided the *Ennahda*'s women. While some, a minority of the *Ennahda* women, were staunch supporters of the horizontal parity principle, others refused to vote in favour of it. Monia Brahim, at the time an *Ennahda* member of the ANC, explained why she voted against it:

> I think the situation of women in Tunisia today is already very
> advanced when compared to other Arab countries. For example,
> in every other Arab country, women are treated as a minority, as
> if they are incapable of participating in political life. In Tunisia, on
> the contrary, that is not the case: Tunisian women are active in
> politics, economics, in the social domain. They can be elected
> to important posts. I don't want the women of Tunisia being
> treated as if they are a minority, as if they are incapable or even
> handicapped. A Tunisian woman is capable herself to get to the
> highest level of politics.[17]

Although the *Ennahda* had no problem in adopting vertical parity in 2011, most members of the *Ennahda* eventually voted against horizontal parity in the 2014 electoral law, even though this parity is required by Tunisia's new constitution (see Article 46: 'The state works to attain parity between women and men in elected Assemblies'). In the end, the *Ennahda* remains a traditionally conservative party, which was probably most clearly illustrated when the *Ennahda* members floated the idea of complementarity, rather than equality, of gender roles in the 2012 draft of Tunisia's new constitution. Complementarity, a principle to be found in all Abrahamic religions, asserts that men and women have distinct biological features and therefore should take different roles within the family, traditionally implying that women are mothers first and foremost. Due to staunch opposition, especially from Tunisia's very vocal secular civil society, the *Ennahda* ultimately removed the term from the draft while claiming that 'the Arabic term had been mistranslated'.[18] Although the *Ennahda* had become a more moderate party a long time before the 2011 popular uprising (Cavatorta and Merone 2013), for secular feminists the complementarity incident illustrated how the *Ennahda* was forced to gradually and pragmatically adapt to Tunisian society after having come to power in 2011. As Bochra Belhadj Hmida, a well-known feminist lawyer, puts it:

> It took them [*Ennahda*] three years to realise to what extent the Tunisian society was different than what they thought. They realise this now, they were into an Islamism that was not Tunisian but imported. They have changed and I think that's an asset for Tunisia.[19]

Secular feminist opponents of the *Ennahda*, especially those belonging to long-standing feminist associations like the Association of Democratic Women (ATFD), remain sceptical about the *Ennahda*'s women's rights discourse. While acknowledging that the lack of women as *tête de liste* is a general, cross-party problem in Tunisia, they dismiss the lack of women in other, quasi-secular parties as a temporary flaw; 'at least they are convinced of the principle of equality, they just seem to forget it from time to time in practice'.[20] The *Ennahda*'s lack of women in its party structures and its conservative women's rights discourse is seen as more dangerous, since it is 'inherent to the Islamist ideology to think a woman is not equal to a man. There exists an ideological-religious frontier, because their frame of reference will always be the Quran'.[21]

However, looking at the *Ennahda*'s history, it is clear that the *Ennahda* has been consistent in its support for Tunisia's 'progressive' personal status code. While its predecessor *Mouvement de la Tendence Islamique* (MTI) still attacked this family code as un-Islamic in 1985 (Borsali 2012), the newly named *Ennahda* movement decided in the late 1980s to no longer oppose the code. In fact, its leader Rachid al-Ghannoushi announced in 1988 that his movement would respect the constitution and the personal status code (Chapman et al. 2003: 1058). This concession happened in the context of a short opening-up of the political sphere under Ben Ali. As Cavatorta and Merone rightly argue:

> of course, such acceptance might have been purely instrumental and tactical in order to benefit from the inclusion into the very brief liberalising period of the late 1980s, but the point is that Ennahda did not go back on it when repression hit the movement and when a more radical attitude could have been expected given that there were no benefits to be gained by this position of tactical moderation. (Cavatorta and Merone 2013: 861)

Moreover, when the *Ennahda* obtained legal recognition after the popular uprisings in 2010/11, a democratic momentum that could have been seized to change their position, they never withdrew their support for the family code. This, together with the presence of female critical voices within the party and the fact that the future generation of political leaders within the *Ennahda* is increasingly female ('look at the young people of *Ennahda* in parliament, for every young man you have ten young women'[22]) conveys the impression that the *Ennahda* will gradually (be forced to) improve its record of women's representation within the party structures.

Women's political participation in *Nidaa Tounes*

Created in the summer of 2012 with the goal to unite the 'secular' opposition against the Islamist-led government, *Nidaa Tounes* managed swiftly to become Tunisia's second major political party. A cross-ideological mix of leftists, liberal progressives, *Destourians* and former partisans of Ben Ali's party, the *Nidaa Tounes* coalition was at the time only unified in its aversion for the *Ennahda*, as Wolf also describes in detail in her chapter in this volume. *Nidaa Tounes* not only managed to win the October 2014 parliamentary elections, but also delivered the new president of Tunisia, Béji Caïd Essebsi. Of the 1.7 million people that voted for Béji Caïd Essebsi to become the new president, one million were women (60 per cent), which indicates a special relationship between *Nidaa Tounes* and the female electorate (Ben Amar 2016). Indeed, *Nidaa Tounes* rallied for the 2014 elections with an explicit pro-women's rights discourse. Thouraya Hammami Bekri of the *Ettakatol* party explains it as follows:

> You know, a majority of women feared to see the *Ennahda* party in power again. Certain political parties [*Nidaa Tounes* principally] capitalised on that fear by presenting themselves as the sole defender of the women of Tunisia, in line with the legacy of [first president of the independent Tunisian Republic] Habib Bourguiba.[23]

This pro-women discourse was, however, not always reflected in the actions of the party because, as Wolf also suggests in her chapter in this volume, the label 'secular' for *Nidaa Tounes* might not faithfully represent where the party is ideologically. While women represent a significant part of *Nidaa Tounes*' militants, the constitutive body of the party initially counted very few women.[24] Moreover, while female candidates of *Nidaa Tounes* ultimately won 42 per cent of the party's seats (thirty-six out of the eighty-six) during the 2014 parliamentary elections, women activists reproached *Nidaa Tounes'* reluctance to put women on top of its electoral lists. *Nidaa Tounes* chose only three women as *tête de liste*, the same number as the *Ennahda*. Torkia Ben Khedher, vice president of the Tunisian Women's Voters League (LET), a feminist association that campaigns for more political participation of women, argues:

> These so-called democratic parties, they too do no justice to women. *Nidaa Tounes*, for example, which calls for equal chances and rights for women barely puts forward women as *tête de liste*, even though they should give the example. So even within so-called democratic parties, there is no political will to imply women in decision-making positions.[25]

Nidaa Tounes and other 'secular' parties were indeed quickly referred to as democratic and/or modernist parties by media and party members alike, in order to differentiate them from the allegedly anti-democratic and anti-modernist *Ennahda* party. It is not always clear, however, what is to be understood by this democratic identity. In the appointment of women for *Nidaa Tounes'* lists, for example, there was a lack of transparency, as professor of political sciences Jinan Limam argues:

> You know, for example, in the constituency of Nabeul 1, the head of list is a businesswoman; it's a woman with money. So probably she's head of list just because she's financially fortunate. It's not her militant qualities or her leadership skills that brought her there, she's barely known in Nabeul. This while other women who have charisma, who have proven themselves already in their social struggles, in their struggles for democracy, like Bochra Belhadj Hmida, have not been made *tête de liste*. It's really problematic.[26]

Nonetheless, initially hopes were high in feminist circles that this new, quasi-secular party in power would defend the rights of women. Several well-known feminists also decided to join *Nidaa Tounes* (for example, Bochra Belhadj Hmida and Saida Ben Garrach who became head of *Nidaa Tounes'* women's commission).[27] These initial hopes, however, quickly faltered when *Nidaa Tounes* decided (after one failed attempt to exclude the Islamists) to form a coalition government with its major rival, the *Ennahda*. Many (secular, middle-class) women saw this cooperation as treason, as they had used their vote strategically to make absolutely sure the *Ennahda* would not govern again. According to a young former member of *Nidaa Tounes*, Khawla Ben Aicha, Tunisian women have been disappointed by *Nidaa Tounes* on three occasions in the aftermath of the elections:

> First of all, [when *Nidaa Tounes* established] an alliance with *Ennahda*, even though women had voted for *Nidaa Tounes* because they felt their rights were being threatened by the Islamists in power. Secondly, the fact that the Ministry of Women's Affairs didn't go to *Nidaa Tounes*, even though one million women had voted for *Nidaa Tounes* and not for another party. And thirdly, the fact that Mehrzia Laabidi [member of parliament for the *Ennahda*] was appointed head of the women's commission in parliament.[28]

The women's rights record of the inclusive Islamo-conservative government coalition (of *Nidaa Tounes*, the *Ennahda*, the UPL and *Afek Tounes*), which has been transformed into a government of national unity since the summer of 2016 has – to date (early 2017) – been rather poor. So far, only one important law beneficial to Tunisian women has been adopted almost unanimously in parliament in November 2015 (HRW 2015). Presented by the Ministry of Women, Family and Children's Affairs and debated in parliament under the leadership of *Nidaa Tounes'* Bochra Belhadj Hmida, Tunisian women have been accorded the right to travel with their underage children without the father's permission. A new bill dealing with violence against women, which Tunisian women's associations strongly lobbied for, took a long time to be drafted by the government and has been pending in parliament since March 2016. Other important reforms, like a revision of the family code and its unequal inheritance laws, are less likely to see the light of day any time soon. During his speech for Women's Day on 13 August 2015, Essebsi made clear that these kinds of reforms were currently not a priority for Tunisia (Businessnews 2015).

Furthermore, since January 2016, *Nidaa Tounes* has fallen apart. A leadership crisis and subsequent resignations from *Nidaa Tounes* left the second-largest party, the *Ennahda,* suddenly with a plurality of parliamentary seats. After Béji Caïd Essebsi had to give up the party leadership when he became president of Tunisia, a struggle for supremacy broke out between Mohsen Marzouk, then party secretary of *Nidaa Tounes*, and Hafedh Caïd Essebsi, son of the president and then vice president of the party (Cherif 2015). Mohsen Marzouk eventually left *Nidaa Tounes* and launched a new party, *Mashrou' Tounes* (Tunisia's Project). Marzouk was quick to count on women to support and mobilise for his new project:

> I think that all women who support the modernist national project in Tunisia will be on the side of our new political party. I can confirm, without pretension from my side, that if it was true that one million women have voted for *Nidaa Tounes* during the previous parliamentary and presidential elections, those who will mobilise again in favour of our new political party will easily attain more than one million and a half.[29]

In general, the record and discourse about women's rights by *Nidaa Tounes* (and its offspring party *Mashrou' Tounes*) is fairly reminiscent of Tunisia's former authoritarian and top-down feminist project (Debuysere 2016b). While women have been and still are important actors of mobilisation for these secular parties, the political will and courage to ensure equal rights and to allow for women's participation in the highest ranks of the party is regularly missing.

Women's participation in the Popular Front

The Popular Front is a coalition of a number of leftist parties that was formed in October 2012 by Hamma Hammami in order to unite Tunisia's left and to break the two-party hold of the *Ennahda* and *Nidaa Tounes* on Tunisia's political scene. The Front came in fourth in the 2014 parliamentary elections, sending fifteen members to the ARP, among them two women. The Popular Front was, like most parties, heavily criticised for putting very few women as *tête de liste*.[30] In general, women figure marginally in the steering committees of most individual parties of the Front and the limited number of women who do play an important role are often the wives or sisters of the secretary generals of the different parties in the Front.[31] One of the two women who currently have a seat in the ARP, for example, is Mbarka Brahmi, widow of the former secretary general of *al-Watad*, Mohammed Brahmi, who was brutally killed in the summer of 2013. This poor record aside, there are two active women's sections operating within the Front: *Musawat* (Equality), which belongs to the Worker's Party and *al-Hurra* (the Free Woman) belonging to *al-Watad*.

Rooted in the Arab left, which is a mix of nationalism, Marxism, Leninism with some Maoist and some Albanian tendencies, many in the Popular Front believe that gender equality will automatically be achieved once socio-economic problems are settled.[32] The lack of women heading the Front's electoral lists is often quite apologetically explained:

The problem is that we look for the best results. And when a woman is not very well-known ... I do criticise the lack of women, but it is not something [the party] wants, it's not a decision of the party that women should not be presented, on the contrary.[33]

Mouna Mathari of the Modernist Democratic Pole (QOTB), a more progressive party within the Front, clarifies the situation more bluntly, however:

The culture of the Popular Front is to listen to the masses. If the popular mass is conservative, one must avoid rushing them. Unfortunately, most of the parties within the Front are not courageous enough to take up issues like equal rights or the defence of minorities or the abolition of the penal law clause on homosexuality.[34]

As a side note, the poor record on women's participation in (the workers' parties of) the left resembles their absence in Tunisia's major labour union, the UGTT, which is strongly supported by the Popular Front. As a member of the UGTT, Besma Sellami, illustrates it:

Women are not at all well represented in the UGTT, especially not at the higher levels. It's like a pyramid: at the lower levels there are women, but the more you go up it diminishes, until you reach the executive bureaus of the UGTT where there are no women. Zero![35]

Apart from the dominating current within the Front that pays (too) little attention to women's representation, there are some leftist parties that make equal gender representation a priority of their party. Within the Front, there is the QOTB, for example, which emphasises women's right to equal representation. QOTB's counterpart *al-Massar*, which although close to the Front is not a member party of it, also champions gender equality and is in fact the only Tunisian party that has a parity quota enshrined within its own party statute.[36] The problem with this second category of leftist parties, however, is that they tend to be elitist. This explains why *al-Massar* didn't manage to get even one member elected for the ARP:

They were eliminated. When you confront them with this, the former members of parliament [of *al-Massar*] tell you that the people didn't get their message. But it is not the people that didn't get it, it's them who didn't manage to make themselves understood.[37]

To sum up, while the left in Tunisia does not necessarily have an ideology contrary to women's rights or women's representation, most leftist parties in Tunisia seem either unwilling or unable to make a real difference when it comes to women's political representation.

Conclusion

Has the region of North Africa witnessed any gendered democracy paradox in terms of women's formal political participation since 2011? And what has been the importance of the ideology of the political parties in power in creating or preventing such paradoxes? This chapter found that only Egypt, when it initially embarked on a process of democratisation, faced a drop in its share of women in parliament. While an Islamist-led government was in power at that time in Egypt, similar Islamist governments in Morocco and Tunisia have not been responsible for causing similar gendered democracy paradoxes in their countries. In fact, an in-depth study of three major political parties in Tunisia found a cross-ideological lack of political will to entrust women with crucial positions within the political parties, refuting the hypothesis that only conservative or Islamist parties in the region bear responsibility for a lack of women's formal political representation.

As a matter of fact, political parties (whether progressive or conservative) may not be the most decisive actors for realising enhanced women's formal political participation in the region. Quantitative data show that there are today two ways in which levels of women's formal political participation are improved in the North African region. On the one hand, there are those countries, like el-Sisi's Egypt or Algeria, where an authoritarian regime decides to implement gender quotas in a top-down manner. On the other hand, in more 'democratic' countries like Tunisia and to a lesser extent Morocco, improved formal political inclusion of women has been realised through effective bottom-up activism and lobby work by women's associations and civil society more broadly. The important role of civil society in realising women's gains is not surprising given that women are, especially in Tunisia and Morocco, a lot more represented in civil society than in formal politics.

In short, the cautious progress that 'success story' Tunisia has made in terms of women's formal political inclusion – and thus in democratising (in a gender-equal way) – has been largely thanks to Tunisia's civil society, which pushed, for example, for legal candidate quotas on electoral lists. While the parity obligation has increased women's representation in parliament, there is still a long way to go to ensure women's equal representation within political parties. As one female Tunisian politician puts it:

We have been very much attacked by civil society when we drew up our electoral lists. They were right. Civil society needs to keep up the pressure on the parties. They should call out to the parties, expose them, shame them publicly. The matter of women's representation within parties shouldn't be left only to internal party politics to decide.[38]

Notes

1. Unfortunately, the index does not take into account any social and economic parameters. This is a shortcoming since, as we have asserted in the introduction to this chapter, a political democracy cannot exist without social equality. Nevertheless, the Democracy Index of the Economist Intelligence Unit is widely cited in academic journals as a good indicator of a country's level of democracy.
2. Monia Bouali, member of women's association *Tounissiet*, interview with the author, 18 June 2014.
3. Jinan Limam, professor of political sciences at the Faculty of Juridical, Social and Political Sciences of Tunis, interview with the author, 16 October 2014.
4. Najoua Makhlouf, head women's commission of the UGTT, interview with the author, 9 June 2014.
5. Fattoum Lassoued, former *Ennahda* member in the ANC, interview with the author, 29 April 2014.
6. Saida Ben Garrach, head women's commission of *Nidaa Tounes*, interview with the author, 14 October 2014.
7. Selma Mabrouk, former *al-Massar* member in the ANC, interview with the author, 15 October 2014.
8. Nejla Lamjid Bourial, former Democratic Alliance Member in the ANC, interview with the author, 7 April 2014.
9. Khawla Ben Aicha, ex-member of *Nidaa Tounes* and current MP for *al-Horra* (*Mashru' Tounes*), interview with the author, 25 February 2016.
10. Mouna Mathari, secretary and member of the QOTB and member of the *Front Populaire*, interview with the author, 22 February 2016.
11. Wassila Zoghlami, who's in charge of the Bureau of Women's Affairs, and Ferida Laabidi, in charge of the Office of Legal Affairs.
12. Sayida Ounissi, *Ennahda* member in the ARP, interview with the author, 25 February 2016.
13. Basma, member of the *Ennahda's Maktab al-Mar'a wa'l Usra* (Bureau of Women and the Family) in Ben Arous, interview with the author, 23 April 2014.
14. Mouna Mathari, secretary and member of the QOTB (Popular Front), interview with the author, 22 February 2016.
15. Hajer Azzaiez, former *Ennahda* member in the ANC, interview with the author, 30 October 2014. See also Debuysere (2016a).
16. Sayida Ounissi, *Ennahda* member of the ARP, interview with the author, 25 February 2016.

17. Monia Brahim, *Ennahdha* member of the ANC, interview with the author, 12 June 2014.
18. Sayida Ounissi, *Ennahda* member of the ARP, interview with the author, 25 February 2016.
19. Bochra Belhadj Hmida, feminist lawyer, interview with author, 10 June 2013.
20. Dalenda Largueche, professor and former president of the CREDIF, interview with the author, 28 October 2014.
21. Dalenda Largueche, professor and former president of the CREDIF, interview with the author, 28 October 2014.
22. Sayida Ounissi, *Ennahda* member of the ARP, interview with the author, 25 February 2016.
23. Thouraya Hammami Bekri, Vice President of the National Council of the *Ettakatol*, interview with the author, 21 October 2014.
24. This was somewhat rectified, however, when in March 2015 a new political bureau was elected, where gender parity was demanded and obtained. (Khawla Ben Aicha, ex-member of the *Nidaa Tounes* and current member of parliament for *al-Horra/Mashrou' Tounes*, interview with the author, 25 February 2016.)
25. Torkia Ben Khedher, vice president of LET, interview with the author, 20 October 2014.
26. Jinan Limam, professor of political sciences at the Faculty of Juridical, Social and Political Sciences of Tunis, interview with the author, 16 October 2014.
27. Bakhta Elcadhi Jmour, member of the bureau of the ATFD, interview with the author, 28 October 2014.
28. Khawla Ben Aicha, ex-member of *Nidaa Tounes* and current member of parliament for *al-Horra/Mashrou' Tounes*, interview with the author, 25 February 2016.
29. Mohsen Marzouk, speaking in an interview on Shems FM Radio on 13 January 2016. See also 'Mohsen Marzouk table sur le soutien des femmes tunisiennes', available at <http://kapitalis.com/tunisie/2016/01/13/mohsen-marzouk-table-sur-le-soutien-des-femmes-tunisiennes/> (last accessed 4 September 2017).
30. Amel Bouzaiene, member of the *Parti de Travailleurs* (Popular Front), interview with the author, 2 March 2016.
31. Mouna Mathari, secretary and member of the QOTB (Popular Front), interview with the author, 22 February 2016.
32. Mouna Mathari, secretary and member of the QOTB (Popular Front), interview with the author, 22 February 2016.
33. Amel Bouzaiene, member of the *Parti de Travailleurs* (Popular Front), interview with the author, 2 March 2016.
34. Mouna Mathari, secretary and member of the QOTB (Popular Front), interview with the author, 22 February 2016.
35. Basma Sellami, Secretary General of Higher Education of the labour union (UGTT), interview with author, 12 June 2014.
36. Selma Mabrouk, former *al-Massar* member of the ANC, interview with the author, 15 October 2014.
37. Mouna Mathari, secretary and member of the QOTB (Popular Front), interview with the author, 22 February 2016.
38. Mouna Mathari, secretary and member of the QOTB (Popular Front), interview with the author, 22 February 2016.

Bibliography

Aliriza, Fadil (2016), 'How Tunisia's Crooked Cops Are Undermining the Revolution', *Foreign Policy*, <http://foreignpolicy.com/2016/02/09/how-tunisias-crooked-cops-are-undermining-the-revolution/> (last accessed 1 September 2017).

Arab Women's Leadership Institute (2015), *Perception of Women's Political Leadership in Tunisia*, <http://www.iri.org/sites/default/files/wysiwyg/2015-04-22_awli_survey_of_tunisian_public_opinion_february_22-25_2015.pdf> (last accessed 14 September 2017).

Arat, Yesim (2010), 'Religion, Politics and Gender Equality in Turkey: Implications of a Democratic Paradox?', *Third World Quarterly* 31: 6, 869–84.

Bell, Christine, Colm Campbell and Fionnuala Ni Aolain (2004), 'Justice Discourses in Transition', *Social & Legal Studies* 13: 3, 305–28.

Ben Amar, Nihel (2016), 'Women's Political Participation in Tunisia', EUSpring, University of Warwick, <http://www2.warwick.ac.uk/fac/soc/pais/research/researchcentres/irs/euspring/euspring_policy_brief_on_womens_rights_in_tunisia.pdf> (last accessed 1 September 2017).

Borsali, Noura (2012), *Tunisie: Le défi égalitaire: Écrits feministes*, Tunis: Arabesques.

Cammisa, Ann Marie, and Beth Reingold (2004), 'Women in State Legislatures and State Legislative Research: Beyond Sameness and Difference', *State Politics & Policy Quarterly* 4: 2, 181–210.

Cavatorta, Francesco, and Fabio Merone (2013), 'Moderation through Exclusion? The Journey of the Tunisian Ennahda from Fundamentalist to Conservative Party', *Democratization* 20: 5, 857–75.

Chapman, Simon, et al. (2003), *The Middle East and North Africa 2003*, London: Europa Publications.

Cherif, Youssef (2015), 'The Leadership Crisis of Nidaa Tounes', Carnegie Endowment for International Peace, 8 December, <http://carnegieendowment.org/sada/?fa=62216> (last accessed 1 September 2017).

Darhour, Hanane, and Drude Dahlerup (2013), 'Sustainable Representation of Women through Gender Quotas: A Decade's Experience in Morocco', *Women's Studies International Forum* 41: 2, 132–42.

Debuysere, Loes (2016a), 'Tunisian Women at the Crossroads: Antagonism and Agonism between Secular and Islamist Women's Rights Movements in Tunisia', *Mediterranean Politics* 21: 2, 226–45.

Debuysere, Loes (2016b), '"La Femme" before and after the Tunisian Uprising: (Dis)continuities in the Configuration of Women in the Truth Regime of "Tunisianité"', *Middle East Law and Governance* 8: 2/3, 201–27.

Economist Intelligence Unit (EIU) (2015), *Democracy Index 2015: Democracy in an Age of Anxiety*, <https://www.eiu.com/public/topical_report.aspx?campaignid=DemocracyIndex2015> (last accessed 14 September 2017).

Elliott, Katja Žvan (2014), 'Morocco and Its Women's Rights Struggle: A Failure to Live Up to Its Progressive Image', *Journal of Middle East Women's Studies* 10: 2, 1–30.

Fallon, Kathleen, Liam Swiss and Jocelyn Viterna (2012), 'Resolving the Democracy Paradox: Democratization and Women's Legislative Representation in Developing Nations, 1975–2009', *American Sociological Review* 77: 3, 380–408.

Fouad, Ahmed (2015), 'Can Women, Copts Make It to Parliament without the Quota?', *Al-Monitor*, 20 November, <http://www.al-monitor.com/pulse/originals/2015/11/egypt-parliament-elections-quota-women-copts.html> (last accessed 1 September 2017).

Fraser, Nancy (1990), 'Rethinking the Public Sphere: A Contribution to the Critique of Actually Existing Democracy', *Social Text* 25/26, 56–80.

Fraser, Nancy (2013), *Fortunes of Feminism: From State-Managed Capitalism to Neoliberal Crisis*, London: Verso.

Human Rights Watch (HRW) (2015), 'Tunisie: Une avancée pour les droits des femmes', 13 November, <https://www.hrw.org/fr/news/2015/11/13/tunisie-une-avancee-pour-les-droits-des-femmes> (last accessed 1 September 2017).

International Institute for Democracy and Electoral Assistance (IDEA) (2015), 'Gender Quotas Database', <http://www.idea.int/data-tools/data/gender-quotas> (last accessed 14 September 2017).

Inter-Parliamentary Union (IPU) (2015), 'PARLINE Database on National Parliaments', <http://www.ipu.org/parline-e/parlinesearch.asp> (last accessed 14 September 2017).

Inter-Parliamentary Union (IPU) (2016), 'Tunisia', <http://www.ipu.org/parline-e/reports/2392_E.htm> (last accessed 1 September 2017).

Jomier, Augustin (2011), 'Secularism and State Feminism: Tunisia's Smoke and Mirrors', *Books & Ideas*, 29 November, <http://www.booksandideas.net/Secularism-and-State-Feminism.html> (last accessed 1 September 2017).

Jožanc, Nikolina (2011), 'Feminism and Democracy: Are There Women behind Women Representatives?', *Suvremene tem* 4: 1, 6–17.

Kunovich, Sheri, and Pamela Paxton (2005), 'Pathways to Power: The Role of Political Parties in Women's National Political Representation', *American Journal of Sociology* 111: 2, 505–52.

Marzouki, Nadia, and Hamza Meddeb (2015), 'Tunisia: Miracle or Mirage?', *Jadaliyya*, 11 June, <http://www.jadaliyya.com/pages/index/21863/tunisia_democratic-miracle-or-mirage> (last accessed 1 September 2017).

Mervis, Zungura, Eve Nyemba, Florence Mutasa and Caroline Muronza (2013), 'The Relationship between Democracy and Women Participation in Politics', *Journal of Public Administration and Governance* 3: 1, 168–76.

Mhadbi, Amira (2012), 'State Feminism in Tunisia: Reading between the Lines', *Open Democracy*, 7 November, <https://www.opendemocracy.net/5050/amira-mhadhbi/state-feminism-in-tunisia-reading-between-lines> (last accessed 1 September 2017).

Moghadam, Valentine (2011), 'Engendering Democracy: Women and the Mass Social Protests in the Middle East and North Africa', Nonviolent Initiative for Democracy, 24 March, <http://www.nidemocracy.org/en/publications/engendering-democracy-women-and-the-mass-social-protests-in-the-middle-east-and-north-africa/> (last accessed 1 September 2017).

Moghadam, Valentine (2014), 'Democratization and Women's Political Leadership in North Africa', *Journal of International Affairs* 68: 1, 59–78.

Pargeter, Allison (2010), 'Libya', in Sanja Kelly and Julia Breslin (eds), *Women's Rights in the Middle East and North Africa: Progress Amid Resistance*, New York: Freedom House, pp. 283–310.

Paxton, Pamela, Melanie Hughes and Matthew Painter (2010), 'Growth in Women's Political Representation: A Longitudinal Exploration of Democracy, Electoral System and Gender Quotas', *European Journal of Political Research* 49: 1, 25–52.

Pratt, Nicola (2015), 'Gendered Paradoxes of Egypt's Transition', *Open Democracy*, 2 February, <https://www.opendemocracy.net/5050/nicola-pratt/gendered-para-doxes-of-egypt%E2%80%99s-transition> (last accessed 1 September 2017).

Stepan, Alfred (2012), 'Tunisia's Transition and the Twin Tolerations', *Journal of Democracy* 23: 2, 89–103.

Tunisian Constitution (2014), Issued 27 January 2014, <http://www.wipo.int/wipolex/en/text.jsp?file_id=440322> (last accessed 13 September 2017).

Valbjørn, Morten (2015), 'Reflections on Self-Reflections: On Framing the Analytical Implications of the Arab Uprisings for the Study of Arab Politics', *Democratization* 22: 2, 218–38.

Viterna, Jocelyn, and Kathleen Fallon (2008), 'Democratization, Women's Movements, and Gender-Equitable States: A Framework for Comparison', *American Sociological Review* 73: 4, 668–89.

Waylen, Georgina (2007), *Engendering Transitions: Women's Mobilization, Institutions, and Gender Outcomes*, Oxford: Oxford University Press.

Wescot, Tom (2015), 'Libyan Women Vow to Push on for "Irreversible Empowerment"', *Middle East Eye*, 8 March, <http://www.middleeasteye.net/news/libyan-women-vow-recover-rights-1401691957#sthash.GinYf0Jy.dpuf> (last accessed 1 September 2017).

Young, Iris Marion (2000), *Inclusion and Democracy*, Oxford: Oxford University Press.

Zemni, Sami (2015), 'The Extraordinary Politics of the Tunisian Revolution: The Process of Constitution Making', *Mediterranean Politics* 20: 1, 1–17.

Chapter 14

Why did Tunisian and Egyptian youth activists fail to build competitive political parties?

Mohammad Yaghi

Defining democracy as 'a political system, which supplies regular constitutional opportunities for changing the governing officials', Lipset (2000: 48) identifies political parties as the most important institution for democratic survival and flourishing. Political parties aggregate the interests of the social groups they represent into relatively cohesive platforms, and articulate these interests by representing them in government (Aldrich 2011). They also 'act as a training ground for political leaders who will eventually assume a role in governing society' (Doherty 2001: 32). Finally, they provide stability to the political regime, endow it with legitimacy, assist the political integration of different regions and communities, and serve as a structure for the distribution of patronage (Randall 2007).

In processes of democratisation, political parties play three major roles. First, they reduce the level of uncertainty by negotiating an agreement that defines 'the rules of the political game' and governing the transition on issues such as who should be included in the political process, the role of the military, and the nature of institutions that will be created (O'Donnell et al. 2013: 6). Second, political parties involved in negotiating stabilise the democratic transition by channelling street politics into conventional institutionalised patterns (Linz and Stepan 1996). Third, the interaction between political parties contributes 'to the emergence of norms of tolerance and the institutionalization of democratic rights' (Lipset 2000: 48-9).

The success of the 2011 protests in Tunisia and Egypt opened the door for democratic transitions in both countries, with parties indeed taking the lead in negotiating the transition, although powerful actors such as the military in Egypt or the trade unions in Tunisia also played a significant role. However, the revolutionary youth groups (henceforth, RYGs) that initiated and sustained the protests failed to transform into a united political party that represented and advanced protestors' interests after the success of the uprisings. This failure occurred despite the fact that these RYGs came from outside the traditional opposition (Aarts and Cavatorta 2013; Korany and el-Mahdi 2012; Chomiak 2011) and that they overcame their social and ideological divisions during the protests (Shahine 2011; Sawaf 2013; el-Mahdi 2014). This chapter seeks to explain the reasons for this failure. It argues that in Egypt and Tunisia, youth groups suffered from structural and ideological problems that inhibited their prospects of forming unified political parties. Furthermore, youth activists in both countries inherited what can be called the youth's contempt of political parties, a tendency that exists among young generations even in well-established democracies (Sloam 2007; Syvertsen et al. 2011; Desrues 2012).

This chapter proceeds as follow. In the first section we theoretically justify the question: why did youth groups in Egypt and Tunisia fail to establish united political parties after their protests were successful? Then, in two subsequent sections (one on Egypt and the other on Tunisia), we illustrate the structural and ideological problems that prevented youth activists from forming unified parties after the protests' success. In the fourth section, I outline how the legacy of authoritarianism undermined political parties' importance among the youth. The chapter concludes by highlighting both the similarities and differences of the factors that contributed to the failure of youth activists to form united political parties.

The empirical data and the analysis provided in this chapter are based on the author's field research in Tunisia and Egypt during the period from March until late August 2012, and the month of June 2013 in Tunisia.

The question of youth parties

The question of why youth groups in Tunisia and Egypt failed to form unified political parties following the success of their uprisings needs to be justified. Social science orthodoxy holds that youth groups belong to different social classes and should not be treated as a distinct social group. As such, they do not constitute a distinct social or ideological cleavage that stimulates them to form a unified political party that can defend their interests. According to Bayat (2010), young people come from different social classes and vary in education level and socialisation, which shape their political orientations in different ways. Similarly, Bourdieu (1993: 95) argues that talking about young people as possessing common interests, and 'relating these interests to a biologically defined age, is in itself an obvious manipulation'.

Other scholars, however, argue that the existence of a unified culture for young people justifies treating them as a distinct social group with common interests. Young people are viewed from this perspective as constituting a distinct identity that expresses itself in a cultural medium called style, as manifested in youth clothing choice, musical tastes, communication with each other, use of technology, and recreation, which differentiates them from other social groups (Kjeldgaard and Askegaard 2006). According to this analysis, young groups constitute a global homogeneous social unit with a specific cultural identity (Valentine et al. 1998).

In contrast to this cultural approach, this chapter treats youth as 'an age cohort with a shared historical experience' (Neyzi 2001: 103). According to Mannheim (1983), just as a social class position can be defined as a common location in the economic and power structure of a given society, the unity of a generation is constituted by 'a similarity of location of a number of individuals within a social whole' (1983: 167). A generation in this sense is 'a particular type of social location' (Mannheim 1983: 168). In order for a generation to share the same location, Mannheim explains, 'one must be born within the same historical and cultural region' and 'exposed to the social and intellectual symptoms of the process of dynamic destabilization' (1983: 182–3). This nexus between age cohort and social change within the lifespan of the cohort is what shapes a generation's political consciousness. In this analysis, the fact that young people have a similar age 'does not in itself involve similarity of location'; what creates similarity in location is that they, the young people, must be 'exposed to the same phase of the collective process' and 'experience the same events and data' which 'impinge upon a similarly "stratified" consciousness' (Mannheim 1983: 176). This implies that each generation inherits 'definite modes of behavior, feeling, and thought' (Mannheim 1983: 169). To summarise, a generation, according to Mannheim, is described by the three locations: 'a shared temporal location (*i.e.* generational site or birth cohort), a shared historical location (*i.e.* generation as actuality – exposure to a common period or era), and a shared socio-cultural location (*i.e.* generational consciousness – or "entelechy")' (qtd in Gilleard and Higgs 2002: 373). It is the combination of these three locations that makes up a generation and that makes it possible to analyse youth as a social unit.

Applying Mannheim's definition of a generation to the youth groups in Egypt and Tunisia that overthrew Mubarak's and Ben Ali's regimes, we can see salient commonalities between them. First, this generation was born in the era of neo-liberal economic reforms that began in early 1980s. It witnessed the dismantling of state enterprises, cuts to social subsidies, the deterioration of public education and health, state corruption, and the increased role of the informal economy (Erdle 2010; Ismail 2006; Kaboub 2013; Singerman 2013). Second, unlike the previous generation, youth groups born in this era also suffered from the impoverishment of the middle class, which accompanied state reductions in public sector employment of university graduates (Bishara 2012). Third, this generation also experienced increasing police involvement in managing state affairs, including violation of basic human rights (Brooks 2013; Ismail 2012). Finally, and unlike older generations, the uprising cohort was exposed to, and inspired by, the democratic principles and ideals of good governance. In short, members of this generation shared temporal, historical and socio-cultural locations that enabled it to act as a distinct social group during the protests that ousted the Ben Ali and Mubarak regimes.

It makes sense then to ask why these youth groups failed to establish unified political parties after their successful protests in Tunisia and Egypt given their largely shared experiences and considerable commonalities. This question gains further pertinence knowing that the conditions for the emergence and success of new parties are more likely in transition countries for a number of reasons. First, low entry costs for new parties depend to a large extent on electoral institutions – how easy it is to register a party (political parties law) and how easy it is to win a seat (the type of election law) (Tavits 2008; Cox 1997). Both in Egypt and Tunisia, the interim governments eased the formation of new parties and the electoral laws saw the adoption of proportional representation as the main method of election. Second, critical junctures provide opportunities for restructuring the entire polity through the formation and competition of political parties (Shugart and Carey 1992). The uprisings of Tunisia and Egypt were such opportunities to restructure the two states. Third, the literature shows that new political parties are more likely to be formed when their chances to win seats in the legislature and the office of president are unknown for all contestants (Cox 1997; Kaminski 2002). In Tunisia and Egypt, respectively, the former ruling parties, the Constitutional Democratic Rally (RCD) and the National Democratic Party (NDP), were officially dissolved and the Islamists played little role in the uprisings, leaving space for new parties to compete in elections. This seemed to suggest that electoral competitions might not see the straightforward landslide for Islamists that had seemed to be on the cards. Many in Tunisia, for instance, were surprised at the electoral strength the *Ennahda* demonstrated in the 2011 elections, as Debuysere and Wolf indicate in their chapters in this volume. Fourth, the literature holds that new parties that raise new issues of significant concern to the public increase their electoral viability (Mayer and Perrineau 1992; Kitschelt 1988; Bell 1997). In Egypt and Tunisia, youth groups had managed to mobilise people against the two regimes because they raised salient issues that resonated with many ordinary citizens. These issues (jobs, dignity and bread) could have served as a lever for public support during the elections. Finally, in new democracies party identification is weak or non-existent (Carreras 2012; Manning 2005), which provides new parties further opportunities to win seats in the legislature. Except for the Muslim Brotherhood (MB) in Egypt and the *Ennahda* in Tunisia, which developed some degree of party identification during the era of authoritarianism, other extant traditional parties in the two countries did not enjoy high degrees of loyalty. As a result, most voters in Tunisia and Egypt did not identify themselves with any party.

Thus, the institutional conditions in Tunisia and Egypt were in theory conducive for youth groups to establish political parties that would represent their interest. This, however, was not the case. A study of the nature of the RYGs in terms of their level of organisation, cohesion, social class and leadership beliefs points to structural and ideological factors illustrating the reasons why this did not occur in practice. In turn, this failure is partly responsible for the absence of youth involvement in party politics more generally.

Egypt

Until the 1952 Free Officers military coup, Egypt had a multi-party system that emanated from the 1923 Constitution (Brown and Piro 1994). In 1953, the Free Officers dissolved existing parties, prevented the formation of new ones, and established a single party system (Blaydes 2010). A multi-party system under tutelage functioned, however, between 1976 and 2011. In 1976 President Sadat allowed the formation of three political parties that represented the right, left and centre of the Socialist Arab Union, then the ruling party (Abedrabou 2011). Furthermore, he introduced the political parties law in May 1977, paving the road for the formation of new parties. The law, however, prevented the establishment of political parties whose goals contradicted the government's general policies, parties whose goals were similar to existing ones, and parties that were founded on the basis of religion, ethnicity or region (Brown and Piro 1994). Despite the many constraints, twenty-four parties operated legally before the 2011 uprisings. However, the election law, the supervision of elections, and government practices ensured that the NDP, the ruling party, would win more than two-thirds of the People Assembly's seats in any election (Blaydes 2010).

Following the 2011 uprisings, the Supreme Council of the Armed Forces (SCAF) amended by decree the 1977 political parties law. The amendments granted a Judicial Committee the power to legalise the formation of new parties and to monitor their work. They also abolished the constraints on party formation that existed in the original law. Finally, they made it possible for a party to become legal within a month of applying for registration if the Judicial Committee did not reject it (Abdul'ati 2011). As a result, the number of political parties tripled; seventy-six parties, for example, sought seats in the Assembly in the 2011/12 elections (Abedrabou 2011). However, the RYGs that initiated the protests did not seek to create their own party. The reasons are explained below.

Structural factors

The structural factors of the RYGs can be divided into two categories: their weak organisational structure and the limited resources available to them. Beginning with the weak organisational structure, the RYGs that called for protests on 25 January 2011 were small in size, relatively new, with little to no political experience, and scattered over many independent organisations. Indeed, one of the main groups that called for the protests, We Are All Khalid Said (WRAKS) was merely a website managed by an anonymous activist. Furthermore, except for the Revolutionary Socialists (RS), which were active from early 2000, the other youth groups had been set up relatively recently. The April 6 Movement (A6M) appeared in the spring of 2008 to express solidarity with textile workers in El Mahala Alkubra, who were demonstrating for better wages and working conditions. However, the group operated secretly and its activists were subjected to constant repression that hindered its development into a mass-based movement (Tuhami 2013). The Youth for Justice and Freedom (YJF) is a leftist group that was formed a few months before the protests by activists that had left the RS. They believed that the RS focused more on political issues than on the social problems that mattered more to poor Egyptians.[1] These groups did not initiate the protests alone; they had the support of youth activists of other political organisations: the National Campaign for the Support of El-Baradei' (NCFSE);[2] a small group within the MB who defected from their mother organisation when it refused to join the protests on its first day;[3] and the *Karama* party (Nasserist, illegal), the Democratic Front Party (liberal, legal) and the Egyptian Social Democratic Party (centre-left, illegal). Independent individuals, mainly bloggers, supported their efforts.

Besides their small size, these groups did not have leaders sufficiently trained to lead the protests and they had weak ties with social strata beyond the middle class. Thus, when the protests started, these groups had no relative advantage to lead them or to expand their own organisations. This idea is well captured by the narrative of one of the activists in Alexandria, who explained the difficulties that faced them during the protests on the first day:

> once the demonstrators reached thousands of people we became confused as we did not have experience on how to lead huge demonstrations and how to coordinate between big protests in different places. [Our experience] was with small demonstrations inside the universities in which we knew each other by name. In the demonstrations of 25 January we did not know where to take the masses and how to connect the different demonstrations with each other. Also new independent activists appeared and began to direct the protests through their chanting slogans. We did not know who they were but they were doing a great job. Our main goal was to prevent clashes with the Central Security Forces. We succeeded in Hay Alrimal, but we failed everywhere else as we could not control the thousands of people who joined the protests.[4]

Furthermore, the members of the RYGs belonged to the middle class; for example, the social base of support of the A6M and YJF were mostly university students and professionals. However, because of the small numbers of the RYG, they chose to locate their protests in poor neigh-bourhoods in Cairo, Alexandria and the Suez. This strategy succeeded in bringing the poor into the protests but the short period of the protests (seventeen days in total) was not sufficient for middle-class activists to develop ties with the young poor who joined the protests. Moreover, the RYGs focused during this period on maintaining the sit-in in Tahrir Square; they did not seek to expand their membership.[5] Indeed, it was the traditional/conservative Islamist groups (the MB and the Salafis) who benefited most organisationally when poor people joined the protests; they already had a well-established organisational structure in these neighbourhoods. In Suez, Assiut and Alexandria, for example, the MB maintained a street presence during the Tahrir Square sit-in and formed popular committees to observe the prices of commodities during the protests; the Salafists likewise distributed bread to people in Alexandria.[6]

Moving on to the second main factor (the limited resources available), the most important resources that the youth groups lacked during the protests were leadership at the national level and funding. Recognised leaders at the national level serve as a magnetic force discouraging political fragmentation during protests. In the aftermath of a successful uprising, those leaders spearhead the negotiation of transition and become centres for the formation of mass-based political parties. Lech Wałęsa in Poland and Václav Havel in Czechoslovakia are cases in point. Egypt's uprisings did not have such leaders. As a result, tens of independent youth groups appeared during the protests that had no connection with the groups that initiated them. According to the Al-Ahram Center for Political and Strategic Studies, there were 180 youth groups by the end of the protests (Albuheiry n.d.); another source estimated their number to be 193 (Howeidy 2011).

The absence of leaders known at the national level for the RYGs should not be surprising given that state-owned media denied these groups access before and during the protests. At the same time, youth groups that relied on social media to spread their message did not focus on creating national figures from within their own ranks, partly because their priority was to oust the regime, and partly because they were afraid of state repression. Wa'el Ghonim, the administrator of the website of the group of WRAKS, for example, was known neither to the website's members nor to other youth groups (Ghonim 2012). Similarly, some figures of the 2011 uprising such as 'la Abdulfatah from the RS, Ahmed Maher from A6M, Khaled Sayed from YJF and Ahmed Duma from the Popular Current were better-known in the west than in Egypt.[7]

In addition to this sort of media blackout, two other factors prevented the RYGs from nurturing national figures. First, no group expected the protests to be successful; consequently, the leaders of these groups did not want to promote themselves out of fear of repression.[8] Second, the leaders of the RYGs believed that the protests gained momentum because of the decentralised nature of their leadership. They did not want to risk losing this momentum by advancing their leadership.[9]

The RYGs also did not possess sufficient financial resources after the protests to establish political parties. The limited resources the RYGs managed to accumulate during the protests were directed toward the maintenance of the sit-in at Tahrir Square. These were food, drinks and tents provided by neighbourhood committees in Cairo (Uleimi 2011); some wealthy Egyptians, such as Mamdouh Hamza, who had a close relationship to A6M (Mansour 2011); and the MB, which established two tents in Tahrir Square to distribute food.

Indeed, most of the businessmen who funded the protesters, such as Hamza, joined Naguib Sawiris, the Egyptian billionaire, in establishing the Free Egyptians Party in order to compete in the 2011/12 legislative elections. According to one activist, the lack of funds was the main reason he joined Egypt's Democratic Social Party. With the 'party's abundant resources', he said, 'I would have more opportunities to spread my ideas and enhance my political career'.[10]

The army's divide and rule strategy

The SCAF saw a significant threat in the RYGs because they sought substantial changes in Egypt's political system, including the dissolution of the NDP; the conviction of former officials; the dissolution of the State Security Investigations Service (SSIS); and a new constitution that would institutionalise social, civil and political rights. Furthermore, they demanded to replace the SCAF as an interim government with a civilian one (CYR 2011a). The SCAF, which sought to limit changes to the presidency after the uprising, considered these demands a threat to its own interests.

In order to delegitimise the RYGs, the SCAF claimed that the Egyptian youths had no true coalition to represent them and that therefore the demands of the RYGs did not reflect the actual opinions of young Egyptians.[11] To this end, the SCAF asked youth groups to discuss their demands in a proposed 1 June 2011 meeting. One thousand activists attended, collectively claiming to represent one hundred youth movements (CYR 2011b). The meeting was poorly run and was intended to question the legitimacy of the RYGs that were organising protests in Egypt against the SCAF. However, Egypt's security apparatus might itself have formed many of these groups. According to Abu Al'ula Madi, the secretary general of the *Wasat* party, President Mohamed Morsi, the first elected president, informed him that the state security apparatus controlled 300,000 thugs during Mubarak's regime, 80,000 of whom were living in Cairo (Almasry Alyoum 2013). In short, the SCAF's policies disempowered the RYGs.

Ideological and personal rivalries

The youth groups originally involved in the protests agreed on pursuing regime change, holding elections to choose national leaders, and limiting the role of the military in managing state affairs. However, these groups possessed different ideologies ranging from conservatism (constraining individual liberties in accordance with the society's Islamic culture) to liberalism. The most institutional innovation of the RYGs that had a chance to turn into a political party was the Coalition of the Youth of the Revolution (CYR), which was formulated during the Tahrir Square sit-in in order to maintain the protests until the fall of Mubarak. The CYR was composed of fourteen activists: two for each of the five movements that coordinated the events of 25 January, including the A6M, the YJF, the NCFSE, the youth of the Democratic Front Party (DFP) and defectors from the MB; and four others who were independents and bloggers (CYR 2011a). The platform of A6M reflects social democratic values; they emphasise both liberal democracy and social justice. The YJF is a Marxist group that considers fighting neo-liberalism and implementing social justice its top priority. The NCFSE was a liberal group whose main concern was political freedom and building democratic institutions; it downplayed the importance of social justice. The defectors of the MB shared with their original organisation some of its ideological beliefs such as the inclusion of Islamic sharia as the basis for legislation in Egypt's new constitution. The DFP supports a free economy and, like the NCFSE, downplays social justice.

The ideological differences between these groups contributed to their disagreements during the Tahrir Square sit-in and following Mubarak's resignation. During the sit-in, the representative of the NCFSE in the CYR engaged in the negotiation the regime called for on 5 February 2011. This incited colleagues to issue independent statements separating themselves from these negotiations (A6M 2011). Following Mubarak's resignation, these groups could not agree on an approach to the interim period. The defector youth of the MB were closer to the position of their original organisation; they preferred to follow the SCAF's road map. For its part, the NCFSC favoured postponing the people's assembly elections so that more time could be given to the establishment of new political parties. The A6M and the YFJ considered ousting Mubarak as the start of the revolution, which would only end if the regime met a number of demands, including turning the SCAF's power over to a presidential civilian council. The RS called for the continuation of the revolution until the revolutionary groups took power. In fact, the A6M, the YFJ and the RS assigned little weight to the legislative elections, arguing that they would not fare well in them due to their lack of mass-based organisations.[12]

Furthermore, after ousting Mubarak, the RYGs witnessed what can be called the rise of egotism among their leaders. Some of the activists interviewed pointed to the effects of media coverage on the rise of this feeling; they said the media played a game of 'pick and choose' among the youth leaders and that those who were not picked focused on divisive issues to attract media attention. At the same time, the youth leaders who did receive attention from the media no longer felt the need to deliberate with their counterparts from other youth groups on issues related to the transition period. Because they had become public figures, they could disseminate their messages through the media or discuss them directly with the SCAF.[13]

These ideological and personal differences encouraged some members of the CYR, such as Ziad Elalami, Sali Toma, Islam Lutfi and Mustafa Najar, to form their own parties or to join existing ones. Elalami and Toma joined the Social Democratic Party. Lutfi formed Egypt's Current Party and joined a coalition of six parties under the name of the Revolution Continues in the 2011/12 legislative elections, and Najar established the Justice Party. In the elections, these parties fared very badly; they won only 7 seats out of 498.[14] The A6M, the YJF and the RS remained focused on street activism in order to force the SCAF to turn over power to a civilian council; however, they left to their members the choice of whether to vote in the elections.

In sum, the youth activists in Egypt failed to establish a unified political party because they lacked leadership at the national level, experience and financial resources. In addition to that, they had different ideological beliefs and suffered from the SCAF's policies aimed at stripping them of political legitimacy.

Tunisia

Upon independence in 1956, Tunisia had a multi-party system (Angrist 2011). In 1964, President Habib Bouguiba banned political parties; however, they flourished illegally during most of his era (Teimomi 2008). In the early 1980s, Bourguiba opened the political system slightly and granted legality to the Communist Party (CP), Democratic Socialist Movement (DSM) and Popular Unity Party (PUP) (Bishara 2012).

Upon coming to power in 1987, President Zine El Abidine Ben Ali announced his desire to foster a multi-party system and build democratic institutions (Haamdi 2011). In 1988, he called for all parties to sign *Almithaq Alwatani* (the National Charter), a document intended by the regime to restore political pluralism (Almana'i 2011). The Progressive Democratic Party (PDP), the *Ettajdid* movement and the Islamic *Ennahda* signed the charter, but the latter was denied legal status. The political parties law of 1988, however, constrained the formation of new parties in two ways: it granted the interior minister an absolute right to accept or refuse their registration within four months; and it prevented the formation of parties that had similar goals (Bishara 2012).

On the eve of the 2011 uprising, the political parties that existed during Ben Ali's era could be divided into three categories: loyalist parties including the RCD (the ruling party), the DSM, the PUP, the Liberal Social Party and the Green Party; legal opposition parties, which included the PDP, the Democratic Forum of Work and Liberties (*Ettakatol*) and the *Ettajdid* movement; and finally, the illegal parties, which were composed of the POCT, the *Ennahda* and the Congress for the Republic (CPR), in addition to several Marxist and pan-Arabist groups (Storm 2013a, 2013b).

Following the success of the Tunisian uprisings, often referred to as the Jasmine Revolution, the interim government that replaced Ben Ali established a new political parties law that made the formation of new parties easier, constrained state intervention in their work, and imposed regulations to ensure free competition in elections. The new parties law reduced the period of party registration from four to two months, and the minimum legal age of party membership from eighteen to sixteen years. Finally, the law banned parties from providing material support to citizens, especially at election times (Tayyashi 2011). With the implementation of this law, political parties flourished in Tunisia. In October 2014, 120 parties and tens of coalitions competed for the Tunisian parliament's 217 seats (ISIE 2014). Despite the increase in the number of parties, Tunisian youth groups that initiated the protests did not establish their own party to defend their interests. The reasons for this are both structural and ideological, as explained below.

Structural factors

Most of the new youth groups that initiated the protests were small in size and none emerged as a leading group that could unite youth activists in a single political party. Furthermore, like Egypt, these groups did not have recognised leaders at the national level and lacked financial resources.

The protests in Sidi Bouzid began when activists from different youth groups and independents gathered, with the victim's family, in front of the local governorate building to protest the conditions that had led Mohamed Bouazizi to self-immolate.[15] These activists, who knew each other from past activism, came mainly from the PDP, the POCT, pan-Arabist groups and independents.[16] To maintain the peaceful nature of the protests and in order to keep them organised under a single leadership, the activists established what they called the 'Sidi Bouzid Committee for Citizenry and the Defense of the Victims of Marginalization' (Haamdi 2011). The Committee, however, became irrelevant as a leadership body when the protests spilled over to other towns in the Sidi Bouzid governorate. Though the protest initiators in the new locations knew the activists in Sidi Bouzid, they organised the protests on their own because their towns were facing the same socio-economic conditions of marginalisation.[17] With no coordinating body to lead the protests at the national level, the youth groups remained fragmented during them.

Youth fragmentation is also related to the types of youth groups that joined the protests. Here, it is important to distinguish between the youth branches of existing political parties such as those affiliated with the *Ennahda*, the PDP and the POCT, on the one hand, and the new youth groups that emerged during the protests such as the *Karama* (dignity) Youth Movement, the New Generation Youth Movement (NGYM), the Coalition for the Youth of the Revolution (CYR) and the Free Tunisian Forces (FTF), on the other hand. The former groups did not deem it necessary to establish a unified youth party after the protests' success; they maintained their political identity during and after the protests and worked to advance the goals of their own political organisations. The latter groups were composed of new actors who lacked organisational structure, recognised national leaders and financial resources.

Unlike in Egypt, the new youth activists in Tunisia who engaged in the protests from their beginning formed their movements' organisations after the end of the protests. For example, the *Karama* officially formed in February 2011 in order 'to organize the youth', 'express their demands' and 'protect the revolution'; the youth groups the *Karama* aimed to organise were 'the unemployed, the university students, and the workers' (Karama n.d.). The NGYM established formally in April 2011 as 'a framework for struggle, a thinking forum, and a program for change'; its roots, according to its documents, go back to 2009 when some of its current activists offered a 'novel analysis of the crisis of the Tunisian student movement' (NGYM n.d.). Like the *Karama*, the members of the NGYM relied on a network of friendship ties that existed at the universities.[18] The CYR was formed in April 2011 with a view to 'dismantle the dictatorship and the corrupt system', 'promote equal distribution of wealth between regions and citizens' and 'fight the privatization of education' (Als'edani 2012: 89). The FTF, not purely a youth movement, issued its first statement on 16 January 2011. It defined itself as 'a group of activists who have progressive and revolutionary positions' and is composed of elderly and youth activists who 'joined January 14th revolution'; its main goals are to 'spread the notions of good governance and direct democracy' (Als'edani 2012: 92–3).

These new youth groups had local leaders who were known in their communities but unknown at the national level. The short duration of the protests and the lack of media coverage of their activities during the protests prevented these leaders from gaining national profiles. Additionally, none of these groups had funds to spend on establishing political parties. Politics for those local leaders came after their daily jobs, which left them little time to establish or sustain political organisations.[19] Finally, the social base of support of these groups was mainly in the interior regions. As such, these groups' priority remained ending the social marginalisation of their regions. As we shall see below, this factor affected the way these groups perceived their mission after the success of the uprising.

Ideological rifts

Disagreement amongst middle-class activists about what constituted a solution to ordinary Tunisians' grievances also curtailed the possibility of establishing unity among youth groups. While all the youth groups agreed on their diagnosis of the problems driving the protests, namely, economic marginalisation, unemployment, corruption and absence of political freedom, they disagreed on how to fix these problems. During the protests, the youth groups that belonged to organised political opposition pressed the demands of their mother organisations. For example, youth groups that belonged to the PDP demanded more political freedom and a political system that would respect alternations of power (Jribi 2010), while the newly emerged youth groups focused on social justice (see below).

Following the fall of Ben Ali, the ideological rift between youth groups prevailed. We can differentiate between four camps at this juncture, each of which made certain distinct demands. The first camp was a coalition composed of the *Ennahda*, the CPR and the *Ettakatol*. This camp rejected Mohamed Ghannouchi's interim government and sought to replace it with a national unity government drawn from outside the old regime. The second camp was the Front of 14 January. Formed on 21 January 2011, this coalition included the POCT and seven additional radical leftist and pan-Arabist groups. Its platform included, *inter alia*, deposing the Ghannouchi government, dissolving the institutions of the old regime, and solving the country's social and economic crisis by nationalising companies the old regime had privatised (Hewar Mutamaden 2011). The third camp was that of the legal opposition. The PDP and the *Ettajdid* movement joined the interim government of Ghannouchi. According to Issam Chebbi, PDP secretary general at the time, the revolution achieved its goal by ousting Ben Ali, and the country was trapped between military rule and state collapse. To avoid either possibility, he said, his party agreed to join the government in order to keep the state functioning.[20]

The last camp was that of the new youth groups. These groups remained focused on the revolution's main social goals. The *Karama* and the NGYM, for example, called for the constitutional formalisation of the revolution's demands before any election took place. According to Elamine, the leader of the *Karama*, '[those] who have not (the poor people) lack sufficient resources to compete in the elections with those who have everything and embrace free-market policies'.[21] In order to protect their rights, 'the constitution should be written first to guarantee the interests of poor Tunisians because they do not have a chance to achieve their demands through the elections'.[22] In the absence of this condition, he claimed, elections were merely a mechanism for 'changing the guardians of the same polices of neoliberal economics'.[23] What would lead to social justice, according to the *Karama* and the FTF, was not an election, but the continuation of the revolution until the demands of the marginalised are achieved.[24]

Despite the fact that the new youth groups shared three common attributes (disdain for the traditional political opposition, belief in social justice, and a conviction that horizontal networking was a means of organising), these groups remained ideologically divided. The *Karama*'s leaders, for example, were originally progressive pan-Arabists, while the NGYM's leaders were more inclined toward Marxist ideals. Like their counterparts in Egypt, these groups did not participate in the parliamentary elections held in 2011. This had changed by the time the 2014 elections arrived. Although they did not compete in the elections, members of the NGYM cast their votes for the candidates of Popular Front, while members of the *Karama* movement backed the election of Moncef Marzouki for presidency, the first Tunisian president after the uprisings. This was a departure from their initial positions (that is, boycotting the elections), but it was also an indication of the ideological differences that kept the youth groups divided.

It is fair to say, however, from the interviews with the leaders of these groups, and from following these up with an examination of their Facebook pages, that they remained focused on extra-institutional activism, especially in the interior regions where their social base existed. According to the Tunisian Forum for Social and Economic Rights,

Tunisia witnessed 1,095 collective protests in November 2016, 31 per cent of them in Sidi Bouzid, Kasserine, Gafsa and Kairouan in the interior regions. The protesters raised socio-economic demands and the protests included sit-ins, preventing officials from leaving their offices, hunger strikes, and violent and peaceful demonstrations, among other things (FTDES 2016).

In short, like their counterparts in Egypt, the Tunisian youth activists suffered from similar problems, especially the lack of well-known leaders at the national level, funds and ideological cleavages. However, unlike Egypt's activists, the new youth groups that appeared during the protests in Tunisia were more committed to non-institutional activism in seeking their social revolutionary goals.

The legacy of competitive authoritarianism

Besides the structural and ideological factors that prevented the youth groups from establishing united parties in Egypt and Tunisia, there is also a clear contempt for political parties among the youth. For example, in Egypt's 2015 legislative elections, the percentage of youth between the ages of eighteen and thirty registered to vote was 36 per cent, but only 19 per cent of those registered participated in the elections (Husni 2015). In Tunisia, although the same age cohort makes up 30 per cent of the entire population, only 20 per cent registered for the 2014 parliamentary elections (Rajhi 2016) and only 11 per cent of those registered participated in the elections, compared with 17 per cent in 2011 (Barakat 2015).

Not only was youth participation in the elections weak, but youth made up only a very small percentage of the existing political parties' membership. According to the Tunisian ministry of youth and sport, only 2.7 per cent of youth between the ages of eighteen and forty are members of political parties, though they constitute 40 per cent of the population (Rajhi 2016). Reports attribute the lack of youth participation in the elections to low youth representation in the political parties' leadership and the marginalisation of youth in state institutions (Barakat 2015), the political parties' failure to provide solutions to youth problems and the failure of the uprising to achieve its goals (Deutsche Welle 2014), and to the disappointment of the performance of political parties (Rajhi 2016). These insights might be true but they are missing the impact of the legacy of authoritarianism on the youth populations of the two countries.

According to some youth activists, the young hold political parties in contempt because of their experiences with them during the period of authoritarianism. First, members of parties and parliament under authoritarianism were not perceived as policy-makers, but rather as politicians who legitimated incumbents in return for personal benefits.[25] Second, the legal opposition's political parties were perceived as the personal investment of some elites intending to gain access to state resources, rather than as political parties that defended the interests of the social class they claimed to represent. The elites that rallied youth support in their opposition to the old regime, and had their parties legitimised, did so not because they wanted to defend the ideals of their party, but because they wanted to acquire personal bargaining leverage that could induce the regime to co-opt them. Many youth activists who were subjected to state repression (jail, torture, or bans from travelling or working at state institutions), felt used by those elites, and consequently stopped trusting political parties. This distrust was deepened when many youth activists felt, for the second time, that they 'were used as a tool to achieve the elderly leaders' hidden goals', such as gaining an appointment as ministers or employment in the presidential office after the uprisings, instead of advancing their parties' goals.[26] Finally, many of the activists who joined political parties after the uprisings believe that 'it is not fair that some of the decisions which they do not approve should be implemented just because the old guys [the parties leader] decided to vote for it'.[27] This simply reminds them of the illegal opposition's politics during their underground activism under authoritarianism, when activists had to implement decisions taken on their behalf by party leaders without any input from their side. In this sense 'the young were used for mobilization only, without access to the party's decision-making'.[28]

The inherited negative ideas about political parties from the period of authoritarianism did not change after the uprisings because the new parties did not establish new practices to convey to the youth population a different experience. In fact, as the authoritarian regime in Egypt, following the military coup, managed to co-opt many of the leaders of the political opposition, distrust of political parties deepened.

Conclusion

This chapter has shown that the revolutionary youth groups (RYGs) in Egypt and Tunisia that initiated and sustained the protests of 2011 suffered from similar structural and ideological problems. These problems prevented them from forming unified political parties that could further their interests. The structural factors were mainly related to a high level of fragmentation of the youth groups due the absence of unified leadership during the two uprisings, lack of leaders at the national level and lack of funds. Ideologically, the youth activists held diverse worldviews and different priorities.

In Egypt, however, the RYGs were subjected to manipulation by the SCAF that aimed to keep them fragmented and weaken their representation among young sectors of the population. Furthermore, because these groups had small organisations and their activists had little political experience, they failed to organise the broader poor youth population that joined the protests, which ultimately contributed to their further fragmentation. Unlike in Egypt, the RYGs in Tunisia did not suffer pressure from external forces; however, their geographical concentration in the interior regions forced them to focus on ending the social marginalisation of their regions. As such, they remained committed to extra-legal activism as a means to bring about social justice.

Finally, the structural and ideological factors that prevented youth activists from forming unified political parties should be combined with the impact of the legacy of authoritarianism on the youth population in the two countries. The youth in general are contemptuous of political parties; they perceive them as political organisations that advance the personal interests of leaders rather than representing the interests of social groups. This negative attitude towards political parties prevents the youth from participating in the political processes.

Notes

1. Personal communication with Mohammed Nagy, activist in the YJF, Cairo, 25 June 2012.
2. The NCFSE was established in March 2010 following the return of Mohamed el-Baradei', the former Director General of the International Atomic Energy Agency, to Egypt.
3. Personal communication with three defected MB members, Alexandria, 2 July 2012.
4. Personal communication with activist, Alexandria, 2 July 2012.

5. Personal communication with activists from the A6M, the YJF and the RS, Cairo, June and July 2012.
6. Personal communication with activists in the Suez, Assiut and Alexandria, June and July 2012.
7. Those four youth group leaders were arrested and sentenced to three to five years in prison following the July 2013 military coup because of their refusal to submit to military rule (BBC 2015).
8. Personal communication with Mustafa Maher from the A6M, Cairo, 22 July 2012.
9. Personal communication with Ahmed Samir, Alexandria, 13 July 2012.
10. Personal communication with Ahmed, Cairo, 2 June 2012.
11. Personal communication with several activists, June and July 2012.
12. Personal communication with twelve activists from the A6M, the YFJ and the RS, Cairo, June and July 2012.
13. Personal communication with seven activists, Cairo and Alexandria, June and July 2012.
14. The Islamists won 73 per cent of the seats, the liberals 15 per cent and 12 per cent went to the remaining parties.
15. Personal communication with Oueiniah, Sidi Bouzid, 8 May 2012.
16. Personal communication with Elamine, Sidi Bouzid, 8 May 2012.
17. Personal communication with Jasser and Ayman, Manzel Bouzayenn, 9 May 2012.
18. Personal communication with Sghiri, Tunisia, 29 April 2012.
19. Personal communication with eight activists from the *Karama* and the NGYM, April and May 2012.
20. Personal communication, Tunis, 4 May 2012.
21. Personal communication with Elamine, Tunis, 5 June 2013.
22. Personal communication with Elamine, Tunis, 5 June 2013.
23. Personal communication with Elamine, Tunis, 5 June 2013.
24. Personal communication with Aljelassi and Daas, respectively, Tunis, 7 and 8 June 2013.
25. Elamine, Facebook message exchange, 2 October 2016.
26. Ahmed Elenany, Facebook message exchange, 18 September 2016.
27. Ahmed Elenany, Facebook message exchange, 18 September 2016.
28. Elamine, Facebook message exchange, 2 October 2016.

Bibliography

A6M (2011), 'About the Youth Demands and a Rejection for Any Negotiations before Mubarak's Departure' (24 February), in Omar H. Rabe' (ed.), *The Documents of 100 Days of the January Revolution*, Cairo: Al-Ahram Center for Political and Strategic Studies.

Aarts, Paul, and Francesco Cavatorta (2013), *Civil Society in Syria and Iran: Activism in Authoritarian Contexts*, Boulder, CO: Lynne Rienner.

Abdel-Malek, Anouar (1968), *Egypt: Military Society*, New York: Random House.

Abdul'ati, Mohammed (2011), 'Egypt's Election Blocs: The Scene after the Revolution', *Aljazeera Studies Center*, 17 December, <http://studies.aljazeera.net/ar/reports/20 11/12/2011121712482610615.html> (last accessed 1 September 2017).

Abdulmawla, Izeldine (2013), 'The Tunisian Experience in Democratic Transition', *Aljazeera*, 14 February, <http://studies.aljazeera.net/ar/files/arabworlddemocracy/2013/02/201324101039595777.html> (last accessed 1 September 2017).

Abedrabou, Ahmed (2011), 'Egypt's Political Parties and the Parliamentarian Elections 2011/2012', Doha: Arab Center for Research and Policy Studies, 29 November, <http://www.dohainstitute.org/release/e7a331ed-4f67-485b-8d72-5fde1828a653> (last accessed 1 September 2017).

Abedrabou, Ahmed (2012), 'Parties Pluralism in Egypt and January 25 Revolution', in *Egypt's Revolution: Motives, Directions, and Challenges*, Doha: Arab Center for Research and Policy Studies, pp. 183–217.

Albuheiry, Ahmed (n.d.), 'Coalition of the Youth of the Revolution: The Structural Crisis and the Inevitability of Dissolution', Al-Ahram Center for Political and Strategic Studies, <http://acpss.ahramdigital.org.eg/News.aspx?Serial=97> (last accessed 24 July 2014).

Aldrich, John Herbert (2011), *Why Parties?: A Second Look*, Chicago: University of Chicago Press.

Almana'i, Mohammed (2011), 'The Tunisian Communist Party: A Historical Background', *Rational Thinking*, 27 February, <http://manai.over-blog.com/article-68213201.html> (last accessed 1 September 2017).

Almasry Alyoum (2013), 'Madi: Morsi Told Me the Intelligence Established Organization of 300 Thousand Thugs', *Almasry Alyoum*, 26 March, <http://www.almasryalyoum.com/news/details/298281> (last accessed 1 September 2017).

Als'edani, Munir (2012), *The Youth in Tunisia's Democratic Transition*, Sfax: Mohamed Ali House for Publication.

Alshama, Mohamed (2011), *The Days of Freedom in Tahrir Square: 18 Days Changed the Face of Egypt*, Cairo: Shams or Publishing and Distribution.

Angrist, Michele Penner (2011), *Party Building in the Modern Middle East*, Seattle: University of Washington Press.

Appadurai, Arjun (1990), 'Disjuncture and Difference in the Global Economy', in Mike Featherstone (ed.), *Global Culture: Nationalism, Globalization, and Modernity*, London: Sage, pp. 295–310.

As'ad, Ramez Jamal (n.d.), 'The Impact of Political Parties on Democratic Transition in Egypt (2013–2015)', Democratic Arabic Center for Strategic, Political, and Economic Studies, <http://democraticac.de/?p=1231> (last accessed 1 September 2017).

Barakat, Nisma (2015), 'Tunisia's Youth: Lack of Political Participation Due to Old Generation', *The New Arab*, 13 January, <https://www.alaraby.co.uk> (last accessed 15 June 2016).

Bayat, Asef (2010), *Life as Politics: How Ordinary People Change the Middle East*, Amsterdam: Amsterdam University Press.

BBC (2015), 'Alaa Abdel Fattah: Egypt Jails Activist-Blogger for Five Years', BBC News, 23 February, <http://www.bbc.co.uk/news/world-middle-east-31583404> (last accessed 1 September 2017).

Bell, Janice (1997), 'Unemployment Matters: Voting Patterns during the Economic Transition in Poland, 1990–1995', *Europe-Asia Studies* 49: 7, 1263–91.

Bhnhus, Ahmed (2014), 'Egypt's Political Parties between Numbers and Capabilities', Vetogate, 30 August, <http://www.vetogate.com/1193937> (last accessed 20 June 2016).

Bishara, Azmi (2012), *The Glorious Tunisian Revolution* [in Arabic], Doha: Arabic Center for Research and Policy Studies.

Blaydes, Lisa (2010), *Elections and Distributive Politics in Mubarak's Egypt*, Cambridge: Cambridge University Press.

Bourdieu, Pierre (1993), *Sociology in Question*, London: Sage.

Brooks, Risa (2013), 'Abandoned at the Palace: Why the Tunisian Military Defected from the Ben Ali Regime in January 2011', *Journal of Strategic Studies* 36: 2, 205–20.

Brown, Nathan, and Timothy Piro (1994), 'Egypt', in Frank Tachau (ed.), *Political Parties of the Middle East and North Africa*, Westport, CT: Greenwood Press, pp. 93–132.

Buqarah, Abdul Jalil (1993), *From the History of the Tunisian Left: Perspective Movement (1963–1975)* [in Arabic], Tunis: Sras House for Publication.

Carreras, Miguel (2012), 'Party Systems in Latin America after the Third Wave: A Critical Re-assessment', *Journal of Politics in Latin America* 4: 1, 135–53.

Cavatorta, Francesco, and Fabio Merone (2013), 'Moderation through Exclusion? The Journey of the Tunisian Ennahda from Fundamentalist to Conservative Party', *Democratization* 20: 5, 857–75.

Chomiak, Laryssa (2011), 'The Making of a Revolution in Tunisia', *Middle East Law and Governance* 3: 1/2, 68–83.

Coalition of the Youth of the Revolution (CYR) (2011a), 'A Political Paper', in Omar H. Rabe' (ed.), *The Documents of 100 Days of the January Revolution*, Cairo: Al-Ahram Center for Political and Strategic Studies.

Coalition of the Youth of the Revolution (CYR) (2011b), 'A Statement to SCAF', Facebook, <https://www.facebook.com/Revolution.coalition/notes> (last accessed 1 September 2017).

Coalition of the Youth of the Revolution (CYR) (2011c), 'Statement of the Coalition of the Youth of the Revolution', in Omar H. Rabe' (ed.), *The Documents of 100 Days of the January Revolution*, Cairo: Al-Ahram Center for Political and Strategic Studies.

Cox, Gary (1997), *Making Votes Count: Strategic Coordination in the World's Electoral Systems*, Cambridge: Cambridge University Press.

Desrues, Thierry (2012), 'Moroccan Youth and the Forming of a New Generation: Social Change, Collective Action and Political Activism', *Mediterranean Politics* 17: 1, 23–40.

Deutsche Welle (2014), 'Tunisian's Youth Turn Their Back to the Elections', *Deutsche Welle*, 14 August, <http://www.dw.com/ar/> (last accessed 1 September 2017).

Doherty, Ivan (2001), 'Democracy Out of Balance', *Policy Review* 106, 25–35.

el-Ghobashy, Mona (2011), 'The Praxis of the Egyptian Revolution', *Middle East Report* 41: 258, 2–13.

Elhanashi, Abdulatif (2014), 'The Tunisian 2014 Legislative Elections: A Reading in the Results and Their Implications', Arab Center for Research and Policy Studies, 7 November, <http://www.dohainstitute.org/release/9ed6a2a4-ff9f-4b3e-a020-f0965e83feab> (last accessed 1 September 2017).

el-Mahdi, Rabab (2014), 'Egypt: A Decade of Ruptures', in Lina Khatib and Ellen Lust (eds), *Taking to the Streets: The Transformation of Arab Activism*, Baltimore: Johns Hopkins University Press, pp. 52–75.

Erdle, Steffen (2010), *Ben Ali's 'New Tunisia' (1987–2009): A Case Study of Authoritarian Modernization in the Arab World*, Berlin: Klaus Schwarz.

Forum Tunisien pour les Droits Économiques et Sociaux (FTDES) (2016), 'Report on November 2016 Social Protests', Tunisian Forum for Social and Economic Rights, 26 December, <https://ftdes.net/rapports/novembre2016.fr.pdf> (last accessed 1 September 2017).

Ghonim, Wa'el (2012), *Revolution 2.0: If the People One Day Wanted Life*, Cairo: AlShorouk Publisher.

Gilleard, Chris, and Paul Higgs (2002), 'The Third Age: Class, Cohort or Generation?', *Ageing and Society* 22: 3, 369–82.

Haamdi, Bashir (2011), *The Right for Authority and Wealth and Democracy: A Study in the Track of the Revolution of Freedom and Dignity*, Sidi Bouzid: Dunia Barnt.

Hewar Mutamaden (2011), 'Foundational Statement of the Front of 14 January', *Hewar Mutamaden*, 22 January, <http://www.ahewar.org/DEBAT/show.art. asp?t=0&userID=232&aid=242688> (last accessed 1 September 2017).

Howeidy, Fahmi (2011), 'The Coalition Is a Necessity and Not a Luxury', Howeidy personal website, 7 June, <http://fahmyhoweidy.blogspot.ca/2011/06/ blog-post_07.html> (last accessed 1 September 2017).

Husni, Hajer (2015), 'Baseera: 18 per cent the Percentage of Youth Participation in the Election', *Masrawy*, 26 November, <http://www.masrawy.com> (last accessed 1 September 2017).

Instance Supérieure Indépendante pour les Élections (ISIE) (2014), 'The Report of the Instance Supérieure Indépendante pour les Élections', <http://www.isie.tn/wp-content/ uploads/2015/04/rapport-isie-2014.pdf> (last accessed 1 September 2017).

Ismail, Salwa (2006), *Political Life in Cairo's New Quarters: Encountering the Everyday State*, Minneapolis: University of Minnesota Press.

Ismail, Salwa (2012), 'The Egyptian Revolution against the Police', *Social Research: An International Quarterly* 79: 2, 435–62.

Jribi, Maya (2010), 'Press Conference about the Events in Sidi Bouzid', 24 December, <https://www.facebook.com/photo.php?v=150263485024124&set=vb.10000121 4196100&type=2&theater> (last accessed 1 September 2017).

Kaboub, Fadhel (2013), 'The Making of the Tunisian Revolution', *Middle East Development Journal* 5: 1, 1–21.

Kaminski, Marek (2002), 'Do Parties Benefit from Electoral Manipulation? Electoral Laws and Heresthetics in Poland, 1989–93', *Journal of Theoretical Politics* 14: 3, 325–58.

Karama (n.d.), Facebook, <https://www.facebook.com/chabab.karama/notes> (last accessed 1 September 2017).

Kitschelt, Herbert (1988), 'Left-Libertarian Parties: Explaining Innovation in Competitive Party Systems', *World Politics* 40: 2, 194–234.

Kjeldgaard, Dannie, and Søren Askegaard (2006), 'The Globalization of Youth Culture: The Global Youth Segment as Structures of Common Difference', *Journal of Consumer Research* 33: 2, 231–47.

Korany, Bahgat, and Rabab el-Mahdi (2012), *Arab Spring in Egypt: Revolution and Beyond*, Cairo: American University in Cairo Press.

Linz, Juan, and Alfred Stepan (1996), *Problems of Democratic Transition and Consolidation: Southern Europe, South America, and Post-Communist Europe*, Baltimore: Johns Hopkins University Press.

Lipset, Seymour Martin (2000), 'The Indispensability of Political Parties', *Journal of Democracy* 11: 1, 48–55.

Mannheim, Karl (1983), *Essays on the Sociology of Knowledge*, London: Routledge.

Manning, Carrie (2005), 'Assessing African Party Systems after the Third Wave', *Party Politics* 11: 6, 707–27.

Mansour, Ahmed (2011), 'Mamdouh Hamza: A Witness on the Revolution, Part 3', *Aljazeera*, 19 October, <https://www.youtube.com/watch?v=eQrCZYkkBU0> (last accessed 31 July 2014).

Mayer, Nonna, and Pascal Perrineau (1992), 'Why Do They Vote for Le Pen?', *European Journal of Political Research* 22: 1, 123–41.

New Generation Youth Movement (NGYM) (n.d.), Facebook, <https://www.facebook.com/mouvement.nouvelle.generation/> (last accessed 1 September 2017).

Neyzi, Leyla (2001), 'Object or Subject? The Paradox of "Youth" in Turkey', *International Journal of Middle East Studies* 33: 3, 411–32.

O'Donnell, Guillermo, Philippe C. Schmitter, Laurence Whitehead, Cynthia J. Arnson and Abraham F. Lowenthal (2013), *Transitions from Authoritarian Rule: Tentative Conclusions about Uncertain Democracies*, Baltimore: Johns Hopkins University Press.

Rajhi, Isam el-Din (2016), 'Why Tunisia's Youth Do Not Engage in Political Participation', *Noon Post*, 25 June, <https://www.noonpost.net/content/12527> (last accessed 1 September 2017).

Randall, Vicky (2007), 'Political Parties and Democratic Developmental States', *Development Policy Review* 25: 5, 633–52.

Sawaf, Zina (2013), 'Youth and the Revolution in Egypt: What Kinship Tells Us', *Contemporary Arab Affairs* 6: 1, 1–16.

Shahine, Selim (2011), 'Youth and the Revolution in Egypt', *Anthropology Today* 27: 2, 1–3.

Shugart, Matthew, and John Carey (1992), *Presidents and Assemblies: Constitutional Design and Electoral Dynamics*, Cambridge: Cambridge University Press.

Singerman, Diane (2013), 'Youth, Gender, and Dignity in the Egyptian Uprising', *Journal of Middle East Women's Studies* 9: 3, 1–27.

Sloam, James (2007), 'Rebooting Democracy: Youth Participation in Politics in the UK', *Parliamentary Affairs* 60: 4, 548–67.

Storm, Lise (2013a), 'The Fragile Tunisian Democracy', in Nouri Gana (ed.), *The Making of the Tunisian Revolution*, Edinburgh: Edinburgh University Press, pp. 270–90.

Storm, Lise (2013b), *Party Politics and the Prospects for Democracy in North Africa*, Boulder, CO: Lynne Rienner.

Syvertsen, Amy, Laura Wray-Lake, Constance Flanagan, D. Wayne Osgood and Laine Briddell (2011), 'Thirty-Year Trends in US Adolescents' Civic Engagement: A Story of Changing Participation and Educational Differences', *Journal of Research on Adolescence* 21: 3, 586–94.

Tavits, Margit (2008), 'Party Systems in the Making: The Emergence and Success of New Parties in New Democracies', *British Journal of Political Science* 38: 1, 113–33.

Tayyashi, Fadl (2011), 'A Reading of the New Parties Law', Alchourouk, 14 October, <http://www.alchourouk.com/Ar/_A512930> (last accessed 1 September 2017).

Teimomi, al-Hadi (2008), *Tunisia (1956–1987)* [in Arabic], Tunis: Mohamed Ali Hammi Publication.

Tuhami, Mohammed (2013), 'Political Parties in Egypt', *Alhewar Almutamaden* 17: 2, <http://www.ahewar.org/debat/show.art.asp?aid=345988> (last accessed 1 September 2017).

Uleimi, Nuha (2011), 'Why the Revolution of January 25th Succeeded', *Masress*, 22 February, <http://www.masress.com/rosasabah/103818> (last accessed 1 September 2017).

Valentine, Gill, Tracey Skelton and Diane Chambers (1998), 'Cool Places: An Introduction to Youth and Youth Cultures', in Tracey Skelton and Gill Valentine (eds), *Cool Places: Geographies of Youth Cultures*, London: Routledge, pp. 1–34.

Conclusion and perspectives

Chapter 15

Arab parties in context: lessons learned

Francesco Cavatorta and Lise Storm

While the systematic examination of political parties presented in this volume highlights some region-specific trends about the way in which they function (or not) and operate in competitive authoritarian systems as well as in politically unstable countries, it is important to underline that wider tendencies also emerge that speak to the way in which party politics works elsewhere, including in established democracies. Thus, rather than reiterating the significance of political parties in the Arab world, this concluding chapter briefly looks at how the findings connect with what occurs elsewhere when it comes to political parties and party politics more broadly, suggesting that there is very little that is 'exceptional' about the Arab world when it comes to party politics.

The first significant finding is that the Arab world is no exception when it comes to the weakness of left-wing parties with a political programme based on considerable wealth redistribution and with a class-conflict discourse. As Resta argues in her chapter, socio-economic conditions in the region would be theoretically ripe for the emergence of strong parties linked to left-wing politics capable of addressing the profound dissatisfaction that neo-liberal reforms have provoked. If anything, the Arab Uprisings were in fact a struggle against social and economic injustice (Achcar 2013) rather than against authoritarianism per se. The weakness of powerful left-wing parties is all the more surprising when one acknowledges that ordinary citizens 'demand' redistributive policies, believe that socio-economic difficulties are the most pressing problem their country face, and support greater social egalitarianism and state intervention in the economy (Teti et al. 2018). The Arab left, though, suffers from the inability to present a coherent and effective programme that could rally voters, much like its counterparts in Europe, North America, Australia and, currently, Latin America. While the resurgence of the left in Latin America seemed for a moment in the 2000s to bring left-wing politics back to dominance, a return to lasting, effective social democratic values and policies did not materialise. The success that the Sanders and Corbyn campaigns had in the United States and the United Kingdom respectively should not obscure that the winners of such electoral competitions were Donald Trump and the British Conservative Party. In addition, in continental Europe, the fortunes of genuine left-wing parties are not on the up, as the 2017 French presidential elections demonstrate. The weaknesses of left-wing parties are bound with both historical and contingent factors ranging from the hegemonic ideas of neo-liberalism to the long-term disastrous compromises of the Blairite and Clintonian 'third ways', and from profound internal divisions on the role identity politics should play in left-wing politics to disagreements over international affairs. The Arab left is also no stranger to such weaknesses, highlighting its 'un-exceptionality' when compared with the left elsewhere. As Debuysere, for instance, argues in her chapter, the Tunisian left is still very much divided between Marxists, Leninists, Maoists and supporters of the Albanian model of socialist development. Such 'ideological divisions' that are obscure to most ordinary citizens prevent the left from uniting in a coherent manner and from presenting an attractive alternative socio-economic programme. Similar divisions characterise left-wing politics in continental Europe and Latin America as well. Other significant dividing lines also exist, for instance on international affairs. The position the left should have on the war in Syria, whereby some support Bashar al-Assad because of his struggle against Islamic radicalism while others are opposed to him because he is an illiberal, cruel dictator, is only one example of that (Dot-Pouillard 2012).

The second significant finding that links political parties in the region to wider trends is the rise and rise of populism, which is usually connected with the personalisation of campaigning and politics. While there exist multiple and at times incompatible definitions of populism just as there are conflicting normative meanings attached to it, one could argue that the essence of the term is the appeal made to the common man struggling against a privileged elite and whose problems can be quite easily solved if a rather general and often inconsistent set of policies were applied. In addition, only a charismatic leader who 'understands' what people want and need is charged with implementing such policies. In many ways, Arab political parties and political systems conform to the way in which politics has become the realm where policy complexity and nuances are absent. Arab political systems are often criticised and held to be incapable of democratising precisely because populist leaders or strongmen are in charge and rule through easy sloganeering. Equally, the political opposition, namely the Islamists, are also accused of populism because they rely on simple and simplistic recipes linked to religious beliefs and practices to 'brainwash' people and gain power (Roberts 1996; Colas 2004; Salamey and Pearson 2007). While there is a degree of truth to the assumption that Arab politics is populist in the pejorative sense of the term, this populist trap, however, is not only Arab. Even before the election of Donald Trump in the United States, populism was alive and well in many parts of the world, including established democracies. The cases of the *Front National* in France (Davies 2012), the *Vlaams Blok* in Belgium (Jagers and Walgrave 2007) and *Syriza* in Greece (Stavrakakis and Katsambekis 2014) are just some powerful demonstrations of that (Oesch 2008), which include leftist parties in Latin America (Seligson 2007). The fact that populism is often personified in a 'strong' leader explains in part the personalistic use of political parties both in the Arab world and elsewhere. One of the most significant and yet unsurprising findings in this book is that many political parties in the Arab world have simply become the vehicle for personal advancement. This phenomenon has been on the rise for some time with a strong personality either creating an ad hoc movement to serve his (less often her) political career and interests (Berlusconi's *Forza Italia* or the *Lijst Pim Fortuyn* come to mind) or taking over established parties (McAllister 2007). In turn this takes away from the legitimacy of parliamentary systems, for instance, and forces voters to consider personality rather than policy positions in presidential systems. This does not apply across the board, of course (Kriesi 2012), but the trend seems undeniable (Garzia 2011).

A third significant finding has to do with the flexibility and adaptability of ideology that Arab political parties display. While the rigidity of ideological commitments that many parties across the globe displayed in the past was not necessarily a positive feature of political systems because it often prevented necessary compromises, the current 'end of ideology' is equally problematic because of its effects on ordinary voters. The weakening of ideological commitments and the mixed messages parties send voters at election times are not normally associated with Arab politics, with commentators (Salem 1994) traditionally arguing that ideology has been a most potent force in the Arab world. The findings of this book do not support this though, and what emerges is a picture of parties (from the left to the Islamists and from nationalists to liberals) that show significant degrees of ideological inconsistencies, contradictions and even volte-faces. We therefore have Islamist parties that have almost completely reneged on their previous ideological commitment to economic redistribution and injustice, subscribing now instead to neo-liberal market economics (McMahon 2013). Once inspired by Islamo-leftist thinkers such as Ali Shariati, they are now in awe of market forces and part of their political programme is simply to substitute a current economic ruling elite with one sharing their enthusiasm for social conservatism (Cavatorta and Merone 2013). Leftist parties, as mentioned, are no longer united in their commitment to secular values and tend in fact to 'hide' or misrepresent their secularism because they feel that the majority of the population is socially conservative and would not approve of them. While this might be true, they are selling their ideological commitment short. In addition, many of them have supported authoritarian regimes well beyond what is understandable (Cook 2005). Nationalist-liberal parties with supposedly secular values face a similar problem as the case of *Nidaa Tounes* amply demonstrates. The only 'ideological parties' seem to be Salafist ones, although on closer scrutiny they are very pragmatic (hence their splits and divisions) as well as linked to a specific religious community. This says more about the relevance of ascriptive identities than ideology per se. In short, many parties in the Arab world are ready to ditch quickly their policy positions and ideological tenets to obtain a stake, however small, in the system. Through this stake they have the opportunity to reap the benefits of participation and redistribute patronage down to members and supporters. Scholars like Browers (2009) argue that the relaxation of ideological entrenchment is a positive political development as different sectors of society become capable of finding a stable compromise, but there are significant costs that come with this. Marzouki (2015) labels this type of compromise 'rotten', in reference to the political agreement among different political parties in the aftermath of the 2010/11 Arab Uprisings, because it only works when important issues related to socio-economic injustice are sacrificed in the name of political stability and pragmatism. This, in turn, favours overwhelmingly those who are already privileged and turns the disenfranchised away from participating in the attempts at radical reforms. A similar pattern of 'de-ideologisation' characterises political parties and party systems across the world as 'pragmatism' (in its pejorative meaning) dominates the way in which elected representatives operate. Improbable ruling coalitions are put together, deputies often switch from one parliamentary group to another, and dissatisfied party representatives run as independents. In all of this, radical transformations are often prevented even when they have been electoral promises parties made.

Finally, and more problematically, what emerges from all the contributions is that political parties in the Arab world, as elsewhere, suffer from very low levels of trust among ordinary citizens and voters, leading some to argue that even in democracies the decline of mass political participation through political parties leads to 'rule the void' (Mair 2006). A recent report of the UK parliament makes for very sobering reading in this respect and highlights the following to explain low trust in parties:

> politicians not respecting and not listening to the public; politicians not being trustworthy and not keeping promises; MPs just following the party line and whips; MPs only being willing to engage with the public in a limited way; the conduct of politicians being off-putting; there are too many career politicians; the main parties are too similar or do not appeal to voters; and politicians are not representative of the public. (House of Commons Political and Constitutional Reform Committee 2014: 8)

Thus, despite their importance and unique role, parties and their elected representatives are increasingly perceived, no matter how unjustly, as vehicles for careerism, corruption and patronage with little to no connections with the social reality they purport to represent. Bowler and Karp (2004) had already suggested that scandals in office undermined trust in elected representatives, and more than a decade on, their findings, however limited they were in geographical scope, resonate still. In part, this is the product of the increasing cynicism about institutional politics that pervades electorates across the globe, driving individuals to prefer other forms of political engagement, but such low levels of trust are also the outcome of the actions of parties themselves, as Bowler and Karp (2004) had also noted. This explains why many young people are sceptical about becoming members of political parties, preferring instead social movements active in civil society, as Yaghi also details in his chapter. The absence of formal engagement in political parties on the part of young people is a phenomenon that is visible across different political systems and once more the Arab world is no exception. Furthermore, there is evidence that the decline in party membership has been ongoing for some time and is not limited to young people (Mair and van Biezen 2001; van Biezen et al. 2012). What is considerably problematic is that parties seemed to have become appendages of the state (Mair 2006) and that they no longer have the organisational and ideological capacities to be the defenders or promoters of democratic governance. This is leading towards a convergence of governance (Cavatorta 2010) where authoritarian, democratic and semi-democratic systems implement similar policies and where, crucially, a governing class of politicians, technocrats and businessmen self-select to govern increasingly complex societies with little input from the masses.

In conclusion, political parties and party systems in the Arab world display traits specific to the region and therefore have a degree of singularity when compared with other parts of the world and, in particular, with established democracies. The weight of foreign occupation, the prominence of ascriptive identities and the constraints of competitive authoritarianism generate dynamics that are not necessarily found in other contexts. However, as this brief conclusion also suggests, there are trends that are far from exceptional and worth exploring in greater detail in future comparative research.

Bibliography

Achcar, Gilbert (2013), *The People Want: A Radical Exploration of the Arab Uprising*, Oakland, CA: University of California Press.

Bowler, Shaun, and Jeffrey Karp (2004), 'Politicians, Scandals and Trust in Government', *Political Behavior* 26: 3, 271–87.

Browers, Michaelle (2009), *Political Ideology in the Arab World: Accommodation and Transformation*, Cambridge: Cambridge University Press.

Cavatorta, Francesco (2010), 'The Convergence of Governance: Upgrading Authoritarianism in the Arab World and Downgrading Democracy Elsewhere?', *Middle East Critique* 19: 3, 217–32.

Cavatorta, Francesco, and Fabio Merone (2013), 'Moderation through Exclusion? The Journey of the Tunisian Ennahda from Fundamentalist to Conservative Party', *Democratization* 20: 5, 857–75.

Colas, Alejandro (2004), 'The Re-invention of Populism: Islamist Responses to Capitalist Development in the Contemporary Maghreb', *Historical Materialism* 12: 4, 231–60.

Cook, Steven (2005), 'The Right Way to Promote Arab Reform', *Foreign Affairs* 83: 2, 91–102.

Davies, Peter (2012), *The National Front in France*, London: Routledge.

Dot-Pouillard, Nicolas (2012), 'La Crise syrienne déchire les gauches arabes', *Le Monde Diplomatique*, August, <https://www.monde-diplomatique.fr/2012/08/DOT_POUILLARD/48029> (last accessed 1 September 2017).

Garzia, Diego (2011), 'The Personalization of Politics in Western Democracies: Causes and Consequences on Leader–Follower Relationships', *The Leadership Quarterly* 22: 4, 697–709.

House of Commons Political and Constitutional Reform Committee (2014), *Voter Engagement in the UK*, Fourth Report of Session 2014/2015, November 10, London: The Stationery Office.

Jagers, Jan, and Steffan Walgrave (2007), 'Populism as Political Communication Style: An Empirical Study of Political Parties' Discourse in Belgium', *European Journal of Political Research* 46: 3, 319–45.

Kriesi, Hanspeter (2012), 'The Personalization of National Campaigns', *Party Politics* 18: 6, 825–44.

McAllister, Ian (2007), 'The Personalization of Politics', <https://openresearch-repository.anu.edu.au/bitstream/1885/19199/2/01_McAllister_The_Personalization_of_2007.pdf> (last accessed 1 September 2017).

McMahon, Sean (2013), 'Class Warfare in Egypt', *Counterpunch*, 9 July, <http://www.counterpunch.org/2013/07/09/class-warfare-in-egypt/> (last accessed 1 September 2017).

Mair, Peter (2006), 'Ruling the Void: The Hollowing Out of Western Democracy', *New Left Review* 42, 25–51.

Mair, Peter, and Ingrid van Biezen (2001), 'Party Membership in Twenty European Democracies, 1980–2000', *Party Politics* 7: 1, 5–21.

Marzouki, Nadia (2015), 'Tunisia's Rotten Compromise', *MERIP*, 10 June, <http://www.merip.org/mero/mero071015> (last accessed 1 September 2017).

Oesch, Daniel (2008), 'Explaining Workers' Support for Right-Wing Populist Parties in Western Europe: Evidence from Austria, Belgium, France, Norway, and Switzerland', *International Political Science Review* 29: 3, 349–73.

Roberts, Hugh (1996), 'Doctrinaire Economics and Political Opportunism in Algerian Islamism', in John Ruedy (ed.), *Islamism and Secularism in North Africa*, Basingstoke: Palgrave McMillan, pp. 123–47.

Salamey, Imad, and Frederic Pearson (2007), 'Hezbollah: A Proletarian Party with an Islamist Manifesto – A Sociopolitical Analysis of Islamist Populism in Lebanon and the Middle East', *Small Wars and Insurgencies* 18: 3, 416–38.

Salem, Paul (1994), *Bitter Legacy: Ideology and Politics in the Arab World*, Syracuse: Syracuse University Press.

Seligson, Mitchell (2007), 'The Rise of Populism and the Left in Latin America', *Journal of Democracy* 18: 3, 81–95.

Stavrakakis, Yannis, and Giorgos Katsambekis (2014), 'Left-Wing Populism in the European Periphery: The Case of SYRIZA', *Journal of Political Ideologies* 19: 2, 119–42.

Teti, Andrea, Francesco Cavatorta and Pamela Abbott (2018), *Political, Economic and Social Transformations in the Wake of the Arab Uprisings*, Basingstoke: Palgrave Macmillan.

van Biezen, Ingrid, Peter Mair and Thomas Poguntke (2012), 'Going, Going, . . . Gone? The Decline of Party Membership in Contemporary Europe', *European Journal of Political Research* 51: 1, 24–56.

The contributors

Editors

Francesco Cavatorta is associate professor in International Relations and research fellow at the Centre Interdisciplinaire de Recherche sur l'Afrique et le Moyen Orient (CIRAM), Université Laval, Quebec (Canada). He is the author and co-author of a number of books, including *Civil Society and Democratization in the Arab World* (2010) and *Politics and Governance in the Middle East and North Africa* (2015), and several journal articles on democratisation, civil society and Islamist movements in North Africa.

Lise Storm is Senior Lecturer in Middle East Politics and Director of Research at the Institute of Arab and Islamic Studies at the University of Exeter (UK). She is the author of *Political Parties and the Prospects for Democracy in North Africa* (2013), *Democratization in Morocco* (2007), and several journal articles on democratisation, political parties, and the state of democracy in the Middle East and North Africa.

Contributors

Larissa Alles completed her PhD at the School for International Relations at the University of St Andrews in Scotland. Her background is in Islamic Studies and Politics of the Middle East, with a particular focus on political and social developments in the Arabian Peninsula, and Yemen in particular. In 2013, she was an international observer at Yemen's National Dialogue Conference. Her interests lie in the nature of power and authoritarian rule in the Middle East, non-violent forms of resistance, and conflict mediation.

Aurélie Daher is the Deakin Visiting Fellow at the University of Oxford (St Antony's College) for the year 2016–17. Starting September 2017, she will be assistant professor and co-head of the Peace Studies Master programme at Université Paris-Dauphine in Paris, France. Her work focuses on Hezbollah and Lebanese politics, political Shiism, and the networks of Iranian influence in the Arab world. Her dissertation was published as a book with the title *Hezbollah, Mobilisation et pouvoir* in 2014 in Paris, and is due to be published in English in 2017 with the title *Hezbollah: Mobilization and Power*.

Loes Debuysere pursued a Master of Arts in Middle Eastern studies at SOAS (London) and a Master of Science in Conflict and Development Studies at Ghent University (Belgium). For her PhD, she joined the Middle East and North Africa Research Group at Ghent University where she currently conducts research on gender politics in post-Ben Ali Tunisia. She has previously published some of her work in *Mediterranean Politics* and *Middle East Law and Governance*.

Sophie A. Edwards is an independent researcher. Her research focuses on Iraqi politics, the politics of the Kurdistan Region, conflict and development.

Anass El Kyak is an MA student in International Relations at the Institute for Advanced International Studies (Laval University) in Quebec, Canada. His current field of research is collective security and the multilateral fight against terrorism. He is currently writing his Master's dissertation titled: 'Analysis of the UNSC Collective Action in the Fight against International Terrorism: Effects of United States' and Russia's Strategic Actions on the UNSC Collective Struggle against ISIS'.

Manal A. Jamal is an associate professor of political science at James Madison University (JMU). Her research interests include comparative democratisation, civil society, social movements, conflict to peace and the political economy of transitions, and Middle East politics, including the Arab–Israeli conflict. Her publications have appeared in *Comparative Political Studies, British Journal of Middle Eastern Studies, International Feminist Journal of Politics* and *International Migration Review*, as well as in a number of edited volumes.

Amir M. Kamel is a Lecturer in the Defence Studies Department, and an Associate Staff Member in the Department of Middle Eastern Studies, both in King's College London, UK. Further, Amir currently holds a Visiting Scholar position in Georgetown University's School of Foreign Service in Washington DC, USA. Amir's work is concerned with the political economy of the Middle East, and includes foreign policies towards the region, as well as domestic issues and developments. Amir is currently working on projects dealing with US foreign economic policy towards the region, as well as methodological and theoretical studies concerning political economy in general, and the Middle East in particular. Additionally, Amir has over six years of experience consulting with government agencies, private consultancies and companies, and NGOs on issues relating to the Middle East, Economics, Politics and Security.

Hendrik Kraetzschmar is Associate Professor in the Comparative Politics of the MENA in the School of Languages, Cultures and Societies at the University of Leeds. His main area of research is the nature of electoral, associational and party politics in the Middle East and North Africa. He has published a number of articles in leading academic journals and is the editor of *Opposition Cooperation in the Arab World: Contentious Politics in Times of Change* (2012) and co-editor of *Democracy and Violence: Global Debates and Local Challenges* (2010). His latest edited volume on *Islamists and the Politics of the Arab Uprisings: Governance, Pluralization and Contention* will be published by Edinburgh University Press in 2018.

Raquel Ojeda-García is Associate Professor in the University of Granada and she has coordinated the research project 'Territorial policies and colonization/decolonization processes in Western Sahara'. She has been visiting scholar in Canadian, European and Moroccan universities and her main research interests are decentralisation in Morocco, Western Sahara, Mauritanian political system and public management in local governments. She collaborates with think tanks such as CIDOB, Fundación Alternativas, el Real Instituto Elcano and Centro de Estudios Andaluces.

Zoltan Pall is a research fellow at the Middle East Institute at the National University of Singapore, and a former visiting assistant professor at the Gulf University of Science and Technology in Kuwait. Currently he is working on a research project that focuses on the activities of Kuwaiti and other Middle Eastern Islamic NGOs in Southeast Asia. He is the author of *Salafism in Lebanon: Local and Transnational Movements* (forthcoming) and *Lebanese Salafis between the Gulf and Europe: Development, Fractionalization and Transnational Networks of Salafism in Lebanon* (2013).

Valeria Resta is a PhD candidate in Political Studies at the University of Milan. Her thesis focuses on the role of political parties in transitions from authoritarian rule in Tunisia and Egypt drawing from both the theoretical framework of democratisation studies and that of authoritarian resilience.

Anne Wolf is a Research Fellow at Girton College, University of Cambridge, and a doctoral candidate at the University of Oxford, St Antony's College. She has published numerous articles on Tunisian and Maghreb politics and is the author of *Political Islam in Tunisia: The History of Ennahda* (2017). Her current research focuses on the evolution of the networks of Ben Ali's Constitutional Democratic Rally party and authoritarian resilience after the 2010/11 uprisings.

Mohammad Yaghi completed his PhD at the University of Guelph and is an adjunct professor at Queen's University in Kingston, Ontario, Canada. His research has been published in the *International Journal of Media & Cultural Politics* and he is completing a manuscript on youth movements in the Arab world before and after the uprisings.

Index